**Praise for the *The Giant of the French Revolution*:**

"Spirited and highly readable . . . Lawday creates some great set pieces and striking turning points. . . . He is able to capture the atmosphere of the early Revolution: its inflammable mix of devilment and righteousness, reckless selflessness and flagrant self-promotion. He sees that Danton was more than the sum of his crimes, the sum of his secrets; he celebrates his, 'large heart and violent impulses in an irresolvable conflict'."
—Hilary Mantel, *The London Review of Books*

"Danton—his life is the stuff of opera."
—Bee Wilson, *The Sunday Times (UK)*

"Lawday . . . has brought Danton into full view in an audacious piece of historical writing . . . there is not a better portrait of Danton. There are some tremendous set pieces in the book . . . The last scene of Danton's life is rendered exquisitely. Lawday writes: ' As his Gorgon head touched the block, he reared around to squint up to the exhausted executioner, telling him: "Make sure you show it to the people. It is worth a look."' Lawday's triumph is that he makes Danton's last words not just a defiant last gesture to the world but an irrefutable statement of fact."
—Hugh Macdonald, *The Herald*

"David Lawday strides confidently into the fray and brings back a compelling, highly readable, and very timely account of a paradoxical champion of humanity pitted against ideological fanaticism."
—David Coward, *The Independent*

"Revolutionary turmoil comes dramatically alive in [Lawday's] account . . . [a] spirited tale."        —Edward B. Segel, History Book Club (online)

"World-historical in his ambitions, monumental in his passions, tragic in his final demise, Danton was a figure larger than life—a figure made for the theater. With both empathy and critical understanding, Lawday sets his *dramatis persona* on the stage of the French Revolution, providing an informed and readable account that deserves a broad audience."
—Darrin M. McMahon, Ben Weider
Professor of History, Institute on Napoleon
and the French Revolution, Florida State University

By the same author

*Napoleon's Master: A Life of Prince Talleyrand*

# THE GIANT OF THE FRENCH REVOLUTION

*Danton, A Life*

DAVID LAWDAY

Grove Press
New York

First published in 2009 in Great Britain by Jonathan Cape
A division of Random House Group Limited, London

*Published simultaneously in Canada*
*Printed in the United States of America*

ISBN-13: 978-0-8021-4541-3

Grove Press
an imprint of Grove/Atlantic, Inc.
154 West 14th Street
New York, NY 10011

Distributed by Publishers Group West

www.groveatlantic.com

*To Andrew and Amy*

# CONTENTS

# IMAGES

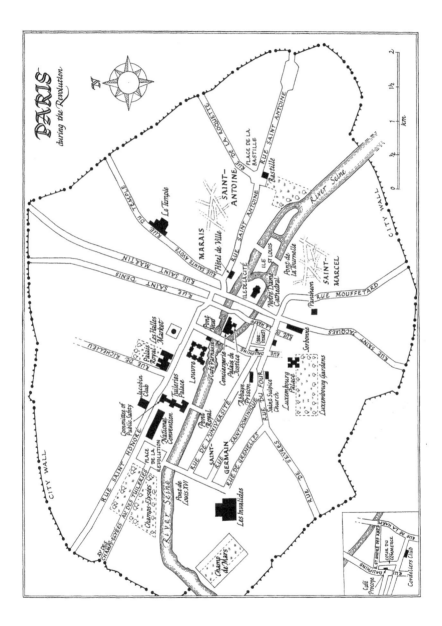

No beast so fierce but knows some touch of pity

Shakespeare; *Richard III*, Act 1, Scene 2

# PROLOGUE

# Paris: 15 July 1789

Yesterday the Bastille fell. Today, an hour past sundown, a giant of a man with a wrestler's chest bursting from a blue military tunic stands at the entrance to the smouldering prison, banging at its breached gate with a sword. From the gloss of the uniform it looks as though he is wearing it for the first time. Behind him stand a score of men armed with rifles and pikes, shouting for the officer in charge of the fallen fortress to give them entry. Cautiously the acting governor shows himself, waving written orders. He looks petrified: not twenty-four hours before he watched the severed head of his predecessor dancing through the streets of Paris on the end of a stonemason's pike.

The big man snatches the paper from his hand. 'What's this rag?' he roars. 'We'll see about this!' He takes the officer by the collar and marches him off in the direction of City Hall on the banks of the Seine, surrounded by his rowdy companions. As the spectacle progresses, people gather in the summer night to watch, spitting insults at the prisoner, flailing at him here and there with pikestaffs.

The miracle that only yesterday lifted Parisian hearts to the heavens seems to have left the street tonight.

Though the jeering onlookers have no idea who the prisoner is, some can put a name to his hulking captor. He is Georges-Jacques Danton, a man destined to bring a violent end to an absolute monarchy that has ruled for almost a thousand years. The comic-opera restorming of the Bastille has its crackpot side, and indeed there is much of the scallywag in Danton. It also suggests an impulsive lust for action that will serve him and the insurrection well. He is twenty-nine years old, robust, high-living and impetuous, the kind of man who can and will overstep the mark. Such taste for action distinguishes him from the liberal theorists, tortured ideologues and genuine crackpots whom he joins in bringing about the most abrupt change in human society the world has known. His physique in particular sets him apart. He stands a good head above his companions, with a massive frame to match. And an alarming face. Gorgon! Gargoyle! Cyclops! Tartar chief! He knows what they call him and he employs his monstrous demeanour to full effect.

Danton is no military man. The uniform he wears in putting his own evening-after stamp on the fall of the Bastille is that of a captain in a new national guard created to keep a measure of order in the free-for-all of popular revolt. Each district of Paris has formed its own militia, loosely attached to the guard, so Danton feels entitled to style himself a guard captain. He leads a populous Left Bank district hard across the Seine from the Île de la Cité, the most radical ward in the capital, and his Bastille escapade is more than anything a letting-off of steam. Why does he do it? For the hell of it. Building a reputation as a champion of the violent Paris street crowds demands derring-do of the kind that the people will notice and remember.

The acting governor of the Bastille will emerge unharmed from his ordeal. Moderate souls at City Hall who have taken charge of the capital in these first days of popular revolt return the frightened stand-in to his post, with an apology. Danton protests, but lightly. He is satisfied with his show.

Like most people alive at the start of the twenty-first century I have come to regard terror as part of life, regrettable but present. For this book I thought of giving Danton the subtitle *Gentle Giant of Terror*. To be sure, it fits him and it about sums him up. Only there can be no associating him with the Bin Ladens of late or with the frightening responses of their mighty targets. Nor with grandmasters of terror such as Stalin. So I unburden him of that dubious honour here.

Danton is no killer by nature. All the same he throws himself into action in an age when people at all levels of society live in fear for their lives; they cannot know when danger will strike and they are uncomfortably aware that no authority is able to prevent it. This is the classic climate in which terrorism thrives. At the height of his career Danton operates within it and thus has his part in the barbarous bloodletting of the French Revolution aptly named the Terror.

His fate is to take charge of the Revolution at a critical moment, when it stumbles and risks collapsing, so that France, the largest nation in Europe by far, faces a return to the failed old order from which passionate reformers and an angry populace have torn it free. He is not the instigator of terror; he resigns himself to it. There is no force on earth, he tells himself, that can stop a revolution from having its dose of blood. Until such time as law and order reassert themselves, men of good will can do no more than stop the dose from becoming a torrent. Such is Danton's intent – and also his weakness: his pity for the guillotine's guiltless victims lays bare his own bull neck.

Throughout history exponents of terrorism have acted from a host of motives, united only by the urge to kill blindly. They range from frustrated nationalists, secessionists and pure avengers to those misled by faith or visited with an obsessive grudge against humanity itself. Leaders of the French Revolution are none of these. There *are* psychopaths among them, but very few. Mostly they let dogged principle and fear run away with their senses. Danton sees the danger of revolutionary terrorism, but is equally aware of the dangers of letting the Revolution run aground. Its failure is unthinkable. What awful vengeance would royalists then wreak? What could prevent all-out civil war? What hope would remain if liberty, once won, were abandoned? Behind his bluster Danton is a practical man and his actions assume an overriding purpose: to save the new France from foreign invaders – Austria and Prussia, joined by England – who resolve to undo 1789.

1789 . . . what a year. The historian Jules Michelet, a great romancer of the French Revolution born in Paris a decade after the event, pictures the whole world watching its progress 'with uneasy sympathy, conscious that France at her own risk and peril is acting for the entire human race'. One scarcely has to share Michelet's full rapture, or even to be French, to feel the pulse quicken. At the same time it is hard even today not to feel something sharper than Michelet's unease – to feel dread, in fact. My own interest in Danton goes back to English classroom recollections of a gang of revolutionary fanatics who are outsmarted – hurrah! – by the ingenious Scarlet Pimpernel as he saves hapless French aristocrats from the guillotine. Baroness Orczy's 'damned, elusive' *Pimpernel* is a wonderful story, right down to the taunting notes her mysterious English hero spirits into the pockets of the masters of the Terror – signed with a little red English hedgerow flower – to inform them of his latest successful venture.

The Hungarian-born baroness rather misses the significance, though, of what her English hero is trying to stop. How to catch its full force? What occurred in France in 1789 and in the five extraordinary years that followed is rated by the historian Eric Hobsbawm, a connoisseur of revolution, as a phenomenon as awesome and irreversible as the first nuclear explosion, producing an energy that sweeps away a benighted old Europe in a mushroom cloud, while England's Industrial Revolution, under way at more or less the same time, intensifies the blast. Karl Marx is equally struck: for him, Danton and company stormed the heavens.

Nuclear imagery gives an idea of the enormous rough house that 1789 produced: harrowing events succeed each other in anarchic confusion, most often soaked in blood. Within two years of the Bastille's fall, suspicion and fear rule: everyone involved is afraid for their skin, or ought to be. Hunger for liberty is in violent collision with the absolutism of France's Bourbon monarchy, yet the conflict has so many sides that the picture grows perilously blurred. Friends kill friends. They send each other to the guillotine no longer knowing why, for what belief, what doctrine, what logic. Blind violence takes over.

The American Revolution which precedes it by a dozen years or so – and likewise launches a republic – is, in terms of social change, a sideshow by comparison, a local happening that permits Americans to continue leading their lives virtually unchanged while the rest of the world also carries on very much as before. The reckless French ride from monarchy to republic, on the other hand, is a mass social revolution that upends Europe's largest state – a country populated by one in five of all Europeans at the time. The upheaval is so uniquely radical in spirit that English liberal firebrands who hurry across to France to demonstrate their support find themselves looking on a little disconsolately, too tame to make a mark. And then comes Lenin, whose Bolsheviks idolise the men of 1789 and like to borrow from them. Lenin stands back in awe at Danton's actions, singling him out as 'the greatest master of revolutionary tactics yet known'.

What manner of man makes such stupendous things happen? And what manner of man allows terror to achieve his ends?

Revolution's record for devouring its own children starts with Danton. He is the tragic hero incarnate. I write of him after first plunging into the French Revolution for another reason – and discovering that there is simply no avoiding Danton whichever way the currents pull. That *other reason* was a life I was writing of France's incomparable statesman, Prince Talleyrand, the ace of diplomats, who owes his reputation as the greatest survivor of the revolutionary age – perhaps of all time – to his own guile, certainly, but more directly to Danton. For it is Danton, boisterous, alarming, yet essentially practical, who saves Talleyrand's precious neck. At his own peril, Danton helps him escape the guillotine, together with others of Talleyrand's old-world stamp, because he deems it a folly to lose for ever the services of such talents.

The vaudeville swordsman at the gates of the Bastille is, then, by physique alone, a giant figure for his times. His family background and the profession he enters boost his revolutionary credentials. He is born into the rural bourgeoisie in the flat, thinly populated southern rim of the Champagne region, beyond the reach of the province's fabled vines – a land where wheatfields pierced by rare village spires spread either side of the looping river Aube, a minor tributary of the Seine. This is *France profonde*. Its greatest chronicler, Honoré de Balzac, awards Danton's birthplace, Arcis-sur-Aube, the badge of pure authenticity: 'Nothing better explains provincial life than the deep silence in which this little town slumbers.'

Danton's family has not long climbed out of the peasant class and its roots continue to tug. All the same he receives a thoroughly middle-class education, one liberally dosed with the Enlightenment thinking that is gripping France and making the rest of Europe sit up and listen. With this behind him he trains for the law. Bourgeois upbringing, liberal ideas, the law . . . what better credentials, as the world will learn, for joining a revolution still ten years off?

The right credentials may indeed place him near the controls of revolution, but to grasp the controls he needs something more, some singular asset that sets him apart. The weapon of revolt that distinguishes Danton is his voice – a perpetual roll of thunder which spurs fellow men to action without his always quite knowing where he intends to drive them. His immense lungs work to no script, expelling rich, earthy phrases that somehow fall into a purposeful pattern to excite bourgeois reformers and street crowds alike. To hear Danton is to hear the heartbeat of revolution.

Peer into the 1789 volcano and amid the flame and fury two principal actors, two complete opposites in style and psyche, soon take focus. One is Danton, the other the puritanical Robespierre. This book only sketches in Robespierre; it is not *his* life. It is hard, though, not to side with the all-too-human Danton, for the death-struggle in which the pair become locked sounds a powerful warning against letting utopian zealotry take charge of men's affairs. Robespierre calls adversaries who disagree with him 'monsters'; Danton calls his opponents 'rascals'. There's a smile in the word 'rascal', a smile that shows understanding for human frailty. Danton cannot hate. He is not the most brilliant actor in the Revolution; he is not the most thoughtful, nor always the most convincing in his impulses. Theory and dogma are not his strong suit. But his heart and his voice drive the common people to action, and this is what keeps the Revolution alive when it is on the brink of going under.

There is a further striking side to Danton – the pent-up brevity of his existence. He wades for all he is worth into revolution at the age of twenty-nine and is dead at thirty-four. So much of him, so reckless and thankless a life, such exertion – all concentrated into barely five years. A short life has the nerve and elan that a long life spread over decades of achievement cannot match. A short life collects no dust; it is somehow touched by martyrdom. Its great mystery is where it might have led.

Perhaps it is better not to know Danton at sixty-four. Better not to know his contemporaries in revolution – friends or enemies – when their hair has turned white. He is far from alone, in fact, in coming to a terrible and premature end. The poignancy of what befalls the hot-blooded Danton somehow embraces them all, including those with ice in their veins. Robespierre goes to the guillotine at the age of thirty-six, having fed it heads by the thousand; Saint-Just, his brilliant scaffold-hand, loses his at twenty-six. And it may be worth remembering that as these scalded sons of Icarus tumble, an ambitious soldier, aged twenty-four, is battling his way towards power of a kind unseen since Julius Caesar. Napoleon Bonaparte already holds a military command.

A curious problem in writing a life of Danton is that he himself hated putting pen to paper. He scarcely wrote a private letter. Not one has surfaced in which he even begins to lay himself bare. There is surely a psychological block here. Even if he had lived beyond the age of thirty-four and had led a full political life thereafter it is unlikely that he would have started writing out his extraordinary speeches in advance, let alone penned private letters. His hand is near unreadable, as a shocked barrister who first takes him under training as a lawyer and examines his copy testifies ('Good God, man. What an atrocious fist!'). Against that, he has a photographic memory for text and recites Cicero and the classical orators by the yard. A prodigious memory encourages Danton to demonstrate mastery of the word with his tireless tongue alone.

All the same I've found myself cursing him for not leaving behind at least some personal reminiscences. It would have been nice to know how his brash bravura in speech translated to paper. His personal indifference to pen and ink is bizarre in one so educated. This was an age of letter writing: the educated sent notes in the morning to friends and lovers they intended to see in the afternoon. It is true that Danton can rely on others to compensate, which may be a factor. His trusty lieutenant Camille Desmoulins is a professional writer who makes full use of his own gifts and is usually at Danton's side, pen cocked. As Robespierre observes: 'Desmoulins writes, Danton roars.' They are all members of the radical Jacobin club, the Right Bank brain centre of the Revolution in Paris, and Danton and Desmoulins double as leading lights of the Cordelier club, its Left Bank boiler house. Leadership of the Cordeliers makes Danton political master of his riotous Paris district, later to be known as the Latin Quarter.

There exists, to be sure, a written record of many of the Danton speeches that so arouse Jacobins, Cordeliers and the nation. The trouble is that they are truncated versions, lacking the booming richness and classical range of the original, since they are printed from notes taken by clerks who cannot be expected to capture Danton's rhetoric, or worse, by notetakers commissioned to sabotage it. The speeches appear, mutilated, in the semi-official government gazette (which continues to publish right through the alarms of the Revolution) and in minutes of meetings held by the Jacobins and Cordeliers. As such, they may seem somewhat shaky justification for his reputation as the hardiest orator of the turbulent age – a voice more resonant than that of the great Mirabeau, another tribune with a remarkably unpretty face. Nonetheless, even the disjointed excerpts of Danton's speeches that come through suggest that the absence of faithful, unabridged texts is a great loss to public oratory.

For all of these reasons it requires a fair degree of intuition and deduction to reach Danton. The record of his childhood and adolescence is sparse and some of it, which I have tried to weed out, is probably pure fancy anyway. So I present this life, yes, as authentic history – page notes doubling as a bibliography appear at the end – but also in some instances as romanced history, for to find Danton you need to imagine him and thus to an extent invent him.

That said, Danton in manhood is probed and skilleted, admired and reviled in a multitude of memoirs written by contemporaries who love him, loathe him or simply stand and watch as the Danton tempest roars past. Fortunately, the revolutionary age is inhabited by numerous perceptive chroniclers – men and women of high and middle society, survivors and victims – who scarcely put their quills down in their desire to bequeath a telling memoir. The new republic's high priestess, the beautiful Manon Roland, who nurses a curiously complex hatred for Danton, is busy at her memoirs until the very moment her executioners rope her into a tumbrel bound for the guillotine. At Danton's trial, luck also takes a hand: the official transcript is so painfully one-sided as to reveal precious little of what really occurred, but a juror breaks the court rules and makes notes, subsequently published, that provide the hellish flavour of Danton's ordeal.

Just as it is hard for anyone with an interest in history's human dimensions to avoid taking sides between the Revolution's two principal actors, it seems downright impossible for professional historians to avoid fighting over Danton's character. He tries academic nerves. He excites extreme views. Corrupt demagogue! Lionhearted saint! Few figures in history present quite so stark a contrast, a sure sign that extreme verdicts do not get him right. The ultimate struggle is between two late-nineteenth-century French historians, Alphonse Aulard (1849–1928) and Albert Mathiez (1874–1932).

Once Aulard's student, Mathiez is a passionate critic of Danton, nailing him for every sin under the sun; his indignation causes him a nervous breakdown, but not before he has scuttled Danton in the eyes of generations of French left-wing purists, who applaud Robespierre to this day and view the Terror as the harsh but vital tool of republican principle. Aulard, an august liberal and holder of the famous history chair at the Sorbonne, which Mathiez covets for himself and fails to wrest from his rival, is strongly partisan on Danton's behalf, though a calmer observer – which only maddens Mathiez the more.

Danton's biographers are in fact rather few in number, perhaps due to the unusual dearth of personal archive material. In the English language a youthful Hilaire Belloc produced what I find the most readable life of Danton. It was published in 1899. The biographical penury may have a further explanation. Danton is a figure made for the theatre. Playwrights indeed have a strong nose for him. Shakespeare would have loved him. He has all the stuff of tragedy – the vigour, the rise to power, regicide, hubris, vulnerability, the spiralling fall. Plus the poignant irony: the wild man of 1789 who starts out as an enemy of moderation ends up losing his life in horrendous fashion for insisting on it.

A good dozen dramatists – from Germany, Italy and the old Habsburg lands, as well as from France – have been moved by the dramatic force of his short life. Of their plays the most popular is *Dantons Tod* by Georg Büchner, a German political dramatist born as Napoleon reaches his military peak. Astonishingly, Büchner was only twenty-one years old (he died of typhoid at twenty-three) when he peered with such empathy into the heart of Danton, and it may be a premonition of his own youth cut short that inspired him. Even as the centuries move on, Büchner's Danton lives; his play continues to be widely performed.

Still, the theatre aims to capture a salient part of its subject, a part that holds an eyeglass to the whole. My aim in this book is to show the whole: to enter the life of a man who stands up, warts and all, for humanity against ideological fanaticism, who reveals how dark are the paths down which patriotism that asks no questions leads. These are conflicts that are always with us.

Let the curtain rise.

# ONE

## *Bullfights*

A countryman born is a countryman for life, and this may be truer of the people of France than of most anywhere on earth. Georges-Jacques Danton was reared in a flat, chalky tract of the Champagne region, and no matter how large a part of his heart he put into driving the great city of Paris to revolution, a still larger part was yoked to his rural birthplace. It was an attachment that would cost him dear.

He was born on 26 October 1759, the fifth child and first son of a couple from the provincial petty bourgeoisie. His father, Jacques Danton, had fairly recently stepped up a class from the peasantry, and peasant roots still clutched at the Dantons as the little market town where they lived, Arcis-sur-Aube, sleepwalked into the turbulent final third of the eighteenth century. The land stretching flat around Arcis was the backside of the wine country to the north and was known as the Champagne badlands, though it was bad – 'flea-ridden' was the description used in cartographic tradition and indeed by the king's provincial administrators – only by the bountiful standards of France's countryside, for it grew wheat and barley aplenty and helped keep Paris, the metropolis 100 miles to the west, in bread. Moreover, its plainness was alleviated by the river Aube which looped across it in a rich green ribbon, hidden by willows and sycamores from strangers passing through. If local eyes were at all open to the outside world, it was due to the tranquil Aube, which was navigable in those days and flowed into the Seine some thirty miles yonder, so that travellers with time on their hands could ride a barge straight from Arcis to Paris, thence to the English Channel if so inclined.

Still, country people knew where best to congregate and the population around Arcis was as thin as its chalky soil. Only within the little town, where the Dantons made their way better than most, did the population multiply. Not many years before Danton's birth, stocking-makers had set up looms in Arcis thanks to a local grandee with influence at the Bourbon court in

9

Versailles, which decided where industries were permitted to set up in France. Arcis' good fortune, then, was to hold a royal charter for the manufacture of woollen and cotton hose, and while its peasantry sowed and reaped, its spinning machines hummed and clacked in local cellars from dawn to dusk.

Even so, the song of the stocking looms failed to break the town's deeper slumber. At the time of Georges-Jacques' birth few in this corner of *France profonde* sensed that the nation at large was alive with discontent, girding for change as never before. Yet in respect of timing the gladiators of social change fairly hovered over the Danton boy's cradle. In the very year that he was born the philosophical bomb that freethinkers called the Enlightenment went off with a great bang: the notorious Voltaire, at his malicious best in exile, published *Candide*; the determined philosopher Denis Diderot relaunched his banned *Encyclopédie*, questioning each and every truth that monarchy held dear; and Jean-Jacques Rousseau was completing his *Contrat Social*, a trumpet call for reform of the French state.

War was declared that year on the old order and on the absolute rule of kings.

In looks, Danton was closer to the barnyard than to the Enlightenment. He was a robust child, an exception in the family. Two of his four older sisters died in childhood, true to a high mortality rate set by five siblings from his father's first marriage, which ended with his wife's death in labour. Danton's own mother, though sturdy of constitution, was unable to provide him with the mother's milk he required and took to having him suckled by a cow from the barn, a common expedient in the countryside. The infant Georges-Jacques was equal to the test until a jealous bull entered the barn and gored his face, splitting his top lip. He carried the vivid scar all his life. A further encounter with a bull at the age of seven crushed his nose, compensating for the first atrocity in so far as it gave his face a certain misshapen balance.

Rural life thus left its harsh tattoo on the Danton boy even as his father, the son of a peasant farmer, moved away from it. Having broken with the family history of tilling the land and turned instead to law, Jacques Danton was edging through the provincial legal orders. From court bailiff and below he rose to prosecutor – still a relatively minor post but one which carried weight in Arcis, combining as it did the duties of justice of the peace and country solicitor; he spent a good deal of his time stamping documents and registering ownership of fields and copses. Prior to his own abrupt death at the age of forty, not a hint of dissent or rebelliousness, not a shadow of political contrariness, marked Jacques Danton's career in the king's service. The one reforming move he made, if such it was, was the break with his peasant class that enabled him to install his second family in a large house backed by a barn and several acres of land on the edge of Arcis where the town's weathered stone bridge spanned the Aube.

Georges-Jacques held no memory of his father, who died when he was three. Parental influence came from his mother, née Madeleine Camut, who had married down, at least in economic terms. Her own father was a building contractor commissioned to keep the king's roads and bridges in running order in the Champagne badlands. His income gave the Camut family a comfortable living and opened up prospects for the younger generation. Madeleine's brother was a village curate, soldiering in the most conservative corps of the kingdom; her two sisters found worthy husbands in the bourgeois class – one was the postmaster in Troyes, the provincial capital situated a morning's coach ride away, the other a merchant in the same city.

Madeleine was a practical woman, slight but of strong constitution, who overcame her husband's premature death and the shock it caused her and her expanding tribe (she bore two more boys after Georges-Jacques) by taking a new husband – an Arcis clothmaker named Jean Recordain – just as soon as the niceties of Catholic Church doctrine allowed. Practical though she was, she was also loving and affectionate towards her children, a combination that rubbed off on Georges-Jacques. He adored his mother and was always close to her, though like her first husband she too was no agitator. By provincial class ratings the Dantons remained a good deal closer to the eternal peasant smallholder than to the occupant of the princely Arcis chateau that rose above the trees across the Aube from their home. Their modest rung of the bourgeoisie manned the king's administrative services – magistrates, lawyers, inspectors, notaries, doctors and civil servants who kept the wheels of the *Ancien Régime* turning. Only on the bourgeoisie's upper rungs – a wealthy elite of bankers, industrialists and landlords – was the middle class on something of a level with the nobility, for all it lacked was enjoyment of the king's favour, which exempted those of blueblood birth and the high Catholic clergy from paying taxes. Nor were the Dantons within earshot of that most energetic bourgeois breed of the day, the men and women of letters – the educated elite of the French masses – who appointed themselves to goad and rattle the monarchy into doing what their hearts told them was fair and right.

If peasant roots tugged at Georges-Jacques through such bourgeois layers it was because in his case they were overpowering. As he grew up, the rural masses indeed began scenting change in the air. But there was something that lulled and pacified peasant minds, something as old as the land itself, and this was the eternal bounty yielded by the French soil. The food. The wine. Who could imagine such marvels ever ceasing?

\*     \*     \*

The boy Danton ate like a horse. He was as big and strong for his age as he was ugly, which granted him protection against the taunts of Arcis boys. To keep her first son from running wild on the banks of the Aube, his mother placed him in the charge of a neighbouring spinster who offered rudimentary instruction in reading and writing and used a stick pouched in her apron to discipline him, when she was able to catch him. Much of the time Danton hid from her and splashed about in the Aube, regardless of his mother's concern for his safety. He tested himself against the powerful current that ran beneath the bridge, for the water there came bouncing across a weir created by riverside threshing mills at which barges bumped and manoeuvred to fill up with grain for the trip to Paris.

As Danton turned eight, his mother recognised the need for more authentic schooling; she placed him in the Church-run Arcis grammar school, where he learned the rudiments of Latin. Here too he was unruly. He cut school regularly to spend the morning playing cards in the grass with fellow truants on a quieter reach of the Aube half a mile upstream from the bridge; there they competed to see who could swim from bank to bank the most times without stopping. Danton was a powerful swimmer with a broad chest for his age. Alas, too much time in the water took its toll. At ten, he caught a chest infection that exposed him to a severe bout of smallpox which further blighted his farmyard face, leaving his cheeks as rudely rutted as a pumice stone. The older he became, the more terrible his countenance grew. While his mother's affection wasn't blunted, her tenderness was slow to impose on her oldest boy the education of her class. Only under pressure from his Camut uncle, the priest, was the young smallpox survivor packed off to Troyes to enter a college that prepared boys to enter a Church seminary.

On first sight the provincial capital appeared to Danton to offer temptations greater than the Aube, for the river Seine ran through its heart. Discipline at the new school, which went at its task in all earnestness, at once killed these fancies. Outside the holidays Danton was not permitted to return home. When he did he let his mother know that he couldn't stand the monotony of the place and its strange customs. After two years there he was convinced that he was not cut out for the Church; he would never understand its ways. He hated all the bells. They never stopped ringing. He particularly disliked the one that rang to end recreation time. 'If I have to go on hearing that much longer, it will be my death knell,' he advised his mother, employing ecclesiastical terminology to convince her. She accepted the advice, though coming from her twelve-year-old it sounded over-defiant; to his pre-seminary teachers it was plain refusal to accept authority.

The following year he entered a lay boarding school in Troyes where pupils took most of their instruction at a next-door college run by Oratorian fathers. This suited him better. The Oratorians were liberal Catholic priests sceptical of hoary Church tradition, who kept abreast of public opinion. They were a renegade part of the Church, cramming Enlightenment thinking into their pupils' heads along with the Latin and Greek classics that were the core of their teaching. Furthermore, they had a progressive constitution – superiors in the order were obliged to take account of novice priests' views – so that Danton, with hindsight, was able to see his Oratorian schooling as a clerical probing shot before the full blast of revolution.

His mother had at last found the place for her son to shine, though bad writing pulled down his average marks. He had an explanation for her about the writing which he was not sure she understood: he remembered the sound of words perfectly, but not the sight of them. (Dyslexia was not yet part of the physician's vernacular, let alone a schoolroom excuse.) To compensate, he excelled in Latin. His recitations from Cicero had his class-mates clapping and his master at times joined in the applause. They enjoyed his performances; his forte was to turn around the most striking words and phrases to give them a still bolder twist. He revelled in Ancient Rome and its republic, memorising whole chunks of Cicero and reeling them off without a stumble. The pure, frightening justice of it all was riveting. The part played by plebeians. The outlandish conspiracies. The personal power struggles. And behind it all the unblinking regard for democracy. Furthermore, pagan antiquity was in fashion: recent discoveries of extraordinary ruins at Pompeii and Herculaneum excited freethinkers, encouraging the republican urge. All this enthralled the adolescent Danton. From his second year with the Oratorians, the prize for Latin discourse was his.

Rhetoric was a second strongpoint, or so he fancied, for when it came to arguing things out it most likely occurred to him that his physique and his alarming face gave him an edge. Rhetoric meant sounding off. Oratorian friars did not discourage speechifying, but what they wanted more from their wards was sounding off on the written page – a logical written argument. Writing again! How it irked Danton. His teachers said he was lazy. They said he could not be bothered to submit to the intellectual grind of written prose. But his fingers just didn't seem to operate with a pen between them. His hand betrayed him. Once a pen held command, even the spelling of words escaped him, words that were perfectly clear in his mind and which he had no trouble using when answering a question in class.

Why was writing so important? Why didn't speech count for more? Speech was the first link between human beings. Danton tested his theory in class one day when a novice teacher rebuked another pupil for not preparing his written work. The offender was a friend of his named Jules Paré, who made things worse by appearing unapologetic. The rhetoric teacher ordered Paré to fetch the rod from a junior classroom for a beating, which brought Danton to his feet. Now aged fifteen, he argued in a shaky adolescent baritone that it was morally wrong to consider inflicting on pupils of their age a punishment meant for minors. The proposition lit a heated debate, which soon brought in Oratorian fathers from around the college. It was a glorious dispute for this liberal establishment to throw itself into, and in the end, while the youthful teacher was somehow saved from humiliation, Paré was spared the rod. Alas, Danton's aptitude for oral argument went unrewarded: he came close to bottom of the rhetoric class that term. There was gratitude, though, from one quarter. Paré, who was no dunce and was to become a government minister at the height of the Revolution, gave Danton his undying loyalty.

Before turning sixteen Danton took a larger risk. When King Louis XV fell ill and died in 1774, his eldest son set 11 June of the following year to take the crown as Louis XVI in the magnificent cathedral at Reims, as tradition demanded. It promised to be a sumptuous occasion attended by the mightiest figures in France, the high society from Paris and Versailles – the cream of the aristocracy, bishops, statesmen and generals with their elegant ladies and mistresses. The Oratorian fathers in Troyes, both fascinated and perplexed by the coming event, made it the subject for the annual college essay prize.

Reims was not a world away from Troyes. It was situated in medieval glory in the north of the Champagne region, the hub of the sparkling wine trade, and was reachable, Danton calculated, within a day's coach ride. Driven by adolescent bravado, he determined to go there. 'I want to see how a king is made,' he announced to classmates. Once he had declared the intention, there was no letting them down. His bold feats in Latin recitation made them look to him for action. Moreover, it occurred to him that the essay prize could come within reach if he had rich content to compensate for bad handwriting.

Naturally it meant playing truant, for there was no chance that permission would be granted. Paré and a few other confidants pooled their coppers to help pay his way. When the time came he started out for Reims on foot, anxious not to be caught boarding the stagecoach before he was clear of Troyes. Once he was able to pick up a coach, it stopped at Arcis, which lay on the direct route to Reims. During the long stop-over Danton sat huddled against the bare upholstery, shrinking from the window: he wanted to see his mother but he could not take the chance that she would haul him off the coach.

In Reims he joined the huge crowd crammed in the forecourt of the cathedral to watch the new king and his vassals proceeding in and out wearing their gorgeous robes of state. To witness the sacred ceremonies from the inside was impossible. A regiment of royal guards kept the populace at a respectable distance and Danton would have felt the sharp end of a guardsman's pike when his part of the crowd momentarily spilled towards the great carved doors. He was excited by the monarchy, thrilled by it, though not enamoured, for in rhetoric class they had been discussing the royal justice. The Oratorians frankly criticised it. That the king could dispatch offending subjects into exile, to prison or to death without trial – merely by a *lettre de cachet*, a slip of paper bearing his signature – did seem strange in the age of Voltaire, and who were the Oratorians' charges to disagree with their teachers' outrage?

Danton could not hear the oaths sworn in the cathedral by the new king. But no one present in that vast throng outside expected Louis XVI to deviate an inch from his divine right to rule, and he did not disabuse them. The truant from Troyes watched the young king emerge at last in his crown from the cathedral; he watched him ride in the royal carriage a few turns of its high wheels to the cathedral park, where victims of scrofula awaited the king's touch. There were many hundreds of them, assembled in lines. Danton would have run to the park in time to see the stout new monarch walking up and down their plagued rows, touching each moaning sufferer with a fingertip, first on the forehead, then on the chin, then on each cheek, with a rapid little movement, like a bird pecking at something objectionable. He might have heard him repeat again and again, 'May God cure thee, the King doth touch.' And he would have seen him stop at the end of each row, where a trio of chalice bearers waited to cleanse the royal finger, the first proffering vinegar, the second pure water, the third orange water, and after each dip of the hand a separate towel appeared on a golden plate to dry it.

Danton had much to turn over in his young mind on the return to Troyes. The event was too extraordinary not to impress a country boy. And he had to find excuses for his absence, not only for the Oratorian fathers but for his mortified boarding-college head, who was kept in the dark over the trip. He made some headway with a near-truthful explanation – that he wanted to gather eyewitness knowledge of the coronation to enliven his essay – but the monks knew him well enough to suspect that sheer bravado was the motive. In the end he owned that he had made a mistake, which was better received.

When things cooled down, Danton won the essay prize. Inducing the Oratorian fathers to pardon his illegible penmanship would have required some artful work. No record of his essay was kept, but it most likely seduced the monks by weaving the liberal views on social justice they pressed on their charges into a vivid description of the archaic scenes he defied college discipline to witness.

It was soon time for Danton to choose a career. During the final college terms in Troyes his reading broadened beyond the Ancients whose words and rhythms he so admired. He felt the urge to read something different. This was not discouraged by his teachers, who wished to send their charges out into the world as rounded men. He was already a tall, brawny youth with a mashed face and a powerful memory, and into that accommodating receptacle – full of Aristotle, Cicero and Tacitus – there now poured a fresher stream of thought, not aggressively up to date but universal: Molière and Corneille on the home side, with rude support from Rabelais; and Shakespeare and Dante for foreign input, whom he struggled to read in the original, having learned enough English and Italian in class to engage with them. In years to come Danton kept Shakespeare jealously on his bookshelves, accompanied by a contemporary Scotsman, Adam Smith, whose demolition of old economic thinking in his *Wealth of Nations* appeared to critical admiration throughout Europe just as Danton tasted his own solitary prose triumph at school in Troyes.

This bout of bookishness hardly set Danton apart. At the age of nineteen, despite his twist of nonconformism, he was more or less the standard product of a bourgeois education of his day. That he emerged a headstrong young man, more impulsive than contemplative, was more in his nature than in his background. His curate uncle was perhaps entitled, even now, to hope that this boisterous, exuberant nephew could yet be pressed into God's service, and he badgered Danton's mother for support. The avuncular concern was practical as well as godly. A clergyman believed the Church offered career security, as it always had.

Danton's memories of perishing boredom at his pre-seminary school sufficed to kill that revived scheme. The modern outlet for his class was the law. Even his father, a peasant's son, had recognised the law's potential, and now, as shards from the Enlightenment explosion began to rain on Troyes and pinpricks were felt in the Champagne region, the law seemed to call louder than ever. A family caucus attended by the Troyes postmaster and the careful men of commerce on the Camut side agreed that the young Danton should go to Paris for training; the place to succeed in law was the capital. Save for London, Paris was the biggest city in all Europe, the enforcement centre of laws covering 26 million Frenchmen who made up the largest nation in the civilised world, leaving aside Russia. The family would finance his apprenticeship in Paris at the very start; after that he would have to fend for himself.

The family caution was no deterrent. Danton wasn't fretting over money and never really would, even though he pursued his pleasures greedily. He proved his disregard before setting out for Paris. Without fuss, at his mother's bidding, he placed the modest inheritance received from his father in the name of his stepfather Jean Recordain, whose cloth factory had fallen on lean times.

# TWO

# Doing the Palais

Danton arrived in Paris aboard the mail coach from Arcis on a spring evening in 1780. The long day's ride was free, courtesy of the coachman, a family friend. It was an economical start.

In his pocket he had two names: they identified an inn favoured by travellers from the Champagne country and a barrister the Camuts had once dealt with, who was said to recruit apprentice clerks as the mood took him. As the coach bounced through the eastern ramparts into the capital Danton was astonished at the noise and bustle. And the smell. The city walls held it in like a pestilent bladder. It was intolerable – putrid, stifling, faecal – but then, miraculously, after no more than five excruciating minutes, his crushed nose grew accustomed to it and the foul odour became the air itself, the air of the capital.

On the Rue Saint-Antoine the coach passed by the Bastille prison, a grim mammoth of stone. It was a district choking with artisans' workshops: cutting, splitting, filing, welding, sawing, polishing, hammering. Metals writhed and swelled before his eyes. Tanners, bakers, butchers, fruiterers beat and mixed and chopped, their grunts mingling with the cries of hawkers and pamphlet vendors at every corner. This was a grand spectacle, though without much colour, for its actors seemed to be clothed entirely in black.

How could Danton begin to imagine that these people would one day take him as their leader? Become *his* people? There were so many of them. Six hundred thousand and more, so he had heard, not counting the upper classes behind the carved doors of their mansions or the strivers of his own class. If the great bulk of the French nation lived on the land, a vast swarming minority of artisans, stall-keepers, factory hands, labourers – one in five of the population – were city dwellers, and their chief haunts were the narrow, noisy streets of Paris.

From his coach window Danton could spot the Seine, then the Pont Neuf spanning the river at the western end of the Île de la Cité. The tall houses and shops erected on the bridge looked ready to bring it down and sink it in the slow waters below. This was the heart of the capital. The coachman pointed his young Arcis charge a few streets back along the right bank of the Seine to the inn whose name he carried in his pocket, the Cheval Noir. It was close enough to walk. Danton had just a small wooden trunk with him containing clothes and half a dozen of his books. Here on the Seine quays some of the men he saw wore topcoats in brighter colours – blue, green, mauve. They were of a gentler class than the Saint-Antoine crowds in their working black. And elegant private carriages clattered by on the cobbles, their occupants still more colourfully attired, in pinks and yellows, the menfolk included.

The Cheval Noir was a busy, run-down hostelry just north of where the Île de la Cité and the Île Saint-Louis almost touched, offering a view over both islands. For provincials, Paris inns were like clubs: Bretons went to this one, Gascons to that, Burgundians to another. The Cheval Noir was frequented by the natives of the Champagne region, though Danton would not have expected to know anyone there among his fellow Champenois when he gave his name and was allotted a room.

The next day he set out to find the barrister. It was urgent to secure a position. He was twenty years old and bursting to get started, not only in order to save the family purse. The name he had for the lawyer was Maître Vinot, whose chambers were conveniently located on the Île Saint-Louis, a ten-minute walk from the Cheval Noir. On arrival Danton discovered to his discomfort that Maître Vinot had little recollection of the Camuts, or pretended so.

Nonetheless he sat Danton down and asked him to show him his handwriting, giving him a short document to copy, which the young visitor, conscious of his failing, finished with some difficulty.

'Good God, man. What an atrocious fist!' Vinot growled, looking it over.

'Maître, I am not here to be a copyist,' Danton replied. He was used to defending his penmanship.

The barrister was taken. 'Hah! I like a little cheek. We need it in this profession.' He admitted Danton as a clerk, with food and lodging. It was up to him to study for his law examinations while clerking. A week later the burly legal apprentice moved out of the Cheval Noir into the rooms which Maître Vinot provided on the Île Saint-Louis. In view of his handwriting deficiencies he was assigned, in the Paris legal jargon, to 'do the Palais'. This showed sound judgement on Vinot's part. It was an initiation for legal apprentices that entailed familiarising themselves with events and personalities at the Palais de Justice – the Paris Law Courts. The business of the great stone warren in the middle of the Seine, the hub of French justice, was to resolve in its numerous courtrooms the more important criminal and civil suits that came to trial under the king's law. The Vinot chambers dealt in civil grievances, mostly between members of the gentry, so that fraud and malfeasance were its bread and butter. Danton's task was to report back on these matters to his chambers, to try his voice at very minor pleadings, anticipate the judgements of the Palais magistrates and generally find his way in the judicial labyrinth until he knew it well enough to move through it with ease. That accomplished, he might sit the law examinations and take silk. It would take a few years.

With his startling countenance and physique Danton could hardly help being noticed at the Palais de Justice, which was not without professional benefit to his chambers. He went about the job, Vinot quickly concluded, with diligence and intelligence. 'Doing the Palais' was in fact a quick route to advancement in the law. He could listen to the greatest lawyers of the day pleading their cases and study their style at close quarters. What was more, mixing so soon with the Paris legal profession allowed him to feel each day a little more at home in the capital, for which he felt somehow grateful, given that his farmyard looks labelled him an out-and-out provincial. In the evenings he joined fellow clerks and junior lawyers from the Palais in drinking and discoursing in cafés around the Law Courts. Danton's forte was to imitate famous barristers he'd heard that day; he declaimed their pleas, line after line, in a grave, persuasive voice, a feat of memory that impressed his companions. His appetite too impressed. The Champenois naturally regarded food and drink as the first of pleasures and Danton attacked each with vigour, as his physical size suggested he ought, though he set certain outward limits to self-indulgence. His modest resources told him to keep an eye on pleasure's costs, for despite his views on money he could not afford to be in debt.

Some months after his arrival in Paris a letter from his mother bid him look up a young woman from Troyes, a distant relative of the Camuts. She had her own apartment in Paris beside the sprawling Halles food market, where she lived between frequent visits home. Her name was Françoise Duhauttoir and from what Danton could make out, at their first meeting, she had inherited a small private fortune that allowed her to live independently, a rare situation for an unmarried woman of her class. She was older than he – by a good six years – and looked an appealing blend of town and country. He wasn't experienced in these things, but in his impressionable eyes she must have combined the sharp-nosed, pale-cheeked look of the city mistress with the well-set promise of the Champagne peasant girl.

As time went by he began calling regularly at Mademoiselle Duhauttoir's door, stepping over the market produce – potatoes, apples and beef shanks – crated in the street outside. Clearly she was not put off by his looks; she seemed to see manly promise in his burly frame, and she said she liked his voice. In fact she confirmed what he was feeling progressively sure about: he had no cause to hold back because he was ugly. Unsightliness of his rare stripe might even be viewed as an asset. For instance – Mademoiselle Duhauttoir was the first to observe this – his bulbous cheeks, despite the granular flesh, gave him the look of an enormous cherub.

The young woman from home was not his first conquest in Paris – the fresh girls around the market sold their favours for 2 sous – but she was the most dependable. Although there was a suspicion of an older man somewhere in Françoise Duhauttoir's to-and-fro life, a provider no doubt worthier of her time than he, they maintained an intimate complicity that would in time hold additional benefits, for she too knew people in the legal profession.

All the same Danton missed the countryside and the fresh air. The Seine was some consolation. It lacked the tingling pace of the fresh waters of the Aube racing over the Arcis weir, and even the Paris boatmen were repelled on bad days by the half-submerged filth it carried. On better days, though, it was at least a chance to swim. He longed to swim; it was a passion he wanted new friends in Paris to share and, though they didn't know how to do so and had never tried, he talked them into joining him for the experience at a spot a little upriver from the heart of the city, before it discharged the full foulness of its waste. Here there were docks for barges from the interior – grain boats from Arcis among them – and it took fifteen minutes to cleave from bank to bank, even for a master swimmer like Danton. People at work on the quays stopped to watch, curious to see whether he would make it across. It was a strange sight for city folk. The friends who took up Danton's challenge often regretted it as they thrashed and laboured in midstream, counting on him to race up and save them. From the stretch of the Seine where they bathed, close to the city walls, there was a straight view of the Bastille rising in gaunt fastness above the Saint-Antoine district. They could hardly keep their eyes off it. As a newcomer Danton found the stone-grey colossus and its thickset towers menacing as well as overpowering. 'I hate that bloody place hanging over our heads,' he would tell his swimming friends.

Long before Parisian hordes set about flattening the Bastille, the Seine flattened Danton. Within a year of his initiation at the Law Courts the river's soupy microbes infected his bather's lungs, leaving him close to death for over a month. He lay in bed fighting a grave sickness that doctors were unsure how to treat. Their prescription was to wag their heads and to observe – as he began at length to recover – that he was fortunate to have a robust natural constitution. The illness and a frustratingly long convalescence provided a chance, though, to knuckle down to legal studies, and when these grew tiresome, as they might after an hour or so, to read up further on the determined men of letters who were subverting the kingdom of France.

Demands for reform were a constant talking point at the Law Courts, for Paris was a hive of political disputatiousness. Under the Oratorians the philosophical assault on the powers of the monarchy had by no means been omitted from his education, but it had taken second place to the study of the Ancients and their glorious republics. In convalescence, Danton now focused his attention on the great minds who were raising political temperatures at the Law Courts. Stuck in bed with poisoned lungs and a preposterously premature death threatening, he came in full curiosity to Montesquieu, Voltaire, Rousseau and Diderot, memorising their words until he could recite whole paragraphs blind. By the time he recovered, his memory had so tight a hold on Diderot's bulky *Encyclopédie* that his fellow café-goers swore he could recite the entire work by heart, page by page. It was an exaggeration he could live with; no one, he was sure, would ever ask to hear him spout the whole thing. Danton was no fount of original political thinking, but he could carry an audience. And when he heard others come up with ideas that took his fancy, he was often able to put them across with more vigour and eloquence than their authors.

After three years with Maître Vinot, Danton was ready to sit the Bar examinations for his lawyer's diploma. He was close to twenty-four years old and felt he had performed enough clerking. The hours were hard: rise at 6 a.m., lunch at nine, dine at 3 p.m., an hour's recreation, then work until nine at night. Danton was of an age to take his lawyers' robe, though he had not exactly pored over the legal texts, preferring the hurly-burly of the Palais despite the trying hours. It was Maître Vinot, with whom his relations remained extremely cordial, who reminded him that there was a short cut to the Bar. To take the law degree in Paris was a notorious grind; it meant facing examiners known to be uniquely demanding and ungenerous. The process could take months, then end in failure. Instead, following his patron's advice, Danton applied to take his degree in Reims. This looked a better prospect. In the matter of prize-winning, Reims had already proved favourably disposed towards him. It was not necessary to be a native of Champagne to sit Bar examinations in its ancient capital, the process was open to all. But it was known to be easier and shorter than the Paris trial. Indeed, there was dismissive talk among members of the Paris Bar that law degrees from Reims were up for sale. Reims graduates shrugged off the taunts. Parisian scorn had never stopped ambitious young men from the highest rungs of the bourgeoisie from opting to spend a week or so in the Champagne capital to enter the legal brotherhood, for whether obtained in Paris, Lyons, Bordeaux or Reims the diploma amounted to the same thing in the end.

Danton was in and out of Reims before the Law Courts had time to miss him. When he reappeared in Paris at summer's end in 1783 wearing the black robes of his new station, it was to continue working in the Vinot chambers, though for higher gain and with easier hours. As a junior partner he was obliged to seek his own cases to plead. He plugged away at it, forced to take on unprofitable briefs for longer than he'd expected, for grave signs of stress in France's finances were just now taking their toll on the lawyers' trade. In the great rumbling chorus for reform of the social order, who could tell where these latest disruptions might lead?

Perhaps reflecting the state's financial slide, debtors became Danton's standby clients. It was income of a kind. The higher gain promised from partnership with Maître Vinot was real, though in the first years it lingered obstinately below the hopes that lofted him back to Paris from Reims. For a young man about town it would do. Any strong political sympathies he was developing he kept to himself in the courtroom. He was as apt to argue the case of a shepherd against an overbearing landowner – which he did, and won – as to take the high-born landowner as his client. There was no great advantage in representing nobles, except that plenty of them were now joining the debtors' class.

France was a rich country, inherently the richest in Europe, but its wealth was on a perilous slide.

# THREE

# Questions for a Bourgeois Gentleman

For a man of Danton's palpable energies, this was an awkward time. Too slow for his liking, yet also disturbing. By the mid 1780s, Louis XVI's treasury had run so low that there seemed only one feasible way to replenish it – to increase taxes on the middle and lower classes. Unless, that is, the state was to attempt the unfeasible. For there was an insanely provocative tax proposal in circulation, one that turned the existing royal order and its system of privilege on its head, to which the court at Versailles nonetheless gave serious consideration before, at length, rejecting it: to tax the aristocracy. In the end the king went for the conventional remedy – and borrowed heavily to boot. This response was to prove suicidal.

Indeed, there had been every reason for the court's panicky reflections on making the nobility pay up. Vast French outlays on arms, transport, men and loans to support the American colonists in their struggle for independence from England had slowly been emptying the state coffers from the day Danton first arrived in Paris. Here was the source of the financial stress. Now, as he turned twenty-five, everyone was aware of it. The giant from Arcis could not join friends in a Paris café without hearing about it.

Moreover, the agent of France's financial ruin had been easy to spot riding around the capital in a rumpled topcoat from ministry to ministry, running his host's cupboard bare in appealingly mangled French. He was Benjamin Franklin, the rebel American representative to the Bourbon court. Wigless and dishevelled, his lank hair falling over the back of his collar, the paunchy American was a mercurially divided soul who had managed to keep squeezing large war loans out of France – straight gifts as often as not – even as she ruined herself in hostilities engaged by others 3,000 miles from her shores. Franklin's layman's charm coupled with his obvious delight at living in Paris and having access to the Versailles court made him immensely popular. As far as France was concerned, the loans he negotiated would better have gone in the opposite direction. But the courtiers, in particular the duchesses, found 'Monsieur Franklin' irresistible. So innocent, so rustic. And that roving eye of his! No matter that he had not long before leaned towards abandoning the cause of American independence and keeping his British citizenship, the French adored him.

Once a week, as Danton was still finding his barrister's feet, he saw crowds in the street applaud as Franklin drew up in his carriage at City Hall, directly across the river from the Vinot chambers, on his goodwill rounds. Danton was intrigued. How did this shabby republican, a man of the people, a tinkerer with machines and printing presses, a homespun scientist, reconcile himself to frolicking with the noblest of them at Versailles? Perhaps it was his true nature. For it was hard for anyone in France, even for one nourished on Cicero such as Danton, to imagine what it was to be a republican. At Franklin's bidding, the king had thrown arms and troops across the Atlantic. The American's thinking had been as sound as it was simple: he wagered that even the looming prospect of financial ruin would not discourage the French from doing their utmost to bloody England's nose in America. The wager needed to be a safe one, for without French support the American rebel cause was probably lost. And safe it was. The Bourbon court was hell-bent on revenge for England's seizure of all Canada and a cherished string of French colonies stretching from the Caribbean to India – tragic losses dating from their previous conflict two decades past. It would wipe the slate on all the humiliation suffered in that Seven Years War.

So it was that in the years that followed England's defeat on the other side of the Atlantic in 1783, when the American colonies were able to call themselves the United States without further dispute, an avenged France might fairly have expected to see better times ahead. Alas, as young Maître Danton cast around for meatier briefs, hopes raised were hopes crushed. The *Ancien Régime*'s financial agonies persisted, as though peace itself were a ruinous illusion. Luxury and waste at court continued unrestrained; the Bourbons did not feel it their personal responsibility to save the treasury, and the whimsical extravagances at Versailles of King Louis' Austrian queen, Marie-Antoinette, were (so a combative Paris press dared advise the public) the most insolent proof of it.

Franklin remained in Paris for a while after England's defeat, continuing to charm his hosts. But the damage was done. France was unable to halt the plunge into bankruptcy. For common citizens in the cities and on the land it would take a little time and some dire events – successive bad harvests, dramatic increases in the price of bread that left the poor starving, plus a freakishly cold winter – for the full effects to penetrate daily life. For the moment, though, the difficulties afflicting ordinary people hinged on taxes. A system that continued to exempt bluebloods and the clergy aroused greater public wrath against the king's justice than did notorious iniquities such as the *lettres de cachet* empowering him to remove from society, without question or appeal, anyone who offended royal sensibilities.

Who could be held to blame for France's increasing woes but an omnipotent king and the privileged classes? Danton would not have argued with that.

For a while yet, as the 1780s tottered on, Danton's life was unremarkable. He was young and he had an unusually powerful voice, even by the echoing standards of the Palais de Justice. He was up with liberal thinking and mostly agreed with it, but he was not by any means its mouthpiece. There were more than enough pamphlets and news-sheets hawked on street corners to keep up vocal pressure against the monarchy. The royal government's attempts at censorship were ineffectual swipes at a relentless swarm of printing-press bees.

Danton read the news-sheets, both anti-royalist and screamingly royalist, and also enjoyed himself at the theatre, where the level of daring rose as the king's popularity fell. He took a regular seat at the Théâtre Français, the largest playhouse on the Left Bank, which he found well worth the price because although its troupe was paid from the king's purse and mostly performed the classics of Racine, Corneille and Molière, its stars had a wicked habit of playing up politically suggestive lines, pausing over them or throwing their eyes high to alert their expectant audiences. Dramatists were slipping the leash in all genres: comic, tragic, satirical, outright erotic.

Danton was not much concerned by morals, good or bad, but he might have wondered along with the rest of the audience if it was more than coincidence that the collapse of state finances seemed matched by a free fall in the morals of the privileged classes. A blueblood former officer in the King's Army by the name of Choderlos de Laclos was even now titillating Paris with his malicious novel *Les Liaisons Dangereuses*, a stiletto driven into the breast of his own class. Laclos' work had remained immensely popular from its first appearance in 1782 and Danton, like his bourgeois friends at the Palais, was doubly amused to find that those who applauded it the most were those it attacked.

There was much to entertain a young man about town in the few years left before everything turned upside down. Danton continued to swim. He also fenced, and – as Mademoiselle Duhauttoir's main attentions indeed turned to the older man whose presence in her life he had rightly suspected – he dallied more often with young women in the lively Marais district behind City Hall. On becoming a barrister, he had moved to an apartment in the Marais, not much larger accommodation than the lodgings made available by Maître Vinot, but altogether independent. There, and around the Halles market, girls came as plenteous as the apples and peaches on sale – girls from the city and girls from the country.

For café-going, the young lawyer was particularly drawn to an establishment called the Parnasse. It was conveniently located on the Right Bank where the Pont Neuf opened on to the quay, not far from his Marais apartment and right opposite the Law Courts, at the corner of the Rue de l'École (its habitués called it 'Café de l'École' for simpler reference). Thanks to its position, it was one of the best-known *limonadiers* in all Paris and a natural haunt for the legal brethren of the Palais. By 1787 Danton's café circle included his old classmate from Troyes, Jules Paré, now a capable lawyer, and a passionate character named Camille Desmoulins. Camille, as everyone including the waiters tended to address him, was a year younger than Danton and served as a junior lawyer at an august political assembly of notables, mainly aristocrats, called the Paris *parlement*. Its institutional role, like that of lesser *parlements* in the regions, was to propagate laws for the king, except that these days – a sign of the times – it had developed an anarchic streak and as often as not locked horns with the royal court on the important affairs of state.

In appearance, Danton and Desmoulins were almost comically dissimilar. Camille was a slender Picard with dark shining eyes and black flowing locks and the air of an excitable poet. His *parlement* post paid a miserly salary and he often had to write home to his father, a municipal magistrate in Picardy, to tide him over. Camille's needs were a source of conflict in the provincial Desmoulins home since his father, an expert on the minutiae of royal law, judged that his son should have been fending better for himself, or spending less. Danton himself had long since stopped receiving financial support from home, but he sympathised with his friend nonetheless.

Danton's and Camille's judgements on events in France had a similar tilt; they were the products of a like education. 'We were raised in the schools of Rome and Athens, in pride in the republic,' Camille exalted, though in fact he'd been a boarder in Paris. Their talents dovetailed. Camille's gifts lay precisely where Danton's deserted him – in a passion for writing. His ease with the pen was pushing him into journalism. If political pamphleteers set the capital's mood, he had to be part of it.

At the Parnasse, however, Danton's eye was not fixed solely on his friend's ardent political texts. He was achingly aware of the buxom, auburn-haired daughter of the café's proprietor. To address the ache, his tactic was to befriend her mother, the mistress of the till, and this transparent campaign amused the pair of them since the mother was Italian by origin and Danton, reared on Dante, had the habit each time he entered the establishment of launching into absurdly literary Italian to discuss the weather, the clientele or whatever item of café small talk he hit upon. At least the performance brought him close to the daughter, within smiling distance, whenever she assisted her mother at the till. His interest was different from the desire he felt for the Marais girls, though he could not say why, for she aroused him the more.

Danton was in love.

Gabrielle Charpentier was a full-bosomed, full-cheeked girl, three years younger than he, with a natural dignity that allowed her to move about the crowded café, tossing her dark hair, without collecting taunts from boisterous male customers. Her father, François Charpentier, acted the gentleman host, in a grey frockcoat, a small round wig and, to show professional intent, a white cloth on his arm, though he had no need to put himself out. The Parnasse was a good business and furthermore he had purchased – as a secondary enterprise to underpin his fortune – the office of royal tax collector, a remunerative position which the monarchy fielded out to suitable local bidders. This unusual entrepreneurial combination placed the Charpentiers squarely in the Paris bourgeoisie, and the café owner had it in mind to marry his eligible daughter into the legal class, whose members' earnings filled his till.

Gabrielle could not help but be aware of Danton, any more than the Law Courts could. He stood a head above most of the Parnasse customers. And his battered features turned more grotesque still when accompanying the Neapolitan hand-on-heart gestures he practised on her mother. Yet the ugliness grew invisible when he talked; all she saw was a virile, hearty suitor. If people whispered to her how hideous he was, as they did, she only thought how winsome his manliness was. Love, fulfilling its duty, was blind. Gabrielle was won over before Danton asked for her hand.

Monsieur Charpentier was more cautious than his daughter. Danton was not a rich catch, he recognised, but the young lawyer had vigour and self-confidence and, no doubt, promise. He certainly needed to improve his professional standing beyond that of Law Courts lag with irregular briefs, and the café owner told him so. If financing was an obstacle, Gabrielle's dowry might help.

When Danton examined the situation with his friends it was the resourceful Françoise Duhauttoir who proposed a solution. The mysterious older man in her life, whom she presently intended to marry, turned out to be a barrister who was preparing to sell his practice. This was an excellent opportunity for Danton, she said. The practice on offer was the seat held by Maître Huey de Paisy, Françoise's betrothed, on the King's Council, a select brotherhood of lawyers under royal charter. They dealt with appeals against verdicts delivered by courts in Paris and the provinces, attacking or defending them. The council was limited to seventy-three members and because of their small number and the trust placed in them they were considered the elite of the profession, men who knew precisely how the state and French society worked.

This meant quite a leap for a journeyman barrister, but it was not the vault in status or the required expertise that fazed Danton. He had turned twenty-seven and his self-confidence was all that old Charpentier believed it to be. However, a King's Council seat did not come cheaply. Maître Huey de Paisy's price was 78,000 livres, a good portion of which Danton was able to meet through a loan of 30,000 livres from Mademoiselle Duhauttoir, who was impatient to see the sale through. With additional loans from the Camut family chest in Arcis and Troyes, plus the immediate prospect of a dowry worth 15,000 livres deliverable with Gabrielle, he was still 10,000 livres short. This was a problem. Huey de Paisy resolved it by giving Danton a year's grace to make up the missing funds. Except for the dowry, all of it had to be reimbursed. It was a big risk to take, but Danton now jumped at it. If all went well, Françoise Duhauttoir's betrothed reckoned, the seat would yield an income of up to 25,000 livres a year, as it had for him, and there was the added bonus of regular professional contact with the king's ministers and their influential officials, also, at times, with the outer sanctum of the royal court. It promised to be a good schooling in politics.

Danton signed the purchase contract in March 1787 and Louis XVI, beset by popular unrest and sniping from the nobility itself, enrolled him as a council member three months later, on 12 June, in a standard decree declaring the monarchy's 'full and entire trust in the person of the dearly beloved Sieur G-J Danton and in the worth, competence, loyalty, wisdom, experience, fidelity and affection he brings to the office of lawyer in His Majesty's council'. There was precious little search made into Danton's 'loyalty'. It would have taken a king with less stressful matters on his mind to divine just where his new council lawyer's instincts were to lead him.

The decree was the bunting for Danton's marriage two days later to Gabrielle. His mother came from Arcis for the occasion, accompanied by a bevy of aunts and uncles. Their arrival gave the brawny groom a bout of homesickness; they were a glimpse of the Aube, an intake of fresh Champagne air. By all appearances he was now a city bourgeois with a stable career ahead of him, except that his longing for the countryside never left him. It gnawed and pulled, a mysterious hunger. Ever since his arrival in Paris it had drawn him back to Arcis every few months – each time for only a day or so to retake his bearings, for he had his eye on two extra acres of land he thought he might be able to acquire close to the family home, one of them on a riverside copse behind the grain mills. That would have to wait until his new practice began producing funds, but it pleased him to think of the additional acres as his.

As royal authority continued to crumble through 1788, the career stability promised by a King's Council seat was only apparent. The office presented the kind of dilemma that tore at most of Danton's class. How could one serve the king – even as indirectly as he was – and at the same time respond to an ever louder rumbling against the monarch's powers? Danton was not made to finesse. Acknowledging the contradiction, the Arcis bull lowered his head and charged at it.

A first test came from fellow King's Council advocates, for their tradition was to examine a newcomer's credentials rather more closely than King Louis did. The conservative brotherhood perceived from Danton's appearance that it was taking in an original, and it wasn't diverted from that judgement by the silvery wig he wore atop his massive head to mark his social station. Putting him to an initiation ceremony, members laid him a trap. He was required to deliver a discourse in Latin and the theme they set him was this: the moral and political situation of the country in regard to justice. Even without the obligation to address it in Latin, it was, considering the times, a hideous teaser. 'It had me walking on razors,' Danton recalled, for ageing conservatives on the council far outnumbered junior members schooled in new ideas like himself.

But he would not avoid the trap, he would spring it. He was up to speaking in Latin. He began mildly: the king's government must grasp the gravity of what was happening in France; it must respond with simple remedies; the nobility and the high clergy who possessed France's riches must make sacrifices; the common people must be heard, popular grievances addressed. The seniors nodded, impressed at least by his Latin improvisation. The gist of his discourse was not uncommon for the times, though they were disturbed by his booming emphasis on phrases like '*vox populi*' and '*motus populorum*'.

Then came the bull's charge. Danton concluded: 'I sense a terrible revolution on the way.' There was but one hope of avoiding the worst – to contain popular discontent so that the crisis played out very slowly, over several decades. The drop of his massive wigged head showed, however, that he considered that outcome unlikely. He ended, ambiguously: 'Woe to those who provoke revolution, and woe to those who carry it out.'

His conclusion prompted worried council elders into asking him to supply a written version of his talk for their perusal. Danton baulked. Was this another trap? It was not just his aversion to the pen that held him back; he thought it would probably be a mistake to let his presentation reach the eyes of court snoopers at Versailles. 'Written! I haven't written a word,' he replied. The assembly sat in astonished silence. He added, with his mashed smile: 'Should you wish, however, I can repeat the whole speech. I believe every word of it.' The elders retreated, deciding, on a hasty second vote, against obliging themselves to sit through it again.

Once professionally established, Danton left his cramped Marais apartment and moved with Gabrielle into larger quarters befitting a King's Council advocate, an apartment situated straight across the river on the Left Bank. There it was no less noisy and the air no less malodorous; it was best to keep looking up wherever you were in the streets of Paris, for the contents of bedpans and chamber pots rained without prejudice from windows above. The Left Bank ambience was different, though, because here metal workshops and dyers' yards no longer proliferated. This was the parish of Saint-Sulpice, still within easy walking distance of both the Law Courts and the Parnasse café. From the Seine the district extended south in a lively wedge of commerce, professions and the arts to the Luxembourg Palace, the residence of the king's brother, the Comte de Provence, on the rare occasions he cared to stay in Paris.

Danton rented the second floor of a residential building on the Cour du Commerce, a busy, narrow street of cafés, booksellers, printers and other craftsmen that opened at one end on to the School of Medicine, where surgeons learned to cut and sew. At the entrance to his building he put up a plaque announcing: Maître d'Anton, Advocate in Council. The building had five floors and its inclined façade was several shades cleaner than those of its soot-caked neighbours, so the noble tilt he gave his name with the introduction of the apostrophe did not look entirely out of place. He adopted the simple change without anguish: it went with his station, like the silvery wig he wore. In the fraternity he had joined, class counted. He was a practical man.

Danton settled into family life, delighting in wife and home. Within weeks of moving to the Cour du Commerce, Gabrielle was pregnant. She seemed to accept that her main task was to keep Danton happy, which meant cooking to his enormous appetite. He was always inviting lawyers and clients home to dinner, along with people he met in the street – the journalists, bone-cutters and jabbering actors who inhabited the Left Bank. Gabrielle knew the way it would be with him; it was the revolving mixture of professional man and roustabout in Danton that charmed her. Armed with skills learned from her father's café, she was up to the task.

Danton suppers were riotous affairs served with rich vegetable stews, roast duck, juicy meats and strong wines by the bottle – good country fare, the host liked to remind his guests. Budget restraint bowed to natural, indeed careless, generosity. His guests came eight, ten, a dozen at a time, usually including the bright-eyed Camille Desmoulins, so eager to release his fertile thoughts that he stuttered and stumbled over his words and had to refer fellow revellers to what he had written that day to make his point. Another regular was Philippe Fabre d'Églantine, a wealthy cloth merchant's son from Carcassonne in the far south who was trying his hand in Paris as a comic playwright. He'd added the flowery ending to an otherwise unsatisfactory name after winning a gold sprig of eglantine as his prize at a southern horticultural fair. Almost ten years older than Danton, the dandyish Fabre with his bohemian looks and dilettante skills in the arts believed he was irresistible to women, which was true in so far as his success as a playwright to date was limited to liaisons with young actresses he rehearsed for his searing little political comedies. As a songsmith, though, he was faring better, for a charming pastoral ditty he had composed about shepherdesses hiding from the rain '*Il pleut, il pleut, bergère . . .*' looked like becoming a popular favourite; he hummed it around Paris salons as a break from his passionate political discourse.

Feasting with talkative friends was a pleasure of which Danton never tired. Gabrielle must have taken it to be the mark of a country upbringing. He was incurable. No alarms over the sinking affairs of the nation or the rising fury of its people could cut his ogre's appetite for food, wine and talk. The first two were expensive pleasures, as Gabrielle, without malice, sometimes pointed out, reminding him of the large loans he had to repay. During 1788, though, funds were flowing in from his new practice. Despite the times, it looked as though it would indeed bring in the 25,000 livres a year which Huey de Paisy, with his vendor's talk, forecast. Take away the debts to be settled and it offered a comfortable middle-class living. Danton took on his old friend Paré as a partner, trusting he would agree to act more as chief clerk than barrister, for the cabinet work needed organising.

The reliable Paré seemed satisfied with the role. They were immersed in administrative law, mainly in appeals against judgements from high provincial courts. It was not often that the monarchy upheld fairness and impartiality as a principle – 'What is legal is what I wish,' Louis XVI testily asserted at this very time, warding off threats to his authority – but the old King's Council system did have an impartial history and since it frequently involved city boroughs versus boroughs, a town versus a region, an arm of the state versus another, the hard times afflicting lawyers caught up in everyday criminal and civil law largely passed it by. Council barristers' fees came mostly from the royal purse in the end.

\* \* \*

While dependence on royal patronage was something for Danton to reflect upon, it was no bar to a freethinker acting on his impulses. Every middle-class Frenchman practising a profession was directly or indirectly in the king's sinking service. And every middle-class Frenchman was questioning the future. Where will power lie? Who will hold it? Where will I stand? When Gabrielle gave birth to a son, François, in early summer 1788, the questions somehow grew weightier for Danton, head of family, and they had to be confronted.

For many of his class the search for answers passed through Freemasonry. The Masonic movement had the dual attraction of being intellectually underground, which discouraged the police, and highly fashionable. All liberal educated men seemed drawn to it. It was the greenhouse of change in which the lush plants of intellectual dissent flourished, its reforming loam enriched by its strange secretiveness. Danton was drawn to it in the same way that his peers were. It was the thing to do.

With Camille, Danton had himself inducted into a Masonic lodge as soon as he had acquired his King's Council seat. Lodges were more accessible to newcomers than the secrecy inside intimated: ninety-one separate lodges operated in Paris alone, with hundreds more in cities across the kingdom, and they were united in the conviction that absolute monarchy and the Catholic Church's domination of society were twin despots to be fought and brought down to size. Since the government was still doing its ineffectual best to censor the press and suppress public meetings, debate in the lodges was probably the most effective day-in-day-out form of political activity open to reformers.

If anything struck Danton as truly odd about the Masonic movement – odder than its rituals – it was that a prince of royal blood, Philippe, Duc d'Orléans, cousin of King Louis and head of France's second royal house, stood at its summit as Grand Master. For the duke – gambler, man about town, combative liberal – it was, however, an ideal position to occupy. It made him a standing reproach to his Bourbon relations for their ineptitude in landing the throne in its present mess. Better still, it left Louis XVI to ponder the Duc d'Orléans' scarcely hidden personal ambitions, which were to move to a constitutional monarchy in the English manner, with himself as king if things turned out right.

Relations between the head of the Orléanist line and the Bourbon line were therefore strained beyond repair. The queen, Marie-Antoinette, made it plain that she loathed the duke; she believed she saw through his schemes better than her husband. The rift between the royal branches had been developing quietly, through gritted teeth, for more than a century now, from the reign of Louis XIV, the Bourbon Sun King, whose only brother bore the Duc d'Orléans title. Rules governing the succession to the throne had never been written down, an awkward lapse that encouraged blood rivalries. Although the present King Louis threatened now and then to banish the present duke from Paris – and indeed once did so for a while – Philippe d'Orléans felt safe from harsh Bourbon retribution. Thanks to immense Orléanist landholdings he was the single wealthiest man in France, a Croesus who used his riches to sponsor reforming causes, buy influential supporters and engage political agents to promote them. He was convinced that the Bourbons had neither the stomach nor the self-confidence to remove him for long from his splendid Palais Royal compound next to the old Louvre Palace in the heart of Paris, where his standard-bearing liberal presence aggravated the throne's misfortunes.

Danton and Camille selected a Paris lodge named the Nine Sisters on the strength of its distinguished membership. The great Voltaire had been a member there. The current list included the leading luminaries of the Paris salons – liberal aristocrats and sharp-penned modernisers such as the Marquis de Condorcet, a philosopher and mathematician, and the abbé Sieyès, a lapsed churchman with an ungodly flair for politics. Another prominent member was Benjamin Franklin, who wished to show he was a modernist despite his dallying at Versailles. Adherents of the Nine Sisters called it the 'Philosophers' Lodge'.

Nothing was revealed of meetings Danton attended, though the waspish encyclopaedist Diderot, another Freemason, who died four years before Danton joined, had enjoyed recapitulating what he held to be typical Masonic discourse during his final Paris café rounds: 'The people will never be happy until the last monarch is strangled with the guts of the last priest.' This was Diderot out to shock. The prudent Sieyès echoed Masonic distaste for the collapsing *Ancien Régime* with like indignation if less gore: 'A time will come when our outraged offspring will be astounded to read our history, and will give its inconceivable insanity the name it deserves.' Still, modern men of reason – and Danton was now eager to include himself among them – did not wish to kill the king, or even dethrone him. The monarchy as it existed was finished, that was clear. But a new kind was possible. There was room to adapt it to a place at the head of a free society.

As 1788 neared its end the position of the exuberant young giant from Arcis was not, then, inflexible – even if the 'terrible revolution' he had dangled before the King's Council elders a year earlier looked an ever more likely prospect. For the trials of the kingdom by now reached far beyond bankruptcy. Popular unrest was exploding as never before.

The long rumbling turned to a roar.

Bread was the gruel of revolt. That year's harvest was so meagre – the second disappointment in a row – that the price of a regular loaf rose in no time from the standard 8–9 sous to 14 sous. Even if the poor were able to find bread, they could not afford it. Paris and its teeming population were the worst hit, though the provinces suffered too. An unaccommodating climate was not the only cause of distress: a sharp drop in funds going into farm production, a sequel of state bankruptcy, contributed to misfortunes. Food hoarding was a further bane – a widespread practice among speculators and commonplace worriers that grew with the approach of winter even after lynch mobs took to dealing with large-scale hoarders. In Paris, the over-crowded working-class districts in the east – Saint-Antoine surrounding the Bastille and Saint-Marcel on the Left Bank – broke out in violent riots over both bread shortages and surging unemployment. The king's dragoons were sent in to subdue them.

Danton observed the ugly scenes with horror and foreboding. He saw the despair of the masses. It was obvious to him that reforms proposed in the Freemasons' ornate lodges must give the common people justice, not simply change the ruling order. What was reform worth if it failed the people? Around the country hundreds of thousands of the labouring class were now jobless and destitute as a result of a free-trade treaty which the royal government had signed with industrial England two years before. King Louis had meant well, but as cheaper goods poured in from England the agreement crippled France's textile industry, a mass employer in both the capital and the provinces. In Paris alone, 80,000 were out of work. As Versailles realised too late, the treaty ran the old enemy's broadsword through the French workplace.

So it was that when the clerks of the Palais de Justice, Danton's old corps, stopped work that autumn and blocked the heart of the capital in wild demonstrations against the royal government's political ineptitude, the young King's Council barrister could not but recognise that he was in the thick of things. Moreover, his Cour du Commerce home was a stone's throw from a rowdy popular meeting hall in a disused convent where agitators from his Left Bank neighbourhood had lately taken to assembling. The daily gathering in the dusty refectory that once housed the mystic order of Cordelier (cord-belted) friars, men pledged to poverty, was one of numerous district committees and assemblies now forming across the capital to channel radical furies. Danton was drawn to these modern 'Cordeliers' by their prox-imity and the democratic spirit of the times. This was his entry, almost haphazard, into politics. To the rebellious throng at the refectory he brought a startling physique, a ready roar and practice in public speaking honed at the Bar. He seemed cut out to be the bull in the wild Cordelier herd.

If Danton differed, however, from the reforming zealots of his bourgeois class, it was because he was not possessed by demon ideals. Always a practical man, he was driven by impetuosity and heart. These were the contradictions that spun within his burly chest. He was convinced that the people's sense of injustice had to be addressed, rapidly. This was a political necessity. Yet had he been asked why, for all his practical nature, he was on the verge of moving headlong into the unknown, he would perhaps have explained, even now, that it was for the very hell of it.

# FOUR

## *Jumping upon a Tide*

Not all of Paris was as ugly as the mood on its streets. The Duc d'Orléans had lately transformed the closed gardens behind his Palais Royal residence into public pleasure grounds lined by colonnaded boutiques and cafés of a variety and quality unsurpassed in all Europe. This was not, on the face of it, the ideal time for luxury and self-indulgence, but the population responded with enthusiasm.

In the spring of 1789 Parisians from all walks of life converged on the Palais Royal gardens – lawyers and adventuresses, coachmen and whores, fire-spitting radicals and bourgeois matrons – to stroll, to gaze, to shop, to seduce, to eat, to drink wine, to take coffee. And to talk. How they talked. On the gravel terrain between flowerbeds and newly planted rows of trees, stump orators now leaped upon table tops roaring for liberty and human rights. Down with tyranny! Out with the king! The speakers grew in audacity and belligerence, safe in the knowledge that they were in the domain of the Duc d'Orléans, who most often was listening from the balcony of his private quarters overlooking the southern end of the rectangular park. There he stood, an ample figure in princely wig peering down with a slow wave at distant tub-thumpers discoursing on the events of the day.

Danton was drawn to the Palais Royal in that gusty spring. It was an exhilarating arena. For those like him who had begun frequenting radical assemblies in the Paris districts, the duke's splendid grounds offered an additional daily spectacle more intoxicating than their local shows. Late afternoon was the most crowded hour. This was a time for bold words, and the budding politician in Danton delivered some when he saw an opening – not measured speeches but a burst of words that he hoped would capture the blistering spirit of the moment. The crowd invariably stopped and listened, caught by the thunderous voice. The applause excited him. The words came easily, as they did before the Cordeliers. What spilled from his outsize lungs had a natural way of condensing itself, before he knew it, into support for 'the people'. His improvisation always seemed to lead him to that same destination: the people. Rights of the people . . . Power of the people . . . Respect for the people . . .

The message carried. Paris was hungry – and the open attractions of the Palais Royal that drew the citizenry to its gates somehow underscored the deepening misery. Those two bad harvests in a row – a stroke of providence unimaginable for a countryman with Danton's memories of plenty – had by all accounts released popular fury in the provinces too. The family mail from Arcis confirmed it: peasants unable to feed themselves were waylaying grain shipments commandeered by the king's government to feed Paris. Frenchmen were killing for food. It was obvious that what flour got through to the capital was not enough to keep it going. The suffering did not stop there. The winter from which Paris emerged that spring had been the harshest in memory; no one had seen the Seine freeze over before. For want of firewood the poor shivered and died in garrets on the Rue Saint-Antoine. Though the extreme cold for once relieved the city of its smothering stench, its absence was small consolation. A stick of firewood was as hard to come by as a loaf of bread.

Now, in the spring, the industrious Paris that astonished Danton with its hammering and cutting and welding when he first arrived was down to less than half its regular output, leaving bands of resentful workers to roam the streets, indulging in aimless violence. In April Danton was shocked when royal troops shot dead protestors they caught looting Paris workshops. From Brittany in the north to turbulent regions in the south, reports came in that wild crowds were stoning the king's officials and clashing with the king's soldiers.

Through inflexibility, ineptitude and ill chance, the old order had come to grief.

Louis XVI was forced to acknowledge the scale of the catastrophe. Having wavered, he had lately consented to bring together the principal forces in the land – the nobility, the clergy and tax-paying commoners – to raise money and find a solution. The summons was dramatic evidence of the crown's desperation, for it involved convening an Estates-General, an emergency national congress of those three forces. The last time such a congress had been called was two centuries previously in order to re-establish royal authority and close the chapter on civil war after long years of murderous religious strife pitting Catholics against Protestant Huguenots.

The Estates-General was set to open at Versailles on 1 May, and all through the spring of 1789 a great scramble was afoot to choose representatives of the Third Estate – the people, the great subjugated majority of the French nation. Elections were organised throughout the country, and the city of Paris was divided into sixty electoral districts to choose its participants at the Versailles congress.

Danton was beguiled by the prospect, though in truth he had ceased to believe a settlement to keep the *Ancien Régime* in place was possible, however managed. In conversation not a year earlier with the most distinguished of his King's Council clients, the justice minister, Charles de Barentin, he had voiced his doubts in all frankness. He had recently won a difficult case for Barentin, who invited him on the strength of it to consider joining his ministry to take charge of his cabinet. At first, out of politeness, Danton had avoided answering with an abrupt no, and instead outlined for Barentin his ideas on a fairer social system that might yet save the existing order, if the king were to apply it progressively. But at that very moment, as though on cue, King Louis rejected out of hand a virtually identical set of proposals put by far grander thinkers than Danton, who had been unaware of their protest. So when Barentin next sounded him out on joining the ministry, Danton felt entirely justified in refusing. The political situation had now changed, he said. The monarchy was clearly deaf to all reason. He told the king's minister: 'This is no longer about modest reforms. We are more than ever on the brink of revolution.' The minister was distrustful of Third Estate aspirations. Aroused, Danton hardened his warning. 'What! Can't you see the avalanche coming?'

Still, neither his premonitions nor his activities at the Palais Royal and the Cordeliers stopped him continuing to play his part as King's Council advocate. He was incensed, but not insane or irresponsible. He was still able to stand back and separate the affairs of the legal practice that provided his living from the events that promised to wreck it. It was a situation that many bright young men of the law faced. Danton had a wife and son to think of. In him, the family man stood in the way of the thundering radical, but the strain was telling.

The creation of electoral districts across Paris to prepare for the Estates-General handed committed reformers an additional box of explosives to bring on the avalanche. Election meetings swelled the hubbub of defiance sounding from the Palais Royal, the Masonic lodges and local assemblies in the Cordelier mould. The last-named perhaps offered the clearest view of the gathering phenomenon; it was in these ward assemblies that an authentic new democracy was on the march, since shopkeepers, butchers, smiths and market porters rubbed shoulders with bourgeois gentlemen.

The Cordeliers lent their name to the electoral district in which Danton lived. At its heart was the old parish of Saint-Sulpice, a cathedral-like church whose twin towers threw shadows over his Cour du Commerce roof. The Cordelier district's fractious daily meetings were a non-stop fireworks display from morning to night, shaking the refectory to its sainted rafters. Its assembly men were a wild tribe even by the anarchic standards of 1789, with a passionate corps of journalists, writers, poets, playwrights, actors and pamphleteers all eager to draw the common people into their fervent quest for 'liberty'. They were a bohemian set who hurled their republican fancies at the workers and apprentices they pulled in off the street.

There were other riotous Paris districts, especially Saint-Antoine and the poor Saint-Marcel in the east, but in the eyes of cautious liberal gentlemen who assumed charge elsewhere, the Cordeliers were a band apart – a strange mix of romance and practical street politics, almost wilfully non-intellectual. As from that spring, with royal authority patently in free fall, Danton and his colleagues distinguished themselves further: they turned their Cordelier headquarters into something of an inner-city Paris government in street-level charge of their district, policing it, forming a local militia and, when their spirits overflowed, marching to patriotic songs.

Gentlemen reformers from milder districts frowned. But among the Cordeliers, Danton's status was high. The bohemians respected him for his daunting physical presence and the stentorian voice he turned on their discussions, and the hospitality on offer at his Cour du Commerce home confirmed their respect. Other core Cordeliers included Camille, Fabre and Paré, together with a master butcher by the name of Louis Legendre, a fierce political autodidact who liked to appear for debate in a bloodstained apron. Then there was a restless actor, Jean-Marie Collot d'Herbois, who prided himself on his French adaptations of Shakespeare, and a strange, nervous dwarf of a journalist named Jean-Paul Marat.

The Cordeliers lived under each other's feet, within sight of the friars' gaunt refectory. Marat, his skin tufted by scurvy, lived across from Danton in a cellar beneath the Cour du Commerce; here he published inflammatory news-sheets from a portable printing press which he could hide at an instant's notice when a patrol of the king's troop tramped past above. Marat was an irate mole, though at this stage he need not perhaps have kept quite so far underground. The police, still under the orders of the king's government, preferred to avoid trouble; they generally steered clear of both the Cordelier assembly hall and a labyrinthine café nearby called the Procope, which backed on to the Cour du Commerce from the parallel Rue Dauphine and where the tribe mustered after its debates. With its private cubby holes and mysterious corridors, the Procope warren was a perfect place for conspirators. Cordelier regulars loved it. To Camille it was 'the one sure place in Paris where freedom reigns supreme'.

For Danton, the Cordelier assembly hall was an ideal place to test his orator's skills. With Left Bank agitators coming in and out of the old refectory all day, there was no better hall in Paris in which to sound off and send the dust of ages flying. In the Cordelier hall he ran through ideas that would perhaps blossom that same day into a public harangue before the great crowds at the Palais Royal. He used Cicero as a model. Danton understood just why Cicero's strongest support came from the teeming poor of Rome: he employed the mood of the crowd to get his way – he was the people's champion.

The Roman senator's speeches held pride of place still on Danton's Cour du Commerce bookshelves. Among his favourites were Cicero's orations against the brutish Verres, the governor of Sicily, and his prosecution of the corrupt aristocrat Catalina. Running them through his head until their cadence became second nature, Danton committed himself to mastering their deceptively quiet openings and sudden lunges for the jugular. He identified with Cicero on more than one account, for the star of the Forum was as averse as Danton to speaking from a written text; he learned what he was going to say by heart – or it simply came to him while speaking. Moreover, it was satisfying for the brawny young lawyer from Champagne to recall that Cicero had neither the advantages of aristocratic birth nor the military genius that propelled noble Romans to power; he was a middle-class lawyer who swept to the very top of the Roman republic by talking his way there. The fancied kinship with Cicero went further still. By all accounts the Roman believed that triumphant oratory started with careful physical conditioning and he therefore exercised his chest muscles, built up his thighs and went through a strenuous daily series of press-ups with the same fixed purpose that Danton put into swimming the Aube and the Seine – back and forth, bank to bank, until satisfied that if anything was to let him down it would not be his stamina.

Even Marat found time to emerge from his cellar to listen to Danton performing at the Cordeliers, though the praise the obsessive journalist showered on him for his style was not wholly welcome. Danton avoided Marat's company. Gabrielle did not want him in the house; she said he smelled like a rat. And in truth he was a sad fellow who seemed unable to enjoy himself, a diminutive, bony creature who always wore the same soiled green frockcoat and tired suede breeches, the presumed source of the offending smell. It was hard, though, not to admire Marat. He was a merchant of the extreme, skilled in his craft and utterly inexhaustible. He outwrote every agitator on the streets of Paris. To be sure, Camille was also a wonder with the pen, certainly more elegant than Marat – he had already launched a successful news-sheet entitled *La France Libre*, which put a stirring and compelling case for a republic – yet in volume of output Camille was no match for the little cellarman. Marat cranked out half a dozen different pamphlets a day from his underground lair, beating the drum for popular revolt, and he was on the point of single-handedly launching a genuine daily newspaper, which, he told Danton with gimlet-eyed glee, he was calling the *Ami du Peuple*. Considering the author's isolation, it seemed an ambitious title, but Marat was a box of contradictions: a doctor by training who so hated aristocrats and churchmen that he stood not for preserving life but – in their case – taking it; a scourge of the monarchy who for the sake of regular income had until recently served the Bourbon court, tending sick horses in the royal stables; a lowland Swiss by birth who took France's torments for his own. And, by God, what a pen.

In the first days of May, 1789, as the Estates-General got underway, Danton found himself back in Arcis on a despairing personal mission. At that moment revolt seemed to him a small thing; his heart was broken. His infant son François had died on 24 April, barely a year old, and he could not bear the thought of burying him anywhere but in his own Champagne homeland. Gabrielle promised him they would have more children, but his sorrow threw him into a depression and he stayed on in the Danton home at Arcis pondering his loss for several days longer than intended, convinced that the country air was his only cure. Besides, his presence in the capital was not crucial. He had not been one of the half-dozen Cordeliers sent to a Paris-wide electoral assembly to choose the delegates who would represent the city's huge population of commoners at the Estates-General. Nor had he sought the honour. In these first tremulous days of democracy, voting was a complicated, long-drawn-out affair – restricted to property owners or men who paid more than a tidy 6 livres a year in taxes, so that the working class was virtually excluded. The Cordeliers for once acted with caution in choosing their electors, stilling wilder instincts: a leaden civil servant with long municipal experience was selected to head their contingent.

If the Estates-General was convened to bridge France's great social rifts, its enduring contribution was to confirm them. Rather quickly after the opening, the commoners of the Third Estate – backed by a smattering of liberal-minded nobles and churchmen – broke free of the structure of the king's congress and turned themselves into an independent national parliament over which Louis XVI, the monarch absolute, had no more practical control than he had over the weather – short of ordering his troops to crush it at gunpoint.

News of what was happening in Versailles landed first at the Palais Royal. News-sheets alighted there through the day like chattersome town sparrows, and the crowds snatched at them, retiring with their catch to fight for the last vacant leather seats at the Café Foy, the biggest and most comfortable of the Palais Royal cafés. In late June they read that King Louis was planning, after all, to use force to disband the breakaway National Assembly. The name Mirabeau was on everyone's lips, dominating the news from Versailles. Danton had heard Honoré de Mirabeau speak at the Palais Royal and was excited by the effect his huge rich voice and his valiant humour had on the crowd: he had them laughing and ready to die for change at one and the same time. On the day that Danton listened to Mirabeau he was in the company of Camille and Fabre. After the performance the Cordelier trio, profoundly impressed, made for their usual table at the Café Foy. And who was Danton to object when Camille observed that he rather resembled Mirabeau? Danton accepted it as a compliment, though even from a distance anyone could see that the great Mirabeau was as ugly as sin.

One from a line of dissenting Provençal noblemen, Mirabeau was a shaggy, dishevelled monster of a man with a ripe wit and a purplish, knobbly, smallpox-ravaged face who deserted his class for the Estates-General and had himself elected as a commoner. In earlier years the passions that drove Mirabeau had landed him in duels, exile and prison for one excess or another, and it was sometimes hard to remember – before he began speaking – that his reputation came supported by an earnest engagement in reform politics. Mirabeau's gods were a popular constitution, patriotism, liberty and truth, and they hovered in marmoreal splendour over his terrible head when he took the rostrum to confront his adversaries.

As Danton read of it in the news-sheets, it was Mirabeau, with one grand, defiant gesture, who created the people's parliament. On 23 June Louis XVI had given a self-serving summary of events in the realm as the Versailles congress moved to a fruitless close, and the representatives of the nobility and the high clergy filed out after the monarch as he left the restless chamber. Commoners stayed behind, to decide what to do. It was a fateful act. Just by staying put and rejecting a request from the royalist president of the congress to leave, they became a revolutionary parliament. Mirabeau was first to rise to speak. With a twist of his head towards royal troops ringing the hall outside, he addressed the president with unusual calm: 'To avoid misunderstanding, go and tell your master that we are here by the power of the people and that we can only be removed by the power of his bayonets.'

To press home the revolt, Mirabeau had the assembly pass resolutions making each deputy immune from royal chastisement and making it a capital crime to lay hands on any one of them. The troops did not move.

This was political revolution – a *coup d'état* achieved by force of argument and bravado. To Danton, back in Paris from the sad mission to Arcis, it was sublime stuff. It had the true ring of Ancient Rome, the stubborn heroics of the Roman Senate; Cicero's speeches raced through his head. He took Mirabeau as a second model. He was an inspiring rascal – a roisterer, too, who liked his food and drink more than most. Perhaps Camille was right: Danton and Mirabeau *were* alike. It was a warming thought. As joyous opponents of the *Ancien Régime* tasted the first shock of it all, they had only one talking point. Where next?

They debated it beneath the spreading trees of early summer at the Palais Royal, in the Cordelier assembly and in other fired-up Paris districts. With cooler precision they debated it in a multitude of new political clubs formed by educated men in Paris and the provincial capitals, associations that in a matter of weeks would fuse into the Jacobin Society, the brainbox of revolution. Like the Cordeliers, the Jacobins took their name from the place where they met – a Right Bank convent rented from a Dominican order of monks who went by the name of Jacobins. The role of the club was to peer into the future and set the course of revolt. Jacobin club members were middle-class intellectuals almost to a man, sensible, serious-minded reformers, the philosophical brains of the revolutionary campaign – men going public with what they had been debating in the Masonic lodges, for they were the selfsame tribe. Moreover, most of them were also members of the breakaway national parliament in Versailles that Mirabeau led, men such as abbé Sieyès, the priest-agitator with a powerful political tract to his name. His pamphlet *What is the Third Estate?* had fired men's minds since the New Year of 1789 with its drumbeat opening: 'What is the Third Estate? Everything. What has it been? Nothing. What does it wish to be? Something!' It was a challenge that set the popular tone for revolution.

Though Danton may not at once have realised it, the as yet unfinished drama at Versailles was for him a release. What happened there encouraged him to abandon his last vestiges of restraint, to put aside the prudence his King's Council seat asked of him and give himself to revolution. Days later, at the beginning of July, a pro-royalist barrister who had known him from the Law Courts happened to pass by the Cordelier assembly hall. He witnessed a giant fellow with a frenetic voice standing on a table top and summoning patriots to take arms against 'thirty thousand troops who are preparing to descend on Paris, loot the city and cut our throats'. The refectory windows rattled with the force of the discourse. Looking closer, the visitor was astonished to recognise the speaker as Danton, his old acquaintance, whom he had always regarded, for all his high spirits, as a peaceful, self-disciplined fellow.

Cordelier members were likewise surprised by the new fury in his performances and told him so. Danton had a disarming explanation: 'I saw an irresistible tide sweep by, so I dived in and swam with it.'

Indeed, he was not burdened by undying principles or theories. He was a man of his times who could see what was right: the old order simply had to give way. Exactly what order of liberty would replace it he was still not sure, no one was, but it was a goal he was glad to fight for with the weapons at his disposal. More violence threatened, possibly far worse than anything Paris had so far witnessed, should King Louis and his government attempt to undo what was done.

Violence was the rogue current in the wave Danton dived into. Who could tell what mad twists it would take? He had come to Paris at the age of twenty to make his way and now here he was, aged twenty-nine, lover of life, sentimental husband, showman, a lawyer at war with much of the law as it stood and yet living from it, hearty populist – he revelled in spicing his public discourse with crude street oaths to warm the crowd – and, in most aspects, a creature of excess. Though he was not by nature a violent man, not a man to raise a musket in anger or take a club to a guardsman, he could talk violence – and to those who did not know him better his alarming face and sheer brawn gave his words a full supplement of menace.

In the early days of July 1789, immense crowds assembled each evening in high excitement and foreboding at the Palais Royal, eager to hear more about what they had read in the day's press. Danton now ranked as a popular performer. Anyone with the voice and the will could speak there: fanatics, messiahs, dissenters. For the most part, though, orators sought to give the old order a final shove to send it toppling over the brink. Table tops were an open dais: Camille's passions often hoisted him upon them. Danton's huge voice was a storm blasting through the trees, and spectators awarded him a stage name for his assaults on tyranny: 'the Thunderer'.

There was a general assumption that the boldest speakers at the Palais Royal were somehow in league with the Duc d'Orléans. Moreover, the king's cousin was liberal with his great wealth when it suited him; he lent money, or gave it away, without question to those he thought could be useful. Much gold changed hands on the stairwell that climbed to the duke's balcony. Danton was aware of it. Who wasn't? But the giant from Arcis was not there out of greed, he was there riding the tide.

One evening, Camille introduced Danton to an old schoolfriend of his, a lawyer representing a northern constituency at the hold-out parliament in Versailles. He had come to the duke's pleasure grounds to test the mood. He was a clever fellow, Camille no doubt forewarned Danton, though before one got to know him he could appear anything but. The friend had a feline aspect, with joyless eyes. In his over-brushed olive frockcoat he looked like a church usher. Danton must have wondered why the ardent Camille kept up the friendship; they appeared to have little in common.

The visitor acted prim and awkward, and hardly spoke. His name was Maximilien Robespierre.

Camille had briefly explained that he and Robespierre had been scholarship boarders together in Paris at the Louis-le-Grand college, reputed to be the best *lycée* in the capital, which was why Camille's rigorous father insisted on sending him there. The friend was from Arras, a northern cathedral city of blunt Flemish manners. The bishop there had financed his education at the Paris school, selecting him as a promising pupil in need of assistance. The boy from Arras was almost two years older than Camille but they became friends because they hailed from the same damp northern parts; in Paris they felt like intruders from a foreign land. On leaving Louis-le-Grand, Robespierre had returned north and stayed there until he won election as an Arras commoner to the Estates-General, a chance return ticket to the capital.

In the visitor's cold eyes Danton would have wondered whether he did not detect some kind of reproach – some suspicion, perhaps, that the man had of people like himself and Camille, people who spoke out for revolution in the gardens of a royal prince with the habit of distributing his wealth among those who played his game. Well, let the sly devil think what he wished. He was not Palais Royal material, that was sure. He would surely be more at home at one of the new political clubs, waving his papers to request a hearing. There was nothing in this pinched, thin-lipped creature to warn Danton that he was in the company of his executioner, no intimation that he stood face to face with death. To the burly Danton, Robespierre looked half a man, a milksop.

The Cordelier pair's habit after listening to speeches at the Palais Royal was to repair to the Café Foy for refreshment to debate the various orators' skills. Once seated that day, Danton and Camille ordered up red wine from the Gironde. Robespierre shook his head and ordered a glass of milk. His sober assessment of the evening's events was that to defend the people was never wrong, whatever the talent of the speaker.

There was room for dark diversion as well as earnestness in revolution. At the Palais Royal the general assault on the royal regime had grown so discordant that a public speakers' committee was formed to provide some semblance of order, and Danton readily accepted a place on it. For its thrust the committee settled on mockery. Royal justice could appear so barbarously absurd, there was nothing else for it. Did the monarchy not see how disproportionate were the punishments its judges meted out against enemies of the regime? Offenders could still be sentenced to the rack, or yet more horrible medieval torture. The machinery of dismemberment kept its berth in central prisons, and though infrequently used – hanging was the common lot of people sentenced to death – it was a sneer at the legal profession of which Danton and the vanguard of reformers were part.

The committee on which Danton sat decided to match the outrageous savagery of the state with equally outrageous derision. It publicly 'sentenced' King Louis, his brothers and princes of the Bourbon line to death by medieval means most foul – 'the guilty to be drawn and quartered alive, their hearts torn out and bunged into their mouths'. The judgement, laid down in a parody of a Law Courts text and nailed to the trees in the Palais Royal, bore the mark of a well-wined Danton, and indeed carried his name beneath it as signatory. It was easy to picture the committee lions bent over a magnum of claret at the Café Foy rejoicing over each merry, awful word.

What was happening in derisive defiance of the regime at the Palais Royal was an open invitation to popular insurrection. It fell short, though, of orchestrating the climax. That fell to chance. The menacing deployment of royal troops around Paris of which Danton had warned the Cordeliers was real enough, though it looked as though the troops' actual mission was to frighten marauding mobs into keeping off the streets rather than to 'cut throats'.

Whatever Louis XVI and his advisers had in mind, it went awry. From 11 July the king's soldiers began deserting in their thousands and fell in with people's militias formed by riotous city districts like the Cordeliers. Louis sent German and Swiss guardsmen, his most reliable troops, to boost the Paris cordon, which only strengthened rumours of a coming massacre. In a last show of testy ill judgement, the king then dismissed the one figure in his government – Jacques Necker, the finance minister – whom the middle class regarded as capable of even comprehending the state's financial woes. From the defiant assembly at Versailles, Mirabeau fired off his own warning to the king: 'Sire, you have more soldiers deployed against the nation than an enemy invasion would array.' Furthermore, Mirabeau objected, His Majesty's impious foreign mercenaries were singing drunken songs of France's demise at the gates of Paris.

It was Camille Desmoulins who lit the touch paper of revolution. That was how Danton and the Cordeliers would remember it. Camille, buoyed by the success of his *France Libre*, was able, when he concentrated, to keep his tongue almost untied when addressing a crowd. On the morning of 12 July he took the coach to Versailles to see for himself what was afoot for inclusion in his news-sheet. He returned to Paris in the early evening brimming with excitement, unable to contain himself, at an hour when 10,000 people and more were gathered at the Palais Royal. Inspired by the size of the crowd, he leaped on to a table at the Café Foy, his dark hair flying behind him, slender fists pumping the sultry air, shouting, 'Citizens, I have just come from Versailles. Necker is dismissed. The death knell has sounded for patriots. Beware, Swiss and German battalions will fall upon us this very night to cut our throats. There is not a moment to lose. Not one moment. To arms!'

The crowds roared their response. To arms!

They poured out of the Duc d'Orléans' gardens, many of them making for their district headquarters in a scramble for pikes and muskets stacked there by defecting troops. Camille watched the rush, a little chastened by the impact of his words. The language of the Cordeliers did not always mean quite what it said: cutting throats and plundering the poor were a manner of speaking. Of course Camille had exaggerated. 'I was choking with a host of ideas I had to get out,' he told Danton. 'I spoke at random, but my words went straight to the crowd's heart.'

That night and the next day passed in an atmosphere of extreme agitation, intensified by reports from the provinces that peasant bands were torching and looting the chateaux of France's noblest families. Then, early on 14 July, Paris street hordes armed with guns and cannon provided by royal-army deserters converged without particular design, pulled by some great intuitive magnet, upon the Bastille prison with its eight towers wedged across the Rue Saint-Antoine. If the target was not preselected, the surging crowds moved there almost automatically, for the Bastille was the most visible symbol of resistance to social change that they knew: its dark walls reeked of the monarchy's efforts to stifle the Enlightenment. Danton had not missed its significance when forced to stare at it as he did his laps across the Seine years before. In bygone times its inmates were Protestants whom Jansenist jailers tortured into converting; now its inmates were mainly political prisoners – men of letters, thinkers, throne-baiters and all manner of offenders against royal power, men whose ardour the king's government believed would benefit from an indefinite period of oblivion. Paris had a score of prisons but the Bastille was the harshest of them: under Louis XVI its windows had been bricked in and its inner garden and courtyard closed to its prisoners. Parisians had come to regard it as a fastness of terror.

When the attacking horde opened fire, the Bastille guard returned it. But in mid-afternoon, as the attackers drew up a reserve battery of cannon, the governor of the smouldering prison surrendered. That evening the governor's severed head and that of the capital's chief magistrate toured the streets of Paris at the tip of pikes, finishing up as footballs kicked between the flowerbeds of the Palais Royal.

It was not quite the end of Louis XVI's reign, but it was the end of his power. A revolution was under way in Europe's largest land, discharging menace throughout the continent and beyond, for sovereignty had abruptly passed from its God-given owner to the people, and though everyone sensed the enormity of the change, who could make sense of it?

Danton missed the Bastille fray. It was an impromptu climax of popular fury that escaped the control of even the most impatient vanguard of bourgeois reformers. The storming of the Bastille had no bewigged leader with chalkboard and assault orders in hand. As for Danton, he arrived to see it happen after the surrender. His revolutionary energies were expended otherwise, and always would be. He was a man of the rostrum, not the barricades, he liked to tell the Procope, which was in fact where he spent a good part of that extraordinary day, exchanging ideas on the establishment of a rebel municipal government.

All the same, he felt he had not given his all on 14 July and it irked him. The idea that he had put his bull energies into promoting the sovereignty of the people, then simply watched as the people grasped it, left him dissatisfied. Why, Camille had done more! And Camille was a scribe. Was he, Danton, the man of action, to shrink from the front line when such momentous things were happening? Moreover, his position at the Cordeliers was at stake, for the district's hotheads, Marat included, were pressing him to become their elected president. In all but title he was already their leader, for it was plain that Camille and the most passionate agitators deferred to him and his vocal cords; even Legendre, the master butcher, who claimed he deferred to no man, bowed to Danton's natural ascendancy.

Nonetheless, Danton had to work at maintaining their support.

By unfathomable military logic, from the very hour that the Bastille fell, troops who abandoned the king's colours and units that stayed shakily intact merged with militias from the insurrectional districts of Paris into a single loose-knit guard force, so that only the king's Swiss and German mercenaries remained under the sovereign's direct orders. The elements of the new guard came together haphazardly out of some fundamental urge to restore public order after the cataclysm. It was the prettiest irony that the disparate contingents forming this force – the National Guard – mustered under the command of the Marquis de La Fayette, for it was the liberal aristocrat's costly campaigns at the side of the colonists in the American War of Independence that sowed the seeds for the attack on the Bastille.

The beak-nosed La Fayette had not grown in modesty after his transatlantic endeavours. He had three loves of which he made no secret – personal rank, country and civil order – and his aim now was to keep order in the revolutionary capital. However, few could tell what the marquis was planning, since his support for the monarchy appeared to be quite as strong as his support for liberal reform. Moreover, he assumed command of the National Guard without much bothering to gain the formal backing of the Paris districts, so the loyalty of the local militias to his force was only nominal. While Danton's Cordelier battalion, a ragtag civil guard, expressed allegiance, it intended to keep order under its own rules, in the wayward spirit of the district. It was only natural that the capital's most rebellious district should be the wariest about forfeiting its independence.

Cordelier independence suggested to Danton a cure for the mild regret that ate at him over his invisible part in the staggering events of 14 July. True, the cure could quite possibly make him a laughing stock. He was aware of that. But by late afternoon the following day, after a vinous session at the Procope, he threw caution to the wind. Danton was never much held back by timidity and inhibition. His plan was to retake the Bastille. Why? To demonstrate to the street crowds that he was with them. Also, it seemed only right to make sure that all the prisoners of the *Ancien Régime* were freed, every man jack of them. Since command of the shattered Bastille was in limbo – nominally still the king's charge even as La Fayette's guard assumed control – Danton would not have put it past the king's men to retain some of those poor devils. But still more to the truth, Danton had an eye for the stunt. He was twenty-nine years old, still an age to let loose. And was Mirabeau's magnificent action at the Estates-General in Versailles not just that, a great stunt? What better way to win the people's fancy?

Only the week before, Danton had bought himself a soldierly uniform for patrols with the newly formed Cordelier battalion, a smart blue officer's outfit with gleaming buttons to reflect his prominence in the Cordelier assembly. He had not worn it yet. Now was the time. Gabrielle had sewn on a stiff pair of epaulettes, so that with a sword swinging at his side it was unmistakeably a captain's uniform, though the cloth was tight across his ox-like chest and the buttons strained perilously.

The sun was sinking on 15 July as Danton left the Procope with a dozen Cordelier regulars and headed for the Pont Neuf, picking up reinforcements on the Cour du Commerce and the busier Rue Dauphine. It was dark by the time the strange platoon armed with pikes and muskets, now twenty strong, arrived at the Bastille, choking on the acrid dust from spent gunpowder that still thickened the summer stench of the city around the fortress. The huge prison gate had been obliterated. In its place thick wooden beams were drawn across the breach. Drawing his sword, Danton brought it down with a fearsome thud on the stopgap woodwork, calling for the officer in charge. His Cordelier companions, some in gentlemen's hats, neckerchiefs and breeches, others perspiring in coarse woollen workmen's trousers, cheered him on. At length a hesitant figure in uniform – a stand-in for the governor killed not twenty-four hours before – appeared from a broken side-gate flanked by a pair of guardsmen.

Trembling, he refused Danton entry. 'No one comes in. Those are my orders.'

Danton scowled. 'Whose orders? Show me, traitor!'

The orders could only have come from La Fayette. It would not harm to take La Fayette down a peg; the general was adjudging too much authority to himself in the fluid situation created by the colossal event of the day before. 'Show me,' Danton bellowed, observing the mounting fear in the stand-in governor's eyes. Now a crowd was gathering to watch, attracted by the rumpus in the heavy summer night.

'What's this rag? We'll see about this!' Danton roared. 'I arrest you in the name of the nation, you rascal.' Taking the officer by the collar, he marched him off towards City Hall, his platoon falling in behind. More and more people poured from their homes to watch as the curious procession passed by, jeering in unfocused anger at the Cordeliers' prisoner and poking at him with pikestaffs. The man stumbled forward with a frozen gaze, as if all he could still see was his predecessor's severed head dancing on the tip of a pike through these same streets the night before.

Danton and his militiamen reached City Hall to find a provisional revolutionary municipal council in session, in the first throes of establishing itself as a ruling 'Commune' in place of royal authority. By rights Danton should have been there representing his district, except that more moderate district leaders were inclined to sideline the Cordeliers because of their reputation for doing things in their own reckless way.

It was past midnight by now but such was the agitation caused by the events of 14 July that the Cordelier troupe found it hard to manoeuvre their prize catch through idlers still thronging the streets and bridges at the heart of the capital. The embryonic Commune gave Danton a frigid reception. What was he thinking of? What was the purpose of the arrest? Danton had half expected a rebuff. This Commune was made up mostly of level-headed men whose political views he at present had no argument with; they were the electors chosen by the districts to depute the city's representatives to Versailles. What irked him was the presumption of those who were taking charge. Its president – the prospective first mayor of Paris – was Jean-Sylvain Bailly, a starchy Freemason and man of science chosen not for love of theatrics but for the support he gave Mirabeau in confronting the king at Versailles.

Bailly was not the kind to appreciate the antics of a mountebank, which Danton would perhaps have allowed was close to describing his action. Indeed, the provisional mayor sent the acting Bastille commandant back to his battered ruins with a certificate of thanks for his contribution to liberty and an apology for the abuse he had suffered.

In revolutionary Paris, Danton on his side and Bailly and La Fayette on theirs were not made to understand each other.

Everyone had his own idea of liberty. Everyone struck his own balance between action, dreaming and common sense. And on balance Danton was pleased with the restorming of the Bastille. It made him suspect from the outset with the new power in place in the capital. On the other hand it regaled the street people and confirmed him as the man of action at the Cordeliers, the boiler room of revolution.

# FIVE

# The Cordelier Republic

In the dust over the Bastille there hung two great questions. What model of government could guarantee liberty? And how to dispose of Louis XVI? These were staggering issues for a young provincial such as Danton to confront. His working experience of the law was grounded in old custom, which was of small help.

Instinct, though, provided guidance: it told him that if revolution was to work, it had to stay close to the people and meet their demands. Making revolution could not be left to bourgeois sages alone, however enlightened they were. How could the Baillys and La Fayettes in their fine culotte-breeches and silk stockings embody the will of men in rough twill trousers – the rebellious tinsmiths, masons and dyers of the Saint-Antoine ward? The gentlemen of the Commune scarcely even shared the objectives of these sans-culottes. This presented a complication for Danton. To champion the little people in revolution and win their hurrahs was bound to have certain drawbacks. There was the risk that gentlemen reformers would regard him as a rabble-rouser, and in truth he had already heard them say it often enough. It went with his booming voice and his frightening face. He considered himself no less a patriot than the theoreticians of revolution, yet to identify with sans-culotte goals made it harder to endear himself to moderate men of his class who were taking charge of the insurrection. Furthermore, siding with the street compromised his rewarding work on the King's Council, which continued to function and require his attentions after 14 July, in the same quirky manner that a disempowered king continued, in name, to rule France.

But there was no pulling back now. The tide was too strong.

Danton's first thought was to put revolution into practice in the Cordelier district. He pictured his district as the audacious vanguard of change for the rest of Paris to follow. If the Cordeliers didn't show elan, there was a definite risk that the Commune under Bailly and La Fayette would soon enough resume the old order's authoritarian habits at City Hall. That was unthinkable. To avert it, the Cordeliers adopted a stubborn working principle: no law, no decree, no order emanating from the Commune had force in the capital unless validated by the Cordelier assembly. After all, Bailly's authority was provisional. How dare he claim to rule Paris! The Cordeliers had stout allies in the working-class wards in the east, districts ready to march at the first sign of City Hall disdain for their aspirations. The mood in the capital was so volatile that no man had the right to take personal charge.

To make their point, Danton and his team ruled that delegates they sent to sit in the Commune were at all times beholden to the Cordelier assembly. What was more, they were subject to replacement after attending three sessions of the new city council; that way they would not be contaminated. The provocation enraged Bailly and representatives from milder Paris wards, but Danton was adamant about maintaining his district's freedom of action. 'To release revolution, you must stir the sludge,' he advised his Procope companions.

As soon as he was formally elected president of the Cordeliers assembly in September, Danton began improvising local decrees one after the other, all of which, practical or whimsical, were an overt challenge to Bailly's authority at City Hall. He brought to his campaign the lawyer's craft of dressing ideas in legal terms that appeared to lend them unanswerable force. Danton decrees skittered forth: rules to police commerce in flour; to regulate bread distribution; to impose a district tax to aid the derelict; to empower the Cordelier battalion to arrest delinquents anywhere in the capital (one in the eye for La Fayette). Among his boldest initiatives was a decree authorising Cordelier battalion guardsmen to block shipments of gold ingots to provincial mints, this to ensure that all gold pieces were struck in the Paris mint, which happened to be located in the Cordelier district.

It was open warfare. The 'Cordelier Republic' versus the Commune. Danton's ward had become a state within a tottering state – 'the Terror of the Aristocracy', as Fabre subtitled it.

Danton had his assembly. Danton had his battalion. And he had something with more clout still – his promotional division, though it tended to give him as much grief as gratification. After the fall of the Bastille the journalists and dramatists of the Left Bank were in their ardent, excoriating element. Marat's newspaper the *Ami du Peuple* was now up and running, an instant success with the most bloodthirsty fringe of the populace. The same savage words leaped from every line: 'swine' . . . 'murderers' . . . 'scoundrels' . . . 'vultures' . . . 'heads must roll' . . . 'death'. Marat had his paper on the streets each day at daybreak, eight pages of unrelenting vitriol composed through the night and sold for a sou.

Danton found Marat as exhausting to read as he was to have for an ally. He sympathised with Marat's doctor, who used the eight pages as a daily gauge of his patient's health: when the tone exceeded a certain level of violence the physician went straight to Marat's print shop and bled him. Danton was not pleased to have the capital associate the little hatemonger too closely with the Cordeliers. Frankly, he would have liked to disown him. But the sans-culottes loved Marat – and they were Danton's constituency too. In the realm of extremist journalism, Marat had a rival in a hitherto destitute Norman, Jacques-René Hébert, about whom Danton had similar reservations. Hébert joined the Cordeliers as a springboard for his fanatical labours on a homespun rag entitled the *Père Duchesne*, an Old Father William bunion-cure publication which he was fast transforming into a merciless scourge of aristocrats and profiteers, turning a nice profit for himself all the while.

By comparison with Marat and Hébert, Camille Desmoulins made sparkling reading in the Cordelier cause. In general, Danton enjoyed what Camille wrote and applauded it. Indeed some liberal patriots, as well as aggrieved royalists, speculated that it was Danton who dictated the thrust of it to his friend, which was unfair to Camille, who required no help with the pen. It was true that they both enjoyed quoting liberally from Ancient Rome – Danton in his speeches, Camille in his pamphlets. If anything, though, Camille was the more 'Roman'. It would hardly have surprised Danton to see him arrive at the Palais Royal in a toga.

The two headstrong friends were not of course in complete agreement on all aspects of revolution. Camille was an out-and-out republican with no time for monarchy of any sort; Danton, despite his furious verbal assaults on the throne, thought there might still be a place for the king as long as he accepted the transfer of sovereignty to the people and acted by it. Moreover, Camille was not unburdened by vanity, which could lead him down dubious paths. Lifted by the success of his *France Libre* and impressed by Marat's ugly popularity with the sans-culottes, Camille drove himself to publish a lynch-law pamphlet entitled *Discours de la Lanterne* (The Gallows Speak), patently designed to appeal to the basest popular desires for vengeance against anyone connected with the old order. Camille put himself in the person of the gallows: How many of these criminals have escaped me? Why have they released the marquis of so and so? Swine, I shall have you yet! Camille rather stretched his credentials too. He had come to see himself as 'one of the principal authors of the Revolution', as he informed his father in a letter home dated 20 September which, a few lines further

55

down, also begged for funds: 'Please send me shirts and two pairs of sheets as soon as possible.'

If the *Discours de la Lanterne* duly elevated Camille in sans-culotte esteem, its revenues failed to keep him in fresh linen. It was also typical of the ardent wordsmith that he began to regret its savage tone as soon as he suspected that it encouraged aimless street violence. In October hungry crowds inflamed by his pamphlet seized a hapless baker suspected of hoarding flour and strung him up from a lamp post in front of City Hall, unimpeded by guardsmen. Lynchings were taking place every day. The baker's murder dismayed Danton, for practical political reasons as much as anything. Such acts settled nothing. He lectured the Cordelier assembly in a countryman's rebuke for Camille: 'This year the harvest is good, everyone knows it. I'm from the countryside and you may take my word for it. Let us join with all the districts of Paris to force the authorities to change policy. Let them stop requisitioning grain! These brutal tactics only drive peasants and speculators to hide it. On the contrary, we must negotiate with the farmers to ensure supplies.'

Still, there was no stopping Camille. He was on a more promising track with a regular weekly newspaper that he planned to launch any day now with the weightier title *La Révolution de France et de Brabant* – a witty, ironic, inspiring, albeit still angry, rundown on the course of events (so the prospectus promised) designed to appeal to both the news-hungry citizens of France and valiant Belgians simultaneously engaged in freeing their Flemish province from its Habsburg rulers. Camille vowed to use his newspaper to skewer Bailly, which he did. Here Danton probably did contribute some words of his own, for it looked as though the mayor was letting rank go to his head. Bailly had voted himself a huge salary – 'a horrible theft', the first edition of Camille's newspaper called it – and engaged a troop of horseguards to ride before the mayoral coach whenever he left City Hall. Was this not the conduct of an *Ancien Régime* satrap? Had City Hall already forgotten it had changed masters?

Besides its passionate pamphleteers, the Cordelier promotional division could call on playwrights – next-door neighbours of Danton – to bring tears and smiles to revolutionary Paris. There was Marie-Joseph Chénier with an anti-royalist tragedy about Charles IX and his part in the Saint Bartholomew's Day massacre, a play which Danton had found so moving in rehearsal that he leaped on stage to warm up the audience on opening night, whacking his huge palms together to invite applause as the curtain rose. And there was Fabre, the dilettante artist, aping Molière and pouring his feverish talents into a provocative comedy, *Philinthe*, an instant popular success in 1790 that brought in the money he needed to pursue his dandy's lifestyle, which was his first concern. *Philinthe* was thin theatre but Fabre somehow succeeded in capturing the lyrical side of the revolt with his leading player's lament:

> This France! This beauteous part of the globe, this land of thirty thousand leagues, heaven's eternal love, *chef-d'oeuvre* of the elements, this protectress of humanity, this triumph of civilisation – this France o'er long defiled and devoured by a small tribe of evil-doers wearing a human face.

The torrent of words spilling forth from the Cour du Commerce neighbourhood gave collective celebrity to the 'Cordelier Republic'. Admired and feared, applauded and cursed, Danton's district at the heart of Paris stoked the fire of revolt.

In the autumn of 1789 political anarchy appeared all but total. All but . . . for there existed a shaky centre of power that commanded the broad respect of patriots. Mirabeau's revolutionary assembly in Versailles was hard at work creating a new national constitution to bury the old order, and even the Cordeliers, impressed by the serene audacity of its *coup d'état*, recognised its legitimacy as supreme law-making authority.

This National Assembly was full of earnest, moderate men – mostly bourgeois but with a good number of liberal nobles – with specific proposals for reforming French society from top to bottom. To Danton they lacked the high spirit of adventure he thought the times demanded, but how could any right-thinking man disagree with the principles the assembly was erecting as the new law of the land? Mirabeau seemed made for the task, and he had some remarkable men working with him, among them the political strategist Sieyès, the inspired all-rounder Condorcet, and the club-footed Talleyrand – Charles-Maurice de Talleyrand-Périgord – a diplomatic mastermind of exalted aristocratic lineage who understood the harm that a regime of privilege had done to France.

With such hands at the tiller it was hard to imagine there was much steering room left for people like Camille's school friend Robespierre. But perhaps, Danton thought, democracy needed its mediocrities. He did not discuss Robespierre with Camille; there was no need to. Camille knew his opinion.

In the last days of August the assembly had abolished by law the social system surviving from feudal times. The immense privileges that allowed the nobility and the Church hierarchy to dominate the common citizenry vanished at a stroke. The *Ancien Régime* was dead. From now on the French people were of one class – free, sovereign, equal before the law, at liberty to think, act and work as they wished. This was the thrust of the revolutionary constitution; it kept the monarchy in place but with only vestiges of its past absolute power. Private property ownership was upheld and guaranteed – a matter of satisfaction for Danton with his enduring peasant reveries of adding fresh acreage around the family base in Arcis.

The main immediate victim of change was the Catholic Church, which owned half of France's landed wealth. It lost it all. Even the most prescient bishops had not foreseen the scale of the assault on their dominion. For the people's parliament simply nationalised the Church – its priests and all its property – and proceeded to auction off its lands to the public, a colossal step that turned the social geography of France on its head. Across the country the peasant felt a delicious pang of triumph over the seigneur. And if things did not quite happen as the revolutionary constitution intended and Church lands mainly fell to financial speculators, it was still hard not to feel pride in the resonance of the Declaration of the Rights of Man that accompanied it:

> Men are born free and live free with equal rights . . . These are the rights to liberty, property, security and resistance against oppression.

The words echoed the independence declaration issued by American colonists across the Atlantic thirteen years before, but their intent was different. It had to be different, for the French declaration was not remotely about independence, it was about a social contract new to mankind. The Declaration of the Rights of Man was the Enlightenment seizing power. And within days of its passage the document was enthralling all Europe – in admiration in some quarters and in anguish elsewhere, particularly at royal courts aggrieved by so reckless a departure from an old order that they fully intended to preserve.

Louis XVI himself had not yet given up all hope. After the Bastille's fall his two brothers had secretly fled into exile, first to Germany, with a platoon of minor Bourbon princes and royal cousins. Louis himself remained ensconced at Versailles with Marie-Antoinette and their young son, the dauphin – the gracious lichen clinging to an ancient house. It was not pride of home alone, or even obstinacy, that kept him there. His court could surely string the Revolution along. Perhaps he could accept only bits and pieces of this constitution that disempowered him, and thus block the offending whole in spirit. There seemed room for royal subterfuge. The future of the monarchy was the burning issue in the news-sheets, at the Cordeliers, the Commune and – to its acute discomfort – at the Versailles parliament.

Danton found the basic constitutional principles drawn up by Mirabeau and company wise enough – and practical – including the decision to allow King Louis to keep his throne. But to yield the king a veto over parliament's decisions was another matter, and this, in haste, was what a majority in the parliament now conceded. Patriots of radical cast were aghast. A royal veto over parliament subverted the very principles they had agreed. Political opinion was dividing by the day. A vocal minority in the new parliament even wished to call an end to the Revolution there and then and to establish a monarchic government on the English model, with a commons and an upper chamber of lords. La Fayette with his military command in the capital shared this view. Stauncher patriots, though, aimed to exclude the king from power altogether. Their destination was a republic, which meant pursuing the revolution with all zeal.

The republic was as yet only a vague vision. For the moment Danton, like most insurrectionists, leaned towards the concept of a constitutional monarchy – provided, that was, that Louis gave up all thought of retaining sovereignty and abided by each and every item in the constitution without attempting to smuggle in changes. And to take England as a political model worried the Cordelier giant. France was not England. Under the English system the aristocracy held on to power, whereas revolutionary France had stripped the nobility of power and privilege. How could Frenchmen back down and support the return of the aristocracy in a house of lords? To Danton, that seemed out of the question, and at the Procope his companions roared in agreement. Weren't the Cordeliers 'the Terror of the Aristocracy'? Well, that was what they would be. There could be no letting the rascals back into power.

Jousting with Fabre, Camille and his Cordelier inner circle was one of the things Danton enjoyed most in rebellion. It was plain folly, surely, to think of halting the Revolution, to call it over and done with. The people were nowhere near satisfied. Beyond glorious words and the downsizing of a king, where was the gain? Storming the Bastille had not ended the food crisis, or put the hordes of unemployed back to work. The sans-culottes continued to riot in the streets of Paris, resentful of La Fayette and the gentlemen of the Commune.

Danton had sympathy for the people's anger. Indeed, he owned to a portion of responsibility for the turmoil on the Paris streets, in so far as his political kinsmen – Marat in the *Ami du Peuple* and Camille in his *Discours de la Lanterne* – were adept at whipping it up. He understood the people's fears. Were royalists not regrouping with full intent to undo the Revolution by force? Royalist conspiracies filled the Paris air, like the great stench. Popular anguish over the imminence of counter-revolution was a mass nervous disorder, and it deepened with public confirmation of what for days had been rumours that King Louis' brothers, accompanied by court grandees, had indeed moved into strategic exile, waiting for the moment to strike back. Some royalist émigrés made for England, but their warrior core hastened to military gathering points just across the border in Germany. It was some reassurance for patriots that King Louis himself remained at his palace in Versailles, though there were strong rumours – embroidered by Marat – that he was contemplating flight to Metz, an army stronghold in the east close to the exiles' camp.

In the first damp days of October anger on the Paris street peaked. Danton could scarcely believe the extent of King Louis' folly. The monarch had recalled his elite Flanders regiment to Versailles to reinforce the royal bodyguard, and unpatriotic scenes ensued in the charming Versailles opera house, where Louis invited regimental officers to dine. The news-sheets reported drunken subalterns raising aggressive toasts to king and queen and stamping with their boots on the red-white-and-blue cockade that symbolised the Revolution. Louis had apparently let the affront continue unchecked, though he was aware of the cockade's high tokenism, for on occasion he sported one in the royal hatband so as not to display revolutionary unwilling.

What was La Fayette doing about the provocations in Versailles? Such happenings ought to concern the National Guard commander. He was the designer of the cockade – to the traditional red-blue colours of Paris carried by the rebellious hordes that stormed the Bastille, he had thoughtfully added the white of the Bourbon monarchy for use by his guardsmen – but that was of small import. What mattered to the Cordeliers was that La Fayette's revolutionary brief was to maintain order and yet he seemed to have no control over the monarch's conduct, nor to want it. The Danton tribe debated the situation, sensing that popular mistrust had reached a fresh breaking point. King Louis surely could not be allowed to stay in Versailles, toying with the nation. The sans-culottes wanted him in their midst. They wanted him in Paris, where they could keep an eye on him.

The great question was: how to get the king to Paris? The most promising solution that Danton's Palais Royal committee and the Cordelier assembly could conjure up was a mass popular march on Versailles. That would surely unhinge the court. Public pressure for a march spread rapidly through the capital's radical wards. In the Cordelier district posters went up at street corners urging citizens to rise up and converge on the king's resplendent residence a dozen miles away to put an end to what Danton and company billed as dangerous court intrigue.

The time was now!

The march on Versailles that occurred in driving rain on 5 October was composed almost entirely of women in its first surge, fully 7,000 of them – workers' wives, Les Halles fishwives, women of the streets. There was tactical reasoning behind this, though the demonstration indeed reflected women's distress, for bread supplies in Paris had finally run out altogether on the eve of the protest, leaving housewives in the poorer districts to despair for their families' survival. The Palais Royal committee's motive for mobilising women was entirely practical: the king's bodyguard was unlikely to fire on women, unless the soldiers panicked.

Before daybreak on 5 October Danton ordered the tocsin bell rung at the Cordelier church abutting the refectory, and soon alarm bells echoed the call across the working districts of Paris, calling the populace on to the streets. The Cordelier men's battalion got carried away and, discarding the plan, set out on the heels of the departing women's army; only when halfway to Versailles did the menfolk decide to turn back, to avoid provoking the king's bodyguard. Of the men's militia only Marat, on the scent of a rousing story for the *Ami du Peuple*, continued to follow the women. With an umbrella shielding his soiled green frockcoat, Marat for once must have looked almost colourful against the black-clad women's rearguard.

As the rain-drenched column reached the Versailles Palace in the afternoon, a delegation in muddied skirts went to the parliament hall to demand food for Paris. The main body of women marchers flocked around the royal palace, yelling at the troops of the king's bodyguard and the offending Flanders regiment to pin the patriotic cockade to their helmets. Eventually some of the women discovered an unlocked door opening on to a back staircase into the royal precincts. Soaked and ravenous, they flooded through, undeterred by warning shots fired by palace guards. Marat was ecstatic. He watched the women rampage through gilded salons to snatch at court leftovers and shrieking for the blood of Marie-Antoinette, whose Austrian haughtiness they had heard much about. Marat then scurried back to Paris to meet his morning deadline, arriving well past midnight at his print shop, where Danton and Camille heard him whooping as they happened by. Camille noted: 'Monsieur Marat is a bolt of lightning, making more noise than the Four Trumpets of the Last Judgement and chanting "Arise, the dead!"'

Marat clearly fancied he had seen women marchers falling under fire from the king's bodyguard, and that was what he intended to write.

More verifiably, Marat, on his way back to Paris, had crossed La Fayette at the head of 15,000 guardsmen going in the other direction, along with columns of the poor from the streets of Paris who trailed to Versailles some way behind the women. In mounting uproar at the royal palace, La Fayette convinced the king on arrival that it would be safer all round and avoid bloodshed if his National Guard were to replace the nervous royal body-guard there. Hesitantly, Louis agreed. It was to be the king's last night at sumptuous Versailles – the end of royal life at the chateau to which the Sun King, Louis XIV, moved his court a century before in order to close Bourbon eyes and noses to the turmoil and stench of Paris.

The next day, 6 October, a motley horde of La Fayette's guardsmen, women marchers and sans-culottes led Louis XVI and his family back to the capital. The fact that the monarch consented, under duress, to leave Versailles brought him a brief surge of popular goodwill, though it afforded him small joy. For his enforced destination was the Tuileries Palace, a royal residence beside the Seine adjoining the Louvre, its medieval parent palace, and none the more inviting for having languished in disuse, mostly un-inhabited, for the hundred years since the Sun King's decampment. Furthermore, over the Tuileries courtyards – rising from its long, low walls along the river – there hovered extreme odours, since it was the habit of Parisians who were caught short by day or night to defecate at those princely walls, squatting there in scores, hundreds, at a time; as a site for quick open-air relief the Tuileries seemed immensely preferable to the city's dark alleys or to an embarrassed dash into a private home in the hope of finding a privy before being set upon by an irate owner. Indeed, depending on where a citizen's foot landed, the capital to which Louis XVI returned was the most splendid and most filthy of cities. Gentlefolk who had reason to descend into the street from their carriages, which they avoided whenever possible, felt bound to summon a *décrotteur* at each corner to scrape their beturded footwear for a sou before proceeding to the next. And now the Commune's scrubbing crews scarcely had time to remove the top layers of grime and cobwebs and to bung rat holes in the Tuileries Palace salons before the king and queen arrived, virtual prisoners of the common people whose cause Danton was making his own.

The royal move presented an opportunity for the Cordelier chief to display political grace. In Danton's churning imagination there was still a consti-tutional place for a king in the Revolution's new order. He bore Louis no personal grudge and was by no means unconscious of his link to the court through his King's Council seat, though he liked to think he was quite able to divorce that from political events.

Not a week after the king was installed at the Tuileries, Danton headed a small Cordelier deputation to the dusty palace to greet the monarch on behalf of his district. It was a presumptuous visit, for Danton held no city-wide office. He wore his ceremonial best, which Gabrielle freshened up for him – black satin breeches and habit, dark blue-and-white striped waist-coat, white silk stockings and black buckled shoes. Such attire encouraged a gentlemanly performance – for the time being, moreover, he remained Monsieur d'Anton – and while declining to kiss the monarch's hand, which he was sure La Fayette would notice and hold to derision, he made a deep bow and welcomed him to Paris, saying without a hint of sarcasm: 'Sire, Your Majesty's capital greets you. We ask Your Majesty to accept our thanks for your gracious decision to return.'

Louis was perplexed by the welcome and by the giant emissary's alarming countenance. He made no mention of Danton's seat on the King's Council: he had either forgotten that the feral specimen bowing before him owned it, or more likely he never knew of it. Had he informed himself, though, he might have calculated that Danton held an ambiguous place in the Revolution: hero to the Cordeliers and stirrer of street passions, he was now a figure of mistrust, abhorrence even, to many of the middle-class moderates who held shaky charge in the Commune and in the new national parliament. Members of that parliament – the Constituent Assembly under its new title, a deliberately bland choice for so abrupt an institutional rupture with the past – were naturally growing warier still of Danton as they too abandoned Versailles, where there was no further business to attend, and began to engage with revolutionary chieftains in Paris, in due course trans-ferring their chamber to the high-vaulted Royal Riding School beside the gardens of the Tuileries.

Within the walls of the capital, Danton was at war with Bailly and La Fayette. To them he was a demagogue, a wild man out to impress the rabble. Worse, he fought every sou they spent.

To men who spoke in measured tones, the extreme forcefulness of Danton's speech could shock. They were accustomed to Mirabeau's rich dips and crescendos, but Danton's huge voice carried more menace. His powerful rhythms were a veritable bludgeon, and many wary patriots heard in them the coarse cries of the Halles marketplace. The Market Mirabeau! In the pay of the Duc d'Orléans besides! And taking the English penny! That rumour too had its moment: a confidential note written by a French diplomat in London had surfaced in Paris, reporting the presence in the French capital of 'two English individuals named Dantonne and Parr' who were suspected of being paid agents of the London government. Danton and Paré smiled at the misspellings and the nationality confusion, which, they guessed, were contrived to make the report sound genuine.

It was irritating, though, that such allegations tended to stick, at least with those who wished to believe them. Once spread, the most outlandish accusations quickly became actual crimes and misdemeanours in revolutionary Paris. Danton felt he was surrounded by insatiable amateur prosecutors, for worthy men in the Constituent Assembly engaged in installing France's new order nonetheless found time to do pernickety sums implying that he could not repay the loans on his legal chambers unless he were receiving handouts on the side. To be sure, Danton would not pretend that making the repayments was easy; they were up to date, though, and his continuing King's Council revenues lived up to Maître Huey's promises. Indeed, it often struck him as a backhanded tribute to the *Ancien Régime* that the old coach lumbered on regardless without its providential coachman at the reins.

Still, there seemed no end to the sniping. Rumours that Danton 'bought' the Cordelier presidency by paying members to vote for him grew so widespread that the rebellious district published a heated formal denial as winter came. The denial was circulated to all fifty-nine sister districts in the capital to ensure that it got the widest hearing, sent out under Fabre's name, among others, to avoid reducing its credibility under a Danton signature. The wounding rumours, the circular said, were a miserable calumny against the 'pure, unstinting zeal' of the president whom the Cordeliers had elected and re-elected to lead their district; it was their extreme good fortune to have so vigorous a defender of liberty in their midst. 'His unanimous election in vote after vote is just reward for the courage, the talents and the civic sense which M. d'Anton displays as soldier and citizen.'

The soldier-citizen juxtaposition would have appealed to Danton the militia captain, who continued to employ the ennobling apostrophe, yet he was not convinced that the statement would kill the adverse rumours. Supposing he *had* accepted funds that the Duc d'Orléans' whispering treasurer was always trying to press on him? What if he *had* employed the money to maintain his district in revolutionary mode? Cordelier costs were rising: it required funds to administer the independent decrees its assembly enacted and to print all the posters. Was that 'buying' the Cordelier presidency? It was not a matter he discussed, even with Camille and Fabre. The truth of it was that at present he and the duke had a like goal – constitutional monarchy properly installed and accepted by King Louis. It was also the truth, alas, that Danton with his alarming appearance and rambunctious personality was never very good at dealing with slander.

Among front-line patriots Danton had an important admirer, however, in the great Mirabeau. To be sure, the orator regarded the Cordelier chief as a troublemaker. But Mirabeau was an impulsive, emotional man, and he was inclined to like Danton perhaps because he saw something of himself in the young lawyer's brawny eloquence and mashed features. Indeed, Mirabeau had his eyes on Danton as a recruit in his own secretive doings, though it was no more than a thought at this stage and the Cordelier leader was unaware of what was fomenting in Mirabeau's fertile mind.

Mirabeau was all for revolution, all for liberty. Had he not proved it? Yet King Louis' transfer to Paris struck him as a step towards the elimination of the monarchy, and he was not ready for that. Something in his own blue blood, low Provençal strain though it was, wanted to keep the king in the ruling structure – the ermined symbol of a nation in possession of all the liberties it craved. But the feckless optimist in Mirabeau also believed that those liberties were now in place, safe as the mint, engraved in the revolutionary constitution. It pained him, then, to see Louis XVI held hostage by his people in the Tuileries.

Louis clearly sensed Mirabeau's trend of thought. Affairs of state now obliged them to meet frequently in the run-down Tuileries chambers, where the monarch was also witness to the orator's failing health, for by all accounts Mirabeau coughed in the royal presence until his fat chest looked about to burst and complained, politely, of searing pains in the gut. The southerner lived to excess and was paying for it. Still, he remained the bandmaster of the Revolution and, perhaps because of his doubts and his weakening health, within a month of the royal family's arrival in Paris the king's courtiers had begun suing for his private assistance. Louis XVI, despite his plight, had bottomless pockets and Mirabeau, who made a custom of spending more than he had, was open to temptation. Besides, securing the throne amid the great changes that he had helped bring about was a cause Mirabeau favoured. So there seemed to be a fit. Some sort of secret bargain looked more attractive still to Mirabeau when the courtiers advised him that once it were struck he would have substantial funds to distribute among patriots he thought might be inclined to help the king.

Mirabeau, then, was pondering these things. Might the thunderous voice of the Cordelier chief be so inclined? Or so retuned?

In the New Year of 1790 hostilities between the 'Cordelier Republic' and the Commune reached a theatrical climax. The *casus belli* was Marat's blood-thirsty pen.

Rather belatedly Bailly and La Fayette chose to revive a decree for the arrest of the bard of death that was first issued soon after the royal family's return to Paris, when his eyewitness reports in the *Ami du Peuple* were deemed to have posed an unacceptable threat to public order. The arrest decree was subsequently allowed to lapse, but Marat's zest for blood had not diminished as winter set in and the Commune leaders were now determined to silence him. La Fayette went about this task with an impressive show of force. Wary of the Cordelier battalion's reaction, he dispatched 3,000 guardsmen to the rebel district on 22 January in support of a pair of City Hall bailiffs assigned to arrest the journalist.

To show purpose, La Fayette's force rolled up a heavy artillery piece for the occasion, an unfraternal menace that resolved Danton to see off the invaders. It was not that his opinion of Marat and his violent prose had improved. A much larger issue was at stake. Had Bailly and La Fayette forgotten something? Had they forgotten that freedom of expression ranked among the first of the liberties enacted in the new order? Those scoundrels, Danton fumed, only had provisional charge of Paris, yet they presumed to make war on the new freedoms. It was treason! Infamy!

Thus fired up, the Cordeliers, having got wind in advance of La Fayette's 'invasion', pre-empted the guard commander by rushing through a district by-law stating that no one should be deprived of their freedom in Paris unless accused of a verifiable crime. Specifically, the decree established a panel of five 'liberty commissioners' – with Danton at their head – whose approval had to be obtained before a warrant for the arrest of a Cordelier district resident could be executed. The decree savaged the Commune hierarchy: such precautions would remain in force, it stipulated, 'until the great work of France's regeneration is so far advanced that we may put aside fears that men attached to the principles of the *Ancien Régime* and imbued with the old judiciary's false maxims will attempt to stifle the voice of patriotic writers'.

Still, the creation in the heart of Paris of a sanctuary for press freedom designated off-limits to City Hall prosecutors was not enough to dissuade La Fayette altogether. He wanted Marat out of the way. While deciding against leading his 3,000 guardsmen in person, he ordered them to take up positions in the busy morning streets around the Cordelier refectory and to hold these positions as Commune bailiffs entered to inform Danton of their arrest mission.

Danton was there with his kitchen cabinet – Camille, Fabre, Paré – when the bailiffs came. And crashing upon the scene came Legendre, in his blood-smeared apron, warning the bailiffs that his fellow butchers were pulling down their shutters at that very moment and taking up arms. Outside there was uproar as crowds yelled at the 'foreign troops' to get out of the district. The noise went to Danton's head. Dressed for the occasion in his button-straining captain's uniform, he scowled at the bailiffs: 'What are all these troops for? We only need to sound the tocsin and roll the drums and the whole of the Saint-Antoine district will be here with 20,000 men to send them running.'

To the Commune bailiffs this was civil-war talk. Danton observed as much from their shocked expressions. Perhaps he had gone too far. Now he explained to them, with pained courtesy, the ins and outs of the Cordelier decree establishing his panel of liberty commissioners. He refused to retreat an inch. 'Where is the rascal commanding these troops?' he demanded. 'I shall speak to him.' And switching from soldier to lawyer, he told the Commune agents that their warrant for Marat was in any case null and void, since it was made out in an old form now proscribed by the revolutionary parliament.

The bailiffs hurried back to City Hall to seek further instructions, leaving the military escort in place. Danton decided it was a good moment to leapfrog the Commune and bring parliament into the conflict, intending to enlist its sympathy. There and then he led a Cordelier deputation across the Seine to the Constituent Assembly's new Riding School chamber. He gained immediate permission to address the deputies, who were used to receiving delegations of aggrieved patriots, and recounted the day's events in his district – striking proof, he claimed, of Cordelier zeal to support the revolutionary parliament's principles upholding freedom of expression. The reaction of the house was disappointing. It was not only cool, it carried a sting of rebuke. Deputies thanked the giant intruder for his presence among them with a formal note bidding his Cordeliers to show the civic sense necessary to put an end to such incidents.

It was well into that biting January evening before the Commune's bailiffs returned to Cordelier headquarters, their orders to arrest Marat reconfirmed. Nine hours had passed since La Fayette's troops marched in, more than enough time for the editor of the *Ami du Peuple* to make good his escape from his Cour du Commerce den – which he did, his portable printing press in tow. Danton could afford to be a little more flexible now. La Fayette's men were free to search for Marat, he said, though he would not vouch for the journalist's presence. National Guard officers sensed they'd been had. They ordered a rapid search of the neighbourhood before accepting that Marat had slipped their clutches, then pulled the troops out.

It was an astute play by the Cordelier chief, though alas it rebounded on him. His 'threat' to call in working-class hordes from the popular Saint-Antoine district to confront La Fayette's guardsmen had been a rash, spur-of-the-moment response to bumptious bailiffs – empty of real intent as far as he was concerned. But Bailly and La Fayette leaped on it, crying sedition. It became the talk of the Paris streets: Danton and the people ranged against the city leaders. In retaliation, the Commune grandees changed the name on the arrest warrant: now Danton himself was the target.

What began as a tense little sideshow was suddenly a high moment in the Revolution.

A warrant for Danton's arrest on charges of sedition was issued on 17 March 1790 and the Cordeliers at once went on the offensive. The spirit of the counter-attack, led by their president, was righteous indignation. Its thrust was: Jail Danton and you kill liberty at birth! Jail Danton and you insult democracy! Jail Danton and you stifle the Revolution itself!

This was no doubt overstating the case – barrister's licence – but in the people's eyes Danton had indeed grown in stature since the stand-off with La Fayette's force. He could not be arrested like a vulgar miscreant. Besides, he was careful to sue for the support of the revolutionary capital's fifty-nine other districts, alerting them that their rights and liberties were under the same threat as his own. King Louis too grew involved despite his wretched comedown, for though his ministers were now entirely subordinate to parliament they still formed the executive arm of government and this was a case for his justice minister to examine, which he did, concluding that nothing but damage would result from imprisoning Danton. All but two of the Paris districts decided the same, despite the doubts the wealthier wards had about him. The drift of popular and official opinion, encouraged by sardonic commentaries in pro-Danton news-sheets, was unmistakeable: the Commune leadership was abusing its power and the Constituent Assembly must intervene to suspend the arrest order.

Danton was soon joking about his plight, calling it the 'Great Affair' in merry sessions at the Procope. He felt no real danger; ridicule was now the way to dispose of the threat. A pamphlet issuing straight from a snorting corner of the Procope hit the streets with the headline:

The Great Inquiry into the Great Crime perpetrated by
the Great Danton in the Great District of the Great Cordeliers
and its Great Repercussions

When parliament did at length bury the 'Great Affair' at the end of May, suspending the inquiry and the sedition charge, Danton found his revolutionary status changed. The rumpus over his arrest was not quite the fundamental threat to the Revolution he had made out, but he had demonstrated singular qualities that made all Paris sit up: audacity, guile and combativeness.

From the royal court and the benches of parliament to the Commune and the legions of sans-culottes, Danton was henceforth a name on the French nation's lips.

# SIX

## *Travails of a People's Champion*

Leading the Cordeliers was a heady task. It placed Danton in command of the praetorian guard of democracy, a troop of lax discipline but passionate purpose. Some said the Cordeliers coined the slogan that went around the world – 'Liberty, Equality, Fraternity' – and, whether or not this was so, they accepted paternity with pride.

All the same, Danton was aware that outside his radical wedge of central Paris his influence lacked legitimacy, for it was built on street fame alone. To win more solid influence he had to perform in Mirabeau's excellent show at the Riding School or – for a start at least – to join the Paris Commune led, alas, by those who sought to arrest him. Indeed, he had lately reconsidered his initial reluctance to seek election to the Commune: better to steer it from within, he now thought, than fight it from the outside. But how badly did he want power? He pondered the question more and more as the 'Great Affair' subsided and the spectacular summer of 1790 induced a shaken nation to celebrate with pomp and self-satisfaction the first anniversary of the fall of the Bastille.

Danton was not like Marat – or even Camille. Still less like Camille's friend Robespierre, who was making a name for himself at the Riding School, always at the rostrum with that piping voice of his, wearing down even the most ebullient fellow deputies with his pressing abstractions, or more likely sending them to sleep. Mirabeau had sized up Robespierre nicely: 'That fellow will go far. He believes everything he says.' Danton was not like any of these. He truly *had* jumped upon the passing tide. And now he was somewhere atop the wave – equipped, he hoped, with what it would take to ride it to the faraway shore.

With popularity on the Paris street came responsibility as well as satisfaction. What he had won he could not now in all conscience abandon: to do so would be a betrayal of the people who cheered him on. And there was something else that drove him, some inner feeling that he would have found it hard to explain but that had in it something of Arcis and the Champagne badlands, something of life in Paris, something of Gabrielle and the new child she was about to bear, something of the extreme suffering, fury, violence and exaltation now visited upon the land – in sum, all the emotional nerve ends that wove themselves into a love of the bruised, hopeful France that was his. The Revolution fired his patriotism.

Entering the Commune was harder, however, than a man with Danton's overwhelming physique might have expected. Political Paris seemed to slam its doors on him. His verve and boisterous humour attracted disciples, but at the same time Bailly and La Fayette were not alone in regarding him as a bully intent on disrupting their labours. His firebrand history was against him.

The depth of bourgeois mistrust had again become all too clear in May 1790, when Bailly, for his own good reasons, redrew the political map of the capital and turned its sixty districts into forty-eight 'sections'. Clearly the mayor was far from finished as an organiser of the kind of revolution he envisioned. In standing for re-election – this time as mayor proper, not provisional overlord – he planned to take the sting out of independent districts like the Cordeliers and thus make revolutionary Paris more manageable. His method was to cull the capital's power centres. Danton tried to block Bailly's not so subtle scheme, taking his protest to the Constituent Assembly. He only succeeded, however, in getting Mirabeau's patriots at the Riding School to postpone the Paris elections by a week or so – until the end of July, by which time the great turmoil of Bastille anniversary celebrations would be spent.

Danton made a point of respecting the national parliament, never running it down. He might be at war with the Paris Commune but he always bowed to what the parliament decided; as far as he was concerned, its decisions were the coda of the Revolution, for with the collapse of the *Ancien Régime* there was no other crucible of national power. His submission was both genuine and calculated, for it was his best answer to those who branded him a demagogue. He had the Cordelier assembly circulate to the districts a spirited though doleful declaration on the dilution of the Paris wards, which stated: 'We must regard as a vile traitor to the *patrie* any citizen or assembly of citizens that refuses to obey the decrees of the National Assembly, or gives licence to protest against a single one of them.' This was his public genuflection before the new democracy, which he hoped the sans-culottes would emulate. Politically, he was a good sport.

The dilution of the districts was nonetheless a harsh sentimental blow for the Cordeliers. Camille was in tears: 'O my dearest Cordeliers, farewell then to our bell, farewell our old armchair, farewell our beloved rostrum shaking to the voices of our illustrious orators.' What harm had the districts done? By God, it was the districts that made the Revolution, Camille lamented.

Now the Cordelier district was merged with a contiguous slab of the Left Bank running east below the flat spires of Notre Dame – the whole of it named the Théâtre Français section, in honour of the famous playhouse at its heart. In redividing the capital, Commune surveyors with geometric compasses and Bailly's instructions in their pockets put landmarks above neighbourhood soul.

Still, it was from this new Théâtre Français section that Danton sought the broader political legitimacy he lacked. From here he stood for election to the Commune and when the votes were counted at the end of July his majority was almost as large as any he had won for president of the Cordeliers, for in truth his old district formed the bulk of the new section. It was now, though, despite the landslide majority, that he re-encountered the full blast of bourgeois mistrust.

To promote some level of harmony in the Commune, the ballot rules stipulated that deputies elected from any one section had to be confirmed in office by the other forty-seven sections. This was Bailly's small print; in Danton's case it was a capital-letter summons. He was blackballed by no fewer than forty-two sections, ejected from the Commune before seeing his seat. The humiliation did not end there: of 144 deputies elected – three from each section – he alone was so ostracised. He could curse all he liked that Bailly had put tame sections up to rejecting him, and this was no doubt true, but it was obvious that the Paris middle class largely feared Danton, and since the working class in practice remained barred from voting – even under the revolutionary constitution – his popularity with the bulk of the citizenry in this case gave him small leverage; out of a population of more than 600,000, only 14,000 Parisians, the property owners and higher taxpayers, had the vote. Furthermore, he could see Bailly laughing at him, for the scoundrel was re-elected mayor by a landslide.

Danton swore that as soon as he was in a position to do so he would rewrite the new constitution on suffrage. It was awkward and sensitive terrain that Mirabeau and the Riding School shrank from crossing. But what was liberty if it was restricted to a class? The Declaration of the Rights of Man proclaimed equal rights for *all* citizens. Where was the logic in a constitution that set out the law and granted the vote only to men of material worth? The bar was placed conveniently high to limit voters to the middle class and up, for the bourgeois pacemakers of revolt preferred not to have peasants and urban toilers influence their endeavours; the underclass's lot was to remain 'passive' citizens. Danton vowed to convert the sans-culottes into 'active' citizens voting with the best of them. Sensitive it might be, but it was an issue that was not difficult to redress. It could be done with a thump of parliament's hammer.

For now, though, humiliation stunned him. He was not in the national parliament; he was not even in the Commune. Gabrielle implored him to step aside from revolutionary politics and concentrate on his law office. She held their month-old son, Antoine, in her arms as she pleaded with him. She was worried. Her intuition told her that her husband was in danger. Even in joy, he was reckless. Straight from the baptism, he had hoisted the newborn into the crook of his beefy arm and strode across to the Cordelier assembly to raise the mite before his fellow revolutionaries, roaring at the rafters: 'Tremble, you tyrants, you courtiers, you ministers, a new Danton is born to tread in the footsteps of his father. Rest assured, his first words will be "Live free or die."' The Cordeliers cheered.

The performance with baby Antoine came before the humiliation. But it could only have confirmed to Gabrielle what in her heart she knew: her emotional husband was not made to stand aside. Danton did not take Gabrielle's warnings lightly, though it was mainly to mend his stricken pride that he now repaired to Arcis with her and their infant son, to think things over. It was high summer, a chance to show little Antoine to Danton's mother and to purchase the copse beside the Aube he had long had his sights on. He concluded the acquisition in August with a small down payment and a promissory note to pay the rest over two years; he had to be careful with his outlays, for while the King's Council still provided an income he was paid nothing for the Cordelier duties that monopolised his time. The Arcis air and the joy of owning that dappled patch of willows combined to soften his harsh electoral disappointment, though it was not until he returned to Paris a week later that he squared up to the choice Gabrielle put to him: to keep riding the perilous wave of revolution or jump off.

Camille's lamentations over the disappearance of the Cordeliers were, it turned out, romantic flummery. The tears were meant to stiffen members' loyalty. For he and Danton had quickly decided how to meet the situation, and indeed the response was in place before Danton left for Arcis. The Cordeliers simply converted themselves from a district assembly into a political club, a fashionable agency of revolution. Otherwise they went on as before, cantankerous and riotous as ever, though they met in the old friary's chapel instead of the refectory, which the careful Bailly had requisitioned for the municipality. Their famous militia, the Cordelier battalion, remained at the ready and Danton kept his captain's uniform pressed. The difference was that their task was no longer to enact harum-scarum by-laws for the Left Bank but rather to raise the alarm against officialdom's violations of human rights in the new order – and, beyond that, to debate the broad course of revolution.

It was more than anyone could ask of Danton to forsake his beloved Cordeliers, whether they were a local parliament or a club. He was still their leader, despite the electoral setback. He hardly needed to spell out his choice to Gabrielle, for the way he now threw his brawn and lung power into Cordelier clubmanship said it all. There was one aspect of the boundary changes, however, that called for a response; as a club, the Cordeliers were politically upstaged by the Jacobin Society, who had opened their Paris headquarters next door to the Tuileries and the National Assembly as soon as the king was forced into residence in the capital.

There seemed something sacred about the Jacobins in these early days of the new order. Their enterprise had the aura of a revolutionary semi-nary with the collective brainpower to direct events and set the moral compass; their club was a righteous bourgeois eye watching over the wild march of revolt. Moreover, unlike the Cordeliers, the Jacobins kept a printed record of their debates from the start so that they knew where they were going and why, and by the careful expedient of charging an annual member-ship fee of 24 livres, plus a joining fee of 12 livres, they closed their daily brainstorming sessions to the sort of street riff-raff that jammed the Cordeliers, for it was a sum well beyond the means of sensible artisans. Nonetheless, the Jacobins, with fully 1,000 members in Paris, were a motley collection who were more often than not at odds with each other: aggres-sive reformers, tepid reformers, backers of the Duc d'Orléans, republicans, federalists, moderate royalists, closet royalists, supportive Englishmen, Germans, all concurring on just one thing – rejection of absolute royal power. On that, Danton too wholly agreed. And since the Jacobins included in their ranks most of the Riding School deputies and leading Commune members, political reality pressed the Cordelier chief to join the rival club as well. The clubs were not mutually exclusive and it was clear that even the most powerful revolutionary voice risked losing force unless it could be heard from the Jacobin pulpit.

Still, when Danton, along with Camille and Fabre, joined the Jacobins, it was as proud Cordeliers that they paid their dues and sat on the hard benches.

Danton attended his first Jacobin meeting in late September 1790 and it left him feeling a little low. As usual, the session began in mid-evening and as the earnest debate proceeded it became increasingly clear that the most active participant was Camille's friend Robespierre. He came across as a fastidious notary overloading the settlement of a will with tiresome details that expectant heirs would dearly have passed over. At times, rowdier members burst out laughing at his banalities. Derision did not stop him; he piped on regardless as more tolerant souls held up their hands to halt the catcalls. There was something frightening, though, in his sense of purpose. The Jacobin club had been going for less than a year and already the unsmiling lawyer from Arras seemed to be taking charge by sheer persistence. No doubt it struck Danton that since he first saw him at the Palais Royal his pallid face seemed to have withered, grown still paler and drier. Robespierre was only a year older than Danton, but he looked to be fifty. It was harder than ever to imagine the exultant Camille maintaining a close friendship with Robespierre.

This Revolution was a confused spectacle – an impossible interlocking of friend and foe, violence, aspiration and envy. Riots sparked by food shortages continued to wash the land in blood, and the mass settling of feudal scores multiplied the havoc. Gentlemen revolutionaries were horrified. Half the deputies at the Riding School now shared Bailly's and La Fayette's urge to call a halt to political change just where it stood: thus far and no further. The republic of which Camille dreamed as the Revolution's proper destination was not in sight.

Danton's instincts told him that to freeze the Revolution was neither right nor possible. Permit that, and sure as fate counter-revolution would follow, returning a broken country to square one of the *Ancien Régime*, where liberty suffocated and died. But provincial hearts in many parts of the land were already swaying once more, recaptured by royalists and Catholic priests. Even Mirabeau – particularly Mirabeau now – was for finishing with the great national revolt. All through 1790 Mirabeau had been shifting his position. It was an open secret, disclosed and discussed by jeering news-sheets, that the same peerless orator who had humbled the monarchy was now in its pay, distributing the royal manna to secure the king's safety.

Danton had first-hand experience, in fact, of Mirabeau's conversion. Only recently, in late summer, a day or so after Danton's return from Arcis, Mirabeau had invited him to pass by his home in the fashionable Faubourg Saint-Germain, neighbouring the old Cordelier ward. He asked him to come alone. No one refused Mirabeau – he was the monster centrifuge around whom reformers tumbled – and Danton duly accepted.

How guileful he was too, this Mirabeau. Of necessity the meeting was secret. But commentaries and after-the-fact reconstructions by the pair's friends and enemies that appeared in the Paris news-sheets, fed to them no doubt by the principals, gave a picture of what occurred. The two men had sat inspecting each other in silence for some minutes, impressed by each other's ugliness. Danton was further struck – indeed astonished – by the luxury of his famous host's property, situated among the high-doored town houses of the old aristocracy and the offices of the king's ministers. Such elegance made an absurd contrast with Mirabeau's extreme shabbiness of person, which Danton assumed was deliberately cultivated. An appetising ham sat beside them on a flowered serving plate, next to a magnum of Pauillac and two crystal glasses the size of church bells. Mirabeau, short of breath, was thought to have begun by outlining the reasons why he believed the Revolution had obtained its essential goals: France was now a constitutional monarchy under the law, so the people were free. True, King Louis had been given a veto over parliament's decisions: to deny him the veto would have been an unnecessarily brutal rupture with French custom. It would perhaps be possible in any event to rescind the veto when things at last calmed down. The old order, then, was finished. Abolished. So what would Danton do with the king? Banish him? Murder him? Danton declined to say; his mind was not made up. The Cordelier chief listened to his host's seductive voice establishing Louis XVI as the personification of France's history, a figure who united past and present and anchored the new democracy in the country's traditions. Transferring sovereignty to the people was all well and good. But where was the anchorage? If the people tried to eliminate the king, Mirabeau was sure that Danton would help rescue him. The king would be grateful, very grateful, and would show it. After all, Mirabeau added, Danton had a voice bigger than his own.

It must have occurred to Danton on leaving Mirabeau that the great man had insulted his intelligence. He was reminded of something that Camille – also a target of the great orator's seductions – had told him in light-hearted self-reproach some months before. Camille, who had a weakness for being courted by men of rank, had eagerly accepted invitations to stay at Mirabeau's residence in Versailles before the parliament moved to Paris. He had written of the experience to Danton: 'I do believe that his over-elegant, overloaded table corrupts me. His Bordeaux wines and cherry liquors have a price that I try in vain to hide from myself, and it is really the devil of a job to return afterwards to my republican austerity and my loathing for aristocrats, whose crime is to put on the most pleasurable suppers.'

Camille's words encapsulated what Danton felt on leaving Mirabeau, the taste of wine still caressing his palate. But this was different. Here was the hero of France's great lurch into democracy not merely treating him to his rich table, but making a definite proposition. *The king would be grateful, very grateful.*

Surely Mirabeau was aware that his golden shuffle to the king's side was the talk of Paris. And surely he could not imagine that he, Danton, was able to take on a private mission of which everyone would soon learn and which not one of the Cordeliers, even stretching personal loyalty, could view as a contribution to the revolt they lived for. He was pursued by enough damaging rumours as it was, without inspiring another. Besides, he truly had not decided what the king's fate should be. He was not deaf to Mirabeau's argument concerning tradition. Indeed, he was torn. But he somehow foresaw that events – not political manoeuvring – would dictate the course of revolution. And who could control events? Or anticipate them? When they happened, that was the time to act.

It was an event of apparently small consequence occurring far from Paris in late August 1790 that threw Danton back into the Revolution's front line. Out to the east, in the garrison city of Nancy, soldiers in a regiment manning France's frontiers with Germany mutinied against their royalist officers. The revolt was ruthlessly crushed by the army commander in the east, the Marquis François de Bouillé, who slaughtered the mutineers to a man. When news of the Nancy 'massacre' reached Paris, La Fayette feted Bouillé as a hero and the Riding School passed a vote of congratulation, though as details of the revolt and its suppression filtered through during the autumn, and Bouillé's extreme devotion to the monarchy became apparent, popular opinion soured. True, the mutineers were mainly Swiss mercenaries, but they were no less children of the Revolution for that.

At the Cordeliers, Danton put through a motion expressing grief over the massacre. The king's minister of war became the butt of ironic abuse in the Paris press, with Marat screaming for his head. And soon the Riding School itself had to review its stand as the outcry against the war minister mushroomed into a formal parliamentary motion to sack the entire government. This, the Riding School rejected. But by November the Paris sections were determined to make heads roll. Acting together, bypassing the Bailly-La Fayette apparatus, they designated Danton as their spokesman – in the name of the people of Paris – to go before parliament and demand the resignation of incompetent government ministers, specifically those in the top posts; they were a danger to the nation.

Having boycotted Danton, it seemed the sections now needed his voice. They knew their man. To him the members of the government were the enemy because they were named by the king, representing neither liberty nor democracy. To give their démarche weight, the sections pressured an embarrassed Bailly into presenting their delegation to the National Assembly, which meant putting his arch municipal enemy in the limelight. The mayor knew that if he refused, it would be taken as an admission that he had lost control over the sections he created.

So on 10 November, in the well of the Riding School, Danton enjoyed watching Bailly grit his teeth to present him to the house. The massive Cordelier had chosen his attire with care for the occasion: black habit, embroidered moiré waistcoat, black breeches and tightly drawn black stockings, his thick fair hair pulled back in a ponytail and a full white cravat knotted up to the chin, covering his bull neck. This was his suiting, approved by Gabrielle, for formal appearances before the assembly or the Commune, the sober elegance devised to discourage the political class from viewing him as a street-corner rabble-rouser. As soon as Bailly finished his grudging introductions, Danton set about his prosecution task with both gravitas and his trademark Ciceronian scorn. Are we to be governed by men so steeped in privilege that they do not even know they betray the people? Rhetorical question after question belittled the king's aristocratic ministers one by one, casting them as counter-revolutionaries – if indeed, he observed with stinging irony, they had the brains for that. Assembly deputies felt as if they were attending a series of executions. Of the four senior ministers, Danton spared only one, Armand de Montmorin, the foreign minister, noting in gentler tones that the people had judged his intentions and found them honourable.

Danton's indulgence towards the Comte de Montmorin, a moderate aristocrat, brought blank looks from deputies, since he was generally thought no more deserving a patriot than his fellow ministers whose political heads lay on the parliament floor. He was, though, a close ally of Mirabeau, which made him part of the orator's not-so-secret schemes to re-establish the king, a detail Danton chose to ignore. The let-out for Montmorin intrigued deputies and some began to jeer, but the Cordelier chief took no notice. Let them shout. He preferred not to burn his bridges with Mirabeau, not yet at least. Moreover, he had had courteous and amicable dealings very recently with Montmorin during a case he argued for the foreign ministry before the King's Council, and both he and the minister were gratified by the successful outcome. Danton stood by friendships.

In the end, deputies were a little too shaken by the directness of the Cordelier leader's assault on the king's cabinet to vote there and then on removing the ministers. What was this giant intruder's place to make such demands? He was neither from the Riding School nor the Commune hierarchy. The house thanked him for his presentation and awarded him the honours of the chamber, but later, when it did divide, a majority voted to retain the ministers.

Their reprieve was brief. Danton's vigorous public censure ensured their fall. Mortally wounded before public opinion, the stately trio of king's men he had targeted resigned within a week.

The giant from Arcis was back in buoyant mood, then, when Camille announced some joyous news: he was at last set to marry the love of his life. Camille shyly confessed to having first met his wife-to-be when she was thirteen and she was out walking in the Luxembourg gardens at the end of the Cordelier ward with her mother. Lucile Duplessis was now a modern young woman of twenty – ten years his junior – and a true daughter of Rousseau. She was as grand a passion with Camille as the Revolution itself. The cause of Camille's long, heart-tearing wait for Lucile was not her spiritual father but her real one, a King's Treasury official who went by the old order's paternal code. For years the rigorous M. Duplessis shook his head at Camille and his low financial means. He was unimpressed by the young man's Bastille exploits and refused to yield until he was able to verify that the lovesick journalist's newspaper labours were showing a profit. His last look at the accounts had brought not an effusive smile but, miracle of miracles, a nod.

Camille's triumph was a delight for the Danton household, for during the long courtship Lucile had become a close friend of Gabrielle. The pair spent hours together. Lucile, headstrong and erudite, would say with a little smile that she wanted to learn from Gabrielle how to keep a man contented and to raise a child. To Danton, Camille's bride-to-be was a perfect mixture of bluestocking and sensuous maiden. He took pleasure in seeing Lucile and his wife out walking.

All would have been rejoicing in the Cordelier inner circle had Camille, generous, exultant Camille, not done a curious thing in the thrill of the moment. Swayed perhaps by his habit of ingratiating himself with men on the rise, he introduced his increasingly prominent bachelor friend Robespierre to Lucile's older sister, Adèle, and the lonely Jacobin – christened by his club 'the Incorruptible' for the moral integrity that he said drove him – at once began calling on the Duplessis home decked out in a new topcoat and expensive wig. Camille had felt sorry for Robespierre. Indeed, to encourage his rare rush of emotion, Camille also invited him with Danton and several other rising stars of the Revolution to act as a witness at the wedding, which was celebrated on 29 December in Saint-Sulpice.

As revolutionary hotbloods crowded that day into the freezing parish church, their breath misting its marble pillars, Danton glanced at Robespierre. He seemed entirely unmoved by the occasion. The Cordelier headman would not have bet a loaf of bread on Robespierre's chances in love, and he remarked as much to Fabre, who was standing next to him and was likewise intrigued by the Jacobin striver's presence. In a whisper Danton added, 'The man's a eunuch.' Perhaps the Incorruptible sensed the Cordelier disdain, for later, as a noisy reception came to a close, he politely but firmly passed up an invitation from Danton to repair to the Cour du Commerce to continue the festivities over champagne. He returned instead to the Jacobin club.

Danton and his friends were never killjoys. They were united in finding enjoyment in the Revolution to counter its high tension and uncertainty. Fabre, for example, was something of a celebrity himself now through his play *Philinthe*. The spoof on Molière was still filling popular Paris playhouses and he was applying his financial gains to investments in trading ventures of which Danton was only dimly aware, except that they were of a kind he most likely would not have made himself. The fact was that financial speculation was wilder now than under the old older; it was as though nothing monumental had occurred over the past two years to restrain the chase for quick money. But Danton did not judge his Cordelier friends by their foibles; he judged them by the good company they were and by the heat of their passion for revolt. If he, Fabre and Camille were to start judging themselves by their excesses, they would no longer be on speaking terms.

Still, Danton decided to make an effort to get on better with Robespierre and not judge him by his want of passion. For if there was one thing to be said of that cold personage, he appeared to be in deadly earnest about not allowing the Revolution to perish.

In the New Year of 1791, Danton's success in 'sacking' the king's ministers and the notoriety that came with it brought him a windfall promotion in revolutionary political ranks. Though he had not campaigned for it, it was balm for his still-bruised political soul.

The leg-up resulted from the new administrative division of France into *départements* introduced after the fall of the Bastille, and the Paris department, the weightiest of them all, now elected him to its governing council to help run the capital and its surrounds. This was flattering. Not only was Paris the biggest of eighty-three departments covering the length and breadth of the land, it was, in theory, the political overlord of Bailly's Commune. Danton was aware, however, that the position was not all the revolutionary statutes made out. For although the post of Paris regional administrator, unlike the Cordelier presidency, carried a worthwhile salary, he acknowledged to himself that in practice – when it came to revolutionary action in the capital – it was those charlatans Bailly and La Fayette at the Commune who still held the whip hand. Nonetheless, the post at least threw open the door to the legitimate power that eluded him and he determined to make the most of it, particularly since it was unlikely to take up much of his time.

The promotion was billed as a triumph for patriotism in the radical news-sheets. At the Jacobin club, where radicals were gaining ground on the moderate majority, a motion was passed congratulating Danton. And though his private sense was that most members of the Paris department's assembly were a 'pack of donkeys' beholden to the monarchy, he was in fact in lofty company there: Mirabeau and Sieyès were fellow administrators, doubling up on their national responsibilities, and so was the superior Talleyrand. Indeed, it struck Danton that it might have been Mirabeau who cleared the way for his entry to the department's governing council, hoping no doubt to make use of him there.

In a measured letter of acceptance of the department post, which he took up on 2 February 1791, Danton promised not to disappoint those who saw in him 'a marriage of boiling patriotism and moderation' – the twin stuff, he noted, of liberty and revolution triumphant. He made candid mention of the damaging rumours spread about his allegiances. 'Whatever the ebb and flow of opinion on my public life . . . I pledge to let my actions alone answer my detractors and to avenge myself only through my ever increasing attachment to the nation, to the law and to the king, and through my eternal devotion to upholding the constitution.'

This was altogether acceptable to members of the Paris regional assembly, particularly the part about the king. Indeed, so acceptable that assembly men could not believe their ears; they asked their chairman to read out the letter a second time to make sure they had heard it right. Had Danton been called upon to read out his own letter, he would surely have expected the scepticism – or amended his vows a little. The pledge of loyalty to Louis XVI was not one he would have made to the Cordeliers, or to the Jacobins, and it was asking to be tested.

The test came sooner than he could have foreseen. For the events that Danton had been telling himself were bound to dictate the course of revolution now began happening apace.

On 2 April, with Easter a fortnight away, Mirabeau died.

Whether heart seizure, a much-abused liver or cancer felled him, it was a life of excess that carried away the great ringmaster of reform at the age of forty-two. His passing left a colossal void in the Revolution. Not only was he the guide, creator and astute manipulator of a new order that terri-fied the royal courts of Europe, he had fully one third of the members of France's revolutionary parliament in his pocket. This was a count made by

Jacobins who aimed to eliminate the king altogether. Whatever tricks Mirabeau had been up to, he had performed them well.

Danton was as shocked as anyone by Mirabeau's passing. After all he had ranked Mirabeau with Cicero as his speaking model. And if anyone shared Mirabeau's excitement at the very sight of a rostrum, it was Danton. These thoughts filled him as he marched through the streets of Paris behind Mirabeau's coffin, his huge head bobbing above 500 official mourners at the state funeral awarded the great man, then watched the body laid in the Left Bank church of Sainte-Genevieve, rededicated by Bastille warriors as the pantheon for heroes of the Revolution.

With the shock came a certain relief mixed with expectancy. Not that Danton regarded Mirabeau as a political swindler, as some sceptics now did. Camille greeted the death in his newspaper with oblique sarcasm: 'O Mirabeau! Patriot, people's tribune, father of the Constitution, friend of slaves, you have exercised the sole dictatorship that our nation permits – the dictatorship of the word!' But Danton could not despise Mirabeau. What he had done was to grasp power from the aristocracy and the Church and to take reward for pursuing that stupendous change only as far as he thought was right for France. If Danton felt relief, it was because he thought he might now be rid of the allegations and innuendos that stalked him while Mirabeau breathed. Furthermore, someone had to take the departed orator's place. For close on two years Mirabeau had electrified bourgeois reformers and sans-culottes alike with his fulminating wit and passion, and with his death the Cordelier brethren at once began clamouring for their giant favourite to stake his claim as the natural successor. Danton had the terrible face for it. The voice for it. And the people loved him.

If the likely consequences of Mirabeau's death set Danton's mind racing, they put the fear of God into King Louis. The mood of the prisoner in the Tuileries Palace sank from anguish to deep alarm. A private warning issued only months before by Mirabeau rang in the royal ears: 'The royal family is lost if it does not leave Paris.'

Easter came in mid-April in 1791 and the king grasped at the holy week as a belated chance to heed Mirabeau's urgent advice and slip his confinement at the Tuileries. He made his plans public, so as not to inflame suspicions. He and Marie-Antoinette intended to spend the holidays at the royal chateau of Saint-Cloud on the wooded slopes above the Seine just west of the city, there to breathe the fresh air and – though this was not made explicit – to take Easter mass celebrated by priests who remained loyal to the Pope. The intended mass was a risk for Louis. A defiant minority of priests spurned the recent nationalisation of the Church with its edicts requiring the Catholic clergy to swear allegiance to the Revolution; many objectors had gone into hiding, harried by crowds to 'swear or swing'. But it would not hurt the monarchy, the king's courtiers decided, if the loyalist mass at Saint-Cloud were seen as a mark of royal repugnance for the edicts, for surely no one had any illusions regarding Louis' sincerity in recognising the new state church – he had been forced into it, as the clergy were forced into switching allegiance from the Pope. The king was a devout Christian of the old school.

Danton was not much concerned by King Louis' religious preferences, but there were larger matters to consider. Was the royal family's pre-announced breakout from the Tuileries as innocent as it was presented? The Paris street thought not. Sans-culotte opinion was strongly aroused by rumours that the king aimed to proceed from Saint-Cloud to Brittany and the Vendée region of the lower Loire to take command of royalist forces gathering in the staunchly Catholic west to smash the Revolution. A majority at the Jacobin club also thought not. Jacobin eyes were on what was afoot on France's borders, where the threat from abroad appeared to be mounting.

As royalist émigrés mobilised across the Rhine for a counter-strike, it was plain that Austria and Prussia, the main continental powers, were merely awaiting the right opportunity to lead it. Revolutionary Paris still buzzed with concern over the Austrian army's march into Belgium only four months previously to retake the Habsburg possession from an independence-minded population dazzled and inspired by the fall of the Bastille, and the result was that Austrian troops were encamped on France's northern border. More threatening still, England was finally coming down against the Revolution as a dangerous contagion, having blown hot and cold over its impact on mankind.

Was Louis XVI aiming to flee west to join his supporters? Or to the Rhine to join a vast invasion force? There was usually some element of truth in rumours abounding on the Paris street and in this case the contents of a secret letter addressed by Louis to the King of Prussia would have proved them right on the mark, had the letter come to revolutionary eyes. What Louis kept from his subjects was a specific request to the Prussian monarch to lend active support in undoing the Revolution.

Without knowledge of Louis' secret communications, it still seemed obvious to Danton that a sortie by the king from the Tuileries, innocent or not, was a high risk for the Revolution too, a potential spark for civil war. In consultations with the Cordeliers he therefore acted to stop it. If the rumours were at all true, the king was acting as a traitor to his people. So on Easter Sunday morning, after La Fayette deployed a strong National Guard contingent around the Tuileries to protect the king's departure, the

Cordelier battalion and ragtag forces from other radical wards converged on the palace in superior numbers to prevent it.

In the Tuileries courtyard the royal family, impatient and frightened, sat in a row of shining coaches waiting to leave. As the guardsmen fixed bayonets, the crowd brandished pikes and rifles. The stand-off appeared total; La Fayette's order to his men to do their duty and clear a path for the royal convoy by force went unheard. Danton emerged from his battalion to make a grab at the reins of the horses harnessed to the first royal coach. La Fayette, his long, thin face crimson with anger, retired to City Hall to obtain a proclamation of martial law. If he was not given martial law, he hissed, he would resign.

This was a matter for the Paris department. Hastily convened, the first administrators to assemble inclined towards indulging La Fayette. But then Danton arrived from the Tuileries, having heard of the resignation threat. He roared at La Fayette: 'Only a coward deserts his post in time of peril. What's more, it is not the Paris department that appointed you. Go and take your resignation, I dare you, to the forty sections that made you a general!' It went without saying the Cordeliers' Théâtre-Français section was not one of them.

There was no declaration of martial law – and no royal departure.

At length, in mid-afternoon, the king and queen stepped down wearily from their trapped carriages in the Tuileries courtyard and returned to their private chambers. La Fayette, thick-skinned to humiliation, deigned to stay in his post, although Danton made the most of their latest confrontation. Before leaving the emergency session of the department, he co-authored a blunt warning to the king, in language scarcely becoming a King's Council lawyer: 'Keep away from the enemies of the constitution. Proclaim to foreign nations that France has made a glorious constitution for herself and that you are now the king of a free people.'

Later that evening, at the Jacobin club, Danton delivered a fierce speech affirming that La Fayette had wanted to open fire on the people. This was not far from the truth in so far as martial law authorised the use of firearms to restore order, but it was nonetheless an inflammatory reading of his adversary's motives. The Jacobins listened intently; some were incensed against La Fayette, some against Danton, protesting that he was misrepresenting the incident. All the same, Danton achieved his objective: in the court of popular opinion the charge that La Fayette was only waiting for the chance to fire on Paris street crowds clung to the general's uniform like spent gunpowder in the field from that day on. What was it about La Fayette that was so unappealing? The pomposity? The self-assurance? He and La Fayette hardly seemed to be engaged in the same revolution now. The general had taken to talking of himself in the third person: 'La Fayette disagrees . . . La Fayette intends to leave . . .' It was intolerable. He was only two years older than Danton, but the valiant young rooster of the American war had become the smuggest of political peacocks.

To be sure, Danton was not averse to seeing his own reputation embellished. The Cordeliers seized on the Easter drama to lionise him. In inventive mood at the Procope, Camille and company put it around that their brawny chieftain had personally taken the lead pair of royal horses by the bit and led them back to the Tuileries stables, with the king's carriage rumbling behind. It was mostly fantasy. But the Revolution needed its myths and the Cordeliers were more than ready to supply them.

# SEVEN

# A Wilful Woman in the Way

For French patriots it was impossible to ignore the gathering menace from abroad. England with her financial might was always ready to put the world in her pay and as the year 1791 advanced she seemed, in her covert manner, at least as great a threat to the Revolution as were Austria and Prussia with their plans for invasion.

The blanket foreign hostility afflicted Danton, not least because he held England in high esteem. The English were a dogged commercial nation, expansionist to the core, yet they were serious about their liberties and produced doughty reformers who never let up. He felt honoured, then, to rub shoulders in Paris with England's 'Mad Tom' Paine, who was drawn to the crucible of revolution like a fire-raiser to a good blaze. Having put a match to the American Revolution, the Englishman became a regular participant at the Jacobin club from the day of his arrival in Paris in early 1791; he spoke through an interpreter, spreading the down-to-earth wisdom of his revolutionary bible *Common Sense*, his call to revolt across the Atlantic.

Danton became acquainted with Mad Tom at the Jacobins and also invited him to sit in at the Cordeliers to give him a taste of French revolt in the raw. Had they been able to communicate a little better, Danton would have spent more time exchanging ideas at the Procope with the burning-eyed Englishman, who liked his wine, but Paine's French barely stretched beyond the word '*liberté*' and Danton's bookish English was not up to spontaneous discourse. It did strike Danton, though, that Paine ultimately placed small faith in the common people; he seemed to prefer revolution carried out from the top down. Perhaps he was less mad than Americans had baptised him. Paine had in fact first come to France two years before the fall of the Bastille, not to sow rebellion but to pursue a business brainwave – to build a single-span iron bridge across the Seine in Paris. It was a revolutionary scheme, since few were convinced that a single-span bridge bereft of solid stone was at all safe. The idea had come to him during his time in America, in contemplation of an iron span across the Harlem River in New York.

Though Paris chose to reject Paine the bridge-builder, it took Paine the political inventor to its revolutionary heart. He was nothing short of a hero to the Cordeliers, and to most of the Jacobins. His fame reached radical new heights just as Louis XVI's plans for an Easter break came to nothing in the Tuileries courtyard. For it was then that Mad Tom followed up his triumphant *Common Sense* with a similar incendiary device for the French Revolution. The appearance of his new work, *The Rights of Man*, was both an intellectual and emotional boost for the revolt in France: translated in a trice, it was destined to outsell any book previously published and was snatched up with particular curiosity by readers in England and France. Patriots who delighted in the presence of this radical Englishman surmised that his underlying aim in praising their revolt was to foment civil resistance to the monarchy in his home country. Their hearts swelled at his prediction that the Revolution was destined to reshape the entire world. They thrilled to his conclusion that their rebellion was a contagion so strong that no foreign court in Europe could hope to repel it.

Alas, these were the predictions of just one Englishman. When Danton turned from reading *The Rights of Man* to the latest Paris news-sheets, reports from London gave a different picture. Though England was not at present at war with France, public perception there seemed to be heading once more down that familiar old path.

To French patriots this was a disturbing trend since the English people, unlike the Continental nations, had given the Revolution a rather warm welcome at first. There were those like William Pitt, the prime minister, a cautious leader, who did so mainly because anything that knocked the old enemy off her stride could be considered a good thing; and there were high-born humanists in the liberal opposition who did so because they greatly admired the Revolution. The most enthused liberals were exuberant, none more than Charles James Fox, their leader, whose praise for France's revolutionary constitution had Danton and his friends gasping in astonishment at the Procope. In the House of Commons, Fox termed the constitution 'the greatest fabric ever raised by human integrity since the creation of man'.

But now the tone across the Channel had changed. The Revolution had begun to provoke division and hatred, even public violence. The conflict came to a head in the House of Commons on 6 May 1791 in a debate as acrimonious as any that England's parliament had ever witnessed; the Procope company had to read the reports three times over to grasp just how ferocious it was. The normally gracious Fox had fallen into an emotional slanging match with Edmund Burke, political author and parliamentary orator supreme. The two statesmen, both opposition Whigs to make matters worse, lost their heads. The crusty Burke, whose Whig loyalties stopped short of tolerating what was happening in France, cursed the Revolution as a contagion of imminent danger to public order in Britain. Fox told him he could not be more wrong: 'I believe it is one of the greatest events in all history . . . an arbitrary system is abolished, replaced by one dedicated to the good of the people.'

Back and forth the argument went, more biting with each exchange. French revolutionaries, said Burke, invented their Rights of Man through intrigue, murder and assassination; their new constitution was a detestable document that would have abominable consequences. To praise such ideas was to grow a deadly tumour without providing a scalpel to remove it. On the contrary, argued Fox, the revolutionary constitution destroyed a tyranny, a goal all right-thinking Englishmen could not help but share. Should the French be blamed for throwing off slavery and human misery? This was not to suggest, Fox added, that what was happening in France should be ferried across wholesale to England; it was, nevertheless, a wondrous advance for democracy. Nonsense! cried Burke, a choleric character at the best of times: the revolt across the Channel was a grave threat to the English constitution itself, because it encouraged home radicals in their intent to overthrow the British system of government. That threat had to be eradicated. War was the proper response. Better to take preventive action than wait to catch the disease without knowing a remedy. What disease? asked Fox of the Commons. 'Is there a man among us so short-sighted as to wish for man's liberty and happiness to be confined to English soil?' Rubbish, said Burke. English liberals were letting a monster loose on English soil. The present state of France was ten times worse than the tyranny of its past. 'The French will go from tyranny to tyranny, oppression to oppression until this system crumbles with the ruin and destruction of their unhappy, errant empire.' Those in England who supported such a thing, Burke concluded, were not simply mistaken, they were bad men.

Long years of friendship between Fox and Burke ended on the Commons floor in insults and tears. The irony of it was that Burke was in many respects a moderate man.

It was perhaps clearer to Danton than to most French radicals how dark the mood was growing across the Channel, for he had a sharper sense than most of the power of public orators to swing popular opinion. War looked close. Danton had no grounding in foreign affairs, but instinct told him it would be good for the Revolution to try to keep England off her warhorse.

*　　*　　*

The English were not to be kept out of the Revolution, even though the interference was not always deliberate. Through the spring and into the summer of 1791 moderates at the Riding School, many born nobles among them, persisted in trying to foist on France the English system of government. Only a vociferous radical minority was hell-bent on experimenting with a republic, and neither Danton nor Robespierre, from his perpetual perch at the Jacobin rostrum, lent his voice to their cause.

A new parliament was scheduled to replace the Constituent Assembly in the autumn and a decision had to be made on the form it would take. The moderates, looking to the English model, wanted a house of lords to counterbalance a revolutionary lower house, all under a constitutional monarch (whom they envisioned as Louis XVI). Had the irascible Burke back in London been less incensed by the Revolution, even he might have been reassured by their initiative. To Danton, however, it looked monstrously wrong. The people would only see it as the restoration of aristocratic privilege. They would not stand for it. Much as he admired England, this was a backward step for the Revolution and he put all his orator's energy into preventing it. When the moderates pressed for a vote at the Jacobin club on 20 June, Danton took the rostrum – legs planted apart, left hand on his hip, right hand gesticulating, the classic orator pose he now made his own – and began, quietly at first, to undercut the prominent support for a house of lords: 'I would remind members that as a people becomes truly great, men who consider themselves great can no longer be held in reverence.' Growing more heated, he branded as traitors those who aimed to muddle institutions that served the cause of liberty. 'They hope to remain noble despite the horror that the nobility inspires in all France. For that, they want two houses of parliament. I say no!'

The Jacobins postponed a vote. It was not long before the house-of-lords concept dropped out of sight.

On that same night, 20 June 1791, as Danton walked home to the Left Bank with Camille after the long Jacobin session, content with his performance, how little he knew that the seeds of a distinctly more direct foreign intervention were being sown beneath his very nose. To reach the Pont Neuf and the Cour du Commerce the two friends took the riverbank route; they passed a little before midnight beneath the shadowy walls of the Tuileries Palace on the Seine side. From the palace courtyard they heard muffled activity – a bump of carriage wheels, a neighing of horses – and thought little of it beyond remarking on the curious hour for such movement; it was probably Swiss guardsmen preparing some ceremony for the morrow.

\*     \*     \*

At eight the next morning Danton was woken by Fabre, who rushed in from the street. 'Listen! Listen!' he shouted, charging past Gabrielle, who was making coffee.

From his bed, Danton, a late sleeper, dimly heard a tocsin ringing. It was the alarm bell sounding from City Hall. Then it sounded closer, from the Cordelier church and from Saint-Sulpice. 'The king has gone,' Fabre said.

'The king? Where?' Danton was already out of bed.

'Where! Christ knows. The whole family has gone. Every one of them. In the night.'

Fabre was willing Danton to get dressed, throwing him his breeches. Danton instinctively pulled out the black frockcoat he favoured for important appearances at the rostrum.

Before nine o'clock on 21 June they were at City Hall, where members of the Commune and the Paris department were congregating. The entrance hall was in uproar as city fathers flung rumours and counter-rumours at each other; Mayor Bailly maintained that the king had been abducted against his will. There was the same wild hubbub at the Riding School, where deputies also traded theories of flight and abduction. Crowds gathered at the Tuileries to chant abuse at the departed king; they swarmed in larger numbers to the Palais Royal, as if expecting the Duc d'Orléans to make a move for the throne. Danton was convinced that La Fayette had to be behind the king's flight. All anyone seemed to know for sure was that the royal family had left the Tuileries in secret after midnight and headed east.

It would take two full days before Paris began to learn what had happened. It was a preposterous escapade. The royals had left in disguise – Louis as a valet, Marie-Antoinette as the governess of their two children and Madame Elisabeth, the king's timid, gentle sister, as travelling dame – though the size and opulence of the carriage incredibly selected for the escape, together with its three coachmen in resplendent yellow livery, would have told anyone who saw it roll quietly by on the night roads heading east that it carried no ordinary bourgeois family.

The royal destination was a fortress held by the regular army – still the King's Army – at Montmédy, hard on the border with the Austrian territory of Luxembourg. The commander at Montmédy was General Bouillé, the same ardent royalist who had presided over the massacre of dissident troops at Nancy. Once the destination became known it did not take a fortune-teller to deduce that Louis XVI intended to rally loyalist troops to his side at Montmédy in order to recover his full God-given royal rights by force, or to take refuge in Luxembourg with the Austrians and prepare for an imminent invasion. A note which Louis left at the Tuileries listing his grievances against democracy and parliament left no doubt about his general intention. The curtain fell on the royal pantomime, however, a few tantalising hours short of Montmédy at the forest town of Varennes, where a local postmaster, a confirmed Jacobin, suspected something odd was afoot as the disguised royals pulled in for a change of horses. The postmaster alerted the revolutionary town guard – a force in neither contact nor sympathy with the regular army – which performed its patriotic duty of identifying the king and taking him into custody.

In ignorance of this outcome, confused politicians in Paris reassembled at the Jacobin club on the afternoon of 21 June after a morning spent in indecisive disarray. As Danton strode up the Rue Saint-Honoré to the meeting, the crowd chanted his name. '*Vive Danton! Vive Père Danton!*' He smiled at the spontaneous award of paternity, shouting back: 'You're right. You're right. Your leaders have betrayed you.' But he had deeper things on his mind. Since Fabre had woken him, he had gone through a transformation. His revolutionary focus had changed. Louis XVI had indeed betrayed his people; whatever deceptions royalists devised to defend him, the king was a traitor. If constitutional monarchy now stood the remotest chance of survival, the Duc d'Orléans would have to take the throne – and perhaps, just perhaps, that was still possible. Against that, the very idea of monarchy appeared mortally wounded at a stroke, so that one alternative now placed itself before any other in Danton's reckoning: the time had come for a republic.

It was as if, in the brief time between snatching his morning coffee from Gabrielle and a missed midday meal, he had disposed in his pounding heart of eight centuries of dynastic monarchy and become a republican. Until this day he had been riding the tide of revolution – now he had a definite direction in which to swim.

He had to await his turn at the Jacobin rostrum on 21 June while statesmen arriving from the Riding School frothed over the royal flight. As he took the stand, it was announced that La Fayette and the king's ministers were on their way to the Jacobin meeting, which lifted his rhetoric. Danton was seething. He roared: 'If the traitors come here, I demand that we raise two scaffolds. I consent to die on the one if I fail to prove to their face that their heads must roll on the other, at the feet of the nation they have conspired against.'

As if on cue, his quarries entered the Jacobin hall. Still at the stand, Danton addressed himself to La Fayette, reminding him that as head of the National Guard he had sworn responsibility for the king. Then Danton enquired with savage irony whether the general imagined he was acquitting himself of his debt to the nation by appearing in penance at the Jacobins. Fist clamped on hip, the other pointing, he added:

You have sworn that the king would not leave. You have stood bail for him. Either, then, you are a traitor who has betrayed his country, or you are a dunderhead who has taken responsibility for a person you cannot answer for. In the best of cases, you declare yourself incapable of holding your command.

La Fayette paled but stood his ground. He regarded Danton as an anarchist. What had become of the Jacobin club! It was a disgrace to admit such hellraisers to its midst. He swore to members that his actions since 1789 had saved France, not betrayed it. And he won applause with a pledge that his guard officers would scour the country to rescue the king from the enemies of the Revolution.

Danton shuddered at the hypocrisy. La Fayette was not pursuing revolution, he was pursuing the status quo. The guard commander had a strong residue of support, though, in the genteel middle ground of reform. The fact was, the Cordelier chief's enduring battle with La Fayette was far from won. And in the commotion caused by his fierce personal assault on the general and the continuing blank on news of the king's whereabouts, Danton conceded that this perhaps was not the moment to talk the Jacobins into creating a republic – or to erect that pair of gallows he had sworn by. No, the thrust for a republic would come better from the Cordeliers, the soldiers of the 'Cordelier Republic'. Camille had been pressing for a republic for a good year now and had lost none of his verve: even without knowing what had become of King Louis, Camille was demanding in his stop-press pages the head of the 'beast king'.

The very next day, then, at Danton's request, the Cordeliers produced a republican manifesto to put before the Riding School. The appeal was blunt, but not inflexible: Louis XVI had abdicated his throne, so henceforth he was nothing to the French nation, if not its enemy; whether there was any benefit to be had from maintaining a throne remained to be seen; for the Cordeliers, however, the situation was crystal clear – royalty was incompatible with liberty, as the people could no longer place an ounce of faith in a public functionary named 'king'. The manifesto ended in a dramatic appeal to the Constituent Assembly: 'We summon you, in the name of the *patrie*, either to declare France a republic without further ado or at least to take a vote of all the nation's departments on this vital issue before once more throwing the greatest empire in the world into the paralysing chains of monarchism.'

There it was. *Declare France a republic*. But for all his impetuous style, Danton was a realist. The either-or twist at the end was a sop to the Revolution's soft temperate centre. Consciously, he went out on a limb before pulling himself back to safer terrain. That was also his style, a guard against negative reactions, which was all to the good in this case because the Riding School was unresponsive. Robespierre's reaction captured the general doubt. In an icy play of ignorance, he asked: 'What is a republic?' His hostile innocence brought a hush to the meeting, for it was clearly meant to take the wind out of Danton's sails.

For once Danton was left searching for words. In truth, none of them had the answer to Robespierre's rhetorical poser. In practical terms they had only the American model of a republic to go by, and this mainly from hearsay. Back at the Riding School, the moderate majority felt it wise simply to ignore the Cordelier summons as soon as they knew for sure that King Louis was on his way back to Paris from the north-east frontier, under the eye of commissioners dispatched to retrieve him. Parliament did vote to suspend Louis temporarily from his functions, but a majority shrank from dethroning him for treason. Rather than provoke Austria and Prussia into attacking France, most deputies preferred to pretend that Louis had been misled into leaving the Tuileries by incompetent advisers. To cap his innocence, it ruled him beyond the reach of revolutionary law; the king was 'inviolable'. That, deputies thought, should further discourage foreign armies from invading France to rescue him.

This decision struck Danton as ludicrous. It showed the gulf now separating people and parliament. On the streets of Paris and provincial cities popular resentment against the king was on the boil. How could the people's representatives, supposedly reasonable men, make believe the king had done no wrong? How could they reject the idea of a republic? In his newspaper Camille caught the absurdity of it in a spoof on the king and his plight, reducing the monarch to the common man's level after his return under guard from Varennes. He pictured Louis XVI slumped in an armchair at the Tuileries:

'It's damned hot,' Louis sighs to his custodians. 'Well, I've buggered up the trip. Still, it was worth a try. I'd been thinking of doing it for some time.'

His warders shuffle their feet.

King: 'Well, I have as much right to my fun as the next man. I'm hungry. Come on now, bring me a chicken!'

A royal valet appears.

King: 'Ah, there you are! And here am I.'

Danton took a more aggressive tone, though also spiced with humour. Returning before the Jacobins to restate his case, he targeted King Louis in person this time. His angry words landed like shells on the packed benches. Parliament, he said, must confiscate the telltale note which the fleeing monarch left behind in the Tuileries; it must interrogate him in public session.

If he confesses, he is most definitely a criminal – unless he is classed an imbecile. What an abominable spectacle to show the world! To have the entire universe watch us choose between judging a king to be a criminal or an imbecile!

The choice must be imbecile, he allowed, if only for appearances. But there were rules against having a madman as king.

What was to be done? Danton had by now examined Robespierre's wicked little question. Furthermore, he was aware that the Duc d'Orléans had just publicly ruled himself out of the succession to the throne, and though many suspected this was a ploy to ignite popular support, which it no doubt was, the Riding School was taking it at face value. Danton therefore came back to his proposal to sound out the nation's departments on the creation of a republic, only this time he fleshed out his ideas: the departments should elect twelve wise men to form a national council in place of the monarch, each holding office for two years before having to seek re-election.

Danton was earning his stripes as a policy-maker, however rash and unpredictable. But progress towards creating a republic was frustratingly slow. The liberal minds who had produced so much change in the two years since the fall of the Bastille seemed exhausted, blind to the path ahead. In the Riding School's fatigued ranks precious few were ready to go into battle for the most sweeping change of all. At the Jacobin club, on the Rue Saint-Honoré, members were so badly split that a large section of them – two hundred and more upper-class moderates, including La Fayette and Bailly – had recently broken away to form a rival club across the street in their urge to avert 'tyrannicide', adopting the gentle name of Feuillants, after yet another order of monks from whom they rented their premises.

The strongest pressure to abandon monarchy came in any case from voices outside parliament, not least from the eccentric Tom Paine, who responded to the Varennes fiasco by prowling the streets of Paris before dawn to nail up posters demanding a republic. The posters were produced by a small republican club he had just formed with a rising politician named Jacques-Pierre Brissot, the lawyer son of a rich provincial hotelier and a man with a revolutionary itch for journalism. Brissot, a Jacobin and an ally of the sage Condorcet, had energy to spare; when he was not promoting the republic he was crusading for the end of the slave trade, another fashionable mission. For war too. Like certain other idealists of radical persuasion, he believed that going to war with nations that were threatening France would not only be a cleansing experience for the Revolution but a liberating one for any defeated enemy. The dream of the Brissot set was liberty in its widest possible sense – universal liberty.

In Paris, no doors were closed to Brissot. Aged thirty-seven, he was an engaging fellow with dark enquiring eyes and a cleft chin who carried the excellent stigma of having once been imprisoned, briefly, in the Bastille for running into debt when publishing material inimical to the crown. Now an established writer, he was a creature made for politics, an idealist with polish, strong-minded and sociable, and he drank at the very fountainhead of republicanism, a salon run by a beautiful newcomer to revolutionary Paris, Manon Roland.

Madame Roland completed a move to Paris from Lyons with her husband, an inspector of industry and commerce twenty years her senior, in 1791. As Jean-Marie Roland immersed himself in the Jacobin club, she employed her charms and brains to turn their rented Left Bank apartment, situated beside the mint in the old Cordelier ward, into a political salon – the kind of gracious, well-mannered haunt for people with ideas and style that had all but disappeared with King Louis' downfall and the self-imposed exile of the cream of Paris society hostesses. She could not match the gilded mirrors, the exquisite armchairs, the amorous alcoves and string quartets provided by the aristocratic hostesses in their noble mansions, but perhaps this was all to the good. Against the trend, Manon Roland's enterprise prospered.

Male republicans swarmed around the Roland honey pot, for this was how many of them regarded her salon. The hostess – the daughter of a master engraver with Rousseau's dreams etched into her heart – was as comely to the eye at the age of thirty-seven as her political ambitions were naked. Her bluestocking façade made her all the more irresistible, for how could the earnest young radicals who came to her salon not torment themselves with doubts and fancies over the strength of her attachment to the string-bean pedant she lived with? They only had to look past a door leading from the salon to see that the couple had separate beds. Jean-Marie Roland, in his late fifties, was as dry as she looked ripe – a thin, bald, pettifogging man who wrote manufacturing manuals on peat production and wool-spinning techniques, and had nonetheless a strong desire to serve France as best he could.

Madame Roland held Brissot among her favourites. Under the alluring pseudonym 'Roman lady', she wrote erudite pieces for his political review the *Patriote Français*, a trumpet for the republic. Danton she abhorred, or acted as though she did. The more his reputation grew, the more disdainful she became. Danton could not miss her reaction on those occasions when he stopped by at the Roland salon, only a step from the Cour du Commerce, with Brissot, then a friend of his, and braced himself to drink the sugar water she handed round. She seemed if anything to be overly aware of him, for after his first visit it filtered back to him that she had put her lovely hand to her mouth and whispered, 'Which cave did they drag this one from!' He was too much for the adopted gentility of her gaze. This bull of a man with the pocked farmyard face, tree-trunk thighs and fierce language violated everything the master engraver's daughter had come to regard as seemly, which showed in the first impression she penned of him: 'However much I told myself that one cannot judge people on sight, that I knew nothing against him for sure, that the most honest of men was bound to have two sides to him, I could not for the life of me see a good man in this face. Never have I seen anything that so perfectly captures the recklessness of brutal passions and astounding audacity, half-masked by an air of great joviality, feigned frankness and good humour.'

From the start, she visualised Danton with a dagger in his huge fist, yelling on a gang of assassins. Perhaps, next to her husband's pedantry and the imploring looks she got from her salon regulars, Danton's outright virility frightened her. She owned to finding him bold, with a hard eye. She fancied she saw 'a debauched smile on his lips'. However, he was not entirely the stranger she made out, for she had heard him in full throat from a gallery for members' wives at the Jacobin club. But whether or not she agreed with what he said, she chose to place him in the category of patriots she would not abide, along with the bloodthirsty Marat. Danton, she decided, was from the Revolution's gutter. Moreover, she also saw him as a potential obstacle to the political career of her husband, which she was committed to promote. Though she led Jean-Marie Roland by the nose, his rise was her own ladder to power and influence.

Most of this Danton saw through; it amused rather than angered him. How could he despise Madame Roland? Her nunnish coquetry was a treat. She played the queen of virtue. With her sloe eyes and full mouth she paraded her physical appeal, yet acted aggrieved when it produced its inevitable effect. She made penance before she sinned, he joked at the Procope, though not in scorn, for he welcomed her ardent spirit and desire for reform as a fresh gust in the Revolution. Admiringly, she wrote of herself:

> My mouth is a bit large, but it would be difficult to find a smile sweeter or more engaging than mine. Though my hand is not small, it is very

elegant because of my long, slender fingers, which point to subtlety and grace. My teeth are white and straight and I enjoy the fullness of excellent health. Such are the treasures with which nature has endowed me.

Her admirers observed additional treasures, since her 'excellent health' was matched by swelling hips and full breasts, which in the fashion of the times she did as little as possible to conceal from their regard. Her patent method for dealing with the passions she aroused was to tell victims that they must be content with her friendship, though it perhaps occurred to Danton with some relish that her unveiled hostility towards him was somehow linked to the boredom her husband brought her.

Those who had campaigned for a republic since the fall of the Bastille or who, like Danton, had lately warmed to the prospect were not prepared to let the Constituent Assembly, now serving its last weeks at the Riding School, have its lame way. Its vote to absolve Louis of blame for fleeing to join the enemies of the Revolution gratified royal courts from London to Vienna; such lenience was more than they could have hoped for. It looked to the outside world as though the Revolution was tottering; a small push and it would be flat on its face. Accordingly, Emperor Leopold of Austria, the brother of Marie-Antoinette, joined by the King of Prussia, gave it a frank prod with an open appeal to fellow sovereigns to commit themselves to restoring King Louis' former rights. It seemed quite possible that an actual invasion was no longer required.

In this highly charged atmosphere the Paris populace displayed some reserve on 14 July 1791 when celebrating the second anniversary of the fall of the Bastille, though the colossal Fatherland Altar built for the first anniversary, as high as a city church, was ceremoniously re-erected for the occasion at the Champ de Mars festival grounds by the Seine. The sansculottes bristled with contempt for the king and his defenders, but the dampened festivities went on.

To catch the restrained popular mood, Danton and the Cordeliers – assisted by Brissot and, curiously, the Duc d'Orléans' entourage – drew up a petition to be hung from the altar for the Parisian masses to sign. This was street politics of the classic kind: the aim of the petition was to panic parliament into rescinding its infamous decree absolving King Louis of guilt in the Varennes escapade. Danton saw no other way to move the Revolution along. The street must do it.

At the rostrum of the Jacobin club, where the atmosphere had turned increasingly radical since the Feuillants, with their lingering royalist sympathies, broke away, he thundered: 'If we have energy, let us show it. Let those without the courage to raise their heads as free men shrink from signing our petition! Do we not need a purifying moment? Well, this is it!' The petition was addressed to the Riding School itself, the proclaimed objective being to avoid the anarchy that would result from total disaccord between parliament and the people. It ran:

> Everything gives us the right to ask you, in the name of all France, to rescind your decree, to consider the crime committed by Louis XVI proven and to declare that the king has abdicated; to accept his abdication and . . . proceed in a truly national manner to bring him to judgement and to organise a new executive power to replace him.

If the petition did not specify a republic as the solution, the 10,000 working-class Parisians who streamed in red caps and bonnets to the Champ de Mars to sign it on 17 July were not ignorant of the objective. On the way there, at every crossroads, in every corner of the city, they stared at notices put up by Mayor Bailly publicising the Riding School's decree of royal innocence.

It was a scorching summer's day and the mood was almost festive, more purposeful than riotous, as the masses milled around the huge altar waiting to sign. Vendors pushed through their ranks selling sweets and cakes. The core of the protestors came from Danton's Théâtre-Français section, many of them women with children out for the day. Madame Roland was there at the altar in layered skirts inviting them to sign, despite the petition's mixed paternity. Danton, Camille and company were also present, though they kept to themselves on the fringe of the crowd to avoid causing an uproar, also to head off any attempt by City Hall to arrest them for incitement to public affray. They had heard strong rumours that they were at risk.

Numbers counted most in a demonstration of this kind and the guardians of public order were impressed by what they saw: by midday a swirling, bobbing red-topped mass filled the festive fields and spilled over on to the banks of the Seine. As guard commander, La Fayette considered the protest illegal, a public defiance of parliament, and he deployed his most reliable troops, a veteran gendarme brigade supported by cavalry, to police it. As a precaution, La Fayette called for a declaration of martial law and this time he got it, purveyed in person by Mayor Bailly, who came to the Champ de Mars in the early evening with a platoon of guardsmen waving the red flag that signalled martial law was in force. At the sight of the flag the troops cocked their rifles; the crowd tensed, many started running. From a hillock behind the altar, stones flew, bombarding La Fayette's men. Rifles fired back.

No order was given to open fire, save that given by panic. Suddenly the cavalry was charging into the crowd, sabres drawn. Fifteen minutes later, as the smoke of gunfire lifted, the dead lay heaped at the base of the altar and across the field. Hundreds more lay injured. A score of corpses reached the morgue, many of them women; others were thrown into the Seine. At least fifty people were killed. The looser news-sheets put the number of dead at 150. No one – not even a hapless La Fayette – doubted that a massacre had occurred.

The Commune's response was to issue arrest warrants for the petition-makers it blamed for provoking the massacre. It suspended the 'Cordelier press' – Marat's and Camille's newspapers and the *Orateur du Peuple*, an aggressive anti-monarchist sheet run by another Louis-le-Grand graduate, Stanislas Fréron, a lively, conscientious chronicler of events who disdained his old classmate Robespierre and was now drawn into the Danton circle. For good measure judges placed seals on the doors of the Cordelier club itself, throttling the entire movement.

To head off persecution, Camille had taken the precaution, before the guns fired, of creating an alibi for Danton, Fréron, himself and various other Cordeliers in the event that they were accused of inciting to riot by taking a front-line physical part in the Champ de Mars demonstration. His story was that they were out in the country all day on 17 July for a relaxing lunch at the leafy suburban villa which Gabrielle's father had bought for his retirement from the café business. With hindsight, in view of the horrors that ensued, it sounded an offensively glib tale. But neither Danton nor any of them wished to rot in a Commune prison cell.

The obvious place for Danton to lie low was his beloved Arcis – obvious to him because it attracted him so, but also obvious, alas, to his pursuers. No sooner was he back in the Champagne countryside than bailiffs commissioned by the Paris Commune came knocking at doors in Arcis. The little town was not prepared to give up its native son and the bailiffs hardly dared take him; he might have felt quite safe there had he not received a curious private note from Cordelier friends in Paris warning that the butcher Louis Legendre, one of his oldest comrades in revolt, had accepted a huge bribe – 50,000 livres – to assassinate him. It sounded wildly incredible and Danton, no paranoid, wished to ignore it, especially since Legendre was on the Commune's wanted list too. Besides, who would want to pay him that much? Still, it troubled Danton. Much as he admired Legendre's cleaving taste for action, he trusted him little more than he trusted Marat, a view Gabrielle shared. The thought of being riven by the master butcher's meathook was disagreeable. The deeper anguish he experienced in Arcis was more likely caused by what he had witnessed at the Champ de Mars. Danton was devastated. Many of the victims were from his old Cordelier ward. And was he not to blame? Blood spilt on this scale was new to him, new to the revolt that had swept him up. There was lynching, shooting, burning and violence aplenty across the land – a revolution, he had long accepted, required its dose of blood, but a massacre such as this broke new bounds. It seemed an omen of worse to come. For once his heart did not swell at the brave defiance of the people; he was sickened.

To put all this and Legendre out of mind, in so far as that was possible, Danton made a snap decision to leave for London with his stepfather, Jean Recordain, the clothmaker, who planned to purchase a spinning jenny in the land of industry. Danton's mother urged him to go, as a rest from revolution: her husband spoke no English and Danton could help him. Gabrielle did not try to stop him; she feared for his safety at home. The day he left in late July, she held out their infant son to say goodbye. It was the first time they were separating. Gabrielle sobbed when she glimpsed the pistol in his pocket.

On arriving in London three days later, Danton very soon gave up any thought of receiving a hero's welcome from liberal England. At best he found himself an object of dark curiosity. He lodged at the Soho home of a keen republican, Dr Thomas Christie, a likely conduit into circles sympathetic to the Revolution. Liberal grandees knew of Danton, vaguely, but Fox and his supporters were now very much on the defensive, for events in France had upset England's civil order to a painful degree. It came as a surprise to Danton to learn that even as he had been organising the fateful petition in Paris, Englishmen of a republican mind had celebrated the second anniversary of the fall of the Bastille with some fanfare in the industrial city of Birmingham. Their festivities enraged those loyal to the crown. Loyalist mobs ran riot, torching buildings that were used for the anniversary party and sacking the homes of local republican sympathisers. It took the king's dragoons two days to quell the riots. As a gesture to Birmingham's property-owning class, the crown prosecution had three rioters hanged. All this had blown up little more than a week before Danton crossed to England from Calais – a measure of how the English popular press, feasting on the recent emotional confrontation in the House of Commons between Fox and Burke, had succeeded in fanning events across the Channel into a burning topic that set Englishmen against Englishmen.

This was not the time, then, for Danton to advertise his presence in London. He came across his fellow Jacobin Tom Paine, who was shuttling between Paris and London on the strength of his *Rights of Man* and was by chance on home ground at that moment. Mad Tom was the most controversial figure of his day, regarded by Prime Minister Pitt as 'a dangerous disease'. Paine expounded to Danton how he thought France must proceed to a republic: the king must not be manhandled or physically harmed, for that would dishonour the Revolution's glorious achievements. What Paine most wanted, Danton understood, was a serene process that would ease the spread of republicanism to England.

Paine also recounted a recent brush he had had with death, for which, in all good humour, he blamed Danton. He had been in Paris on 21 June, when the Cordelier chief was engaged in arousing the populace against the king's flight. He had found himself in the middle of an angry crowd at the Tuileries and because he was not wearing a cockade in his hat some of them took him for a royalist sympathiser. Before he knew it, brute hands had swung him from the ground and were about to lynch him when a mysterious calming voice from somewhere in the crowd identified him as an American. The voice saved him; the murderous hands loosened their grip. Most sans-culottes knew that Americans were not soft on kings. Paine said he never established who his saviour was, though it was probably a Jacobin. The idea that he stirred up Frenchmen enough to make them want to kill him plainly delighted him. He joked about it. By God, all he needed now was a second miracle to deliver him from Pitt's executioners!

The good Dr Christie proved an extremely obliging host. Through his many contacts among the high-born liberals in the Whig opposition he smuggled Danton into a meeting with Fox. The encounter was too brief to be of much consequence, though Fox surely talked persuasively of his desire for peace with revolutionary France and this was to stick in Danton's mind through the frenzy of war to come.

For the demands of his political career, Danton certainly stayed too long in London – six weeks. No spinning jenny ever took as long to buy. Camille and Fabre, and Brissot too, were urging him to return. An important election awaited him in Paris.

# EIGHT

# The Revolution at War

Danton returned to Paris on 9 September 1791 in good heart and impatient after the journey from London. He was fairly sure by now that he would not face arrest, for the Commune had rowed back on its dubious decision to prosecute authors of the Champ de Mars petition for incitement to riot, and the Riding School was offering an amnesty. As for *lèse-majesté*, it hardly stood as a crime these days. His fellow accused had already been released or, like Camille and his bogeyman Legendre, come out of hiding. The Cordeliers were back in business.

Of more pressing concern to Danton were elections to the new national parliament that was to replace the Constituent Assembly at the Riding School. The fate of the Revolution depended on the make-up of the new body. Would it stop the revolt against monarchy in its tracks, deciding it had gone far enough? Or whip it on with new zeal to launch a republic?

Danton was eager to enter the new assembly. Frankly, he thought it was his due. He had left himself no time to canvass, however, for voting in Paris was set to start in mid-September and finish before the month was out. He had to rely on reputation – and his, large as it was, had its flaws. For one thing, the vote in effect remained confined, even now, to the middle and upper classes, so the street people who lionised Danton were unable to take part. For another, the furious Marat, while wishing to boost him, had done Danton a profound political disservice in the eyes of moderates in the days that led up to the Champ de Mars disaster; indeed, it was more than likely that Marat's machinations had convinced La Fayette and Bailly to try to place Danton under lock and key.

One of the many problems that went with having to count the little harbinger of death as an ally was that his political vision veered with events. His current obsession was the need for a dictator – only an outright dictator, Marat had decided, could purge revolutionary France of her 'rotten souls' – and he saw Danton as the man for the role. He hammered away at his dictatorship idea in the *Ami du Peuple* and bent patriots' ears with his arguments on why Danton was right for the part whenever he was able to tear himself away from his printing press. Marat perhaps missed the irony of seeking to exchange a commoner dictator for the royal one. Still, his demands in his scandal-sheet for a strongman to take hold of the nation caused dismay in every reforming quarter, for what he preached in the *Ami du Peuple* tended to go straight to the hearts of the sans-culottes.

However absurd and misplaced Danton found Marat's proposal, it stuck to him as an electoral curse. Had he not proved his commitment to liberty over and over again? Had he not shown his attachment to human rights? What truck could he have with dictatorship – for himself or anyone else? He was appalled by Marat's thinking and made that plain to everyone in the Procope as soon as he was back in Paris: 'Dictatorship! What a present. What the hell does he want me to do with it? Why not the crown! And a coronation with sacred oils!'

But Marat's ink was, alas, indelible. Even Brissot was alarmed at the spreading dictatorship talk, while Madame Roland, taking her anti-Danton prejudices as confirmed, aired them with renewed pleasure in her salon, to the satisfaction of the sharp political tongues around her. At the Jacobin club Robespierre, too, bristled at the strongman talk, tucking it away in his rigorous mind for future exploitation; his own goal for the new order was some perfect constitutional monarchy that existed only in his mind.

All the same, the Jacobin club, where Robespierre laboured, gave Danton a spontaneous ovation on 12 September at the first session he attended after his return from London, as if members appreciated his difficulties with Marat and were excited to have back in their midst a prize performer with brimstone in the belly to balance the tedious northerner. Robespierre made no attempt to stop the applause. Danton sensed that he somehow feared him, that this dry stick of virtue was confounded by the cries of '*Vive Danton*' that echoed round the Paris streets.

The returning Cordelier chief had a further lift the next day, though it came in an entirely unexpected fashion. Danton was present at the opening sitting of Paris electors, representing the Paris sections, as they began the long solemn business of nominating the capital's deputies to the new parliament. No sooner was the session under way than a court bailiff – ignorant of the Champ de Mars amnesty, or more likely disregarding it in hope of collecting a bounty – burst into the hall to arrest Danton on the expired warrant. The electoral assembly hooted the Commune official off the premises, condemning his intrusion as an affront to the Revolution and a flagrant breach of public liberty, and guards hauled him off to the prison where he had hoped to take Danton. The Cordelier leader treated the episode with disdainful magnanimity, demanding the bailiff's release, an act of generosity that earned him another rousing ovation. The giant had a heart to match that massive frame. There was, moreover, an extra little slice of satisfaction in the incident for Danton, this part hidden, for he had plainly recognised the bailiff as the same dogged fellow who the year before had attempted to arrest Marat. Having now twice sent the wretch packing, it would have tickled Danton to spare him. Afterwards, as the story passed around, there came taunts that he had somehow stage-managed the whole scene to win back attention after his long absence. The carping was irritating, but he brushed it off as the ritual response of those gentlemen reformers who refused to grant him a single saving grace.

In truth, despite a number of handicaps, there seemed little that could stop Danton's election to the national parliament. The Cordeliers considered it a certainty, especially after his new ally Brissot secured one of the Paris seats. Moreover, Robespierre had perhaps unwittingly opened parliament's doors to newcomers like Danton, for at the Incorruptible's behest outgoing members of the Riding School were barred from retaking their seats. Since Robespierre founded this curious restriction on political rectitude, few members cared to oppose it for fear of tarring themselves as self-servers who put personal ambition above high democratic principle. One thing it did was to ensure that the Riding School, renamed the Legislative Assembly, lost its upper-class bias. While this was no doubt among Robespierre's objectives, the exclusion of so many high-born moderates also deprived parliament of all its most experienced reform hands – the genteel liberals such as Talleyrand who had turned the dreams of 1789 into law.

In fact their job was done. A great new dilemma hung over the Revolution and it was up to a fresh class – younger, inexperienced, brasher, humbler of origin – to come to grips with it. Powdered wigs yielded to taut ponytails, and the serious young men who knotted their hair at the nape of the neck came in to make a stark political choice. Should the Revolution hold back from war against all Europe? Or should it go at war full tilt?

Danton was not elected.

Here was a setback that hit him harder than previous failures. Despite the trend towards a younger, bolder intake, the bulk of the capital's seats in the new parliament still went to less controversial nominees than Danton. There seemed simply too vast a weight of unfavourable political opinion surrounding his name. He had to accept it: his face frightened – and the brute force of the street that cavorted behind it frightened the more.

It was of little comfort that the Paris electoral college was, perversely, among the most conservative in the land. Certainly it had stood up for him against the preposterous arrest attempt, but it was packed with Feuillants of the La Fayette school who tended to nominate men of their own stripe. Had he stood as a candidate from hellraising Marseilles in the south he would have been elected hands down, the Procope circle assured him, seeking to ease his humiliation.

It was a fact that his name was known the length and breadth of France, at least to anyone who so much as glanced at the press, for it was not possible to be Cordelier headman, to perform to packed audiences at the Jacobins, to co-administer the Paris region and lead the campaign for a republic without gaining a national reputation. Even in defeat, his friend Fréron's *Orateur du Peuple*, back in lively form, pictured him as Hercules, thrusting his hand into the lion's jaw, seizing the furious beast's tongue and hurling it to the ground at his feet. Fréron's loyalty was appreciated, though the imagery drew a rueful smile that day from its crestfallen subject. For here was the nonsense of Danton's situation: he possessed the national reputation, but not the national rank. Would it forever elude him? He had to wonder. They called him a braggart. What was there to brag about now? On the night of his non-election he buried his sorrows with a feast at his Cour du Commerce table, surrounded by faithful Cordeliers. Gabrielle was still in Arcis, where he had left her with little Antoine, so Camille offered his young wife Lucile's help with the cooking. The only thing for it was to make merry.

As the wine went round and round, the host leaned back, threw his napkin on the table and made an announcement: he was leaving for Arcis, at once. The company was stupefied. Just back from six weeks in London and now off again! Camille, Fabre, Fréron, even the reserved Paré, took turns to warn him that to leave was folly. Did he not see the risks? His bond with the people would snap. His popularity would not last for ever. The new parliament was due to convene in three days' time, on 1 October, and fresh faces were already manoeuvring to take charge. New idols would emerge. New ideas would take root. New disputes erupt. Everyone could see the mood turning to war. And the Jacobins? Robespierre would be in his element; having excluded himself from the incoming parliament out of calculated principle, he would have firmer control than ever of the Jacobin agenda. Perhaps Danton was unaware of it, they warned him, but during his absence in England the fair Madame Roland's salon was abuzz with talk that he had 'gone to the enemy'. If he left again, the talk would surely turn nastier. Did he want to give his enemies the chance to brand him an émigré – like the traitors encamped across the Rhine preparing to attack the Revolution?

All the same it was plain to Danton that Paris did not want him, not for the moment. And he longed to be with Gabrielle and his son. Gabrielle was again with child and had been waiting for him in Arcis for more than two months now. Moreover, he had personal business to attend to in Arcis; it was more than just the fresh air of the Champagne badlands that pulled at him. He could tell them now: only yesterday he had received final confirmation from the state treasury that the King's Council was disbanded with the rest of the *Ancien Régime*'s quixotic legal institutions, and holders of its seats were to receive compensation. He refrained from going into the details with Camille and company, but his share was calculated at 69,031 livres, payable on 11 October. This was several thousand less than he had paid for his practice but more than generous, he allowed to himself, in the circumstances.

Indeed it was a major windfall he had not counted on, particularly in the confused state of the national treasury, for the ministers of the king's government and the revolutionary parliament both scrabbled in that chest to keep going. Danton's initial loans were by now paid off and it had not taken him twenty-four hours to decide he would invest a portion of his compensation in further acquisitions in the land he loved – the tranquil fields and woods along the river Aube. The countryside was an inexhaustible lure.

To go to earth in Arcis at this moment nonetheless looked to be a tactical mistake of astonishing insouciance, as though Danton found pride in dropping his political guard. Nothing that he said convinced the Cordeliers it was a move he could afford to make; everyone would think he was running away from political defeat.

And yet, as chance had it, Danton's fresh departure for Arcis turned to his advantage. First, his bliss was complete. From the King's Council compensation he bought a smallholding farmed by monks, a Church property auctioned off by the state that made a nice addition to the expanding Danton domain, and also made substantial repairs to the family home, where his mother lived. For exercise, he went back to his old love of swimming in the Aube, upriver from the grain chutes, and took little Antoine with him for a first ducking. There was, to be sure, evidence all around of the Champagne peasantry's first lunge for freedom: many of the region's noble chateaux and abbeys lay in ruins, ransacked by countrymen eager to burn the deeds of their serfdom, scratch their names from the tax rolls and loot besides. It was a picture to be seen across France but, ugly though it was, it hardly marred Danton's bliss. Like him, the cannier peasants were spending what they had on buying parcels of Church land at rock-bottom prices.

The happy interlude continued thus for some weeks, through October and into November, when things abruptly changed for the better for Danton back in Paris, without him having to lift a hand. All at once the two men who always stood in his way, La Fayette and Bailly, were gone. Public opinion had not forgiven them for the Champs de Mars massacre; it was they, not the Cordeliers, who had the blood on their hands. On 16 November, Mayor Bailly – who had never been able, moreover, to ensure that his sullen, anarchic capital had enough bread to eat – was replaced by a front-line anti-monarchist, Jérôme Pétion. Danton knew Pétion well: he was a veteran revolutionary from the Riding School, most recently a fellow accomplice of Brissot in backing the Champs de Mars petition. Pétion was in good standing with the sans-culottes because he had been one of the Constituent Assembly's commissioners who brought the king back from Varennes and treated him with a firm disdain that pleased working-class ears. Better still, this Pétion had annihilated La Fayette by a two-to-one voting margin in the run-off ballot for mayor, a post the general thought was rightly his once Bailly lost it. And to cap it all, the price of defeat for La Fayette was his removal from the National Guard command and transfer to a regular army command in the east, where he was to organise France's defences against the expected onslaught from royalist émigrés and foreign foes.

So the Commune was now an entirely different place – and the Cordelier tribe leaped at the chance to ensure that their chief obtained a position within it befitting his prestige. The first thing was to get him back post-haste from Arcis, for further important Commune posts were up for election, including those of Paris prosecutor and deputy prosecutor. These pos-itions had considerable political weight in a capital which was setting the course of the Revolution, and Danton now responded to his supporters' fresh appeal for him to return to Paris, though again he left himself a scant few days to campaign. His apparent nonchalance over the need to put himself out in order to win influential elective office was beginning to look like a major flaw in his political make-up. It was a problem the Cordelier wordsmiths felt obliged to address in their jabbering news-sheets and in appeals made at the Jacobin club. 'Danton will save France if you give him the chance,' they put it to the Jacobins. 'You need men of great character, men who know how to confront our enemies and make them tremble.'

While the Cordelier drum-beating secured formal Jacobin recognition that Danton was a patriot who had served the Revolution well, the club preferred not to interfere in the democratic process by actually directing its members to vote for him. On a first Commune vote, then, both the Paris prosecutor posts eluded Danton. It seemed the electoral gods were forever against him. But here it was that chance played its hand. One executive task left to the miserable King Louis was to appoint government ministers – and for the vacant interior ministry he happened to choose the man elected that day as deputy prosecutor, so a fresh ballot was required to fill that Commune post.

This time Danton was handily elected, by a two-to-one margin over his next rival.

Deputy prosecutor! It perhaps lacked the ring of highest authority, but it strengthened his official presence at the precarious hub of the Revolution and it carried, besides, a decent annual income of 6,000 livres.

More than status or money, his election brought immense relief. Danton had broken the string of rejections. It was high time. He had just turned thirty-two. However reluctantly accorded, the election as deputy prosecutor could be taken as a salute from those otherwise alarmed by his Gorgon head and his bellowing lungs. The relief was liberating; it unlocked his innermost thoughts on what had transpired since July 1789. These he laid out before revolutionary Paris in his acceptance speech to the Commune at City Hall, a lengthy oration which for once he took time to map out before delivery, though to resist improvising was beyond him. He considered it the most important address he had yet delivered – the Danton political manifesto. And he wanted to show that he could behave himself. It mixed revolutionary fire with moderation, so that as he spoke he seemed to charge in and out of the flames, as though he wanted to make sure he was always able to find safety before leaping back in. To attest to his integrity, he contented himself with some throwaway irony to ridicule his detractors and to show what he thought of their endless rumour-mongering. Why, they were even now upsizing the Church smallholding he had just acquired into 'immense estates paid for by God knows what agents of England and Prussia!' Perhaps they were unaware that he had been reimbursed for the loss of his legal practice. Was it not obvious how he had paid for it? He left unanswered the rumours circulating about his supposed dealing with the defunct Mirabeau – but that would do for now; it was enough for him simply to say that he rejected the reputation his enemies foisted on him. The true Danton was the man the Commune saw standing before it – the 'man of the people', the man whose mangled farmyard face, he declared, was a badge of liberty, not of evil:

> Nature has given me the frame of an athlete and the rough face of liberty to match. I stand unburdened by the misfortune of coming from a caste privileged – bastardised, rather – by our old institutions. I have created what I am on my own and maintained my full native vigour without once ceasing – in private life or my chosen profession – to show that I know how to marry cool reason with a burning soul

and steadfast character. If I have felt the seething swell of patriotism from the very first days of our nation's renewal, if I have consented to appear excessive so as never to appear weak, if I have risked arrest for saying loud and clear what kind of men they are who have wanted to halt and to judge the Revolution – or for defending those they call the madcaps of liberty – it is because I saw just what to expect of the traitors who have blatantly protected the vipers of the aristocracy.

And now he was off, unstoppable, riffing, his huge voice rising and falling to its own rhythms. *Excessive so as never to appear weak.* The self-portrait disclosed his method to the world, as if pulled from a Danton coat of arms. And here was his revolutionary outlook, here where his sympathies lay: Paris, indeed the whole of France, was divided into three classes – first, the sworn enemies of liberty and equality, the spoilers of change whom he would 'fight to the death'; then an elite of ardent patriots, the stout hearts of rebellion whose side he would never leave; and third, that large contingent of well-meaning men who sought liberty but feared the storms that brought it, men who would rally to the stout hearts in time of peril but who regarded their reckless energy as an equal peril. For this third class he expressed his respect, while pledging to do his utmost as Paris deputy prosecutor to win it over.

Furthermore, his new office charged him with an overriding responsibility – to uphold the revolutionary constitution, 'nothing but the constitution'. He had had his quarrels with the latest revisions of the constitution, choked on some of the powers it left the king, but now it was done it would serve as his sacred text, for he regarded it as the supreme will of the people. If the king too were to respect it, he roared, 'then constitutional monarchy can last longer in France than all the centuries of despotic monarchy'.

The Commune was on its toes. Was this the same man of the people who only months before had branded King Louis either a criminal or an imbecile? The same people's champion who had gone to dire lengths to demand a republic? To their ears he was now rowing back rather hard, and this struck them all the more when he added for good measure: 'Let royalty be the sincere friend of liberty, the sovereign of liberty, and it will last as long as the nation itself . . . Yes, gentlemen, I must repeat, whatever my personal opinions were on the revision of the constitution, now that it is sworn I shall demand death for the first person to lay a sacrilegious hand on it, be he my brother, my friend, my own son even. Those are my intimate feelings.' In closing, he offered his life in sacrifice to the people: 'I shall die if need be to defend the people's cause. The people alone will have my dying wishes, for they alone deserve them. Their yearning and courage have rescued them from abject nothingness; their yearning and courage make them eternal.' His broad forehead glistening, he stepped down from the rostrum, moved and a little surprised by cries of 'We'll die with you!' that resounded from the Commune benches.

Considering that he was merely embarking on the post of deputy prosecutor, weighty though it was, all this verged on the apocalyptic. He was aware, though, that each time he stepped to the rostrum the audience expected a performance; his voice did the rest.

To preside even in his limited new capacity over the fortunes of the tormented French capital, he judged that he had to reach out to patriots of all persuasions and if this meant indulging that majority which wanted to keep the king, or which was not sure it wanted to dethrone him, then so be it. Accommodation came naturally to him, as naturally as his flashes of anger. Personally, he would have wagered that the Bourbon dynasty was congenitally unable to knuckle down to the constraints of constitutional monarchy. But why alienate the moderates beyond recall? A king in ermine was part of the revised constitution that he had just made his mistress. And the Revolution still needed the moderates, if only to calm things down, for the food shortages that enraged Paris and drove its citizens to kill were causing equal havoc in the provinces.

The bleak fact, Danton also recognised, was that the march of revolution and the rush of liberty had so far done precious little to brighten the daily lives of Frenchmen. That peasants were buying land was some satisfaction. But in the main, hopes raised were hopes unfulfilled. Executive government was paralysed, indeed had ceased to exist since the monarchy's collapse. Harvests had recovered after the disasters of 1787 and 1788, but food distribution, for want of organisation, never seemed to catch up with the more bounteous yields. In the countryside, vagrants took possession of the roads and brigands terrorised the villages. In Paris, as bread shortages eased at the end of 1791, other staple items like sugar left the marketplace. At the onset of winter the price of sugar tripled within a few days from 1 livre or so a pound to 3 livres and more, causing further rioting in the poor districts of the east. Where was the reward for the sans-culottes who stormed the Bastille, for the people in whose name Danton had cut his revolutionary path?

Half of the inhabitants of Europe's largest city were sans-culottes, property-less masses who lived by their manual labour – tanners, pavers, smithies, bakery hands, cobblers, weavers and every manner of apprentice in the pay of master artisans and small entrepreneurs who often scraped by on only a few sous more than they were able to pay their employees. They had settled on a uniform which was now the most familiar sight in the streets of Paris: the floppy red bonnet of the Revolution, dark cloth trousers buttoned to a short jacket, and a long-staffed pike. They mainly lived squeezed together – families of four to a single rented room – on upper floors and garrets in the heart of the city and the slums of Saint-Antoine and Saint-Marcel stretching east, where the great municipal odour was thickest. Perhaps the sole sans-culotte gain from rebellion thus far was to tread where they wished in the capital. Until the Bastille's fall, the Paris poor had been strangers to the wealthy districts of the Faubourg Saint-Germain on the Left Bank and the Chaussée d'Antin and Saint-Philippe du Roule on the Right, where nobles, bankers and prospering bourgeois had their town houses. These days they ventured throughout the city, walking its avenues head-high when off work for the small pleasure of having won the privilege to do so. If the motor for their constant agitation was hunger, they were also powered by the right they believed the Revolution accorded them to engage in violent action, for the right to resist oppression was engraved in the Declaration of the Rights of Man as the Bastille still smouldered. What was resisting oppression if it was not sounding the tocsin and rising in arms? The pike the sans-culottes carried was the symbol of their new right, a daily reminder of the turbulent events they had inflicted on the old order since 1789.

Events. More than ever Danton sensed that it would be events that resolved the monarchy mess. Unforeseen, unpredictable, uncontrollable events. Perhaps, though, it also occurred to him from his new perch of officialdom that he might be able to initiate some of them.

The people's champion kept himself on a leash, however, as winter turned to spring in 1792 and the great stench of Paris resumed in full glory. Gabrielle had given birth to their second son, François-Georges, on 2 February. The happy event both delighted and preoccupied Danton, for his hard-working wife, now back in Paris, made a slow recovery. Her health worried him; she seemed nervous about so many things, even about his new post. She was distraught over the rumours that were put about against him. She knew her mountain of a husband better than anybody; he had his faults, blatant faults – he was impulsive, quick-tempered, excessive in most things, incurably larger than life. But it made her mad to think that anyone could regard a man with a heart the size of his as a monster of vice. Gabrielle was convinced that those who spoke ill of him were ignoramuses who thought that a man of his feral demeanour must have a bad soul. There stuck in her mind a remark he had made to a young Englishman he had brought home to supper one night after his election as deputy prosecutor. With war on the horizon, the English were rare visitors to Paris these days, except as spies. The guest was Lord Holland, nephew of the liberal leader Fox, whose admiration for what was going on in France her husband often talked about to his Cordelier friends.

As the evening at the Cour du Commerce wore on, Lord Holland had begun enquiring about who was in whose pay in Paris. He wanted to know where Danton himself stood. In boisterous mood by this time, Danton told Holland, 'Listen, you can pay Danton 80,000 livres, but you can't buy Danton for 80,000.' Gabrielle would have understood that he was talking of the compensation he had received for his legal practice, rounding up the sum in his usual expansive way. For her, her husband's response summed up exactly where he stood.

Danton's concern for Gabrielle's health increased his urge to show that he could behave himself. It would not pay to call down the wrath of revolutionary gods with rolls of thunder every time he addressed the Commune. This he accepted. Likewise he made an effort, not always successful, to hold himself in check at the Jacobins, where he devoted himself to discussion of practical issues, including the imminent introduction of a towering new machine they called the guillotine for carrying out the death penalty. In tests, the guillotine's hissing blade had proved extremely efficient – humane too, claimed its promoter, the Paris physician-politician it was named after – in decapitating the condemned, which was a matter of interest to Danton as deputy prosecutor.

Like Gulliver, Danton was tied by a thousand little strings of proper conduct that he felt he could snap at one go with a shake of his brawny chest, only he refrained from doing so. As pledged, he had to advance his ideas under the law. Thus he niggled at the king rather than continuing to confront the void of his majesty head-on, though this approach backfired over a side matter he would have done better to ignore. The problem arose out of a Jacobin campaign to organise a relief fund for the troops who mutinied at the Nancy fortress in 1790 and survived the massacre ordered by the royalist General Bouillé. Jacobin indignation had only recently secured the mutineers' release from hard-labour prisons and King Louis himself donated 110 livres from the royal pocket for their welfare – a civic gesture in the circumstances, if paltry. Danton chose to make a mountain of it at the Jacobin club, forgetting his current reserve. He expressed disgust at the meagreness of the royal contribution. It insulted the people's dignity. Did the court think this atoned for its faults? His intervention brought loud applause from rowdier Jacobin ranks. He continued: 'How does the royal family dare offer such alms? Do we dare ratify such insolence?'

But when he demanded that the Jacobins reject the royal donation, they refused, deciding that to return the king's money was a larger insult than the contribution. Robespierre, whose beavering organisational work gave him unrivalled authority at the club, bid them turn to more important matters. The caution brought an embarrassed hush to the proceedings. No one missed the Jacobin gatekeeper's dry reprimand for the giant Paris prosecutor.

Indeed, there were more important matters. War was the first. War now took over the Revolution. Progressively, the war issue dominated debate in the new parliament, at the Jacobins and in the Commune. And it caused a deep crack in the insurrection. Patriots sensed with mounting awe that everything they had achieved was about to stand or fall by war. The new class at the Riding School had already taken the initiative with vigorous decrees aimed against the émigrés, who included Louis XVI's two younger brothers, sundry princes of royal blood and the soldierly heads of France's oldest aristocratic houses. The men in ponytails summoned them to disband their camps on the Rhine and return home, or forfeit their lands and property. At the same time they issued an ultimatum to German Rhineland sovereigns, ordering them to expel the émigrés or else. These were hardy responses to the provocative open pledge made the previous summer by the Austrian and Prussian monarchs – after Louis' failed escape at Varennes – to assist the émigrés in saving their king.

At first Danton stood with a foot either side of the war abyss, recognising nonetheless how crucial a matter it was for the Revolution. Indeed, he considered war inevitable and told the Jacobins so, with the level of clarity his canny peasant forebears would surely have admired: 'I want us to have war, it is indispensable. We must have war. But before all else, we must exhaust all means to prevent it.'

The reason for his rich ambivalence was that the arguments for and against war were part of an impossible jigsaw puzzle, for there was a piece that refused to fit. This was King Louis. The king desired war, purely in order to lose it. France's defeat alone could restore his traditional powers.

At the head of the anti-war party was the cautious Robespierre, backed by a coterie of Jacobins, though not by the new breed at the Riding School. Robespierre worried that war against the rest of Europe would scuttle the achievements of the Revolution – inevitably so in the case of defeat, probably so in the case of victory, since a conquering soldier with no regard for human liberty would likely emerge to take power for himself. For Robespierre, the fortunes of France and liberty could not be left in one man's hands, except perhaps his own. But more important still, as he tirelessly repeated to the Jacobins, the Revolution must turn its guns not on angry European monarchs but on the enemy within – the royalists, the priests and the forces of counter-revolution poised in ever increasing numbers in the west and in large provincial cities like Lyons to reverse the work of 1789. Besides, the idea that the Revolution's task was to liberate the rest of the world was to Robespierre's mind foolish: no one liked armed missionaries.

Whatever Danton's sentiments towards Robespierre, which were currently somewhat soothed by his own efforts to keep himself in check, the Jacobin high priest's put-down of the war party rather appealed to him. Maybe Robespierre had more wit than he gave him credit for. Was this why Camille stood by him? Certainly Robespierre left himself open to abuse by standing in the way of the rush to war. Armed with his own ambivalence, Danton was even moved to defend him as the political tide turned against the pale northerner on the war issue. At a tense spring session of the Jacobins, when some members began jeering and whistling at Robespierre's piping reiteration of his anti-war position, Danton sprang to the rostrum to shut them up, saying they were driven by base envy. 'Monsieur Robespierre has never imposed upon us anything but the despotism of reason,' he roared. Yes, he owned, he had found it painful to keep his silence in recent weeks. Now he felt obliged to speak out on Robespierre's behalf: 'There will come a time – and it is not far off – when we must call to account those who have been attacking a sense of virtue that is consecrated by the entire Revolution. I grant you, his is a virtue that his detractors prefer to see as obstinacy and single-mindedness, but they have never come to scorn it as they do today.'

Danton's defence of Robespierre came out a little more double-edged than he had intended upon jumping to his feet. All the same, it somehow strengthened his stature within the Jacobins: it was not everyone who was able to drum up applause for supporting the guardian of revolutionary morality while at the same time damning him.

War did prove inevitable. At the Riding School the new Legislative Assembly with its vociferous pro-war cabal declared war on 20 April 1792 – initially against Austria, whose army had retaken Belgium, the Revolution's sister-in-democracy. Days later the declared foe became Prussia too, as they marched with the Austrians.

The Revolution's reasons for going to war were as imprecise as the destination to which it was driving French society. Perhaps the most compelling reason was that the notion of war against nations determined to keep Louis on his throne was popular with the masses: the sans-culottes were all for ending the king's double game. The bravura of it appealed, despite working men's daily hardships. Alas, such pride would very soon be deflated.

With the declaration of war – and with foreign adversaries at once militarily engaged in their campaign to destroy the Revolution – Robespierre's logic of concentrating on the enemy within no longer stood up. The practical Danton quickly dropped his hesitations: war was no longer a moral issue; it was a major crisis to be met. At the Jacobins, the Cordelier giant minimised any alarm he felt. 'The play will have its end,' he observed with uncharacteristic phlegm.

It was hard to tell where power resided, even for those exercising it, but a rough pattern was now visible: the Jacobin club, through its debates, served as guide to the Revolution; the national parliament at the Riding School, through its votes, effected the turns; and the Paris Commune, where Danton officiated and his Cordeliers had their noisy say, supervised the great nest of revolt – a charge bound to grow heavier with the prospect that foreign enemies would make occupation of the French capital their first goal.

Ironically, the path to war had been opened by an institution with no real power left at all, King Louis' court. The monarch's preparatory ploy in March of sacking his Feuillant ministers and replacing them with a pro-war cabinet of Brissot's allies, including Madame Roland's earnest husband, Jean-Marie, did the trick. Roland, named interior minister, had by now worked his way into political prominence through what looked like a fussy desk job at the Jacobins – maintaining contact with club cells in the provinces – but which, with his wife's unstinting help, made the pair of them a bridge across which insurrectionary action was bound to pass.

Brissot, the Rolands and the 'liberation war' party were united in pursuit of turning France into a republic and they had strong support among provincial members of the renewed parliament at the Riding School, particularly those from the south-west and the Gironde estuary region. The backing grew from a further shared outlook – a powerful reluctance to let the raucous Paris sections dictate the course of the Revolution. A wary capital baptised them Girondists – a party label they hardly attached to themselves, for they regarded themselves as a broader, more exalted force for liberty than the name implied. Among them was Pierre Vergniaud, a republican lawyer from Bordeaux and the most persuasive of pro-war orators, who, Danton's friends allowed, had a voice quite as vehement and eloquent as their own champion's; another – one who would soon cause Danton grievous trouble – was Charles-François Dumouriez, a popular army general who had liberated himself from the old martial order and now entered the king's government as foreign minister.

Had Danton not been a confirmed political independent – a rare provincial who recognised from the outset that the Revolution must live or die in Paris – he might in fact have been part of the Girondist clan. But he could honestly say he belonged to no party. The party of rigid principle that

Robespierre had drawn around him was not for Danton and never could be; his spontaneous defence of the northerner's virtue could not change his aversion to ideological do-goodery and the politics of obsession.

Instead of boosting popular pride, the coming of war frayed nerves in Paris. News in early May that opening battles on the northern border went badly for the Revolution caused deep dismay among the citizenry. Austrian and Prussian armies, poised for action before war was declared, went about their invasion objectives with all speed. Soon one question preyed on the population of Paris. How far was the enemy from the gates of the capital? Three days? Two? Calculations were exaggerated but no less frightening for that.

The tension grew unbearable that spring. The hunt was on for citizens who might wish to help the enemy. Street crowds returned to the rampage, chasing down anyone who looked like a royalist sympathiser, hanging them from lamp posts for municipal cleaners to dispose of the next morning, if they had time. The National Guard was disinclined to intervene. Anyone could be a traitor. Anyone a spy. The cornershop baker? The sour-faced café waiter? It was enough for someone in the crowd to point a finger. Marat was in his element. He was getting the heads he craved.

What struck Danton, who bore a certain responsibility for the capital's security as Commune deputy prosecutor, was the inadequacy of the forces the Revolution sent out to meet the enemy. Except for a handful of regular Royal Army regiments still intact and willing to turn from their old master in the Tuileries to fight for France, its soldiers were untrained and unfamiliar with war. And so thin in number. At the very sight of weathered Austrian and Prussian professionals approaching they stiffened like rabbits before a forest blaze. It did not help, thought Danton, now with increasing unease, that a general such as La Fayette, with his sympathies for the monarchy, held high command against an enemy whose war mission was to save the monarchy. This was blind folly; it was asking for disaster. Nor did it seem enough for the Riding School to organise a hasty call-up of 20,000 volunteers to man the approaches to Paris in hope of stopping the feared enemy march into the capital.

The war effort looked hopelessly confused. The priority now was to give it focus – and manpower – before it was too late.

# NINE

## The End of a Thousand-Year Throne

On 20 June 1792 the war tensions that gripped Paris erupted in a sans-culotte assault on the Tuileries Palace. Street hordes wielding pikes and sticks swept into King Louis' residence in their thousands with no apparent objective other than to vent their anguish. The attack climaxed weeks of worry and confusion in the capital over the menace of invasion, and since there was not a citizen who had not deduced by now that Louis wanted the foreign enemy to prevail, the monarch was the natural target. At the head of the wave of demonstrators was the butcher Legendre in his bloodstained apron. Were they to kill the king? Abduct him? Or merely terrify him? The volatile mood of the crowd would tell.

The popular assault on the Tuileries seemed precisely the kind of event – uncontrollable, spontaneous – that Danton foresaw would break the monarchy crisis, though in truth he had given it a preliminary push. In his apron, Legendre carried a petition that Danton had helped compose on the city's behalf: it told the king in the bluntest terms not to look for salvation from France's enemies. As the demonstrators swarmed through the palace, the Tuileries guard, unprepared and overwhelmed, put up little resistance. Breaking into the king's private chambers, Legendre shouted at the head of the Bourbon dynasty: 'Listen to us! You are here to listen. You have always deceived us. You are a traitor. The people are sick of being your plaything.'

King Louis, on his feet, swaying, was virtually without protection, for the grenadiers of his personal bodyguard were holding back to avoid a blood-bath. As jostling fellow raiders bayed for the monarch's head, the Cordelier butcher pulled from his apron the petition drawn up by Danton's Théâtre-Français ward and the rest of the Paris sections. Legendre read it out in a market-stall bark, furthermore ordering Louis to abide by the constitution which the Revolution had made for him. Louis did listen, essaying good humour, and, as Legendre finished reading, a demonstrator in the milling crowd thrust a pike at the monarch with a red bonnet dangling at its end. For several terrible seconds Louis inspected the cap. Then, with a strained smile, he unhooked it and placed it on his bewigged head. The royal gesture calmed the crowd and almost won it over, for among loud cries of '*Vive la nation!*' that resounded around the palace chambers over the next four unruly hours there even came an occasional '*Vive le Roi!*' It took Pétion, the new Paris mayor, who sympathised with the protest but was concerned that king-baiting reflected poorly on his authority, a further two hours to coax the crowds into going home.

That night, when Legendre reported on his exploits to the Cordelier club and made much of the monarch wearing the red bonnet, Danton turned away in disgust. He had learned to forgive Legendre for his rumoured (moreover, entirely fictitious) part in taking a bribe to kill him, but this was downright foolish. 'Where does that get you, imbecile?' he scowled, for once putting a chill on a Cordelier celebration. Danton had not taken part in the Tuileries invasion – his role was to drive the street crowd, not run with it – but humiliating the king to his face struck him as counter-productive as well as stupid. A great explosion of popular protest, why not? The Tuileries invasion, yes. The petition, certainly. But its authors had imagined it would be presented with some degree of decorum. Danton feared that the crass baiting of the wretched monarch that day would only revive sympathy for the throne at the Riding School and in indulgent Jacobin ranks.

It was Legendre's turn to scowl. He was damned if he knew what Danton wanted.

Indeed, it would be rash at this point to pretend that Danton knew where he was going. He was full of contradictions. Legendre was right. But who in this stupendous social revolt really knew where they were going? Not Robespierre, not Marat, not La Fayette, not Brissot, not the comely Madame Roland. All had their ambitions, but the Revolution was unencumbered by rhyme or reason.

All the same, the moment when Danton saw just where he was heading was close at hand. After the June invasion of the Tuileries his tactics and manner changed; his concern for decorum went by the board. Any lingering thoughts that constitutional monarchy might work evaporated. His mind was set on something bigger – a second revolution.

Throughout the summer of 1792, Danton put his lungs and his quickening political wit to work in ridding France once and for all of her monarchy. He shook the Jacobin club with a promise to 'bring terror to a perverse royal court' – a pledge delivered without further elucidation, though it was his first mention of terror. Then he bid parliament force King Louis to repudiate his Austrian queen and send her back to Vienna. She had no place in France, he said, for Austria had always wished harm on France. Out of regard for her feminine person, she should be expelled with all the respect, courtesy and security due to her station. Despite the considerate touch, nothing could be more calculated to stir up popular opinion than to tilt at Marie-Antoinette. The sans-culottes had never liked her or her distant Habsburg manner; besides her reputation for caprice and extravagance, she had now come to personify to Parisians a physical enemy – an enemy whose troops had France's revolutionary army on the run in Flanders and the Ardennes.

These were bombshells that Danton fired with an eye on stage management. Each time he had something important to say from the Jacobin rostrum he waited until the general debate grew heated, then rose to propose an adjournment until the morrow, at which time, he promised, he would deliver the goods. It was an orator's device borrowed from Cicero, one that ensured maximum impact, for his Jacobin audience would most likely be packing the benches in increased expectation as the hour came for his turn at the rostrum the next day. He endeavoured not to disappoint. In a vigorous debate on 14 June on the collapse of public order – after he had risen to request an adjournment and entered his name to speak as deputy prosecutor first thing the next morning – he took a full Jacobin house on an excursion to Ancient Rome. A truncated Jacobin club record related it thus:

M. Danton spoke concerning a law passed in Rome after the expulsion of the Tarquins by Valerius Publicola, a law that permitted any citizen, without judicial resort, to kill any man held to have expressed an opinion contrary to the law of the state, the only obligation being to prove thereafter the guilt of the person killed.

Coming from a public prosecutor, this sounded an abominable suggestion to members who, like the Jacobin scribe, missed the context of Danton's classical diversion. They jumped to their feet, jeering, thumbs downturned, thinking the Cordelier ogre was calling for the indiscriminate slaughter of anyone who might be overheard sympathising with royalty. Had they been following the speech more closely, they would have understood – as a bewildered chairman of the session at length consented – that it was part of a muscular Danton peroration listing emergency law-and-order decrees enacted down the ages. Danton and friends jeered back at the incensed antagonists. Where was their sense of history?

Still, this bull of a man was never far from the door of the china shop. The Valerius Publicola jaunt was a nice dip into his bag of classical learning

– and a demonstration of his prodigious memory – yet it was more than likely to confirm the opinion of those who counted him a dangerous rabble-rouser. It reflected both what cautious patriots feared in Danton and what violent sans-culottes expected from him.

The greatest obstacle that summer to Danton's preparations for a second revolution – the dismantling of the throne – turned out to be his old nemesis La Fayette, who was supposed to be out of the way leading the revolutionary army in the east. Indeed he *was* on the eastern frontier, leading his forces from retreat to retreat. Unwittingly, though, La Fayette had lit the fuse for the people's June assault on the Tuileries.

From his latest fall-back position in the Ardennes, La Fayette had addressed a blunt letter to the Riding School demanding more men, rations and cannon. In the same extraordinary letter, he also laid down that the monarchy must remain inviolable. His most imperious demand he left for his sign-off – that parliament must 'annihilate' the Jacobins and Cordeliers. The revolutionary clubs could not be allowed to usurp the power of the nation's elected representatives, he insisted. The letter instructed the Riding School: 'Let the reign of the clubs that you destroy yield to the reign of the law. Let the power they have usurped yield to the firm, independent exercise of constitutional authority, let their errant maxims yield to the true principles of liberty, their delirious excess to calm, constant courage.'

La Fayette had a point, but he was confusing matters to suit his purpose. The Jacobins in particular had developed great political clout. The chief victim of their ascendancy, however, was not the Riding School – which exercised full law-making powers subject to Jacobin club influence – but the king's sorry cabinet of ministers. What La Fayette most wanted to protect was ministerial power, in the hope that it offered a slim remaining chance of buttressing the throne. It took the barest scrutiny of La Fayette's letter to recognise that Danton, like Robespierre, was a specific target. The Paris prosecutor was outraged. What did La Fayette know of liberty? Besides, the letter stank of blackmail! Was the general not threatening to let the Austrians and Prussians march on Paris unhindered unless parliament did his bidding? The letter, which reached the capital just two days before Legendre and the street hordes swept into the Tuileries, presented in any event a heaven-sent opportunity for Danton to show the people who was the villain in the stand-off over the monarchy. Picking his moment at the Jacobins, Danton began, almost gaily: ''Tis a fine day for France when La Fayette at last throws off his mask!' Here was a soldier, he continued, turning serious, who presumed to lay down the law to the nation. But there was an excellent way to stop him: the Riding School must order him to return at once from his command

and submit to questioning. If he refused, his supporters would no longer dare take his side and he would no doubt cross to the enemy. If he obeyed, parliament should strip him of his command because soldiers could not be permitted to dictate the nation's policy. 'Either way, all his plots are aborted,' Danton concluded, his fury with La Fayette running over. 'For there can be no doubt that La Fayette is the head of this nobility that sides with all the tyrants of Europe, and if it is true that liberty has descended from the heavens it will help us exterminate all our enemies.'

While the fireworks over La Fayette's letter impelled the Paris sections to release their pikemen on the Tuileries, Danton's challenge to its author to answer for it before parliament was not, it transpired, the decisive blow against the prince of hypocrites that he imagined. This should not have surprised the Cordelier giant, for a certain respect for the founder of the National Guard persisted at the Riding School. Moreover, who in the new national parliament could disagree that the clubs, the Jacobins in particular, intruded upon the body's rightful pre-eminence in the stewardship of democracy? It was in the Jacobin club that issues were first thrashed out and policy made. That was clear.

Furthermore, La Fayette did not lack spunk. As soon as he heard of the assault on the Tuileries and King Louis being forced to wear the red bonnet, he galloped to Paris to demand the very hearing before parliament that Danton wagered would destroy him.

The soldier spoke for five indignant minutes. Danton wisely decided not to attend, not being a member of the Riding School, for he would have had to endure in silence a white-faced La Fayette, his long nose thrust high, demanding the arrest and punishment of instigators of the 20 June violence and the outlawing of 'sects' that tyrannised citizens through the 'atrocious projects' they favoured. Having thus reiterated his call to close down the Jacobins and the Cordeliers, the general hastened to a rendezvous with the king, departing through an honour guard improvised by members of his old National Guard. La Fayette's sally threw the Riding School into confusion. After a bruising debate, it voted neither to interrogate him on his letter nor relieve him of his army command, though it was some consolation to Danton that it took no steps, either, to outlaw the Jacobins or the Cordeliers.

The fate of the Revolution was by now unfolding too fast for rows with La Fayette to matter. There were breaks in the tension, but few.

On 6 July Camille's young wife, Lucile, gave birth to their first child, a son. The Desmoulins couple lived in the apartment above Danton's on the Cour du Commerce, and over the next few days Camille ran up and down the narrow stairway dividing them, the baby tucked under an arm, to parade his heir. The birth was a fete for the narrow street, in particular for the Procope. Camille named his son Horace, in honour of the Roman lyric poet, who, he proudly reminded the Procope fraternity, was the son of a freedman. Robespierre called by to congratulate his old schoolfriend and with an effort at jollity dandled the baby on his thin knee.

Not long after, the Incorruptible called again at the Cour du Commerce, principally to discuss with Danton ways to hold off any lingering threat to the Jacobin club, and again sported with the infant Horace. Danton would have noticed how ill at ease Robespierre looked with the child. But how else could it be? For Robespierre lodged alone with an obscure carpenter and his wife, within walking distance of the Jacobin club, the centre of his life, and for social diversion saw only his landlord's unbecoming daughters.

As the joy of the Desmoulins household flowed, all distraction suddenly ended for the men leading the Revolution. On 25 July, 1792 the regime of liberty was shaken to its uncertain core, in like degrees of anguish and indignation, when the head of the newly combined Prussian and Austrian armies, the Duke of Brunswick, addressed a savage public warning to the population of France, and in particular to the citizens of Paris, who hardly needed reminding of the perils they faced. Just a few days earlier, the Riding School, taking full stock of the revolutionary army's setbacks, had issued its own warning to the nation: 'The *patrie* is in danger.' The alarm, read out by town criers across the country, brought tens of thousands of young volunteers to the colours.

For its brutality and clumsiness the Prussian field marshal's manifesto struck patriots as more barbarous than anything previously heard from across the Rhine, even from the extremist fringe of the émigré camp. It announced that inhabitants of French cities, towns and villages who dared obstruct his troops, or fire at them in the fields or from their doors and windows, would be executed on the spot and have their homes burned. The duke was still more explicit regarding Paris. On behalf of the Emperor of Austria and King of Prussia, he proclaimed:

Their Majesties will hold personally responsible, on pain of death, without hope of pardon, all members of the national assembly, the Paris department, the districts, the municipality, the National Guard, justices of the peace and whomsoever it may concern . . . for any action to force or insult the Tuileries Palace, or for the slightest violence, the slightest outrage committed against His Majesty the King, the Queen and the royal family. If immediate measures are not taken to ensure their security and freedom, Their Majesties will exact exemplary vengeance that will live for ever in memory, delivering the city of Paris to martial law and total submission, and putting its guilty rebels to the harsh death they deserve.

To French ears it all sounded frankly incomprehensible, coming from an enlightened prince who knew France well and confessed himself proud to have conversed with Voltaire. Karl Wilhelm Ferdinand of Brunswick had the reputation of being anything but a brute.

The Brunswick Manifesto pledged to end anarchy in France and restore the old order. It was posted around Paris clandestinely by monarchists who read in its lurid lines their ultimate salvation; patriots read in it their death before indiscriminate Germanic firing squads. Danton, like all patriots, was aghast at the brutish swagger, if somehow amused by its absurdity. Destroy Paris! Slaughter the population! What were the king's friends thinking of? The more Danton reflected on it, the more, in his anger, he knew what to do; it was a moment of revelation. Something within him stiffened his pride in being French, something swelling from the Champagne country and from the anarchy and anguish of Paris alike. A monarchy saved by a German duke swimming in French blood was so alien to his hardened pride and patriotism that it did not bear thinking about. And even though King Louis publicly repudiated the Brunswick Manifesto and called on the nation to fight, it changed nothing. Only the coming of a republic could save the France in which Danton's pride rested. And the republic – the sweetest fruit of the Revolution, its ultimate sense and meaning as he now saw it, in sharpest clarity – was obtainable only through the physical demolition of the monarchy.

Intimidating the king, pressing him into line, would no longer suffice. The demolition had to be swift and irreparable. It would take force. What would then remain for a Prussian field marshal to save?

At the Jacobins, Robespierre hesitated over how to counter Brunswick's menace. He cautioned against a rash response, trapped as ever in his hatred for 'traitors' inside France: the nobles, priests and their numberless dupes among the common folk who took up arms to undo the work of the Revolution. It was still very hard for Danton to understand Robespierre – the elusive personality, the strange spirit that drove him. It seemed the manifesto cut no closer to Robespierre's emotions than some Jacobin speech contradicting a point of order he had just made. Robespierre had no heart for action; his liberty was abstract. 'That bugger couldn't cook an egg,' Danton told Fabre, though not in total derision, for he recognised the sinew in Robespierre's persistence.

The effect the manifesto had on most patriots, from bourgeois gentlemen to street rowdies, was otherwise electrifying – and precisely the opposite of that intended by the Duke of Brunswick. Nerves frayed were nerves emboldened. And Danton, through his rank in the Commune and his muscular influence in the Paris sections, was well placed to mobilise the tremendous rush of fool's courage that came of it. His recruiter's voice already resounded through the capital, for he had added a swift rider to parliament's proclamation that France was in danger. The Théâtre-Français section voted through a demand, carrying Danton's name as president, for an immediate end to the military system surviving from the old order, under which only males qualified to vote were called upon to serve. Scrap all voting distinctions, the Left Bank reformers insisted. Put the non-voting masses in uniform. With the *patrie* in danger, it was every man's job to defend it.

By pure good fortune the balance of forces in the capital at this very moment favoured the spectacular response to the Brunswick Manifesto that Danton now prepared to spring. Many thousands of combatants from the provinces – lumpen civilians mainly from Marseilles and Brittany and not without their share of ruffians and cut-throats – had converged on Paris to celebrate the third anniversary of the Bastille's fall on 14 July and were still camped in the capital hoping to prove their worth to the nation under siege. They were a symbol, turning more debauched the longer they stayed in Paris, of the federal political system and federal army that the Rolands and their Girondist friends pictured as mainstays of the republic they ardently desired.

The Marseilles contingent, 600 strong, placed itself more or less in Danton's charge. The insurrectionary renown of the Cordeliers was a mighty lure to these intemperate sons of the south and they bivouacked on the floors of the Cordelier convent, where Danton had an eye on them and was hopeful of keeping them on a leash, though Gabrielle swore they looked a sight more fearsome than even he. The men from Marseilles were certainly undisciplined, an attack dog unmuzzled, but they were valiant marchers and they tramped with their red bonnets and two oily cannon to a rousing new war song that troops from the south had picked up when lately garrisoned on the Rhine at Strasbourg. The song caught the fancy of the Paris sansculottes, who joined the chorus and called it the Marseillaise.

As Danton put in place the many pieces of his plan to end the monarchy once and for all, he kept the Marseilles warriors in the dark; they would know of their part soon enough. His closest Cordelier partners were abreast of the details, as were Brissot and select republicans, and in particular the Paris ward leaders he trusted, for they were the key to the operation. While it was important to avoid provoking the National Guard into pre-emptive action, it was also hard to keep the plan secret and the capital fairly raced with rumours that something momentous – quite apart from the feared arrival of invading Prussians – was about to occur.

Once he had locked the plan up as best he could, however, Danton grew jittery. It was exceedingly dangerous; it could easily miscarry. If he was not beset by fear for himself, it could not have escaped him that he might lose his life as the action took its course. Nothing in the Revolution was predictable: its every event thus far might easily have taken a different turn from the one it took. Accordingly, he would have disclosed little to Gabrielle, who seemed permanently afraid for him. What if he were to fall into the hands of royalists? What if he were delivered to that tall efficient scaffold machine just sanctioned by his own Paris prosecutor's office? Indeed, the guillotine blade was a sharp reminder that he had domestic ends to tie up, family farewells to say. So even as he set a provisional date to put the plan into action with the Paris sections, the eternal peasant in Danton took over once more from the headstrong revolutionary.

He left for Arcis.

If it were possible to imagine a still less propitious occasion than the last, the previous autumn, to disappear from the bridge of revolt, this was surely it. But there was nothing for it. He took the night post-chaise to Arcis on 6 August – four days before the tentative deadline set for an operation to demolish all that was left of France's old order. Before the Arcis notary, Danton made over residence rights in the family home he owned to his mother and his stepfather for as long as they lived. In haymaker's boots, he walked across each acre of land he owned, through every copse, down every riverbank, as if it were his last communion with that silent domain. In particular he bid farewell to his mother and took her in his arms, endeavouring to mask the appearance of a final adieu. He was thirty-two years old. In so far as his mother was not to know what lay behind his visit, it was a melodramatic stay, though Danton had always been a demonstrative son. As rural belfries pealed away the hours, each coach that pulled in from Paris brought messages from Camille and Fabre urging him to return. Rumours of the impending action had grown so strong, they cautioned, that the appointed hour could not be postponed by even a day. The operation had to have a leader, and he was it.

Before sundown on 9 August Danton was back in Paris.

That night the capital sweltered in the summer heat, its grand faecal odour heavy in the air. It did not surprise Danton to find the population in a state of extreme agitation; men in overalls and red caps beat drums at darkening corners, calling citizens to arms. The stifling heat and the drumming were a drug that made heads spin. Guardsmen on horseback galloped this way and that, without orders. Bands of sans-culottes swinging rifles swept from avenue to alley shouting '*Vive la nation!*'

Danton went first to the Cordeliers, where Camille was telling excited members that a single day of anarchy would do more to establish liberty than four years of the current parliament. Climbing to the rostrum beside his fiery-eyed friend, Danton swore that tomorrow the people would triumph, or he would die. He wore a new red frockcoat he had been saving for his return and people in the street picked him out, shouting '*Vive Danton!*', as he hastened from the Cordelier meeting to City Hall, where the Commune was in permanent session. In its anterooms, he strode between ward leaders, huddling longest with those from the poor, densely populated Saint-Antoine and Saint-Marcel sections in the east; the ward leaders assured him they had done what was asked of them.

Returning to the Cour du Commerce an hour or so after Camille, Danton found the Desmoulins couple finishing supper in their apartment with some rough-hewn guests, the leaders of the Marseilles irregulars. They were in good spirits, well wined, and he invited them all to his apartment below. There at last he issued instructions to the Marseillais. Gabrielle listened, her eyes filling with tears. Lucile giggled, uncontrollably, out of fear. Fréron came to join them, slumping beside Danton. 'I'm tired of life; I am determined to die,' he said. None shrank from a little play-acting, though the fear was real.

Shortly before midnight, Danton went to bed. He was exhausted. He threw himself on the mattress, removing only the red frockcoat and his buckled town shoes. For an hour he slept. He was awakened by a pair of Cordeliers arriving in haste from City Hall. He hauled his giant frame out of bed and returned with them to the Commune, accompanied by Camille, who to Lucile's horror carried a rifle. On the way, Danton ordered the tocsin rung at the Cordelier chapel and by the first hour of the morning alarm bells pealed from every parish in the capital, a flat, insistent chorus, summoning citizens out into the streets, ready to march. At City Hall things were going to plan: a new insurrectionary Commune had just then taken charge. This was crucial. Section leaders had each put up insurgent representatives to replace Mayor Pétion's cautious regime, and with Pétion himself absent, ferrying between the Tuileries and the Riding School, trying to calm things down, the elected body died away overnight without a fight, less than sure it had the sympathy of the masses gathering in the streets of the capital.

Danton's coup appeared poised to succeed more efficiently than he could have hoped: no blood was spilled, for the moment. The insurrectionary Commune wasted no time debating what to do: its excited members knew why they were there – they were the first block set in place in the erection of a republic. Danton's public-prosecutor rank gave the insurgent body a thin façade of legality, and its first order was to lift a National Guard blockade of the Pont Neuf, an order that removed cannon placed there to stop the Marseillais and Left Bank street crowds from marching on the Tuileries. Provided things continued this way, Danton was in charge of Paris.

The Tuileries Palace, however, was a realm apart. This time the court had no illusion over the danger it faced. Its defences were organised, with misgivings, by La Fayette's successor at the head of the National Guard, Marquis Jean-Antoine de Mandat, a former captain in the King's Army, who also had 900 Swiss troops of the king's own guard under his command. He placed cannon at the gates, concentrating his sights on the Carousel Square entrance closest to the heart of Paris and the Left Bank, where the people were gathering. But even as the tocsin rang across the capital, Mandat warned the court he was desperately short of gunpowder: 'I have three shots, and a lot of my men have only one.' This was soldier's talk, but from the royal chambers to its servants' quarters the deepest dread permeated the palace. Should martial law be declared? It seemed too late for that.

Listening from a window in the king's chambers as distant drumming and clatter grew louder, Marie-Antoinette turned to ask an attendant city official when the Marseilles fighters planned to leave the capital – a capricious query though not wholly innocent, since she had heard that her ministers were offering them 20,000 livres to decamp. The king's sister, Madame Elisabeth, tried to soothe royal fears. They should not worry, she said, 'Danton will save us.' How naïve her calculation! The royal family had heard a lot about Danton, about his contradictions, about the large heart behind the feral aggression, and it was natural that he should be on their minds, but if Madame Elizabeth was talking of the safety of the monarchy as an institution she was pitiably wrong.

An hour before first light, when court attendants urged the royals to flee from the Tuileries and seek refuge in the Riding School, King Louis prevaricated. His place was on his throne! He was not thinking clearly. Perhaps he had managed to catch some sleep but he would still have been groggy, which showed. One side of his hair was flattened, his cheek bare of powder, while the other side of his head was in curled and powdered royal order. Marie-Antoinette was sure the palace defences would hold; she desired forceful resistance.

At sunrise on 10 August the air remained hot and heavy, with scarcely a breath of wind. Throughout the night, Mandat had received messages from City Hall bidding him go there to report on the situation; he was reluctant, believing his priority was to defend the palace. At 6 a.m. he relented, pressed by royal attendants who thought his presence at the Commune might fore-stall mass violence. Only when the commander arrived, elbowing his way through taunting throngs at the entrance, did he learn that insurgents had taken charge of city government. In the vestibule, men with hammers were smashing a marble bust of La Fayette. Mandat responded angrily to the insurgents' requests for information on what was happening at the Tuileries, certain they only wanted to accuse him of ordering his forces to fire on the people.

Eyeing Danton, who had been directing operations at City Hall since leaving his bed, Mandat said: 'I am responsible only to the genuine Commune, to honest men.' In one menacing stride, Danton was towering over the National Guard chief. He roared: 'Traitor! You will learn to obey the new Commune. It is we who save the people you betray.'

Placed under arrest, Mandat was dragged outside on to the steps of City Hall, where the crowd was too dense for his captors to make a passage. Someone – a renegade guardsman, a sans-culotte madcap, it was never estab-lished who – raised a pistol to his head and blew his brains out. Danton was aghast. He knew the perils of the mob enraged; it could be led, but not controlled. To a degree he accepted that. But to what degree? To decide that would perhaps never be possible. Like it or not, he had practically signed Mandat's death warrant, and the murder – its horrifying rapidity – deepened his apprehension over the day now dawning. The first strides towards a republic were taken, but the conclusive move lay ahead.

Without its commander, the National Guard at the palace broke apart. Guardsmen dropped their rifles first in twos and threes, then by the score, refusing to fire on fellow citizens; cannoneers melted away. At 7 a.m., when confirmation of Mandat's death reached the Tuileries, Louis XVI consented to abandon his residence and take refuge in the Riding School, overcoming his queen's objections, for the only defenders who could be relied on now were the Swiss mercenaries. Huge crowds, the king was informed, were converging on the palace from the popular districts, wheeling a dozen cannon before them.

The Riding School was a short walk away, on the north side of the Tuileries, and in single file the royal family hastened there through the palace gardens as the red dawn lit the day. Royal attendants soothed the king's fears that deputies would reject him; they reminded him that two-thirds of the house had declined to punish La Fayette, which suggested it had not lost all faith in constitutional monarchy. The parliament was in emergency session as the king arrived, and he addressed hushed members from the well: 'Sirs, I have come here to avoid a great crime, and I believe I could find no greater safety than in your midst.' Not unambiguously, the president gave him the protection of the house, pledging the assembly's support for 'the authorities as constituted'.

An hour later, the tide of marchers, Marseillais, Bretons and Théâtre-Français forces at their head, flooded into the Carousel Square in front of the Tuileries and breached the palace gates to the roar of their cannonry. The Swiss troops and a number of National Guard royalists, uncertain of the king's whereabouts, resisted. From the Riding School, the king sent a note ordering the Swiss to cease fire and retire to their barracks, but it was too late: battle was engaged and it was unrelenting. For four hours it raged. As the Swiss ran out of ammunition and fell back into the palace gardens, the insurgents surrounded and slaughtered them, then pursued and killed those Swiss who remained inside the palace, hacking down royal butlers, chefs and chambermaids who cowered on stairwells and in the maze of corridors. By noon, the shattered palace belonged to the insurgents. The defenders were annihilated: of the 900 Swiss who fought, only a score or so survived; sixty who were taken prisoner and escorted towards City Hall were lynched on the way. Hundreds of attackers also died. The Marseillais probably took the brunt of the losses, though the Mediterranean rough-necks re-formed and marched back to their Left Bank base late in the day, singing.

Lucile and Gabrielle, certain by now that their husbands were safe, were out on the street to watch. 'God, what a sight! How our hearts tightened,' Lucile recorded in her diary.

Danton stayed at his Commune command post throughout 10 August, appearing on the street only once, in mid-morning, as the battle continued. On that brief outing he rallied stray citizens into reinforcing the insurgent forces at the palace. He returned to the Cour du Commerce for supper and sank into the deepest sleep, too tired to reflect on the importance of what he had helped bring about. A second revolution was launched. One thousand years of monarchy were over. Europe's most powerful throne was demolished. The republic was at hand. Many had dreamed of it, many desired it. Danton supplied the graft that made it possible.

The Cordelier chief's sleep was again brief. At 3 a.m. on 11 August, Camille and Fabre burst into his bedroom and shook him awake. He could not grasp what they were saying at first, so excited was their babble.

'You're a minister,' they repeated. 'Minister of justice.'

He pulled Camille to him by his velvet lapels. 'You're sure? You're quite sure I am named?

The pair threw their arms in the air. 'Yes. Minister of justice.' Fabre, an artist with a speculator's eye for the main chance, beamed: 'I shall be keeper of the seal!'

'And I your secretary!' said Camille.

In fact, the exultant Cordeliers understated the rank, for as soon as they had heard the permanent session at the Riding School naming members of a new executive to govern France, in the early hours, they left the public gallery and raced to the Cour du Commerce without waiting for details of parliament's vote. The parliament, which had no idea what to do with the fugitive monarch in its midst, had given Louis its physical protection only to strip him of his last remaining political rights. In haste that night, deputies seized the right to terminate the king's token cabinet of ministers and replace it with a provisional revolutionary government armed with full executive powers. Had Camille and Fabre waited to hear the final vote count, they would have known that Danton received the overwhelming support of 222 of the 285 deputies present, far more than any other minister appointed. He was first among ministers in a revolutionary government. If none was formally named head of government, to all eyes he was it. The Riding School was plainly in awe at what the Cordelier chief had brought about.

As for the monarchy, it no longer represented the slightest competition. To keep Louis XVI out of the clutches of the sans-culottes, the Riding School dispatched him and his family into private prison quarters at the Temple, a gaunt medieval priory with sharp spires near the fallen Bastille, there to stay until the Revolution decided their fate.

Even to many of those who voted for Danton, to put him at the head of the revolutionary government was to give the bull the run of the porcelain works. But who else was to take charge at this extraordinary moment? There was nothing for it – it had to be the victor of 10 August. Danton was lord of the people. The Riding School's task was to placate the masses who destroyed the monarchy. It was a huge turn in the nation's history.

The prudent Condorcet, a sage of the Riding School that gave temporary shelter to the king, spoke for many fellow deputies in casting his vote: 'We need a man who has the confidence of the people whose agitators have overturned the throne. I choose Danton, and I do not apologise. May his rise restrain the most despicable elements in a worthy, glorious and essential revolution.'

Camille in his excitement was more succinct: Danton, he wrote, came to power by the grace of the cannon.

# TEN

# Courage, Patriots!

Danton came to power with a clear view of his mission. Still only thirty-two years old, he perhaps lacked the temperament to rule – even the proper ambition, certainly the experience – but he was settled on his priority from the outset: France had to throw back her foreign enemies. What use were ideology and Robespierre's virtuous theories if the country was lost? The nascent republic had to put armed men in uniform, hundreds of thousands of them, more than any French king had ever dreamed of putting in the field.

Of course, the new man in power also had to bring down the temperature on the street, the first thing that was expected of him. It was a problem he confronted, in spirit at least, within hours of Camille and Fabre raising him from bed. That same day he went before the Riding School to accept his nomination, assuring the house: 'In all times, and especially at present, where the action of justice starts, popular vengeance must stop.' He produced no key to turn off the violence; he did not possess one. But to those many deputies who feared for their own physical safety, let alone the king's, he swore to protect them. The insurrectionary Commune he had organised to dispose of the monarchy was not about to dispose of them. Deputies applauded hopefully, though the corpses piled high in the Tuileries fore-court within view of the Riding School appeared small cause for optimism.

In truth, the events of 10 August took the stuffing out of the Legislative Assembly that put Danton in power. It had played so little part in the final overthrow of the throne that it now seemed impossibly soft and bereft of authority. Those who held the political ascendancy in the house, in particu-lar Brissot and the Girondists, were the first to agree with the insurgent Commune that it would require a fresh parliament – a National Convention – to establish the republic. It would take six weeks, however, to get the Convention under way.

Until the Convention came into being, then, the deflated house was a limp partner in the task of saving the state from foreign invasion. Even the Jacobin club, with Robespierre fussing at the helm, seemed more preoccupied by the creation of the Convention than by the extreme military crisis. A critical fortnight went by before Danton, in the face of the limited assistance, was ready to announce new practical measures to safeguard the Revolution – by which time the Austrians and Prussians had made crushing headway with their invasion. In the north they had overrun French Flanders and marched on Picardy; in the east they took a great French fortress at Longwy in Lorraine, subdued the patriotic stronghold of Verdun and crossed into Danton's Champagne homeland. Parisians now had real cause to be frightened, even if the initial bout of municipal panic after the declaration of war had been a little premature. By mid-August 1792, the enemy was truly within ninety miles of the capital, pincering from two directions, and – considering the weakness of French forces – it was likely that foreign troops under orders to behave with extreme harshness would be in Paris in three or four days, a week at most, if they kept pressing forward; the Duke of Brunswick's savage threats loomed in citizens' minds.

Some in the capital attributed Danton's delay in announcing new military countermeasures to indolence on his part, a character flaw they chose to see in his frequent retreats to Arcis. Rather, the delay was caused by a blur of peripheral developments that each required a response, perhaps the most spectacular of which was the defection to the enemy of La Fayette, though this hardly surprised Danton, whose long-held opinion of the hero of American independence stood confirmed.

After learning what happened on 10 August, La Fayette, displaying his true monarchist colours, abandoned the supreme army command recently given him on the eastern front and galloped to the Austrian camp. His flight left French forces in increased disarray. Furthermore, Paris could only presume that La Fayette was sharing French military plans with the enemy. A further calamity occurred inside France: in the Vendée region on the Atlantic, where royalist sympathies and loyalty to the Church ran high, a fast expanding counter-revolutionary army – a thousand or so peasants led by young nobles and priests – captured a string of provincial market towns to the ominous battle cry of 'Death to Parisians'.

It was as if Danton had come to power over an increasingly lost cause. So his presentation of emergency military measures required more than grit and motivation – it had to be uncompromising and speak straight to the people. His chest straining his red frockcoat, he told the Riding School:

It is a national convulsion that has overthrown despotism. It is only through a great national convulsion that we shall repel the despots.

So far we have waged only La Fayette's war of pretence. Now we must wage a more terrible war. It is time for the people to throw themselves en masse upon our enemies.

The measures Danton announced included rushing commissioners to every department of France to drum up recruitment, with full authority to draft all men who owned guns in every town and city they came to, as well as to commandeer all remaining private weaponry for the country's defence. To a great burst of applause, Danton declared: 'Everything belongs to the *patrie* when the *patrie* is in danger.' To further applause, he insisted: 'There must be 80,000 men with rifles at the ready in Paris alone. Well then! Let those who are armed fly to our frontiers. For how have peoples who won their liberty kept it? Let me tell you, they have rushed to meet the enemy, not waited for the enemy to come. What would France say if a stupefied Paris waited for the enemy to arrive?'

His sternest proposal also centred on Paris. Since 10 August, he reported, the gates of the capital had been kept closed to permit a bare minimum of passage, facilitating the arrest of traitors who sabotaged the war effort. Now, impulsively, plucking a figure from the air, he vowed that even if there were as many as 30,000 traitors left free in Paris, each one of them must be seized without a moment's delay. To accelerate the operation, he proposed door-to-door police raids in the Paris wards.

Deputies accepted the proposal in silence. Danton sensed their coolness but held to his demand. Was it incitement to terror? So be it. The war demanded all-out effort, no holds barred. He was a lawyer; he knew that arbitrary justice was justice trampled upon. But the *patrie* had to be saved before the majesty of the law got in the way. First things first. He remained, above all, a practical man. Patriots, moderates included, watched him operating with some awe. One saw him as Neptune: 'He smites with his trident on all sides, and all the tempests on earth are released.'

The house-raid decree was one that Danton very soon came to rue. Instead of calming the sans-culottes, as he had so recently promised to do, it waved a red rag at them. How could they take it as anything but an invitation to denounce fellow citizens and sate the desire for popular vengeance? And thus it was. In no time, commissars in the Paris sections rooted out and jailed three thousand and more suspect citizens – stay-behind aristocrats and their families, priests loyal to the Pope and lumpen monarchists.

In public, Danton did not address such actions. Instead, five days later, on 2 September, as volunteers and conscripts rallied in their tens of thousands to his initial summons, he delivered the speech of his life, again to the parliament. In its excess, it had a more gloriously stirring ring than anything the Revolution had heard, and it won an immediate place in revolutionary lore.

He had not prepared the speech: it was an intervention by the first minister in a debate on war policy, as spontaneous as any he had ever made. But that day Danton was in truly bullish mood. He felt somehow convinced that the country was capable of saving itself once the spirit was roused; it required blood, sweat and tears. 'Everything is in movement, everything bristles, everything burns for the fight,' his great voice boomed. The people had a sublime mission. Then, unable to restrain his ardour: 'We demand that whoever refuses to serve or to give the *patrie* his arms be punished by death.'

The climax was yet to come. He concluded, to thunderous applause, his left hand planted on his hip, the right scything the air with terrible vigour:

The tocsin we shall now ring is not an alarm, it sounds the charge against the enemies of the *patrie*. To vanquish them, gentlemen, we must be bold! Bolder still! Ever bolder! And France is saved.

If ever a single flash of oratory sent volunteers rushing to hold the frontiers with fire in their hearts, this was it. The words were sparks from the anvil of Mars that flew through the capital and provincial cities. 'You were sublime,' consented Vergniaud, the golden-tongued Girondist oracle, clapping his back.

It was Danton at his best, but also at his impulsive worst. He was sinking deeper into violence himself. The gratuitous call for the execution of those who failed to enlist was, in truth, no more than a figure of speech from his fierce lexicon. Yet its effect on the volatile popular mood was predictable, particularly since Marat was simultaneously baying in the *Ami du Peuple* for street patriots to kill all aristocrats and priests they could lay hands on. Gabrielle, who was present with Lucile in the Riding School's raucous public gallery, felt both proud and sickly fearful. Her husband scared her. She had a premonition, she told him afterwards, that those who applauded him today would have his head tomorrow.

Heading the six-man government was exhilarating, and at times extremely tiresome. Danton was generous to his Cordelier friends – overgenerous, had he borne in mind the political proprieties. Fabre, Camille and his old classmate Paré took the top posts at Justice, on handsome salaries. The moribund parliament voted him 550,000 livres in ministerial funds, the bulk of it for secret expenditures, in which he at once dug to pay an army of government commissioners, agents and spies, sending them forth to establish what was happening in the war and how to address it – to the provinces, to England, to enemy lands across the Rhine. More funds went towards buying off the enemy agents who infested the cafés and hostelries of revolutionary Paris; they seemed to be everywhere, strolling in the Palais Royal gardens in their English-cut jackets and German leather hats and fighting for seats in the Riding School galleries whenever an important debate was posted.

The tiresome part for Danton was cabinet meetings, mainly because a majority of his fellow ministers were Girondists with their own agenda, including the interior minister, none other than Madame Roland's onerous husband. No matter what the issue – war, security, justice, education, bread – Jean-Marie Roland opposed him on it. He niggled over every public sou Danton proposed spending, as if they were managing France in a time of cloudless peace. The cabinet met in the justice ministry, to which Madame Roland made clear her objections, on the grounds that it humiliated her husband, who she believed was better equipped to be first minister. On matters that counted, Danton invariably got his way thanks to the seniority accorded him by the Riding School vote, thanks also – perhaps in greater measure – to his intimidating physical presence. 'Why do I do what he wants?' the navy minister confided to Roland, who was trying to establish a blocking cabal. 'Because he scares the hell out of me and he'd give my head to the people otherwise.'

Danton's natural joviality, the other side of the ogre, also helped him get his way. More often than not, cabinet meetings ended with disarming assurances to deal with problems personally, as if the conduct of war, diplomacy and the national welfare were one and the same responsibility, and it was his. The odd thing was that although he was a man of action with no great lust for power, when power came to him his overwhelming personality made him hog it.

Roland was not, in fact, oblivious to the invasion peril. The prospect of Paris falling to the enemy so disturbed him that he led a muffled Girondist chorus for the removal of the national government – ministries and parliament – to the placid city of Blois, in the Loire Valley, to keep them out of enemy hands. Moving the capital out of harm's way to Blois fitted in rather well, moreover, with the Girondists' federal ideas and their allergy to almighty Paris. Danton was outraged. He was pleased to find that Brissot on the Girondist front bench was not a conspicuous part of such defeatism. Did Roland and his dominating wife have no backbone? He told the cabinet, beating his chest: 'We shall not retreat. We shall die in the capital, in its ruins. But our enemies will die with us.'

Yet talk of abandoning Paris persisted at the Riding School as the prospect of enemy occupation grew ever more real. By now the Duke of Brunswick's troops were within sixty miles of the capital, though the Prussian seemed intent on taking his time over a final strike. Danton felt obliged to address the house to stiffen its resolve. 'They ask you to leave Paris,' he said. 'You know full well what our enemies think: to them Paris is all France. To surrender Paris is to surrender the Revolution. To retreat is to lose all. We must therefore maintain our presence here by all possible means. Boldness alone shall save us.' He went further. There was a secret royalist command centre in Paris in daily contact with the Prussians, he reported. How reliable this intelligence was he did not elaborate. Indeed, it was perhaps pure rumour, for he owned that the government was unable to locate the command centre's seat and it was never uncovered. Still, such deadly links with the invader had to be broken. 'We must strike fear in the royalists. Yes, we must strike fear in their hearts.'

Danton's logic on the importance of Paris stopped serious talk of decamping to Blois. To silence its propagandists, he informed them he had just brought his own mother to Paris from Arcis, a hostage to his determination to save the capital from foreign occupation.

Old Roland's obstinacy in cabinet did not deter Danton from frequenting his wife's salon, which she now held in the gilded interior ministry, a setting better suited to her purpose. The Rolands made the ministry their residence, while Danton, for the time being, remained at the Cour du Commerce, where Gabrielle felt happier. When he initially called at Madame Roland's salon as first minister to pay his respects, she treated him as an intruder, hardly acknowledging him. It was almost comic. She had changed her style, no longer sitting at an escritoire as she had at her Left Bank home, demure and deferential, watching and listening and occasionally breaking into her male guests' conversations with a gem of bluestocking wit here and an engaging proposal there. Now she made herself the centre of activities, leading the salon talk with the radiant confidence of Paris hostesses of the old school since departed beyond the Rhine.

Despite the cold reception reserved for him, Danton kept inviting himself to the Roland salon. 'I come to ask for supper,' he announced the next time, mock humble, no doubt throwing an atrocious grin at Brissot as he held forth in a silk-draped corner. Though Madame Roland invited him to stay, she made little attempt to be gracious or even polite. He was accompanied by Fabre, whom she made perfectly clear she could not stand either, despite his way with women. Danton perhaps realised that he ought to pay her more attention, though the Cordeliers had small patience with women who meddled in politics.

In truth the beautiful Manon Roland brought out Danton's peasant side: with her he was the rough-hewn farmer at the fair, in the presence of a creature whose price and bloodstock he was unable to calculate. Conversely, he could tell that in her eyes he was Rabelais incarnate, a coarse male ruffian. He wondered at the real source of her hostility and the haughty intellectual tone she adopted with him. Perhaps, as he had first guessed, and not without a tingle of pleasure, her behaviour indeed had something to do with comparisons in maleness that she drew with her husband. But there was more to it, he decided. Madame Roland was a snob. The classic bourgeois snob. Hers was the implacable rancour of the petty bourgeoisie on the rise. His class, his education, his family's standing were more than a match for hers, but he simply wounded those high aesthetic sensibilities that the engraver's daughter wished to parade in the Revolution, *her* revolution. And once this was clear to him, Danton could not resist playing the ruffian and picking her up on her pretensions – not to her face, but making quite sure it was in her hearing and that she was aware she was included. 'We're trash. We come from the gutter,' he lectured a little group gathered around him at the salon, 'and don't ever forget it if we want to avoid the worst mistakes. It's the people, the populace that brought us to power. Don't think you can stop the Revolution at the hour you set your watches.'

Nevertheless, Danton eventually submitted to Madame Roland on the venue for cabinet meetings. It was hard to deny her. She, at least, was bold. He agreed to her new proposal to hold the cabinet sessions on neutral ground – a courtyard building in the Tuileries, where the institutions of the forthcoming republic were to sit in place of the monarchy. And so the cabinet moved house, though Danton found it a pettifogging point to labour in a panic-stricken capital. Moreover, his pre-eminence remained unaffected: the cabinet continued to accept pretty much what he wanted. To France at large, he *was* the government, all ministers rolled into one. Important correspondence from provincial administrators came straight to him, and he passed their letters on to the aggrieved Roland at Interior as he saw fit.

Still, he should have been warier of Manon Roland. How could he predict that her pretensions would so nag and tear at his prestige as it reached its peak as to pull him down.

There was a terrible price to pay for the explosion of patriotic fervour inspired by Danton's oratory. He had held executive power for scarcely more than three weeks when Marat's provocations turned that fervour into calamity. As volunteers and conscripts chanting the Marseillaise left Paris for the frontier in droves, the *Ami du Peuple* ran lurid warnings of the carnage that royalist conspirators would likely wreak on the defenceless families they left behind. Where were those conspirators? In the prisons, to be sure.

It was into the capital's four remaining central prisons, lesser hulks than the Bastille, that police in the Paris sections had thrown those suspected of holding pro-royalist sentiments, seizing them in their homes, in the streets, in the parks, in every corner of Paris. The mass round-ups both enthralled and terrified the population. The insurgent Commune fed the mood by posting at the gates of each of the prisons the names of royalist suspects held inside – counts, countesses, their children, men of the Church, liberal statesmen from the aspiring early days of the rebellion, their servants, their bootmakers, anyone heard speaking of the king without proper malice – names that willed the crowds outside to hate them.

On 2 September – the very day that Danton scaled his 'ever bolder' heights of oratory at the Riding School – several hundred cut-throats armed with knives and clubs broke into the four central prisons at sundown. Marat's inflammatory warnings over defenceless families left at the mercy of royalists had maddened the most violent fringe of the sans-culottes. As justice minister, Danton was informed of what was happening soon after it began. Prison guards were overrun, or more often stepped aside before their wild-eyed fellow townsmen. There was no civil force to call upon to stop the violence: the National Guard kept its head down, pretending not to see; the insurgent Commune, in which Marat now headed a surveillance committee to hunt down royalists, lent its encouragement; the Riding School was impotent. Paris was by now a lawless capital where civil society had imploded in the war panic – and the largely unpunished bouts of rioting, looting and lynching of the past three years proved it.

The prison carnage was merciless and complete. The sans-culottes had their share of thugs and killers, just as the moderate multitude of bourgeois reformers had their outright fanatics and extremists. The killing went on through the night and into the next day and the next. Workers, artisans and apprentices in the killing parties moved through the cells slitting the throats of the occupants and clubbing them to death, roared on in their bloodlust by men and women streaming into the prison yards from the street, intoxicated by news of the event.

The massacre took the lives of some 1,600 prisoners. Among aristocratic victims was the gentle, mild-mannered Princesse Marie Thérèse Louise de Lamballe, daughter of the sovereign of Savoy and a high favourite at the Bourbon court, whom Marie-Antoinette counted her closest friend. Dragging the widowed princess from her cell in what remained of her court attire after three weeks' confinement, the cut-throats taunted her: 'Swear you love liberty! Swear you hate the king, the queen and all royalty.' Trembling in their grip, petrified, she answered: 'I shall swear the first. I cannot swear the second. It is not in my heart to do so.' A prison warden, touched, urged her, 'Swear, for God's sake!' – but she was already being hustled into the prison yard, where the crowd set upon her. Within seconds, a sword blow delivered from behind split the back of her head. Two men from the crowd lifted her from the ground, inviting others to slash at her body. There was no shortage of apprentice butchers in the killing ranks. At length, they cut off her head and carved out her heart, fixing them on pikes and parading them by torchlight through the streets of Paris.

As the triumphant street procession reached the Temple, where King Louis and his queen were imprisoned, Marie-Antoinette peered down from her high windows into the sudden illuminations, enquiring what all the noise was about. 'It is the head of Lamballe,' a guard coldly informed her. The queen collapsed in a faint.

At the justice ministry, Danton for once seemed frozen into inaction. Except for Marat and his raging clique at the Commune, the imperilled capital felt sickened and numb. A dark blanket fell over men's minds, shrouding the prison horrors in near-universal silence. At the Jacobins, Robespierre said nothing. Only Roland, pressed by his wife, raised his voice in public to call the assassins to account, condemning the massacre as a horrific abuse of revolutionary principles; it was the task of government and parliament to halt the assassins at once or lose all credibility as guardians of the law. The Rolands were forgetting, though, how deep Paris had sunk into lawlessness. Danton's authority lay in forcing the nation to save its sovereign skin, not in saving royalists' heads.

Still, the first minister brooded over his inability to act. To be seen to be closing his eyes to such a crime was to be seen as party to it. He was, after all, specifically in charge of justice. If he had gone out and placed his massive frame at the prison gates and used his voice, the voice of the people's champion, to call off the assassins, it might have worked. But he did not. For that, Madame Roland was out to crucify him: in her eyes, he was the 'chief of the horde of killers' even if he was not personally engaged. She wrote to a political ally: 'You know my passion for the Revolution. Well, I am ashamed of it! It has been ruined by scoundrels. It has turned hideous.' Danton was only too aware of such talk. All the Girondists, Brissot included, came to heap blame on him, and with the screams from the prison cells still ringing in the capital's ears it was hard to respond. All around Europe, as civilised society began hearing of it, the massacre poisoned what remained of political sympathy with the Revolution. Danton too was ashamed of it. And how could he reasonably reject blame?

His political instinct was to tough it out. To do otherwise, he decided, could break the spirit of the war effort. This was no time to appear soft. He put a lock on his inner feelings. Popular fury had to be given its dose of blood in revolution. To quench the immediate bloodlust was to prevent further excesses. 'To hell with the prisoners! Let them save themselves,' he yelled at cabinet colleagues in pure exasperation, his tone reflecting his sense of utter helplessness. For public consumption, he maintained, half apologetic: 'No power on earth could have stopped the national vengeance from spilling over.'

The terror continued, however, and Danton continued to shrug. Just several days after the prison massacres, he received an urgent visit from the Mayor of Versailles to warn him that a convoy from the city of Orleans containing a large body of prisoners suspected of high treason was about to leave for Paris, and that cut-throats were plotting to waylay and kill them as they passed through the royal town. Among the prisoners being sent for trial in the capital, the mayor reported, were distinguished figures from the early days of the Revolution, including ex-members of the Constituent Assembly and a pair of former government ministers.

Danton stared for a long minute at his agitated visitor, then turned away, murmuring, 'Those men are guilty enough.'

So they were, the mayor nodded, but it was the task of the law to find them guilty.

'What! Don't you see!' Danton shouted, rearing back at him. 'I would already have given you a different answer if I could. And what are these prisoners to you? Get back to your post. Stop worrying about them.'

The following afternoon, 10 September, assassins surged out of the Versailles forest, stopped the convoy, dragged the prisoners from their carriages and cut their throats, leaving fifty-two bodies of public rank in the forest brush. It was not Danton's business. But if he was indeed help- less, his reputation in the eyes of the Girondists grew ever darker: his shrug- ging looked to them like profound callousness, an attitude struck by an accomplice to barbarity.

Only behind the scenes did Danton allow his heart to act. His continuing roars against those he rated as genuine traitors gave him some cover to save those gratuitously accused by Marat and Robespierre's Jacobin hardheads. Those he personally saved from the guillotine were men he simply could not class as traitors to France – a score of them, fifty perhaps, statesmen such as the Lameth brothers, Charles and Alexandre, astute liberal aristo- crats who had kept things running at the Riding School; or Talleyrand, the prince of diplomacy, who helped craft the Rights of Man declaration and whom he had fraternised with in the Paris regional administration.

Danton had to be careful in helping such luminaries make their escape, for their flight put him in danger himself, even as first minister. At least Talleyrand had recognised the risk they both ran. It was a tribute to the noble statesman's unfailing tact that on the night before the prison massacres he had presented himself incognito at the justice ministry, hobbling in on his cane at midnight and wearing a common man's leather breeches and pigtail, a departure from his silk-and-powder finery which allowed Danton his single smile in that grim week. Even so, to avoid raising suspicions of a political alliance between them, he made Talleyrand wait around for a day or so, after which he issued him a passport permitting him to make a bolt for England, where, moreover, he trusted the diplomat would employ his celebrated skills on the Revolution's behalf.

In parallel with these risky personal interventions, Danton hit upon a broader method of limiting summary executions. The trick was to bar outlying departments from sending royalist suspects to Paris as fodder for the guillotine; he ordered them instead to detain suspects locally until further notice, which Marat correctly read as their reprieve. Perhaps an exasperated Marat understood better than most what drove Danton: his cursed, indestructible humanity. At this stage, Danton was engaged in a constant battle with himself to keep it down. The trouble was, he bore no grudges. As fierce as he was, he was not ruthless. It was a contradiction that saved him in Gabrielle's tender eyes and nourished her faith in him. Even the hostile Roland benefited. When Marat now demanded the interior minister's arrest for insulting the sovereign people with his lonely call for punishment of the prison assassins, Danton halted the frothing journalist's enterprise forthwith. Still, a big heart was not much protection in these violent times. It was a flimsy shield against the stigma that the September massacres attached to him, in both moderate revolutionary hearts and his own.

The fact was, his first concerns lay elsewhere.

Danton's patriotic oratory, together with the strong-arm methods of his recruiting commissioners in the provinces, achieved remarkable success in driving large numbers of conscripts to the frontiers. Yet the military tide stubbornly refused to turn. Even as Paris washed itself in its own blood, the question that still gripped its population was when – in how many days? how many hours? – the sons of Frederick the Great's intrepid warriors would march in.

Something was changing, though. The replacement of La Fayette as commander-in-chief of the revolutionary armies by the popular General Dumouriez, released from the post of foreign minister to put fire in new recruits' hearts, was having a rapid effect. The appointment of Dumouriez, a King's Army veteran already well into his fifties, was largely the inspiration of his fellow Girondists, though Danton supported the choice without reserve. The general's patriotism was not in doubt. Who could question the motivation of a soldier who had spent two years before the Revolution planning to relieve the British crown of the Channel Islands and, more valiant still, the Isle of Wight? Though the fall of the Bastille forced the postponement of that particular enterprise, Dumouriez, who hailed like Mirabeau from the Provençal gentry, remained a military professional down to his lustrous boots; he was irascible, headstrong and ambitious. There was precious little time to train the new flood of recruits and volunteers, but he made time – time to drill them, give them rudimentary instruction in warfare and accustom them to the unnerving sight of advancing Prussian helmets. Harsher discipline was a further Dumouriez input: the prospect of a month in irons for failing to stand and fight reduced disorderly retreats. Morale began to rise; to march to war behind banners inscribed 'Liberty or Death' lifted the hearts of the Revolution's new defenders. Still, no one expected a miracle; at this juncture, the best Danton hoped for was enough spirited resistance to keep the enemy out of Paris.

But a miracle there was.

Two revolutionary armies linked up in extremis at Valmy in the Champagne country on 20 September, 1792 to give Dumouriez victory over the Duke of Brunswick's 80,000-strong force, which withdrew from the field, as if accepting defeat, mainly because Brunswick did not like the look of the flat terrain. The news from Valmy was at first greeted with wide-eyed disbelief in Paris, then with overflowing optimism. The invasion was halted! The Revolution was saved! France was saved! It could only be a gift from the gods to the French republic, which was born, lo and behold, the very next day.

The months to come would show how overinflated such optimism was, but for the moment sheer relief drove an incredulous capital to regard the Prussian pull-back in the rosiest possible light, despite the fact that Brunswick's forces suffered only light losses and were still encamped far inside France. The battle itself was largely a day-long artillery duel, with neither side cutting into the other's ranks. If Dumouriez was justified in claiming victory at Valmy, it was because his ragtag conscripts at last proved they could stand up to the best soldiers of the age.

Valmy, then, was a stupendous turning point because Frenchmen wished to see it so. They were not alone. Goethe, the German literary idol, who was fascinated by the Revolution and was present with his Prussian patron, King Friedrich Wilhelm, at Brunswick's Valmy headquarters, was quick to see its poetry, sighing to dejected Prussian officers: 'Here, this very day, a new epoch in the history of the world has begun, and you can boast you were present at its birth.'

Danton was a raw hand at diplomacy. His experience of negotiating with foreign powers was limited to his recent sojourn in London and the private exchanges he had had there with English liberals. But Valmy was an opening not to be missed. While he was acutely aware of Brissot, Roland and company looking over his shoulder from one side, and Robespierre from the other, he did have his own notion of what might now be achieved. There was a chance, he thought, that England would be sufficiently impressed by the outcome at Valmy to prefer peace to Continental war.

To test the English, Danton put to work the numerous agents he had engaged with funds from the secret war chest awarded him by the Riding School. A pair of his agents were on the spot in London, lately reinforced by Talleyrand, who had previously spent long months there inducing William Pitt to remain neutral in Europe, or at least to refrain from military action. It was no doubt Talleyrand's influence that encouraged Danton to make peace with England his paramount diplomatic objective.

After Valmy, he fancied the clouds had cleared a little in France's favour. If only Pitt would be more amenable, though. Intelligence from London suggested that England's prime minister, much disturbed by the sack of the Tuileries on 10 August and now the prison massacres, was actually leaning hard the other way. And Tom Paine, all honour to him, was not helping. Danton still looked up to Mad Tom, as did most French revolutionaries, but unfortunately the timing of his latest exploits inhibited the diplomacy Danton favoured. The appearance of a second part of his *Rights of Man* in early 1792 had further poisoned the cross-Channel atmosphere. In Pitt's eyes, this second part was still more inflammatory than the first: in essence, it called for the repetition in England of what was happening in France – a national revolt and the end of any form of hereditary rule. Pitt diagnosed 'Paine-itis' as a disease deadlier than cholera and hauled Mad Tom into court in the summer to answer charges of sedition and libel, so that by September 1792 England's archpriest of popular revolt had no choice but to flee to France to avoid imprisonment, a solution backed by an acid London press which hollered that he should indeed feel more at home there.

So bargaining with Pitt would be difficult. It looked a naïve objective, blind to the political realities. Still, Danton was used to swimming against the current, and the benefits to be had from an assured truce with England seemed worth the effort. As long as Pitt could be dissuaded from taking outright military action against the Revolution, the mission was more than half accomplished.

Fortunately, Valmy also presented more immediate benefits. Harvesting them was a task that called upon the peasant in Danton, since what in effect had to be negotiated with the Duke of Brunswick was the possession of land. Danton's objective was that of any landowner confronted by trespassers coveting his pastures: to get them off. What would a clever peasant do? Wave an inducement at them and talk them off.

The commander-in-chief of the combined Prussian and Austrian forces, reinforced by French émigrés, had no military need to evacuate Champagne, let alone all of French territory, as a result of Valmy. Certainly the occupation of Paris had receded as the Duke of Brunswick's goal, perhaps for good, but his army was intact and strong in number, and from where he stood he could maintain intense pressure on the Revolution.

Danton, however, had lately placed a team of personal commissioners in Dumouriez's camp, among whom was Fabre, who knew little of military matters but was intimately aware of Danton's designs. Since Fabre was inclined to irritate by throwing his weight around in the French camp, Dumouriez preferred to leave it to a harder-headed Danton agent, François Westermann, an Alsatian man-at-arms who had led the 10 August assault on the Tuileries, to open negotiations with the Prussian army. These had to be secret because Jacobins and Girondists back in Paris were adamantly opposed to bargaining with Brunswick as long as his troops remained on French soil. By way of inducement, Westermann assured Brunswick's representative that Danton's government had no desire to wage war to the finish with the Prussians and that their army would be allowed to leave French soil without harassment – an offer Dumouriez fully endorsed, since his personal ambition now was to head north with the revolutionary armies and take Belgium from the Austrians; he preferred not to be held up by endless further encounters with Brunswick's troops.

The trespassers, then, would not be prosecuted.

While Brunswick sought to condition any accord on the restoration of Louis XVI, his readiness to bargain with the 'criminals of 10 August' looked like a sure sign that he accepted the fait accompli of the king's dethronement. On Danton's behalf, Westermann responded to the Prussian condition with a peasant's half-nod. Thereafter, in less than two weeks, Brunswick's army rolled back east beyond all the strongholds captured from France – beyond Verdun, beyond Longwy, finally beyond the Rhine.

The withdrawal during early October was a bitter blow to French émigrés, who spread a fanciful tale that Danton paid Brunswick to leave. The millions used to pay off the Prussian commander came, they claimed, from the theft of the Bourbon crown jewels from the Royal Storehouse adjoining the Tuileries less than a week before Valmy. It somehow consoled the exasperated émigrés to find a reason for Brunswick's otherwise inexplicable retreat, especially if it also incriminated the hated Danton. The first minister could again only shrug his massive shoulders at the charge, though this time with a belly laugh. Now he was the fence for stolen Bourbon diamonds! The thought of anyone presuming to assemble a bribe to bend Germany's wealthiest prince, the head of Prussian armies, into shameless flight seemed truly derisory. Dumouriez himself dismissed the 'Brunswick bribe' as fiction. It was not the worst of allegations that Danton's detractors flung at him, though it was perhaps the wildest and it was a sign of the madness of the times – the murderous jealousies, the striving for dominance, the vicious swing of denunciation, charge and countercharge – that the Girondists, a level-headed movement on the whole, gave it some lingering credence even after a gang of mere fortune hunters went to the guillotine for lifting the crown jewels from the Royal Storehouse.

Moreover, the Prussian retreat, though extraordinary, was not as inexplicable as the émigrés found it. King Friedrich Wilhelm did not want his forces bogged down in France, a risk that Valmy clearly increased, for he was wary of being outplayed by Austria in Central Europe. If Prussia and Austria were fighting together today, they were nonetheless rivals in their extensive backyard. For his part, Brunswick feared that holding fast in Champagne would cut him off from his rear and was concerned by an epidemic of dysentery in his ranks. All this was intelligence that Danton received from Westermann and it convinced him that the best course of negotiation was to try driving the wedge deeper between Prussians and Austrians. What harm was there in letting Brunswick know that Dumouriez's main force, once free to move, was chafing to head north and enter Austria's possessions in the Low Countries?

The Prussian withdrawal swelled Danton's prestige. Sans-culottes hurrahed and moderate men applauded: more than any other political figure, Danton had fought the war and he had won it. As promised, the France of liberty looked to be saved.

# ELEVEN

## *Long Live the Republic*

The new national parliament, the Convention, that assembled on 21 September 1792 abolished the monarchy and declared France a republic. Compared with its floundering predecessor, it looked a purposeful body. From the start, it aroused high public expectations of the kind fired by Mirabeau's pioneering parliament at the fall of the Bastille and, as it digested the news from Valmy with its promise of liberty striding into the future, Danton was its idol.

Elected to the Convention by a landslide in Paris, Danton held the stage at its opening session in the manner of a Roman consul with a phalanx of admiring senators as his escort. Leaving his official carriage to Gabrielle, who was pregnant once more, he walked there from the justice ministry with the Cordelier faithful proceeding behind. Along the narrow Rue Saint-Honoré they went, surrounded by well-wishers crying '*Vive Danton*', before cutting back to the Riding School at the side of the Tuileries, still the home of parliament.

It was hard to believe that Danton was taking a seat in a national parliament for the first time. With the coming of the Convention, voting rights were finally extended to the masses as he had demanded two years before, and though the working class failed to take advantage of the reform in any great numbers – even now suffrage remained hemmed in with niggling restrictions – this clearly helped him. Parisians nominated an electoral college that gave him 638 of its 700 votes, the highest tally won by any of the capital's Convention deputies and almost twice the score obtained by a sour Robespierre, who was likewise elected from Paris. Alongside Danton, all the leading lights of the old Cordelier tribe entered the Convention, its romantics and its fanatics: Camille, Fabre, Fréron, Legendre and inevitably Marat, whose renown with the street people remained high despite his sinking relations with Danton. Of twenty-four deputies elected from Paris, ten were founder-members of the Cordeliers.

The Convention was altogether an ambitious democratic body, weird and wonderful in its make-up. The stately Duc d'Orléans, in whose Palais Royal pleasure gardens democracy took seed, was elected under the adopted name of Citizen Philippe Egalité, which he considered a badge of revolutionary worth as well as a guard against the vengefulness of people like Marat. (From prince to streetcleaner, everyone was now Citizen This or Citizen That.) Robespierre, remaining bitter, put it around that Danton sponsored the Duc d'Orléans' candidacy in the belief that a drop of royal blood in the Convention would impress a hostile Europe, though in truth Danton merely raised no objection to it. Room was even made for an Englishman in the person of Tom Paine. Mad Tom was the member for Calais, having been elected upon landing there from England and granted French citizenship to celebrate his escape from Pitt's clutches.

From across the country, meanwhile, Girondists entered the Convention in droves: Brissot, Roland, Pétion, Condorcet and the honey-voiced orator Vergniaud led their charge. Such was their cohesion now that they formed a party from their various provincial strands and filled the benches on the right of the Riding School speaker. They were the radical bourgeois cream of the Revolution, united in the desire to stop Paris and its sections grabbing overall charge. On the left – known as the 'Mountain' because the benches rose more steeply there, almost to the roof – sat a smaller but feistier congregation of Jacobin purists, ideologues, Cordeliers, political clubbers and sundry agitators determined to give no quarter to enemies of the Revolution.

If the Mountain constituted a party, Danton personally was not of it. He took his place there, with Robespierre and Marat, because the spirit of the sans-culottes and the Paris sections darted between its ridges. But he felt himself to be an independent. Indeed, he publicly maintained that he belonged to no party, and he pressed his Cordelier friends to take the same stand.

Independence was a position he maintained with pride. The fact was, he really did not adhere to any strong set of beliefs. He was his own man – a people's champion, yes, but not entirely out of sympathy with certain Girondist views and always listening out for applause from a third group, the largest in the Convention, a shambling collection of moderate-minded patriots whose views shifted this way and that as orators succeeded each other at the rostrum and who sat in the flat well of the Riding School – the 'Plain' or 'Marsh'. What Danton sought at heart was union between all sides: if those who made the Revolution did not pull together, he sensed, there would be no final victory in the war against Europe and no end to civil war.

While Danton's prestige at the opening of the Convention was unrivalled, there was a hitch. His presence there tested its democratic rules, made to prevent the accumulation of powers in any one person. To hold down both a government ministry and a seat in parliament breached Convention by-laws and he was aware of it, as was Roland, who shared the dilemma. In Danton's mind there was strictly no contest. He knew where he had to be. Every reformer and revolutionary of note was now assembled in the Convention, the birthplace of the republic. Its very existence undercut the Paris Commune and sheared the power of the executive government which the Cordelier giant led.

But the matter had to be handled carefully. Danton remained closely involved as first minister in the secret negotiations with Brunswick, and he had to see them through. On the other hand, if he insisted on staying, it could stoke the old dictatorship charges, for they were far from extinguished. Ever since 10 August, reproachful Girondists had likened Danton to England's Oliver Cromwell, whom none-too-distant history taught them to regard as a regicidal bully as well as a failed republican. Even now they were reheating their campaign against any kind of dictatorship with scare talk of a budding triumvirate – Robespierre, Marat and himself. Danton could scoff all he liked at the thought. How could anyone seriously see him running the republic with that pair? Yet implausible though it sounded, mere talk of it unsettled moderates.

The speech the first minister made in his straining red frockcoat at the opening session of the Convention was vintage Danton. To address the dictatorship issue, he began with a surprise. Announcing his resignation as head of government, he said:

> I now stand before you only as a representative of the people and it is in this capacity that I shall speak . . . Here is what you may tell the people. The empty phantoms of dictatorship, the extravagant notions of a triumvirate – all those absurdities invented to frighten the people – they are now nothing but thin air. From now on, nothing is constitutional unless the people approve it.

From Mountain to Plain, the house erupted in shouts for him to carry on as head of government. These days Gabrielle had taken to attending important sessions at the house, squeezing into the raucous public gallery, between Lucile and a pretty adolescent neighbour from the Cour du Commerce, Louise Gély, a big-sister companion to the two Danton boys. Danton would have looked up to his wife now for a smile of encourage-ment. He knew her fears but he needed her support. For while he had every intention of stepping down, he also aimed to continue in office until deputies chose his successor at Justice, which could take time – time enough to complete his work in cabinet, which was far from done. At this precise moment he had not yet received confirmation from Dumouriez of the joyful news from Valmy.

The warm reception from the Convention prompted him to lay down markers there and then for what he wanted the new republic to be: a just, orderly, property-owning society free of social privileges and relieved of the threat of civil war. Coming from Danton, it sounded an oddly conservative agenda, though the language was as robust as ever: 'Our laws must now be as terrible against lawbreakers as the people have been in crushing tyranny; our laws must punish all the guilty, then the people will no longer desire to take punishment upon themselves.' How the house applauded, hearing it as both a tirade against lynch law and a warning to royalists to halt their treachery, or expect the worst. Against zealots from the Mountain who wanted the republic to expropriate all private property, he was equally forceful: they were surely excellent citizens, he said, but they misdirected their passion for liberty and they were fanning the flames of civil war: 'Let us spurn such extremes here and now! Let us declare that the right to own all property – land, industrial and personal – shall be eternally upheld!' Applause again erupted on all sides. If the Revolution wanted a workable republic, Danton's call struck sane reformers as the core of it. It was a call that issued from both Danton the politician and from that irrepressibly practical fellow within him, the Champagne landsman.

The very next day he returned to the charge against civil war. 'We must give the people justice so they don't take it into their own hands,' he insisted before the Convention. 'Let the law be terrible, and everything will come right. Prove that you want the rule of law, but prove also that you want the people's safety. And before all else, spare the blood of Frenchmen.'

The speech drew a huge ovation. No one could turn on applause like Danton. And since France's judges were invariably survivors from the old order, to restore popular faith in justice he now proposed unseating the lot of them. His urge was to replace them throughout the land with magistrates elected by the people. His reasoning was simple: 'The judges, like the priests, have forever deceived the people.' After his career as a barrister, Danton might have felt entitled to hold certain views on judges, but the proposal nonetheless sounded reckless to many deputies, including Tom Paine, who was not so mad in the realm of justice. The author of the *Rights of Man* confronted Danton directly. Jumping to the Convention rostrum, eyes bulging, Paine argued in rushing English that it was folly to throw out all judicial experience at a stroke. Who would control the new political power? The republic was, to be sure, a wondrous creation, but like all power structures it needed to be controlled by a trained judiciary, not by local vote-getters.

Danton listened. A low buzz in the house told him that while the foreign strains may have perplexed members, Paine was not alone in his doubts. So while maintaining his proposal, Danton pulled back, as he often did when opposed, to placate the opponent. Behind his feral countenance was the ever-present spirit of a conciliator. Furthermore, he held the Englishman in high respect. So he strode back to the rostrum, allowing that he quite agreed with 'Citizen Paine', though the deputy from Calais should know that the existing judiciary was not, alas, as qualified as he appeared to believe. In his personal experience, many judges were imposters who recited empty legal jargon in complete ignorance of the texts. Granted, though, it was perhaps unnecessary to get rid of them all. There was a compromise solution: the people could re-elect those magistrates who warranted their confidence.

The war cabinet received formal confirmation of the triumph at Valmy two days after the event, with Danton still in the first minister's chair. No one except the most hostile Girondists – who now, as a party, tweaked their name to the perkier 'Girondins' – had wanted him to leave the government in haste. Accordingly, the Convention decreed that it was lawful and indeed desirable for him to remain first minister until it named a successor at Justice. This was bound to satisfy Dumouriez, who even before Valmy had signalled his displeasure at the prospect of the departure from the cabinet of his ace recruiting sergeant. 'I need your head!' the general told him in a personal note from the front that no doubt had them both grinning.

There could have been no prouder chronicler of events at Valmy than the stripling officer who confirmed the happy outcome to the cabinet: he was the Duc de Chartres, the eighteen-year-old son of Philippe Egalité, the Convention's renegade royal. As a novice officer on Dumouriez's staff – the noblest of the bluebloods who still dominated the revolutionary army's officer corps – Chartres had galloped to Paris on the general's orders straight from the battle. Danton smiled as the youth ended his account with an appeal to the cabinet to overturn orders he had recently received for his reassignment. His orders were to leave the fighting front and take command of the garrison at Strasbourg. He wished to stay at the front, he said; he was too young for garrison work. The Girondin minister of war, Joseph Servan, a former army engineer with little time for war's romance, shook his head, saying he was being reassigned for his own safety. Servan, who was struggling with a bout of flu, had left his sickbed for the cabinet meeting and was feeling particularly out of sorts.

Minutes later, as the proceedings ended, Danton pulled the youth aside. 'Servan is an idiot. Don't listen to him,' he growled. 'Come and see me tomorrow. I'll settle your problem.'

Chartres hurried to see Danton in private the next day, receiving his assurance that everything was duly arranged for him to stay at the front. As he was about to leave, though, Danton again turned him back with a massive fist, observing as if in afterthought, 'A word of advice before you go. You have talent. You will succeed. But you have a fault you must correct. You talk too much.'

The heir to France's second royal house gaped.

'Yes,' said Danton, 'you have been back in Paris for twenty-four hours and you're casting blame all round for the prison business.' Gossip travelled fast in Paris, and Danton, it seemed, had heard that Chartres spent the night at the Palais Royal, the Orléans family residence, where he had expressed disgust to everyone present over the September massacres and astonishment at the failure of the authorities to halt them.

Chartres collected his nerve. How was it possible, he asked, to feel anything but horror over what happened?

'Of course it's horrible! What massacre isn't?' Danton roared. 'It was a matter of laying a river of blood between the people of Paris and the émigrés. You are too young to understand such things. Now go back to the army. And don't forget to hold your tongue.' If this was not accepting personal responsibility for the horror that scarred his soul, it was as close as Danton came to it. Yet he was still shrugging; he refused to discuss it and he did not want others to discuss it.

As the autumn of 1792 advanced, Danton watched the season's high political promise fade. The unity he believed vital for the infant republic seemed to be sliding out of reach. Rivalries, partisanship, individual fear and loathing, all somehow combined to slow the Convention's first brave flush of purpose. What was more, there hung over these divisions the terrible question of what to do with a king who was no longer king.

Dispute over the ultimate fate of 'Citizen Capet', as the scathing popular press delighted in calling Louis XVI, cast a long shadow over the new republic. To many it was obvious that the blood descendant of Hugh Capet, the monarchy's medieval progenitor, represented a mortal danger to republican aspirations as long as he lived. Even in his present prison quarters at the Temple, locked in its towers with Marie-Antoinette and the little dauphin, he was a danger. All the same, there appeared to be more than one way to dispose of Louis XVI's royal person, and honest patriots, pulled this way and that by their heartstrings and their sense of history, differed on what it should be.

Danton,
a face to
strike fear

The Danton family home, Arcis-sur-Aube

## THE CORDELIERS

(*Above*) Camille Desmoulins, the romantic,
with Lucile and son Horace

(*Below*) Philippe Fabre d'Eglantine,
the playwright

(*Right*) Louis Legendre, the butcher,
without his apron

WOMEN OF INFLUENCE

(*Above*) Gabrielle Charpentier,
the first Madame Danton

(*Right*) Louise Gély,
the second Madame Danton, with
Danton's son Antoine

(*Below right*) Manon Roland,
the nemesis

MENTORS

(*Above*) Comte de Mirabeau, voice of revolt

(*Right*) Duc d'Orléans, alias Philippe Egalite, patron of revolt

TROUBLESOME SOLDIERS

(*Below*) Marquis de LaFayette, Danton's bête noire

(*Below right*) General Dumouriez, the cross Danton had to bear

THE GIRONDINS

(*Above left*) Jean–Marie Roland,
their organiser

(*Above*) Jacques-Pierre Brissot, their champion

(*Left*) François Buzot, Madame Roland's lover

(*Right*) Anti-Girondin forces at ease –
Danton's people, the sans culottes

DANGEROUS ALLIES

(*Above*) Maximilien Robespierre,
the purist

(*Top right*) Antoine de Saint-Just,
the purist's apprentice

(*Above right*) Jean-Paul Marat,
hungerer for heads

(*Below right*) Jacques-René Hébert,
hellraiser

The Committee of Public Safety – the green room in lethal debate

(*Left*) 'Mad Tom' Paine,
an English friend of the Revolution

(*Below*) Prime Minister William Pitt,
a stern English foe

The execution of Louis XVI at the Place de la Révolution, 21 January 1793

Danton, hands tied, on the way to the guillotine, 5 April 1794

Danton had yet to reach his own firm conclusion on the king's fate as he made good his promise to stand down as first minister. He left the post on 9 October – a little over two weeks after first announcing his intention to go. By now the Duke of Brunswick's forces were back across the Rhine, displaying in their speed of retreat the renowned proficiency that forsook them at Valmy, and their departure accelerated Danton's own. He confined himself to telling the Convention that he was surrendering his ministry to uphold the dignity of the new house. This was a scruple that Roland, usually a stickler for the rules, declined to observe, fortified by the campaign his fellow Girondins mounted to make a special case for keeping him at Interior, an important ministry from which Madame Roland calculated her husband would rule the roost after Danton's departure.

There was something manic in Madame Roland's desire to do Danton down. It was an obsession. Beyond her snobbery, who could tell what fevered feelings lay behind it? There seemed more to it than the determination of this mistress of the political arts to have her way. Certainly she felt obliged to put up her feminine shutters against his regard. In souvenirs she would write of him, it was apparent that his 'bold eye' caused her particular unease. She determined to resist that bold eye, adding: 'The excess of his oratory, the violence of his gestures, the brutality of his oaths all betray him.' Whatever was turning in Madame Roland's fertile mind, the infant republic was reared in part on her urge to destroy him.

If power alone was her objective, Danton was unmistakeably *the* enemy to overcome. In the Convention and in the street his stock was giddily high. Stepping down from executive government left his status undiminished; alone among deputies from the Mountain, he was appointed to the Convention's select Constitution Committee, a nine-man panel created to give enduring shape to the republic and write its constitution (most of its members were Girondin brains, though England's arch-republican, Tom Paine, was also inducted). By comparison with Danton, then, Robespierre looked a secondary adversary in Madame Roland's reckoning. Robespierre certainly enjoyed unrivalled stewardship of the Jacobin club, where revolutionary ideas continued to bubble and froth, but his laborious oratory and his reluctance to take the kind of action that Danton revelled in wounded his popularity among patriots. There seemed no need to fear Robespierre. Would even ten eager men, let alone 100,000, have marched to his reedy trumpet call?

It was not power alone, though, that drove Madame Roland. She was the Revolution's sprite; what excited her was to campaign, to guide, to pursue her fancies to the end. She yearned for the utopian world she had glimpsed in the pages of Rousseau. Alas, among the high performers of the

Revolution, all her penetrating, good-fairy gaze detected were parrots and poseurs, brutes and blowhards. Among her stubbornest fancies was the belief that Danton had it within him to be a brutal dictator, another that he was a corrupt buccaneer pocketing the state's scarce riches under the cover of war and the destruction of the old order. Both theories served to protect her husband, and she took them in her charming teeth and shook them to death. Seeing things only in black and white, she seduced the Girondin champions into discrediting Danton. It was a struggle that enthralled France's shaky democracy in the last months of 1792, pushing aside matters of extreme national urgency.

Danton found himself endlessly exasperated at the time wasted. At length, he decided it was best to break publicly with Marat to dispel the dictatorship charges. It was the most direct way out, and politically not unadvantageous besides. Not only had Marat been the first to raise the idea that the Revolution needed a dictator, he was now the Convention's chief bogeyman, his shrill judgements approved only by the crazed fringe of the working class. Danton's opportunity to distance himself once and for all from the sanguinary Marat was handed to him, unwittingly, by his Girondin adversaries. Testing their strength, the friends of Brissot and Roland had the curious idea of trying to expel all twenty-four Paris deputies from the Convention on the grounds that they endangered public freedom. The Paris contingent, which included Danton and Marat, must go, the Girondins argued, because its members wilfully subordinated the interests of the nation to those of the capital alone.

In taking the rostrum to refute the charge, Danton allowed that the Girondins perhaps had a point with regard to just one of his Paris colleagues – Marat. It was true, Marat was not made of republican stuff. He was a divisive personality. He could not imagine why people thought of linking him with Marat! Why, he had even heard it said that he, Danton, penned certain of Marat's articles for him. What nonsense. The *Ami du Peuple* was the outpouring of a tortured mind, he said, adding with a final lunge: 'I believe the caves he inhabited have ulcerated his soul.'

Thereafter, there was little chance of mending fences with Marat, though the journalist did admit to the house, with uncustomary grace, that if anyone was guilty of pressing for a dictator to purge the Revolution of rotten souls, it was he, Marat: neither Danton nor Robespierre, he vouched, had ever supported his vision. But having disposed so unequivocally of his ties with Marat, Danton now proceeded in the same speech to turn the tables on the accusing Girondins and their anti-Paris campaign, declaring in a burst of rising fury:

As for myself I do not belong to Paris. I was born in a province towards which my sights turn with an eternal sense of pleasure. But there is not one of us who belongs to this province or that – we all belong, each one of us, to the whole of France ... They say there are men among us who would wish to divide France! Let us abandon such absurd notions! Let us pronounce the death sentence against those who promote them. France must be one and indivisible. She must have unity of representation. The citizens of Marseilles wish to hold out their hands to the citizens of Dunkirk. I demand therefore the penalty of death for anyone seeking to destroy the unity of France.

The words welled with patriotic fervour. There could have been no more heartfelt rebuke for the Girondins, and there could be no doubt it deepened Madame Roland's abhorrence for her chosen adversary, not only because of the theatrical death threats, but because an excited house with a show of hands decreed republican France there and then to be 'one and indivisible' – a statute destined to last for all time.

Danton was indeed liberal with his demands for the death penalty. It was as if they surged with the air itself from his barrel chest after he reached the rostrum to release his feelings, unrestrained by texts or notes. Much of it was parliamentary theatre. Was it also Marat's contagion? In violent times, violent speech held men's ears. Unlike Marat's constant demands for heads, though, Danton's death threats came across as a furious figure of speech appealing for a halt to whatever he thought obstructed his grand nebulous notion of liberty.

Heads were not Danton's business, though naturally he backed a new law sentencing all émigrés to permanent banishment – or to the guillotine should they be caught returning to France. He considered the émigrés military foes who had to be crushed. They had abandoned the *patrie* in its hour of danger. France must strike the wretches from her breast for ever.

Danton's mood seemed to swing between violence and conciliation. If this confused fellow revolutionaries, it perhaps confused him as well. For only days after the Convention enacted the anti-émigré law in late October, and while his desk at Justice was still warm, he heard a rapid knocking at his door at the Cour du Commerce. It was a curious hour for a visit. Dawn had just broken over an autumnal Paris and he was at the breakfast table with Gabrielle, tossing over in his head a speech he intended to make on religion and education, how the republic should grapple with them. Gabrielle ran to the door, pulling it open before he could get up.

A nervous figure entered, looking somewhat comforted by Gabrielle's engaging smile but staring around him as if perplexed by the Danton apartment, a modest abode by high statesmen's standards, furnished in the functional, carved-wood spirit of the provinces, with mirrors everywhere, testimony to Gabrielle's polishing labours in the Café de l'École. What was the visitor expecting? Luxuries in the Danton home were not sat upon and admired, they were consumed – roast duck, beefsteaks, Burgundy, claret, sugared tarts, the extravagant fare that pulled Cordeliers of an evening to their chief's open table. Danton's closeness to the poor was political, a question of human justice; it did not stretch to sitting down to a bare supper table. That morning, sitting alone at breakfast, he was startled to recognise his visitor.

Before him stood Alexandre de Lameth, one of the high-born pair of brothers who had helped organise the revolutionary parliament's affairs until the monarchy came crashing down on 10 August. Danton himself had personally helped both brothers, Charles and Alexandre, escape abroad in the shadow of the September massacres. This Lameth who came calling was a good fellow who believed in liberty, a cavalry captain who had fought in America for the American colonies' independence. He was an active Jacobin from the club's early days who had managed to compromise himself, however, by sticking to his goal of constitutional monarchy when the republic was already a certainty. Danton stared at him in disbelief.

'What are you doing in Paris?' he asked. 'I thought you were safe. Where have you come from?'

'From London.'

'Are you mad! How can you tell me this! Don't you know you face the death penalty?' Danton was in deadly earnest, for Lameth could only be classed an émigré now.

'No, I know that,' the clandestine caller said, hoping to God he had not been recognised by the artisans unshuttering their stalls as he slipped past on his way to the Cour du Commerce. 'But you were ready to save my brother's life and mine. The one mark of gratitude I can give you is to place my life in your hands now.'

On Danton's Tartar features there appeared what Lameth saw as a grimace of satisfaction. 'As you will,' Danton said. 'But you haven't come here without a motive. What do you want?'

'To give still greater proof of my confidence in you. And at the same time to show you your own one path to safety, for by destroying France you ensure your own destruction.'

'You are not shy!' said Danton. 'But you don't seem to grasp it. To reach liberty we must tread through the mire of democracy.' What was happening was for the best. The present turmoil would pass in time. 'I shall slow the chariot of Revolution.'

Lameth saw an opening in Danton's apparent doubts. He was gambling on his compassion. He had deliberated before coming and was confident that Danton would not hand him in, though he was the most powerful man in Paris. The braver you were with this fearful man, Lameth believed, the more he respected and would back you, provided he believed you were driven by noble feelings; his loyalty, once formed, was sacred. When Lameth had first come to know Danton, he recalled him too favouring a constitutional monarchy, and this was the ground he now engaged Danton upon, expressing his fears that those who had imprisoned King Louis in the Temple tower were about to commit 'a final historic crime'.

'Save him!' he implored Danton. 'You did not put him there, not directly. Save him, and you will have a place of glory in history.'

'Everything you fear he has brought upon himself,' Danton said.

The two men entered a vigorous exchange on the king's merits and failings, Lameth recounting touching tales of Louis' royal concern for the poor, Danton countering with warnings that praise for the king would only irritate and strengthen the purpose of the many patriots who seemed determined to have him executed. If Louis were put on trial, Danton said, he was lost. Still, the Girondins had heart, he allowed; they were a large party and he could not see them condemning him to death.

Danton's reckoning only encouraged Lameth to beseech him further to step in and save the king's life. The host turned blunt. 'Let's get this over with. I don't wish to look better or worse than I am. Here is what I really think and you can decide for yourself. I am not at all convinced that the king deserves to go unpunished, but I think it is fair, and useful too, to save him from his present situation. I shall do what I can, boldly but with caution. I shall expose myself if I see a chance of success, but let me tell you, if I lose all hope I do not intend to lose my head with his and I shall be among those who condemn him.'

Lameth asked why he added the harsh rider.

'To be sincere with you,' Danton said, showing him the door. 'Isn't that what you wanted?' He advised Lameth to leave France again at once, if he could. Otherwise he faced arrest and the guillotine for sure.

It was now early November 1792. A decision by the Convention to put Louis XVI on trial was imminent.

Fighting the Girondin offensive against his handling of state expenditures became an altogether trickier business for Danton than disposing of the dictatorship myth. This was particularly galling since the republic was now tasting the fruits of all he had done to throw men into the revolutionary army. Dumouriez, buoyed by Valmy, marched north into Belgium, where the forces of its Austrian overlords withdrew before him, leaving him in charge of the Habsburg land; elsewhere, expanded revolutionary forces crossed the Rhine and camped in the heart of the German Rhineland, took the Mediterranean province of Nice and were all set to annex the Alpine kingdom of Savoy, where there was scant opposition.

By late October 1792, the Revolution was truly on the march. It was not Danton's ambition to conquer foreign lands, though he endorsed the concept of France within 'natural frontiers' – the southern Alps, the Pyrenees and, more contentiously, the left bank of the Rhine up to the North Sea – which stretched the homeland further than it was at present. To be subjected to the Roland couple's tireless harassment over monies he had spent to achieve all this was aggravating in the extreme. The funds put at Danton's disposal as first minister were a matter of record; the way he had used them was not. The Girondins were demanding a detailed accounting with receipts.

In the frantic effort to stave off invasion Danton had certainly spent freely on agents, commissioners, spies and secret negotiators in order to place France in as favourable a tactical position as possible to confront the Prussians and Austrians. The men he paid were fast-moving characters, some of them roughnecks and none overburdened with scruples, which made them expensive. 'Who did you think I should use? Young ladies?' he challenged the Girondins on the floor of the Convention. Could Madame Roland and her favourites not see that they risked driving him against his will, against his instincts, to the side of their real rival, Robespierre? To their natural enemy? To the virtuous autocrat who despised them and was even now levering them out of his Jacobin club?

But there was nothing for it. The Girondins believed they were the true founders of the republic and it irked them to see that Danton, in stepping aside as head of government, had in fact forfeited precious little authority. As the largest figure in the Convention, power still revolved around him: he appeared to have charge of Paris and the army, though with no specific title to it, and even kept up his appearances at the Jacobins, elected to its rotating presidency that autumn to further sour looks from Robespierre. Danton, then, was the one the Girondins believed they had to save *their* republic from.

To be sure, the Cordelier chief was on awkward ground as regards the ministerial accounts and he knew it. He would have been the first to admit that he had not applied the most fastidious accounting standards to the emergency funds allotted him. In fact, he had been rather loose with them. Not all of the careful peasant had rubbed off on the giant from Arcis. At his King's Council chambers he had left that side of things to his old friend

Paré, who was good at it. Still, he presented the Convention with an initial instalment of the by now notorious accounts – figures relating purely to his Justice budget – as soon as he stepped aside from government in October. There was a din in the house, heightened by catcalls from Girondin benches, as he dropped his list on the presiding officer's desk. As the stuff of scandal it proved something of a disappointment. Out of 100,000 livres granted him in provisional budget funds, it showed him disbursing 68,684 livres during his hectic two-month tenure and returning the entire remainder to the treasury. All the same, there were some curious outlays, not least 30,000 livres on new pikes for the Paris sections, an item more in keeping with the war ministry than the Justice budget, though it confirmed that Danton had taken everything under his wing when calling the nation to arms. Then there were 16,590 livres in quarterly gratuities to the large staff at Justice, a helping hand of 333 livres for the good Paré and 2,400 livres paid to a *tapissier* to furnish the apartment of a lesser Cordelier with high duties at the ministry.

These paltry figures only made Madame Roland's tribe hungrier for details of the fate of much larger sums – 400,000 livres evenly split between 'secret' and 'extraordinary' funds – put at Danton's disposal to mobilise a halting Revolution against the Duke of Brunswick and his army. Danton faced no legal imperative to account for these. They were, as designated, secret – or extraordinary, which amounted to the same thing under the statutes. In the circumstances, though, with the Girondins in so inquisitive and hostile mode, he was under severe pressure to offer an explanation.

Madame Roland was a demon at maintaining the pressure: through her salon, through her husband, through lunches for ministers she took it upon herself to host, through her determined presence in the public gallery of the Convention during important debates, through the spell she cast on doting young Girondins, she was a formidable choirmistress. The pressure on Danton increased when old Roland maliciously volunteered his accounts at Interior, every last bill and receipt to hand, which brought calls in the house for a decree making it incumbent on ministers to detail secret expenditures as well as budget outlays. The best Danton could do was to affirm that he had put his secret expenditures before his fellow ministers in cabinet, which had approved them. Not only that, the cabinet had agreed that the outlays should remain secret and not appear in the cabinet record. To this, his fellow ministers attested. Their confirmation went some way towards satisfying the Convention, though Roland countered that he had been absent through illness from the cabinet session in question and thus had not signed off on Danton's figures, which in his view made the cabinet accord invalid. For her part, Madame Roland had another version of what happened in cabinet: her nemesis had grown so powerful that ministers were terrified of offending him.

Danton leaned hard on patriotism to maintain his honour. 'Remember! The *patrie* was in danger,' he bellowed in an appeal to the house. 'We were accountable for liberty, and we made good liberty's account.'

Roland, though tenacious, had no hope of besting so fervent an outburst. All the same, such was the pressure that a few days later Danton felt obliged to elaborate. 'There are expenditures that cannot be declared here. There are emissaries it would be unwise and unfair to name. There are revolutionary missions in the cause of liberty that demand great financial sacrifices.' From the Mountain and the Plain came shouts of support. He ploughed on:

When the enemy took Verdun, when among even the best and bravest of citizens took fright, the [old] parliament told us: 'Spare nothing, spend all you must to restore confidence and inspire the entire nation.' And so we did! We were forced into extraordinary expenditures and I confess that for the most part we have nothing very legal in receipts. Everything had to be done fast, too fast. You wanted ministers to act together and we did, and therein lie our accounts.

This was not unconvincing, in particular the disarming admission that he had 'nothing very legal' to show as proof of the secret operations. Only later, when on the defensive, did he concede that he had given Fabre, installed as a high functionary at Justice along with Camille, a fairly free hand to disburse the secret funds. There was nothing illicit in that, as he pointed out, though it was surely unwise. He would have done well to realise a little earlier that Fabre, a novice speculator, was not a rock of responsibility in financial matters.

In truth, Danton was careless with money because he did not worship it. Money got things done. If he felt uneasy over the accounts and the stink raised by the Roland tribe, he certainly did not feel guilty: they would not find a sou from those funds feathering his own nest or paying for new properties at Arcis. The debate in the Convention petered out towards the end of October, leaving Danton bruised but whole – still the idol of the house, or of most of it. All the same, this was a bone of which Madame Roland never let go and the fanciful rumour persisted, embellished by newly minted anecdotes, that Danton indeed used a considerable chunk of the funds to 'bribe' the Duke of Brunswick into withdrawing his army from French soil. For his part, Danton dropped the matter. The Brunswick 'bribe' was too absurd to worry about. But long after the debate, hardly a session of parliament went by when he came to the rostrum without taunting voices from the Girondin benches crying 'The accounts!'

Danton was no saint, and it would have taken one not to hit back. The openings were frequent. His resignation from the government, while a balm for the Rolands, was also a nettle that stung them into finding a decent excuse for the interior minister's reluctance to do likewise. Much feinting and gesturing was involved: Roland himself pretended in public to be on the point of resigning, while Madame Roland's favourites, Brissot and a clutch of younger hopefuls, lobbied the Convention to display its devotion to the *patrie* by maintaining him in government. By the time they asked for a vote, Danton was tired of the charade and was moved to sarcasm, declaring with a long, ironical shake of the head:

> No one gives Roland his due more than I do. But I must tell you, if you invite him to keep his ministry you should also invite Madame Roland, for the whole world knows that Roland has not been alone in his department. Me, I held mine alone.

Puncturing the dominatrix provided some satisfaction, though the laughs it produced turned rather quickly to rising murmurs of protest from around the Riding School. He had been discourteous. The Convention had strange unwritten rules: to yell for men's heads was permissible, to ridicule a patriot couple was out of order. But it was irresistible. Danton must have pictured the sprite of the Revolution as a caped nun in the Inquisition, her full mouth smiling as she pressed into the torturer's hands a curved cane to flay his male parts. His head continued to race with reasons why this dullard's wife was quite so determined to destroy him. Did she really want to lock him in the cold embrace of Robespierre?

# TWELVE

## The Execution of a King

In his heart Danton probably did not want Louis XVI to die. To have told Lameth so was no lie. Less straightforward was his conditional promise to do all he could to save the king from execution. It was a swinishly difficult issue, made still more awkward for him by the harassment of the Girondins, who likewise did not want Citizen Capet's head to roll. It was hard to turn round and link arms with the Roland-Brissot tribe after all they had thrown at him. Besides, he regarded their policies and their disdain for political unity as an outright invitation to civil war, the prospect of which perhaps now fused in his mind with the king's fate.

Standing constitutional law made the imprisoned Louis XVI 'inviolable' – except if he deserted the kingdom, took charge of a foreign army or refused to take the oath creating a constitutional monarchy. But that was the hasty law manufactured over a year ago, in the summer of 1791, to protect him against accusations of high treason after his flight to Varennes, and not only did the birth of the republic and the preparation of a new constitution render it moot, there was not a man in the Convention who was blind to Louis' serious flirtations with all three proscribed acts.

The king was, then, guilty. Public opinion was convinced of it.

Robespierre, Marat and the radicals of the Mountain argued that there was no need for a trial; Louis had to pay for his treason with his head. To dissuade the Convention from going through the process of judging the king, Robespierre contrived some artful legal questions: if the king were brought to trial before a court, did that not mean he had to be presumed innocent? In which case, the Revolution would likewise be in the dock. But the minds of most patriots were too set on a trial to be swayed by legal conundrums and, on 13 November 1792, the Convention voted to sit in judgement on Louis XVI just as soon as the prosecution documents were ready.

The ghost of Oliver Cromwell again joined the fray. It was a relief for

Danton that Cromwell's name was thrown around this time without targeting him personally. Roundheads and the republican interlude they introduced across the Channel lived close enough in history to hold the Revolution's attentions and to invite its questions. Had England's Lord Protector gained anything for his cause by taking Charles I's head? Could Charles' execution have been the mistake that ultimately defeated England's revolution? A second Englishman entered the debate, too, headlong as usual. Tom Paine, an honorary Girondin who nonetheless liked to vary his seat in the Convention and these days planted himself as often as possible next to the mighty Danton, campaigned for a show trial of monarchy itself. Danton again recognised Paine's motive: it would stand as a trial *in absentia* of the British monarchy too.

In Paine's view, Louis' wretched person should be considered beneath parliament's notice now that the republic was in place. In practical terms, he thought it best to spare the king's life – to hold him in prison until the revolutionary wars were over, then banish him. Lust for bloody revenge against his person was itself despotic. Much as Paine hated and abhorred monarchy, he professed that his compassion for the unfortunate, whether friend or foe, was stronger. Such sentiments could not have been far from Danton's own, for the pair discussed such things at length without falling out. Danton received a private note on the subject from the deputy for Calais, who appeared to consider him the man of all influence in France. In the note, Paine set out his thoughts on the king and stressed that the new republican constitution on which they were both working should 'speak for other nations that cannot yet speak for themselves'. Though the Englishman aimed to abolish the death penalty altogether, he was clearly prepared to make allowances for Danton's broad – and frequent – calls for death to those who dared offend the spirit of liberty. Like the anxious Gabrielle, Paine must have chosen to see these demands for what they were: the hot irons of the orator's craft.

The pressure on Danton from patriots such as Paine was rather gentler than that applied by royalist sympathisers. A letter bearing the signature Bertrand de Molleville, a former navy minister whom Danton knew only because he had once argued a case for his department in the King's Council, was delivered by messenger one night at the Cour du Commerce. It claimed that papers had come into the writer's possession purporting to show that Danton had received a series of sweeteners from the court the year before. These papers, Molleville wrote, carried specific dates for the transactions and included a receipt bearing Danton's signature.

The threat did not need spelling out: should Danton speak against the king at his trial or fail to defend him, the 'incriminating' dossier would be presented to the Convention. He did not reply. To his mind, Molleville's case was a fabrication, an attempt at blackmail manufactured out of those old rumours of his dalliance with Mirabeau. (The letter was certainly founded on trickery, since Molleville was later to admit that the supposed documents were not in his possession, as he told Danton, and never had been; he had simply been shown them by an outgoing minister.) Still, Danton had to give the threat his consideration. Though it was unlikely that Molleville would make the trumped-up story public – to do so would risk his own neck – there was an outside chance he would persist. If so, the blackmail had the makings of a spectacular sideshow that could get out of hand when the Convention came to vote on the king's fate.

There were already sideshows enough surrounding the king's trial. In mid-November, a safemaker poking around in the deserted royal chambers at the Tuileries came across a secret iron safe built into the wall; it was stuffed with the king's private papers and the safemaker at once notified Roland at Interior of his find. Danton first heard of it from Camille, ever the newshound despite his busy days at the Convention. It seemed that Roland had rushed to the palace, boxed the neatly stacked bundles of documents and correspondence disgorged by the safe and returned to his ministry to empty them upon his wife's trembling lap. Danton could just imagine the couple poring with excited eyes over the correspondence, examining each letter line by line to find his name and material to damn him or anyone else who stood in their way.

From the day the safemaker gave the alert it was almost a week before Roland presented his trove to the scrutiny of the Convention on 20 November, a delay allowing the minister to manage its impact. On each document, on each item of royal correspondence, he had stamped his department's seal to ensure that none inconveniently disappeared in some house committee.

Was Danton compromised? Miraculously, given Madame Roland's feelings towards him and her husband's possible manipulations, not a bit. It was King Louis, Mirabeau and La Fayette who emerged as principal villains in patriots' eyes. Louis came out particularly badly: he was shown to be ungrateful and disdainful towards his would-be saviours and, worse, in secret league with his wife's family in Vienna, who ruled an empire at war with France. The letters revealed Mirabeau's demands for funds to finance a huge public-relations campaign on Louis' behalf, with proposals to enlist front-rank revolutionary politicians and journalists to calm the sans-culottes in the capital's rebellious boroughs – the first documentary proof of the great orator's corruption.

However far Mirabeau's machinations had gone, they had not worked, and although it might be presumed that he kept a figure such as Danton –

the 'Marketplace Mirabeau' – in his sights as a prospective collaborator, the Cordelier chief was not once cited in the royal correspondence. Nowhere in all those private royal pages so closely inspected by the Rolands did the name Danton appear. It was as if he were whitewashed of the pernicious charges long levelled against him.

While the forcing of the royal safe in fact gave Danton something of a personal boost, to King Louis and the ghost of Mirabeau it delivered a terrible blow – as the imprisoned monarch was very soon to discover, and as the orator's bones experienced when, by order of a shocked Convention, they were removed from their sublime place of honour in the Pantheon and reinterred in disgrace elsewhere in Paris eighteen months later, the site undisclosed.

Still, the prospect of participating in the king's trial depressed Danton. Owing to his stature in the house, he would be expected to take a leading part. All sides, from the king's sympathisers to the king's would-be executioners congregating around Robespierre and Marat, were counting on his support. He could picture the wretched king having to respond to jeering, insolent questions, and to what purpose? Tom Paine was right: for all its social symbolism, the whole crude rigmarole in store was beneath the dignity of the republic.

It hardly grieved him, then, to have the ideal let-out.

Although there was no retreat to Arcis this time, Danton did leave Paris – ten days before the trial opened on 11 December. Great events were taking place on France's borders and the Revolution needed a man of power to influence them to its optimum advantage.

With hindsight, Danton might have questioned a little more closely the wisdom of undertaking a foreign mission, however important, at this juncture. He might have reflected with a keener sense of self-interest on what was happening at the top of the Revolution. The insurrectionist Paris Commune which he had set up and which had had things its own way for a while, urged on by Robespierre and Marat, had since bowed to the supremacy of the Convention. Yet this brave new parliament was already beginning to look like a prisoner of its own in-house wars.

Where did authority lie? Not with the stay-put Roland and the cabinet. Not, for all their guiding influence over revolutionary policy, with the unelected Jacobins. The truth was that as 1792 drew to a close the Revolution floated perilously in an institutional power vacuum that begged to be filled. For the moment, power resided in the size of men's reputations, in the size of their lungs, the size of their wit, the size of their personal ambition. By most of these measures Danton possessed power. Indeed, he possessed all the attributes of an outstanding politician, except the last – the lust for power itself.

Since no power vacuum ever lasted for long, this was not a scene on which a man driven by ambition would have turned his back. Nonetheless, at the express request of the Convention, Danton set out for Belgium on 1 December, aware that he was likely to be absent for several critical weeks. The territorial bounds of the Revolution were in effect his to draw. An extremely awkward situation was developing in the Low Countries and the part he had played in inspiring the revolutionary army, coupled with the privileged relations he had established with General Dumouriez, marked Danton out as the man to resolve it.

Through the autumn Dumouriez had been on the rampage. He was the new republic's first soldier. Before attacking Belgium in early November, he had taken the precaution of returning to Paris in mid-October to test his standing with those he judged to be in power. Despite his political connections with the Girondins, the victor of Valmy made a beeline for Danton, who responded with a will, taking him to the Paris Opera and squeezing him into a seat between himself and Fabre to display their closeness.

The demonstration annoyed Madame Roland. The next night, this time at the theatre, when Danton sat the general in a box next to his and made a point of leaning across frequently to talk to him, she retaliated. Danton, now accompanied by Gabrielle and his mother, fresh in from Arcis, was in a box reserved for government dignitaries and as its door opened for Madame Roland, looking her comely best, she recoiled in a show of disdain and turned on her heel, declining to sit with 'women of low appearance'. She was not prepared to see Danton shine, not if she could cheapen him, though the social scandal she caused at the theatre hurt her more than him in the delighted pages of the Paris press.

Dumouriez's visit coincided with Danton's turn to assume the rotating presidency at the Jacobins. The club staged a reception in Dumouriez's honour. Though Robespierre ran things at the Jacobins, it fell to Danton, as president, to make the speech of welcome, which he opened by lauding the general for his great services to the *patrie*, for rallying the army and never losing hope after the desertion of 'that vile eunuch of the Revolution, La Fayette'. Placing a red bonnet on the soldier's head, Danton, in Ciceronian flow, urged him: 'A still finer career now opens before you. Let the pike of the people break the sceptre of kings. Let crowns fall before the red cap by which this club honours you. And after that, return among us and your name will be written in the finest pages of our history.'

If Dumouriez was listening carefully he would have detected the subtle mix of praise and warning in Danton's invitation to move on Belgium, for patriots' suspicions were already aroused by his evident determination to push north of his own accord, whatever they wished. It was unlikely, though, that the warning registered. A few days later, Dumouriez was back with his troops, vanquishing Belgium's Austrian masters at Jemappes and driving them out to the border with Germany, where their forces encamped, waiting for the wind of war to change. The new master of Belgium indeed had quite different ideas from those favoured by the Convention. To be sure, his intent was to liberate its people, who were already locked in a struggle for independence from Austria, and to that extent he even appeared to be in step with dreamy revolutionary yearnings to liberate all mankind.

But Dumouriez did not want Belgium to fall under the Revolution's control. For all his timely and valorous services to the infant republic, he did not support it. To the ex-royal officer, a republic was somehow against human nature. He remained a supporter of the constitutional monarchy to which the early Revolution aspired. What was taking shape in his mind was an independent Belgium, with perhaps himself at its head. So on marching into Liège and Brussels, where he at first received a rapturous welcome, he proclaimed himself the 'friend of the Belgian people'.

Patriots in Paris already sensed Dumouriez's antipathy for the republic, though not how far it went. Now their suspicions hardened. On the benches of the Convention it took precious little to turn suspicion into lurid accusation. What was Dumouriez up to? Courting the Belgian people to make himself their dictator! And after that? Planning to use his exalted military position to seize power at home! The damning chorus was led by his old political friends the Girondins, who demanded the immediate annex- ation of Belgium. Their annexation proposal served two purposes: it met their generous desire to start spreading liberty far and wide throughout Europe, and it forestalled Dumouriez's suspect ambitions. In late November 1792 the Convention bought this reasoning: France and Belgium were to be one and the same revolutionary republic, governed from Paris.

Danton's mission in Belgium was both to rein in Dumouriez and organise the projected union with France. In a biting December frost, he arrived on the heels of a pack of revolutionary agents previously dispatched from Paris to examine the lie of the land and who, according to an infuriated Dumouriez, had been making pigs of themselves with the natives and stripping Belgian churches of their treasures, their defence being that Belgian riches must pay for the war of liberation. Danton's first priority, then, was to placate Dumouriez, who clearly regarded the 'violence and extortion' of the French agents as an offence against himself.

It was going to be hard to bring the headstrong soldier round. His anger at the prospect of Belgium's annexation ran so high that although Danton and a joint plenipotentiary, Jean-François de Lacroix, a Norman lawyer and scourge of émigrés, were an eminent cut above the offending agents, and although he knew Danton well, he greeted them both with exasperated contempt. His recent nights out in Paris with Danton seemed forgotten. Now Dumouriez chose to see in him an 'oaf endowed with great energy, as ugly in morals as in physique', in Lacroix an 'unprincipled crook'.

The only way to move ahead, Danton saw, was to humour the general. He himself was not especially enthusiastic about the decreed union, though it conformed, just, to his image of France within her 'natural frontiers'. It was obvious that it spelled trouble, serious trouble, with the English, for even his brief experience of international diplomacy told him that England would do almost anything to stop Antwerp and the North Sea trade lanes falling into French hands.

Still, the situation as regards England had changed since his personal manoeuvring for a permanent truce not six months earlier. Then, invaders were marching on Paris; now, the Revolution was on the march. Moreover, his opening consultations with Belgian Jacobins and city leaders convinced Danton that union with France had sufficient popular support to pass – even though opposition was vociferous and the support, he realised, was essentially a cry of relief at the expulsion of the Austrians.

Danton was jovial with the first soldier of the republic, trying to coax him into accepting annexation as the natural outcome of his splendid military feats. In Liège, a prosperous city-principality, where the general had his winter quarters, Danton called in the stars of the Paris Opera to give Belgians an encouraging dose of the French culture they were now called upon to share. He then recruited French actors for a tour of Belgian theatres to promote the spirit of the Revolution – gestures derided by Dumouriez as thin compensation for annexation. A more promising move was to secure the soldier a spell of leave in Paris for the New Year in the hope it would make him more amenable. The Convention was reluctant to grant it, wary of the effect an enraged Dumouriez could have on home opinion, but Danton sent insistent messages warning that the general would resign if leave were refused, in which case the revolutionary army would fall apart. This did the trick.

The victor of Valmy returned to Paris in the middle of the king's trial, on 1 January 1793, seizing the opportunity, as expected, to rail against the union with Belgium and to speak up for the life of the king. If the spell of leave relieved his bile, it did nothing to endear him to radical benches at the Convention.

Remaining behind in Liège, Danton trusted that no one in Paris would regard Dumouriez as his mouthpiece. As the Convention's first commissioner he had effective political charge of Belgium, a responsibility that grew in Dumouriez's absence: he was viceroy by another name. Accompanied by Lacroix, who had briefly presided over the Convention and was an ally of greater integrity than the general allowed, Danton stepped up his fraternisation efforts, touring towns and villages with a prudently large army escort to promote the joyous prospect of union with his land of liberty and bellowing his wrath against war profiteers who had been pillaging the province.

His aim was to please, a policy he did not confine to winning over aldermen. A month away from Paris was too long for this bull of a man to go without women, and it seems he did not much question himself over making up for it. This was no disrespect to Gabrielle, who was quite up to satisfying him in Paris and did so. But his physical appetite was the equal of his brawn, and in wealthy Liège, a riverside city of arms manufacturers, temptation was there in plenty: women gathered around the massive male with the frightening face who came among them as viceroy in their harsh winter. He wined them at his well-laden table and took them to his quarters, French visitors reported. Their accounts reached the ears of Madame Roland back in Paris, who, appending her own fancies, advised her salon that Danton had gone to Belgium 'to enrich himself', to plunder its abbeys, its princely houses and its armourers' daughters.

What foreign pleasures there were did not divert Danton's feelings from Gabrielle and his two baby sons, for he took the rare step in Belgium of taking up his pen and writing affectionate private letters home. 'Don't forget to look after my trees I sent to Arcis, and make sure your father does something about that house of his in Sèvres. A thousand kisses for my little Danton and tell him his papa will try not to stay away too long,' he wrote to Gabrielle a week before Christmas, greatly missing his older son, now almost two-and-a-half. To a distressed reply from the heavily pregnant Gabrielle, who may also have heard the Liège stories and who complained that she had been told by a Cordelier friend that he was likely to be away for as long as two months and more, he wrote reassuringly: 'Our friend exaggerates, making you think my mission will last so long. I'm really hoping to kiss you on 1 January.' It was unlikely that Gabrielle felt much comforted. Her fears that her husband was running – no, hurtling – towards his death were surely hard to shake off.

Danton was not home by 1 January, of course. That was the day Dumouriez returned to Paris and if at first Danton thought of returning with him, it did not work out. The Revolution needed the presence of at least one figure of authority in the land it was taking to its breast.

*　　*　　*

When Danton did return to Paris two weeks later it was to attend the final act of Louis XVI's trial. The Convention called him back, demanding the participation of its strongest orator. He arrived home at the Cour du Commerce on 14 January in early evening, dog-tired but overjoyed to renew domestic life with the swelling Gabrielle and the two infants, delighted also to see Camille, who would have come down from his apartment above to greet him and give him a commentary in his usual fervent, stumbling style on the trial thus far and the pitiful efforts of the king, deprived of his majesty, to defend himself. Fabre and the journalist Fréron no doubt came to join them to set about a bottle of Burgundy – then another, and another – and tuck into the plump pair of chickens which Gabrielle, assisted by two scullery maids she now employed, liked to have ready for such occasions.

In lively spirits, they discussed two momentous votes that were scheduled to take place at the Riding School the next day. Was Louis XVI indeed guilty, yes or no? There the outcome was obvious. The contents of the royal safe made a huge yes vote inevitable. The second vote was more awkward, for although it was largely a delaying tactic devised by Louis' defenders, it had the outward revolutionary merit of inviting the sovereign people to be his judge: should the king's fate go to a referendum in the cities and provinces, yes or no? Danton was against that; he was pretty sure a plebiscite would promote further riots. Parliament had not even considered consulting the people when going to war or creating the republic. Why should it do so now?

The next morning, as his Cordelier henchmen set off in miserable wintry weather for the Convention, a combination of travel fatigue, the warm pull of the family hearth, lack of preparation and – could he admit it to himself? – reluctance to do what he knew he had to do conspired to keep Danton at home, leaving the Girondins and Robespierre's Mountain tribe to guess at whether he was actually back from Belgium in time for the proceedings. The Convention record listed him 'absent on mission' for both votes, the first of which resulted in a near-unanimous guilty verdict, the second in strong rejection of a plebiscite.

That was 15 January. On 16 January, more than twenty-four hours after his return, Danton was there at the tribune of the Convention in his red frockcoat for the ultimate vote: should the king be put to death, yes or no? Now the Cordelier chief's mood was decisive – and unusually curt. Molleville's failed attempt at blackmail surely gave it extra edge. While it occurred to sardonic Girondins that the landslide nature of the votes Danton had dodged contributed to his decisiveness, his succinct tone, disallowing all ambiguity, nonetheless brought gasps from all sides of the house and aaahs from the crammed public galleries. Turning with deliberate effect towards Brissot, Roland and their cohorts, he roared:

> I am not one of that throng of statesmen who fail to understand that you do not compromise with tyrants, who fail to understand that you strike only at the heads of kings, that you must expect nothing from the kings of Europe except what is won by force of arms. I vote for the death of the tyrant.

It was just as he had told Lameth some weeks before: should he judge that no chance remained of saving the king, he would condemn him. While the vote was a lot closer than the preceding ballots – 387–286 for execution – the refrain 'Death', 'Death', 'Death' beaten out by deputies at the rostrum droned grimly through the Riding School, drowning out pleas for the king's indefinite detention or banishment. The gasps from the centre of the house, the Marsh, turned louder as Citizen Philippe Egalité, the king's blood cousin, and Vergniaud, the Girondins' champion debater, breaking ranks with his party, delivered their verdicts: 'Death'.

If that seemed the end of the tribunal, it was not. Like Paine, fifty or so deputies wanted to suspend capital punishment under the law, so a subsequent vote was called the next day on a motion granting the king a reprieve on that ground. Louis' defenders rose to save his neck all over again. Tempers flared. Exasperated, Danton surged from the Mountain to make a point of order, interrupting one of the defenders in full flow. From the Girondin side came a piercing shout: 'You're not yet king, Danton! What is your privilege?' The taunt was a picador's lance in the fighting bull's neck. Danton exploded. 'I demand that the lout who says I am not yet king be silenced and censured.' In the ensuing tumult he resumed his seat, yielding to the member he had interrupted, though not before noting that the Girondin could have nothing new to tell the house.

And soon he was up again, rejecting all thought of reprieve for the king as 'transaction with tyranny'. He expressed respect for Tom Paine and his opinion, which he allowed was important. But the Revolution could not wilt now. He turned his high scorn on the ambassador from the Bourbon court of Spain, who had the diplomatic nerve to deliver to the Convention a clear threat of war if it went through with the execution of King Louis. What insolence! Spain did not even recognise the republic, and now it was dictating the law! Why, if it were left to him, Danton boomed, he would vote to go to war with Spain without more ado.

A reprieve for the king was rejected by 380 votes to 310.

*    *    *

Louis XVI went to the guillotine on the Place de la Révolution – the future Place de la Concorde – on 21 January 1793. He died with simple courage on a brisk, windy morning before the Paris masses, the same excited hordes who stormed the Bastille three and a half years earlier.

It was not a day of joy. The hush of the assembled thousands, craning to see, seemed louder than their whoops and taunts.

Danton did not attend the execution. Gabrielle begged him not to. He had done enough to finish off the monarchy. The mood was likewise short of festive in the Convention, where Brissot and Roland seized upon the grisliness of the occasion to hark back to the prison massacres in September, denouncing the capital's hold on the Revolution and its thirst for blood. The house recognised their real target: Danton.

This was not what he had returned to Paris for, to fight the Girondins. He had come for the vote and to report on his mission to Belgium, where, moreover, he was due to return forthwith to complete arrangements for the union with France and to keep Dumouriez, who had now returned to the province, in check. But this was a special day – to add to its drama, a deputy who voted 'Death' had been assassinated overnight by a parliamentary guard – and there was a lot Danton wanted to get off his mind before leaving again.

Perhaps it was the royal execution that sent him off in so many directions, but his speech that day sounded curiously incoherent. It was no less vigorous for that; he seemed to be laying about with a heavy mallet, bringing it down here, there and everywhere.

First, those September prison massacres. He allowed that he had not said enough in public at the time about the horrors. Now he put words to what he had thought then: 'You should have been told clearly that no power on earth could stop them. They were an explosion of revolutionary rage, a rage that filled all minds. The men who know most about these terrible events were convinced they were a necessary outlet for the fury of people who never had justice.' Then, swinging the mallet at the Girondins, he said: 'I dare all those who know me to say I am a butcher, to say I did not do all I could to keep the peace in the cabinet. I take Brissot himself as my witness! And did I not show extreme deference towards a stubborn old man who should have used all the means he had to restore calm?'

Now he was on the attack. The 'stubborn old man' was of course Roland, soon to turn sixty, who sat glaring at him. It was reckless to blame Roland when everyone in the Convention knew that he, Danton, had held the whip hand in government as the massacres took place, though it was true that Interior had nominal charge of police and public security. Still, Roland's continued hold on the ministry struck him as harmful to the

Revolution. Was it not obvious that he and his wife were setting the provinces against Paris? Animosity against the hub of revolt seemed to have gained large parts of the country. What had begun as provincial resentment against the predatory old order was now turning into hostility towards the Revolution that destroyed it. In the New Year of 1793 a veritable army of god-fearing peasants, now two thousand-strong, clashed repeatedly with republican guardsmen in the lower Loire region in the west. Civil war threatened – and unabating economic hardship pushed it closer. Major cities in the south, from Bordeaux to Marseilles, showed stout signs of disaffection with the revolutionary capital, as if ready to break. Danton accepted that this was not all due to Girondin stirring – provincial favour for God and monarchy was reawakening – but the Rolands' obstinate calls for regional autonomy were surely a part of it. Furthermore, the couple seemed intent on angering the Paris sans-culottes, whom Madame Roland despised anyway; she wanted liberty delivered with better manners.

The Rolands' latest scheme was to form a special guard force for the Convention drawn exclusively from the provinces, with the task of protecting the house from the Paris masses. Such precautions looked insanely divisive to Danton. He urged the house to send Roland on his way:

For the good of the Republic I demand that he leave the ministry. My concern is the public safety . . . Roland imagines that Paris wishes to exert a kind of authority over all our other communes. That is his great mistake! He has contrived to rouse the departments of France against Paris, the city that belongs to us all.

And on Danton went. As if Roland were already gone, he brought the mallet down that day on the power vacuum in France, on the nation's flagging war energies – even on William Pitt and his Aliens Bill, a panicky new clampdown on foreigners residing in England.

This time the blow struck at old man Roland had its effect. Two days later, on 23 January, he stood down from the cabinet, saying he was leaving in protest over the king's execution.

Danton's mallet was not the only implement to knock Roland down. Public humiliation also took a crack, for no sooner was Louis gone than the Convention killed off a propaganda department which Madame Roland had lovingly launched that past autumn, her mission being to hire journalists and publicists to popularise her concept of revolution. The Roland propaganda office, funded by parliament through Roland's interior ministry, had faced problems from the outset. First, the name his wife devised for it – the Office of Public Spirit – had produced wry smiles; then, despite her high hopes for the project, it became a laughing stock among sansculottes. The abrupt decree cutting off its funds nonetheless struck the Rolands as a gross insult, and his resignation immediately afterwards had all the appearance of signalling the couple's withdrawal from the political front line. Old Jean-Marie Roland's star was evidently sinking.

With Madame Roland, though, there was no such thing as retreat. Danton soon became aware that she had found an alternative surrogate to attack him. In the first chill weeks of 1793, not only did the anti-Danton campaign continue unabated in the Roland salon but an eloquent young lawyer from Normandy, François Buzot, made it his business to assail him in parliament from the Girondin benches with a venom so relentless that it seemed programmed. Madame Roland's passionate aggressiveness – only a passion could sustain her onslaught – showed in everything the Norman now threw at Danton. He was a willing Danton-hater. To his mind, Danton had 'hypnotised 600,000 imbeciles' – the entire working population of Paris – into trembling at his words.

Buzot was a true liberal soulmate for Madame Roland – a latter-day Rousseau who in spare moments wandered in woods and fields studying the master's words. But like hers, his romantic nature had a purposeful core. He was a federalist who enthused about the laws of the new United States of America, which he also studied. Was it a crime, he asked, to cherish the kind of government under which America was learning to live, happy and free? It struck him that a government of states – of Brittany, of Burgundy, of Provence, of his own Normandy and so on – was a mode of republican government suited to a great nation. Better still, it offered the precious bonus of halting the tyranny of Paris and its street mob. Like most Girondins, in particular Madame Roland, he had small esteem for 'the people'. To Buzot the common populace was 'vile and cowardly, the cause and instrument in all ages of human servitude and calamity, ready to be bold only against weakness and virtue'. He heaped all blame for the September massacres on Danton, who he nonetheless conceded to himself was not as detestable a Mountain figure as the 'cruel hypocrite' Robespierre or the murderous Marat. But Danton exuded power. If power resided anywhere in the republic, it seemed to reside in Danton.

The giant's great skill, Buzot allowed, was to have depicted the horrific killing spree as popular vengeance slipping its leash. Danton repeated this often enough that the poor devils of the Paris street had come to believe it; they took the massacres to be a triumph for liberty. Danton had played his hand well, Buzot further allowed, for now all those who raised their voices against the massacres were somehow open to charges from Robespierre and the Mountain that they were enemies of the people – supporters of royalty, counter-revolutionaries, agents of foreign powers, traitors.

There was the madness of it. The Girondins were cornered.

Danton perhaps guessed from Buzot's offensive that relations within the Roland household were changing, though Madame Roland kept these matters to herself and her diary. Her husband's loss of cabinet stature was in one sense a release for her: it lofted her into the outstretched arms of Buzot, six years her junior, who had set his melancholy eyes on her at her salon and, alone among the many, succeeded in winning her heart. As with the contenders whom she kept at a tantalising distance, she tried hard to limit her feelings for Buzot to a 'pure love'. 'My sole aim was to preserve my pure soul and to see my husband's glory intact,' she confided to her diary. But maintaining her bluestocking virtue was a demanding task; her passion for Buzot somehow refused to stay within the bounds she set for it.

With due regret, she confessed her love for Buzot to her husband, which made him jealous and more petulant still over his loss of office. She tried to spare the fallen minister's feelings but failed. Indeed, his jealousy only irritated her and she suspended her purity and took the appealing Buzot as her lover. Of this carnal leap, she wrote, with fond candour: 'I cherish my husband as a sensitive girl adores a virtuous father for whom she would sacrifice even a lover. The fact is, though, I have found the man to be this lover, and holding to my duty was more than my ingenuity in living up to it could stand.'

The melting of Madame Roland's heart did not extend towards Danton. The passion of her abhorrence of him matched the passion of her attraction to Buzot. To her, Danton remained the cause of everything cruel and barbaric. It was he who reigned now, he who kept the people on the march, he the abominable 'genius' – yes, genius, she admitted; she could not find another word for it – in whose hands power had come to reside. He was Tiberius, Caligula, Nero wrapped in one, a figure of eternal execration. And neither she nor Danton could possibly have foretold the end to which her hatred was leading them.

# THIRTEEN

# Flames in Flanders

With the king's execution the war spilled across the entire map of Europe. Revolutionary France confronted a continent united in arms. Kings could not stand idly by when one of their kind, the most regal of them of all, was decapitated by his people. The much-widened war was not what Danton intended, but his own rough and ready diplomatic impulses coupled with Dumouriez's martial ambitions only seemed to promote it.

The most powerful new belligerent was William Pitt's England, her neutrality now strained past the limit. In coalition with Spain, Portugal, Holland, the German princes, assorted Italian states and very soon Catherine the Great's Russia, England joined the Austro-Prussian war against the Revolution in February 1793, and if either the French or the English thought theirs might be a brief encounter, they were wrong: it was to last for twenty-two years with dramatic swings of fortune.

As the drums of war beat ever louder, Danton returned to Belgium in the first days of February to complete arrangements for the union with France. Gabrielle, close to giving birth now, put on a brave face at his departure, though he saw how distressed she was. She had been down at heart, he felt, ever since he had taken charge of the government and the attacks had begun on his role in the prison massacres. Could it be that she believed those accusations? Was that why she was sick? Because she thought him a savage? No, he felt sure it wasn't that. It was for his safety that she worried herself sick. But how haunted, how pale she looked. All the same, she managed a little parting jest through her distress. 'When I die,' she smiled, 'I want you to marry our Louise.' It was worth a smile: Louise Gély, the girl from upstairs, a big sister to their sons, her own close friend, had just turned sixteen.

Owing to Gabrielle's condition, Danton had contemplated staying in Paris this time, but dismissed his hesitations. Belgium was his responsibility, the crucible of a vastly expanded war, and he had to see his mission through. This time he would be away for two weeks, no longer. She was not expecting to give birth for three weeks.

A phrase perhaps turned in his head as he left: 'You must expect nothing from the kings of Europe except what is won by force of arms.' They were his own words, defiant words he had spoken on voting for King Louis to die. They did not in fact encompass his range of feelings on war, which were at times contradictory. Much as he recognised the danger of drawing England into the war, much as he had expended his peasant guile and the Revolution's largesse to prevent it in the past, he now set out a policy that was bound to achieve the opposite – to make England a combatant. On the eve of this second trip to Belgium, in a rousing speech to the Convention on 31 January, his nationalist passions getting the better of his untutored diplomatic instincts, he thundered:

The boundaries of France are drawn by nature. We shall attain them on their four sides – the Ocean, the Rhine, the Alps and the Pyrenees. So kings threaten you! You have thrown the head of a king at the feet of kings. Let that gauntlet signal their death as well. So England threatens you! Then the tyrants of England are dead men.

Here was the bravura that kept Danton's prestige a political head above that of other leaders in the house. Judging by the applause from all sides, it set even Girondin hearts pounding.

To Pitt, though, coming as it did on the eve of England's entry into the war, it could only have sounded like full justification for his urge to confront the Revolution by force of arms. Danton surely did not need reminding that to proclaim the Rhine a natural boundary was an assault on England herself, or would be interpreted as such in London. It planted the flag of the Revolution in Antwerp and other Flemish ports that sustained English commerce; the hostile face of insurrection would now stare straight down the mouth of the Thames. Of all this Danton was indeed aware, only he was keyed up, carried away by Dumouriez's military successes, and he simply decided to overlook the inevitable consequences.

Most likely, Danton's vision also remained blurred by what he knew of the admiration of English liberals for the Revolution. By now, however, Pitt had turned a corner: he had succeeded in putting across the notion that England genuinely needed to be saved from the French plague. Right up to the end of 1792, Pitt's great adversary Fox, playing down continuing disorders and clashes in English industrial cities between excited reformers and government loyalists, had been able to embarrass the prime minister on this score. Fox mocked Pitt's constant alarms over the imminent danger of a popular 1789-style insurrection in England. 'An insurrection! Where is it? Where has it reared its head? Good God, no wonder the militia is called out. But where is it?'

Fox's irony at Westminster, inspired by Pitt's repressive Aliens Bill to control foreigners and his general crackdown on sedition, lost its sting as the revolutionary army surged into the Low Countries and King Louis went to the guillotine – 'the foulest and most atrocious deed', as a shocked Pitt described it. England's leader took these events as full licence to confront the freedom-mongers across the Channel. 'Under the name of liberty they have resolved to make every country, in substance if not in form, a province dependent on themselves,' he told the Commons. Unless they were halted by force, he said, they would destroy 'the happiness of the whole of the human race'. Since human happiness was mostly a matter Pitt's party equated with the protection of worldwide English commercial interests, the nation was able to go to war with a will, upholding what was right. The talkative classes in London coffee houses and clubs grew careful when discussing the fruits of the Revolution for fear of landing in jail.

Danton's grasp of English attitudes was based on the nation's abiding love of reform. And there he was stuck – a shade behind the times. He still imagined that English republicans might win the day.

Dumouriez was an awkward devil. Danton found it hard to catch up with him when he arrived back in Belgium in the company of Lacroix and took up his quarters again in Liège. The general was in Antwerp, having decided to build on his conquest of Belgium by marching north on Holland, an independent state of which England was informal custodian. A certain complicity still joined the two men: Dumouriez valued Danton's practical nature and his swiftness to act, while the statesman was convinced that the general's immense popularity with the troops made him irreplaceable.

However, there was an impediment to their understanding, a large one: the first soldier of the republic continued to despise the republican form of government and was not afraid to say so. Bristling with indignation at the constant interference and contradictory babble of the Convention, he was determined to create war policy himself – the very reason that so many patriots distrusted him and wanted him sacked. Marat was the most insistent, his bony hind newly bruised from an impromptu beating received on the Pont Neuf from a Dumouriez staff officer who saw red at an *Ami du Peuple* article maligning the army head as a traitor. Even when reduced to a hobble, Marat was a redoubtable assailant. His attacks on Dumouriez brought to a head the campaign started by Brissot and the Girondins, and now backed by Robespierre as well.

All the more reason for Dumouriez to suspect that Danton had returned to usurp his authority. Tension between the two was inevitable. It was a relief for Danton, then, that with the general taken up by his latest war plans, he himself was able to concentrate without much hindrance on exhorting the cities and communes of the occupied Habsburg land to vote for integration into France. Progress was 'satisfactory', he was able to report to Paris after a first week, though it was plain that French military occupation was undermining the popular goodwill that the first heady days of the Revolution inspired among Belgians. Moreover, the bullying tactics and thievery of the swarming Jacobin commissars had damaged local sympathies to the point where Danton was obliged to offer financial compensation to maintain a measure of popular enthusiasm for union.

He saw little of Dumouriez, who complained when they did meet about his shortage of manpower, weaponry and supplies while nonetheless poring over his battle plans to conquer Holland. Despite the army chief's privateer methods, Danton rather liked the sound of the Holland invasion. Take Holland, he now reasoned, and England and her commerce were done for: Pitt would fall, his despotic game of buying off Europe to stifle liberty in France an instant failure; in his place, the high-minded Whig liberals who saw good in the Revolution would return from the dead to retrieve power.

This was one way of looking at it. Had Danton known more, though, of what was taking shape in the irascible French soldier's mind he might have turned his attentions to stopping him there and then in his military tracks. For Dumouriez saw large. To trusted fellow officers he sketched out his vision: first take Holland, then abolish Belgium's union with France and merge the province instead with Holland in a Low Countries union; after that, march the French revolutionary army out, reinforce it with Dutch and Belgian troops and descend on Paris to dissolve the Convention and re-erect in its place the constitutional monarchy to which the reformers of 1789 aspired. The anarchic capital with the split Convention at its heart, he had decided, could no longer be allowed to run the Revolution. 'Today's Paris is the most wretched and criminal city that ever existed,' Dumouriez fumed. 'All good men are in hiding, and only fools and rogues are left to govern us.'

The first soldier of the republic now had but one end aim: to destroy his employer.

Danton had no inkling of these highly adventurous intentions. The problem he had to deal with was more limited: the general's undisguised anger with the Convention. He tried to placate Dumouriez in his best jovial manner, throwing a massive arm around him and dining him into a more amenable mood, coupling the bonhomie with the promise of more troops and cannon. It was crucial to mollify him, for Danton feared the revolutionary army would disintegrate without Dumouriez at its head. Thus was the path open to the calamity that the invasion of Holland had in store.

It was while juggling with the grievances of Dumouriez and Belgian aldermen that the Revolution's plenipotentiary received a brief message containing devastating news: Gabrielle Danton was dead. She had died in premature childbirth in the early hours of 11 February. It was now 15 February. On reading the message, Danton let out a howl of pain that terrified those around him. The bull was stunned, the heart bleeding. He ordered his carriage at once and flew back to Paris over the rutted winter roads of Flanders and Picardy, his coachmen driven on by deep sobs coming from the shuttered cabin behind.

It was not in Danton's nature to take his wife's death quietly. He had loved Gabrielle as a wife and mother, adored her; the idea that she could be lost to him, lost to his arms, was unbearable. The knowledge that he had abandoned her when she was weak and so close to giving birth increased his pain. And for what? For the Revolution, yes! But only to put out its distant fires. Not for what mattered most to him.

The dash from Liège got him back to Paris on the evening of 16 February. He found his Cour du Commerce home under seals, a Cordelier magistrate's precaution against violation of the premises in the absence of both master and mistress. He had to wrestle with the door to enter. Gabrielle's body was not there. He learned from Camille, Lucile and Louise, who came down to be with him when they heard the noise, that she had been interred two days ago. Her father, old Charpentier, wished it so. A pair of Cordelier parish priests, clerics now betrothed to the republic, had directed the coffin to their corner church for a blessing, and the Charpentier family, the Desmoulins, the Gélys and Gabrielle's two kitchen maids followed down the tight alley, past printers, bookbinders and Procope cooks fallen to their knees lamenting, 'Oh Madame! Poor Madame!' Monsieur Charpentier had wanted her buried in the church, but there was no Danton family tomb at the Cordelier chapel and since random church burials had been forbidden for some years now, for the sake of public hygiene, Gabrielle was interred in the nearest public cemetery, situated in the Saint-Marcel district, the populous working-class ward neighbouring Danton's Théatre-Français section.

All this Danton listened to while blundering around his home, throwing himself from sofa to bedstead, his great chest jerking, hideous face contorted, as if still hoping to find his wife. He had to see her again.

His reactions were never less than outsize. His body, his face, his energy, his voice, his oratory, his temper, his heart, everything about him was outsize. His impulses overwhelmed him. Yes, he had to see Gabrielle once more. He had to keep her close. Through his tears, a solution formed: he would make a likeness of her, a bust he could for ever embrace and ask for forgiveness. The next evening he hurried to see a sculptor he knew, an artist with a workshop in the Saint-Marcel section. The sculptor shook his head. Madame Danton had been dead for a week, he reminded his frantic visitor, in her grave for three days past. A sculptor needed a mould to make a bust and how could he take the mould after she was buried? Danton implored him, thrusting a sheaf of *assignats*, the new paper money, into his hand. The sculptor may not have been impressed by the paper money, which few Parisians believed in, but the bottomless depths of anguish on his visitor's ghastly face made him give way.

Together – Danton in a dark cloak, the sculptor with his tools – the pair of them hurried that same evening to the public cemetery, banging on the gate for the keeper. A cold February rain greased the dark granite paths between the tombstones. The keeper came to the gate, waving them off, but yielded when he recognised the huge distressed face of the people's champion, the man the papers said was running the Revolution. The three of them were alone in the dark. By torchlight, they found Gabrielle's grave; only a foot of loose earth covered the coffin, for stonemasons had yet to get to work there.

'A spade!' Danton demanded.

The warden held back. He had admitted the giant statesman simply to take a look at the grave.

'A spade!' Danton roared. Within minutes they were at work, digging down to the coffin. Between the three of them they carried the muddied casket into the dry of a cemetery tool shed. At Danton's urging, the keeper searched for chisels to open the lid, a task that took half an hour of careful prising. As the lid came off and Gabrielle's waxen head showed in the flickering torchlight, Danton let out another terrible cry. With his huge fists he fumbled below the corpse and pulled his wife out, imploring her to forgive him, hugging her to him, squeezing her and kissing the stiff grey bloodless lips. With a groan he placed her tenderly on the displaced lid and motioned to the sculptor to do his work.

Did he sense the macabre horror of it? The ghoulishness? With Danton it was no long stretch from outsize to grotesque. It could happen in a speech, as the power of spontaneity reached a scarcely coherent crescendo. Through her opaque loupe, Madame Roland may have missed a lot in Danton, but she did not get him all wrong.

*　　*　　*

Gabrielle's death left its mark on the bonds between revolutionary leaders. Among the letters the stricken Danton found awaiting him on his return from Liège was one from Robespierre, who of course knew of Danton's loss before he did. The Incorruptible, though stilted as usual, was also at his most human. He wrote:

> In this sorrow that alone can break a heart such as yours, if the assurance that you have a tender and devoted friend offers any consolation, then I give it. I love you more than ever, until death. In this moment, I am you. Do not close your heart to an expression of friendship that feels all your pain. Let us weep for our friends and let our deep grief defeat the tyrants who are the cause of all our misfortunes, public and private.
>
> I would have come to see you except for the respect in which I hold your first moments of grief.
>
> Embrace your friend.
>
> Robespierre

The weight of guilt and grief disposed Danton to welcome all condolences, yet it was hard to take Robespierre's entirely at face value. The tone was so unlike the grinding Jacobin he knew. Danton had made up his mind about Robespierre's capacity for human emotions long before. To Camille, who still did his best to think well of their Mountain colleague, he had joked: 'You could tear the flesh off Robespierre and not a drop of patriotism's blood would flow.' But perhaps something ran in those calculating arteries after all. Danton could recall his own surprise at seeing Robespierre dandle Camille's baby son, Horace, on his stiff knee.

Then he corrected himself again. It was more than likely that Robespierre's expression of love had something to do with the Mountain's intensifying conflict with Brissot, Roland, Buzot and company. The Girondins loathed Robespierre no less than they loathed Danton, only the Jacobin leader's carapace of virtue was harder to pierce. Gabrielle's death was an opportunity for the Mountain to strike back at their adversaries, though it was not the Incorruptible but the old Cordelier hand Collot d'Herbois, actor and sometime playwright, who latched on to it. Collot's talents as an adapter of Shakespearean tragedy seemed made for the purpose.

'The Girondins killed her!' he proclaimed at the Jacobin club. Yes, Collot reasoned, there lay the innocent Gabrielle sick in bed, awaiting a difficult birth, her husband absent, and the Roland 'cowards' chose that very moment to exploit her helplessness, inventing yet another story – that Danton in person listed victims for slaughter in the September massacres. 'This infamous allegation came as a death blow when Madame Danton read it in the newspapers. Those who know how much she loved Danton can imagine her suffering!'

Collot's charge struck even the darkly nodding Jacobins as the licence of his craft, though it was true that Roland himself had sharpened the massacre charges against Danton when he was away. Nor did such public dramatisation of his loss do anything to console Danton. What point was there in casting blame for Gabrielle's death on Madame Roland's mouthpieces?

It was hard all the same to accept that the Girondins bore no blame at all. For in the early months of 1793 the split between patriots at the Convention struck Danton as the gravest threat that existed to the brave edifice they had created together. The menace of this period had many sides: the war against the combined might of Europe's monarchs; renewed street riots by Paris sans-culottes in March, looting grocery shops across the capital in protest against the ever-spiralling prices of coffee, sugar, soap and the plainest daily provisions; the onset of civil war now bubbling up from the lower Loire like a poisonous geyser to scald the provinces. Yet none of these, Danton believed, imperilled the republic like the hopeless split at its top. For want of credible executive authority the Revolution seemed on the verge of imploding, yet the combatants at the Riding School, on the right and on the Mountain, for the most part acted blind to the danger.

Danton lay low for a while at the Cour du Commerce, leaving his infant sons with his in-laws at their forest villa at Sèvres on the western outskirts, too stricken even to respond to the soothing call of Arcis. It took startling news from the Low Countries to shake him back into action. Dumouriez had overplayed his hand; the invasion of Holland launched on 19 February was a disaster. All of a sudden the conquering revolutionary army in the north faced a rout. If this was the wider war that many in the Convention cheered on – the war against all Europe – then hostilities were off on the wrong foot.

How quickly the world changed, as Lacroix, still in Liège, informed Danton in a note urging him to return, if only to help take his mind off his personal tragedy. Danton's third trip to Belgium as revolutionary plenipotentiary was hectic and, owing to mounting military setbacks, brief. Heavy of heart, he reached Liège on 5 March and moved on to Brussels the next day.

The go-between role he assumed was most likely beginning to feel beneath his stature as a leader of the republic, yet the security of the *patrie* was at stake. While his chief task, set by the Convention, was to ascertain the effects of the Holland rout, he was also determined to calm the fretting Dumouriez, so as to prevent a complete break between the army head and the authorities at home. As for what was going on, the picture was all too clear: Danton's dash back to Paris not three weeks before, the assault on Holland by the general's main force – a mere 20,000 men – had faltered, then been thrown back from Amsterdam. Dumouriez had turned to the merchants of Antwerp for a huge loan to finance his invasion further north, only to find the resistance of Amsterdam's Dutch defenders mightily stiffened by English gold. Worse followed. The French mishaps in Holland encouraged the Austrian army to hasten back into a now thinly defended Belgium, where the population turned on the remaining French occupation forces as if they were a greater curse than the returning Habsburg soldiery. Popular disillusion over union with France had set in faster than Danton could have imagined, though he perhaps underestimated the depth of ill feeling caused by the pillaging French commissars and the over-hasty imposition of strange French laws, neither of which coincided with Belgian dreams of liberty.

As Danton arrived, Dumouriez was cutting south with his forces in an attempt to retrieve the situation in Belgium. Their paths crossed in Brussels. The general was at his most irate, demanding proper material support from Paris and the scrapping of plans for union. Danton heard him out. He had trouble, though, in rediscovering his joviality towards Dumouriez. What he heard convinced him there was little point in prolonging his stay in Belgium; he knew more than enough of the military situation to inform the Convention of its gravity, and the whole scheme for union was by force of circumstance suspended.

The uproar, the panic, the backbiting in Paris were easy to predict. It was there that the wheels had to be turned to redress the republic's misfortunes.

Did Danton place too much confidence in Dumouriez? Keener observation of the general's personal ambitions, let alone Marat's howls and Robespierre's murmurings for his arrest, might have told him to be more careful with his support. The fact was, however, that the soldier's popularity with his troops, even in retreat, was bound to impress the people's champion from Paris. Danton's populist instinct was even now to keep Dumouriez at the head of the revolutionary army to put things right, and he persisted in telling the Convention so: to sack Dumouriez, he believed, was to betray and demoralise the whole army.

It was a lapse of judgement that came to haunt him. Within ten days of his latest return to Paris, Danton was back yet again in Brussels, appalled en route by the sight of streams of ragged French soldiers – deserters, he learned – heading in the opposite direction. This time he came not to listen to the general but to confront him over a shocking letter he had addressed to the Convention. The Dumouriez letter, dated 12 March, was not yet public knowledge because Convention officials had found the tone so aggressive that they hid it, declining to have it read out to the house and trusting instead that Danton would make the army chief retract it. It could only be read as a declaration of war against the parliament, the foreword to a military *coup d'état*.

The thrust of Dumouriez's missive was that the authorities in Paris had piled error upon error in policy towards the Low Countries, subjecting his armies to intolerable suffering and France herself to imminent ruin. Had he not warned them often enough about his plight as commander? Had he not threatened to resign? He had done everything in his power to make them see the light. Now it was time to tear the blindfold from their eyes. All of them, Convention members, Jacobin club leaders, ministers, all were guilty men – as guilty as the brutish and insolent agents they sent to Belgium with criminal instructions to make the province pay for its liberation. Due to the Convention's blunders, the Belgian dream was dead, the general wrote. 'Terror and I dare say hatred have replaced the happy fraternity that accompanied our first steps into Belgium.'

In both tone and content the letter crashed through barriers of political authority that no republican soldier could be permitted to cross. In vain, Danton, on arrival in Brussels, reminded Dumouriez of the protocol restraints that he was under as army chief, cajoling him, threatening him, subjecting him to his friendly bear hug, his ghastly grimace of man-to-man understanding, imploring him to say he wanted the letter torn up, urging him to write a more accommodating one in its place. Their skirmish lasted for hours – through dinner, through endless rounds of wine – with Dumouriez hardly budging, still complaining bitterly about lack of support from home and cursing the enemy for introducing a new field weapon, an explosive shell, that frightened his conscripts to death. He was undermanned, underfunded and now outshelled. By three in the morning, though, he appeared to soften, showing grudging outward signs of repentance. Danton managed to extract his signature to a six-line note asking the Convention to put the offending letter on hold until he had an opportunity to return to Paris to deliver his criticisms in person.

It was better than nothing. Danton hastened back to Paris with it tucked in his trunk, thinking it should serve both their interests.

It rapidly transpired that he need not have bothered. Dumouriez did not return to Paris. The general suspected that 'the fools and rogues' running the republic's affairs only wanted him back to send him to the guillotine. Forced to evacuate Belgium and pull back to France's northern border after a climactic defeat by the Austrians at Neerwinden on 18 March, he broke the tacit agreement with Danton and grasped at the ultimate fancy of attacking Paris, in the belief that he alone could save the *patrie*. In a circular proclamation addressed to municipal authorities in the north of France, he advised them not to stand in his way: 'Paris is engulfed by tyranny, killing and crime. I shall soon march on the capital to halt the bloody anarchy that reigns there.'

Dumouriez thought he might need help to achieve his desperate purpose, and secretly opened negotiations with the Austrian enemy in the hope they would provide it: his priority was to get the Austrians to agree to let French forces leave Belgium in orderly fashion, giving him a free hand to move on Paris. The Austrians did not disoblige. But if there might have been some small chance of carrying off a *coup d'état* with a victorious army, the chances were less good with the beaten, disintegrating force now at Dumouriez's disposal. His officers hesitated, or point-blank refused, while dejected revolutionary recruits accustomed to marching under 'Liberty or Death' banners generally rebelled at striking this reverse blow for freedom. The deserters Danton saw were thronging the roads and fields of Flanders and Picardy that led home.

The great Dumouriez drew his conclusions, proclaimed his break with the Paris authorities in the last days of March, and on 5 April defected to the Austrian enemy, as transparent a traitor to the republic as Marat had contended.

If Danton failed in good time to recognise the army chief's ambitions for what they were, he had set himself with a will to confronting the wider problems that welled up behind them.

In the spring of 1793 Paris had every reason to panic over the turn of military events. It was as if the pages of the Revolution were furled back by nine months, to the past summer, a time when it was on the verge of collapse and Danton's voice rang loudest in summoning the nation to arms. *Be bold! Bolder still! Ever bolder!* That time, as he had promised, France *was* saved. This time was another matter.

On the borders, the misadventures in the Low Countries left France wide open once more to foreign invasion, while inside the country civil war was spreading apace. Indeed, war within now appeared greater reason for alarm than war without. What had begun as angry clashes in the west between God-fearing peasants and republican guardsmen swelled during March 1793 into an orgy of massacres and full-scale hostilities taking thousands of lives in the swampy Vendée region below the Loire, extending ominously north into Normandy and east, in the direction of the capital. The peasant rebels lined up hapless republicans along the walls of burned-out country chateaux and shot them down to display their own rejection of military conscription imposed to stiffen the republic against its foreign foes. In major provincial cities, meanwhile, anti-revolutionary sentiment was gaining the upper hand: from Lyons and Nantes to Marseilles and Bordeaux, the hungering citizenry was on the brink of outright rebellion against the republic, or over the brink; the people of Toulon threatened to hand over the Mediterranean naval port to the English navy (and would do so by the summer). Counter-revolution was under full sail – for God, for royalty and for the restoration of dishonoured traditions in some minds, in others for a daily crust of bread and for the better times the Revolution promised but seemed unable to supply.

Danton stepped into the crisis with all his familiar vigour, as if this too helped lift his private distress. Paris was well enough acquainted with the Cordelier chief's taste for action to keep looking to him for leadership; his nature was geared to action, as other patriots were given to hope, to dream or to avenge. So in between the third and fourth trip to Belgium he had hardly left the podium at the Convention; his presence dominated every anguished debate. To survive, the republic would have to mobilise for total war – on a scale no other European nation had attempted, or even envisaged. It would require a fresh levy of 300,000 men, raised from every province in the country. For a start, he demanded and obtained an emergency conscription drive in Paris to boost the still-haphazard countrywide call-up in place. No one fired the patriotism of the Paris street quite like Danton. He cried: 'I call on Paris, this renowned city, this much-maligned city, this city whose burning public spirit strikes fear in our enemies, I call on Paris to set the example! I summon Paris once more to save the *patrie*. I summon Paris to give France the invincible elan that brought last year's triumphs.'

Breathless, he prevailed on the house to dispatch commissioners into every section of the capital to call out the citizenry and swear more men into uniform. This was before Dumouriez defected, when Danton had still believed it was not too late to rescue him from his misfortunes in the Low Countries. Indeed, he had kept up an often emotional defence of the general during March, telling the Convention: 'He has glory of the republic at heart.' This, clearly, was tempting fate and Danton would have every cause to regret it.

Still, confronting the many-sided dangers demanded action. He had startled the Convention on 9 March with a novel proposal to further increase army strength. As if the solution had just occurred to him, and its revolutionary truth was apparent, Danton exhorted the house:

What are you waiting for? You want all Frenchmen to take arms for the common defence. Well! There's one class of men who have committed no crime, men who have two good arms to fight but are not free to fight. These are the unfortunates jailed for debt. It is a blot on all humanity, on all social philosophy, that when a man receives money he should have to mortgage his person and his liberty . . . No! I ask the Convention to decree that any citizen imprisoned for debt shall be freed, because such imprisonment is contrary to a healthy morality, contrary to the rights of man and contrary to the true principles of liberty.

Even as Danton bulled on, strained looks would have accompanied the storm of applause. Something was missing from his argument. Yes, the right of private property! That 'sacred right' he himself had urged the republic to adopt as a cornerstone of any workable French constitution, the right which the Revolution had bestowed on the largest class in the land, the great French peasantry. A free pardon for debtors might challenge it head-on.

As often happened, though, when Danton got carried away he was able to check himself in full flight, his native prudence calling him to order. At the very edge of the cliff, his instinct was to take a step back. If he appeared reckless – and he knew that the recklessness increased his popularity with the people – he was also the master of his passions. So while holding to his call to free debtors, he now patted the air with raftlike palms, adding: 'Let not property owners take fright! Yes, a just nation will always respect property. But have respect for misery and misery will respect opulence.'

The adjustment made, his oratory flowed the faster. Seldom, even for Danton, would it ring with such passion as on the following day, 10 March. His lungs were an orchestra trained at the Paris Bar and the Roman Forum: trumpets, drums and cymbals blared as 'the people', 'the *patrie*', 'the republic' entered the score; bass violins led in the oaths. And what was now bringing the Revolution to its knees? The shock military reverses were bad enough. But the war in the Riding School between the Girondins and the Mountain was more damaging still; it obstructed every practical measure devised to safeguard the republic. 'All your arguing is miserable!' came Danton's bass horn. 'I know only the enemy. Let us beat the enemy. You tire me fighting over details instead of fighting for the safety of the republic. You are all traitors to the *patrie*! All of you!' Now he was back at the edge of the cliff. 'I don't care a damn for my reputation. As long as France is free, let my name be reviled. What does it matter if they call me bloodthirsty! Well then, let us drink the blood of the enemies of humanity if need be. Let us fight! Let us win our liberty!'

The Marsh stood to applaud; shrieks of support came from excited working men and women in the public galleries who thumped the balustrades in delight. There were subtler reactions, too, that did not reach the orator's ears: scornful glowers from Brissot, Buzot and Madame Roland's friends, who rightly saw themselves as prime targets of the outburst; and sour stares from Robespierre and the sensitive-looking youth seated beside him on the Mountain, scratching notes, whispering things to the Incorruptible, a boy-statesman all of twenty-five years old with a brilliant debating record that already illuminated his name – Antoine de Saint-Just.

But that was only the beginning of the Convention session held on 10 March. Before it was over the Revolution embarked, at Danton's insistence, on a terrible course that came to define it in history.

# FOURTEEN

# In the Green Room

'I summon all good citizens not to leave their posts.' The bellow from Danton halted members of the Convention in their tracks as they strayed from the benches and shuffled about the high doors of the Riding School, heading for a late supper after that interminable session on 10 March 1793. It was close to midnight, and it was plain to most that their debate on how to counter internal enemies of the Revolution was getting nowhere.

The deputies were exhausted. It was surely time to adjourn. The house was deadlocked, principles and opinions angrily divided. Was it right to hunt down nobles and priests and their sympathisers because they were a potential pool of subversion? No! Well, how else to be rid of them? How to square brutal suppression with liberty? On and on it had gone, never close to a decision.

The thunderous summons from Danton produced a strange silence. The house froze, then members filed back to their seats. He bounded to the rostrum. 'What, citizens! You would think of leaving without taking the great measures which the safety of the republic demands!' He was dismayed by the latest information he had received on the situation in the capital; the Paris sections, worked up by Marat's latest seething commentaries, were evidently planning violent new vigilante action against counter-revolutionaries. Fears on the Paris streets of the terrible retribution that royalists would exact if they got the chance had barely subsided since the great invasion scare of the previous summer. Nerves seemed irreparably frayed. Now those fears were back at fever pitch with the revolutionary armies retreating anew and the wrong side apparently in the ascendancy in an increasingly merciless civil war. To sans-culotte extremists in the rowdier Paris wards the solution looked straightforward: kill those who plot to kill us before it is too late. It was because the Convention was aware of the renewed hysteria that it launched that day's debate on how to deal with suspected counter-revolutionaries, with a general view to pre-empting a further bloodbath in the capital. As for Danton, he was no longer able to spend much time at the Cordelier club, where extremists were taking charge, but he was still close enough to the Paris sections to know what sans-culotte hotheads no doubt had in mind: a repeat of the prison massacres – even an armed assault on the Convention itself to assassinate moderates.

Parliament had to act without delay. Never, Danton saw, had the break-down of authority threatened such chaos. And yet he also saw the start of a solution. He had been mulling it over for weeks. It was time to impose it. In the deep silence created by his summons, with the eyes of the entire house fixed upon him, he demanded:

> Let us now do what the Legislative Assembly did not do. Let us create terror to save the people from doing so. Let us organise a tribunal – it cannot be a perfect one, that is impossible, but the least bad we can make it – and put the sword of justice to the heads of our enemies . . . I demand that this revolutionary tribunal be set up forthwith, at this session, to give government the means of action and the energy it needs.

The harangue, though fierce, was not without tactical balance. The more violent his oratory, the better he thought it could assuage the people's blood-lust. Terrifying measures, extraordinary laws were needed to smash the counter-rebellion at home and ensure public safety. But equally the task of the special tribunal he demanded was to stop the common people from drenching themselves in the blood of those they saw as their enemies. If such a court had existed last September, he argued, facing down the Girondins, who continued to blame him for the prison massacres, then that abominable episode would surely not have occurred. 'No human power on earth was in a position to stop that explosion of national vengeance. Let us learn, then, from the mistakes of our predecessors.'

The Revolutionary Tribunal was not Danton's personal brainchild. The idea had germinated among the Mountain's radicals before civil war became a reality, and it was among proposals vigorously debated during the Convention session on 10 March that accounted for members' fatigue. Danton's role was to get it up and running.

It was, as he publicly acknowledged, a contrivance born of desperation – intrinsically 'bad'. Bad in relation to the high principles of justice. Bad, not least, for the liberties he urged Frenchmen to fight and die for. Its mission was to expedite committed opponents of the Revolution to the guil-lotine, though there seemed plenty of room in its stark statutes to execute in a wink any nobles, churchmen and *Ancien Régime* officials who had not fled – their families, servants, wigmakers and carriage builders with them – as often as not on the strength of telltale denunciations by neighbours and by excited street wardens in the Paris sections. 'Intelligence with the enemy' was the catch-all crime for which suspects would henceforth pay with their heads before baying crowds in public squares across the capital.

To secure the Riding School's acceptance of the tribunal, Danton presented it not as a move to override the existing justice system but to improve it. This was flummery, he knew. But it took sleight of intent as well as a thunderous voice even to attempt to reconcile opposing views on the creation of the special court, for on one side there was Vergniaud, the Girondin oracle, predicting 'an inquisition a thousand times more atrocious than that of Venice', and on the other the Mountain, promising that however bad it was, it would still be too good for the scoundrels it judged.

Only with hindsight did Danton come to realise that the Revolutionary Tribunal he succeeded in pushing through parliament was an agent of vengeance reaching far beyond the goals he had for it. He could not have spent long deliberating on its statutes; perhaps he did not have the time. To Danton, the tribunal was a means of saving the people from taking justice into their own hands; alas, its procedures became as arbitrary as those of any lynch mob. It sat in the Palais de Justice, where the Cordelier giant's political career took root. The Paris Commune, increasingly a friend of violent action, named its three judges. An irritable public prosecutor with a wide jaw and crow-black hair, a farmer's son from Picardy named Antoine Fouquier-Tinville, inaugurated proceedings within three weeks of Danton's demand for its creation, at the end of March 1793 – just as Dumouriez, the first soldier of the republic, was poised to deepen the mood of fear and suspicion in Paris by crossing to the royalist side.

After this, no one, not even the most ardent patriots, could count themselves safe from the guillotine. Unable to lay hands on Dumouriez himself, the tribunal was to take the heads of sixty of his senior officers for fighting under his orders. The sum of a suspect's rights was to be tried before a public jury, but the privilege counted for little since its twelve members were too intimidated by Fouquier and the judges to do anything other than accede to their wishes. The tribunal's rule of thumb was to judge and execute those sent before it within twenty-four hours. The unstinting Fouquier became the incarnation of the Terror that Danton rashly unleashed.

At the time, though, what filled Danton's thoughts was the need to bring effective working order to the floundering Revolution. Like Camille, he would shrug his shoulders over the powers given the special court and tell Cordelier friends over supper at the Cour du Commerce that anyone sent before it deserved to be there; the more it terrified royalist plotters and saboteurs, the better the chances of defeating them. 'It needs splitting into a lot of sections so that every day some scoundrel pays with his head,' he growled, determined not to soften.

Moderate patriots who came to Danton's table without prejudice perceived a strategy through the smokescreen of violent talk. 'He acted barbaric to maintain his popularity,' decided Dominique Garat, his successor at Justice and a regular guest, 'and he wished to maintain his popularity to restore in the people a respect for blood.'

Danton was beginning to regain his old taste for food and wine in that wifeless apartment. It was now two months since he had lost Gabrielle. Once or twice in those hectic days he invited supper guests to come early, and with Fabre, the dilettante dramatist, he took them off to the theatre afterwards, laughing at a playwright's talent for deflating the old aristocracy. Besides café life, the theatre and the arts were lonely survivors of the old order's abundant social pleasures and they flourished for that. No news, however dire, from the foreign front or the Vendée held theatre curtains down. Fabre's own popularity was high: like several other revolutionaries, he was both playwright and professional politician, a winning combination with the public. The more pointed the politics in a play, the more bourgeois audiences flocked to it, leaving their anguish at home. Twitting the Convention also pleased, if the humour was light. After the theatre, Danton would repair with his cronies to the smoky Procope, which he continued to patronise however high his rank, there to ask sterner questions of the Convention. How was a credible government to be carved out of that parrot house? 'We must have a government!' he repeated over and again, jovial but insistent. There was no society without government.

Though without a mistress, the Danton home was not without womenfolk. While the two maids looked after the kitchen, young Louise Gély was there to look after his two infant sons once his Charpentier in-laws returned them to Paris from their suburban haven in Sèvres. Louise said she owed it to her friendship with Gabrielle to care for the children, and her parents – her father was a civil servant at the navy office and a militant Cordelier – had no objection. At sixteen, Louise was a competent girl, slim and nicely turned out in lace bodices and full skirts that reached to the floor. Seemingly she wanted to be pretty in the plain republican attire that had replaced the flesh-flaunting fashions of the past, and she succeeded.

Danton liked to have the blushing adolescent around, though she seemed a little afraid of him. Was it his rank that frightened her? Or his ugliness? Or the blatant bull-maleness that upset Madame Roland? He was young, entering his prime, but still Louise was half his age. She was skinnier and daintier than his bounteous Gabrielle but just as pretty, with large bright eyes and fair hair, dusted in powder, that fell below her shoulders. If anything obstructed his thoughts of constructing a credible government it was Gabrielle's poignant parting jest – or was it a premonition? – about him marrying Louise. Well, it was not the time for that, though he would have watched with more than casual attention as the girl moved about his home, mothering the boys and helping out at the supper table with his guests before retiring for the night, with a courteous smile and a rustle of her long skirt, to the Gély household above. How well Gabrielle had understood him. Inside the ogre she had married, twinned with the Arcis peasant, was a bourgeois with bourgeois desires, and what he needed for comfort and satisfaction was a family hearth and a loving, docile wife.

Had Danton and his articulate friends asked themselves in the fraught spring of 1793 what they wanted as the end result of the Revolution, they would likely have been a little nonplussed, then talked of liberty and the miraculous passing of the old order. Beyond that the vision clouded. The republic was still to produce a new constitution, a fundamental rule book for the nation. What kept Danton atop the tide he rode was more patriotism than passion for revolutionary path-beating, and his patriotism was the will to save *his* new France, to make it a stable home for a free people. Behind his actions, behind his impetuous misjudgements, this was the practical end he sought.

The intimidating powers conferred on the Revolutionary Tribunal had the effect of awakening patriots to the issue that worried Danton most – the lack of political authority in the republic. Thoughtful citizens might disagree on how to correct the problem, but all could see that what passed for government at present was a mass of contradictions that encouraged public disorder and violence. The Convention, the Jacobin club and the Paris Commune were its three pillars; that had not changed since the fall of the throne. But the Convention at the Riding School and the Commune at City Hall frequently came out with conflicting decrees, and while Robespierre's Jacobins, in their monkish sanctuary on the Rue Saint-Honoré, pulled the ideological bell ropes – on education, religion and right-thinking revolutionary society in general – all the club reckoned to govern was men's minds. In the eyes of the people, the Convention (full of Jacobin members) was invested with supreme authority, yet the decisions of its key committees – defence, finance, the market, police, agriculture, constitution – as often as not died amid jealousies and divisions on the floor. At the Commune, the excitable Paris sections created eccentric by-laws they aimed to impose on a nation suspicious of everything the capital stood for, then sent boisterous delegations of sans-culotte petitioners to the Riding School to get what they wanted by noise and intimidation. An executive government did exist in name – the council of ministers, which Danton had led until six months earlier. But since the leading lights of the republic, all of them Convention members, were barred by anterior rules from serving as ministers, it was now a phantom executive without a scrap of moral authority.

Danton had to use extreme care when setting about strengthening government to address the republic's crises. A new system had to be invented, but the merest suggestion that he might be angling to put himself in power was bound to draw furious cries of 'Cromwell' and 'dictator' from the benches on the right. His fearsome physique alone sufficed to invite the taunts. So he put all his eloquence into preparing the ground for the consolidation of government. In March, he had told the Convention:

Yes, citizens. You are failing in your duty. The Revolution can only go forward, can only gain strength through the people. A nation in revolt is like boiling bronze that swirls in the pot. The statue of liberty is not yet cast! The metal bubbles. If you don't keep a watch on the furnace you will all be burned.

The imagery was Danton at his vivid best and to stamping acclaim he went on to argue, more prudent now, that to bar elected leaders from executive government was a squandering of the republic's precious resources. That was the crux of his scheme: 'A new power structure,' as he described it, 'one that still comes under the Convention, which can dismantle it at will . . . one that proscribes dictators and triumvirs but which nonetheless has the power, indeed the duty, to exert fearsome authority.'

The 'new power structure' – the Committee of Public Safety – that emerged on 6 April 1793 was indeed a limb of the Convention, as desired by Danton and the Mountain radicals. It was a committee of nine members whose task was to defend and govern revolutionary France in her hardest hour. This tight ruling body was as much the fruit of Danton's personal quest for practical solutions as was the Revolutionary Tribunal. Although Robespierre from the Jacobin pulpit supported the principle of strong government, he at first kept at arm's length from the new committee, obsessed with fears that he would be assassinated if at this fevered juncture he took too visible a hand in running the country.

The Committee of Public Safety nonetheless ranked above all other Riding School committees and became in a matter of weeks the supreme hub of power in France, supplanting not only the Paris Commune but the full Convention to which it was supposed to answer. It stood over political decision-making as the Revolutionary Tribunal stood over justice. And fiercely as Danton swatted aside the dictator taunts, adamantly as he assured the house that he was not asking to lead anything, his protestations did not deter him from assuming its leadership, for the Convention foisted it on him.

In April 1793 Danton was back at the head of France. He was now thirty-three years old.

The Committee of Public Safety was a political oddity. It contained not a single Girondin. Was this why there was something chilling in its bland title? Its composition carried the ominous hint that one side of the Revolution was about to be obliterated. The vocal cords of those gentlemen reformers who had had the greatest say in directing the republic were as if severed at a stroke. They kept talking, but from now on Girondin commands went unheard. Moreover, the process that ruined Roland, Brissot and company was entirely democratic. The worried brethren of the Marsh, who accounted for half the votes in the Convention, for once sided en bloc with the fiery 'Montagnards' in naming the nine men to rule revolutionary France.

Though none of the nine was formally appointed to head the committee, Danton was the most renowned of them, the most popular with the masses, and his overwhelming presence placed him in charge from the start. He had, after all, taken the leading role in creating the new executive. Among prominent Montagnards elected with him – none of them wild men – were Lacroix, his fellow Low Countries plenipotentiary, Joseph Cambon, an expert in finance, and Bertrand Barère, a fairly recent convert from the right. With familiar brio, Danton proclaimed the ruling committee's mission: 'Vanquish our enemies, restore internal order and make a good constitution.'

This was demanding work. Initially the theatre of operations was a gilded rectangular salon with polished mirrors and rich green carpet on the first floor of the Tuileries – a room at the heart of King Louis' former private chambers. In light of the taunts thrown at Danton that he wanted to be king, it seemed an odd choice of venue. Perhaps it merely underlined how absurd he found such accusations. His personal 'ministry' within the committee was foreign affairs, which gave him the main say over the prosecution of the war and strengthened his overall influence.

The Committee of Public Safety left no time for rest. It convened each day to an eccentric rhythm set by members' continuing outside activities. All its sessions were closed; there was no fixed agenda, no order of speaking, no records kept of what was said across the green baize of its oval table; only its torrent of decrees was made public. Danton's carriage drew up in the Tuileries courtyard in mid-morning to get each session under way and thereafter members came and went from the green room through the day as they left to join important debates at the Riding School – a constant call on Danton – or club events at the Jacobins and the Cordeliers. Members who were still present broke for dinner at 5 p.m., each going his own way. At 8 p.m. all nine reconvened and remained locked together to hammer out urgent decrees into the early hours of the next day.

Danton brought all his passion for swift action to the task. On average the committee issued thirty decrees per day for rubber-stamping by the Convention, topping sixty at its most prolific, whether it was raising troops, ordering up military equipment, naming young generals to repair the wreckage left by Dumouriez, tightening security measures at home, dispatching troops and commissioners to halt reverses in civil-war zones, ensuring bread supplies or holding down bread prices. Behind most of its decrees was the intention, one way or another, to stoke up the atmosphere of fear in which enemies of the Revolution lived. Danton harangued, coaxed, bullied and caressed the committee into doing what he thought necessary. He was seldom home at the Cour du Commerce before 2 a.m.

The frenzied recruitment campaign which Danton had launched in the past summer and autumn was still insufficient to ensure the safety of the republic in 1793. In the green room he set about creating a whole new republican army, a people's army formed exclusively of sans-culottes with Montagnard officers. He had faith in sans-culotte valour. 'Each one of our soldiers believes he is worth two hundred slaves,' he told the Convention. 'Your armies did miracles when facing the worst. Think what they will do when they're well supported.' The objective was to raise a further 400,000 new recruits to hold the frontiers and beat back the rising counter-revolution, which Robespierre and Marat, in equally pressing terms, pledged with him to destroy.

This was mobilisation on a scale never before seen, not in France, not anywhere – a *levée en masse*, total war. When voted into law in the summer of 1793, it made every male citizen of soldiering age permanently liable for conscription – the young to fight, married men to make weapons. Legions of commissars appointed by the Committee of Public Safety scoured every corner of the country from Lorraine to Gascony and Brittany to Provence enforcing it. It was a pity that the great manpower call only deepened popular grievances in the rebellious west and the provincial cities that baulked at rule by revolutionary firebrands in Paris, for resentment over such levels of conscription intensified the civil war. It could not be helped. The *levée en masse* was a firewall against the collapse of the republic.

Hard as he pressed on mass conscription, Danton appeared remarkably conciliatory in foreign relations, his broader personal charge. That disaster in the Low Countries had come as a terrible shock. It made him more realistic. Perhaps now was the right time, he thought, to make a hostile and horrified Europe think a little better of the Revolution. Indeed, England and her allies, even the Austrians and the Prussians, had always painted a false picture – for their own ends – of the French people's great thrust for liberty. As he had told himself when last at France's head six months before, peace with England could only be of immense practical benefit to the Revolution, for with it the worst of outside pressures was removed.

But that was before Danton had lost his head on news of Dumouriez's first stirring triumphs, before he proclaimed those extended 'natural frontiers' for the *patrie* that so upset the rest of Europe. Experience had brought a further change of mind. Natural frontiers did not look so compelling now. If there was anything remotely positive to be gleaned from the Low Countries disaster, it was that London ought no longer feel so imperilled by the Revolution, with Antwerp back in dependable hands. And was there not something to be salvaged with Austria regarding Marie-Antoinette? Since King Louis' execution, his young widow had remained locked up with the eight-year-old dauphin in her dismal tower at the Temple, contemplating the same fate. Danton had no desire to send Marie-Antoinette to the guillotine; the prospect repelled him. She was in a pitiful situation. If the Austrian court were to recover the Revolution's prize hostage alive, things could look different to an enemy whose troops were back in France occupying the northern frontiers and mobilising for an onslaught on Paris.

A chance to turn European minds had come unexpectedly, thanks to Robespierre, in a Convention debate on the death penalty on 13 April. The Incorruptible, with the stripling Saint-Just in support, demanded death for any 'cowards' who proposed bargaining with enemies of the republic. Danton's ears pricked up. He had just come across to the Riding School from the Committee of Public Safety, which he had been heading for only a week, and here was this fish-eyed fellow Montagnard pulling the rug from beneath his diplomatic feet. Was it deliberate? Danton couldn't tell, though it was prudent to suspect there was cold calculation in anything Robespierre proposed. Since there was little to gain from confronting the Jacobin captain head-on, Danton came at him by a route layered with a characteristic sarcasm that delighted the house.

Taking the rostrum in a new red frockcoat hastily tailored for his Public Safety function, he plunged into a spontaneous analysis of war objectives. It was time for realism. Time, he said, to put aside the dream of freeing other peoples from their tyrannies by force of arms. Turning his mangled smile on the house, Danton observed that the notion of liberating enemies, while no doubt inspired by the finest of motives, was born in a moment of starry-eyed enthusiasm. Naturally, the republic would dispatch an army to China if rebels staged an insurrection there! He looked up to the rafters, shaking his massive head. No, France would prevail by example, not conquest:

It is time, citizens, for the Convention to show Europe that it knows how to match policy to republican virtues. First and foremost, we must think of restoring government and French grandeur. Let the republic consolidate, let France attract the whole world by her shining spirit and energy . . . Let us decree that we shall not interfere in the affairs of our neighbours! But let us also decree that the republic shall live! That we condemn to death anyone who would propose a transaction [with the enemy] that is not based on securing our principles of liberty.

The closing proviso dealt with Robespierre's irritating blast, though this was no longer Danton's first purpose. His objective had turned, even as he spoke, to letting the world know that France's new government believed the best way to save the republic was to make it succeed at home.

Danton's intervention on 13 April aroused great interest in foreign capitals, not least in London. Here was the man holding the reins of the cursed Revolution turning from aggression to what sounded like a peaceable course. Fox and England's liberal grandees, though disconcerted by what they were hearing of a slide into some sort of officially sanctioned terror across the water, saw a chance to unsettle their adversary Pitt in his war policy; they sent Danton a letter praising his 'wise' stand, calling it a move towards peace. Moreover, Antwerp's fortuitous return beneath England's wing was a gratifying development for London opinion.

Having obtained Europe's ear, Danton assembled those younger members of the old order's diplomatic corps who were still available and sent them secretly around the continent's capitals large and small, hoping their *savoir faire* might pay off in negotiations, for this was no job for the Revolution's rough-tongued commissars from the Paris sections. There were bites from the allies, particularly from the Prussians, who at once agreed to talk about talks. In smaller capitals, in Stockholm, Naples and Florence, negotiations centred on likely allied responses to the liberation of Marie-Antoinette, a prospect for which Austria seemed ready to forgive France a lot.

Alas, Pitt remained unmoved. He refused to believe that a regime he held to be founded on terror and expropriation could last. If the war was to end, it had to end on England's terms: the reversal of the Revolution. It was too dangerous to change policy on the strength of a gentler roar from the bull leader of the republic. Nor was Pitt encouraged by France's extraordinary turn to mass military mobilisation, whatever else Danton's dictatorial committee might say about abandoning the Revolution's aggressive dreams. Surely, no civilised nation had ever resorted to the extreme of turning the entire male population into soldiers.

Rather as Pitt envisioned it, life for the people of Paris grew more fearful by the day as spring turned to summer in 1793. The population seemed haunted. As a resident in the heart of the capital, Danton watched the mood darken. He wondered what part of the blame he carried.

He was aware that his dire oaths expressed rather more than he intended. 'Take my head if I'm a moderate', 'Kill me if I lack in patriotism', 'Let me die if I am wrong': these were phrases that formed in his lungs, expelling themselves while his brain rushed on. He was very often surprised by Camille's vehemence too: Camille was for executing the Girondins, every one of them, Madame Roland included, and of course Danton did not believe for a moment that his romantic friend meant it. All the same, the word now on everyone's lips, the word bandied around with some relish among the radicals of the Mountain, seemed an apt description of what haunted Parisians: 'terror'.

Danton had only to step into the stench of the Cour du Commerce to be assailed by citizens in grubby red bonnets pulling at his arm, demanding bread and denouncing neighbourhood traitors in the same breath. They said they were on their way to the revolutionary committee installed at the Cordelier hall to name names: the iron merchant who 'acted high and mighty' with his workers; the timber trader who asked to be addressed as 'Monsieur'; the master watchmaker who put on 'arrogant airs, and spoke with irony'; the ministry official who hoarded food in his cellar. Traitors all! To the guillotine!

Danton would shrug his shoulders. If they were guilty, they deserved what they got. In the street, he left it at that. The Paris poor had high regard for the guillotine; it was the avenging angel of the sovereign people. The 'People's Axe', they called it, the 'Scythe of Equality'. There were endless popular names for it. They loved that gaunt machine of death. What better end for that class of citizens they resented the most, the *rentiers*, the 'selfish rich' who lived off their income without soiling their hands – the nobles, yes, but worse still the speculators and landlords risen from their own class.

Compared with most of the Left Bank's rank airless alleys, the Cour du Commerce was fairly well swept, though its most famous resident noticed the sans-culottes holding their pikes high off the ground as they accosted him with their grievances and made off through the day's accumulating excrement to report to their revolutionary committee. These were the people in whose name Danton had cut his revolutionary path. Even the most militant and outspoken of them were no more than half-literate, which was a blessing for the cruder end of the Paris press. For their scant education conferred enormous leverage on Marat and his blunt prose in the *Ami du Peuple.*

Marat was not the only beneficiary. The ripe man-in-the-street language of the equally popular *Père Duchesne* made its publisher, Jacques-Réné Hébert, his rival in extremism. Hébert, a Norman goldsmith's son who had come late to the Revolution, was masterful at echoing the prejudices of the sans-culottes, and his influence had recently given him a hold on the Cordelier club – and indeed on the Paris Commune. *Père Duchesne* provided pat solutions to issues that confounded the Convention: the way to deal with counter-revolutionaries, royalists and hoarders, its publisher proposed, was to rope them together, lock them in churches and blast them with cannon until peace was achieved. 'That's the Public Safety I want.'

Danton and his friends, Robespierre too, could agree with Marat and Hébert on one thing: the sans-culottes were an indispensable force in revolt. Agreement ended there. To Marat's kind, the Paris masses were there to exploit, to excite into producing ever greater anarchy and mayhem. The Girondins, though, while ruefully recognising sans-culotte power, generally held the working class in contempt, concerned to keep the republic out of the rude hands of street battlers. To Danton, the people *were* the Revolution: they were the tide he had jumped upon and he respected its force; no make-or-break revolutionary action was possible without the people. The hard thing was somehow to direct it – to ride the wave to a safe shore. But how?

The time that wrote its sinister name in history as the Terror got under way in earnest in the summer of 1793, with the ogre from Arcis at the head of the Revolution. In truth, terror was a new departure only in men's frightened discussions, for it was part of the revolt against the *Ancien Régime* from the start. Its seed was the question that indeed haunted common folk: who is going to stop us? Who is going to take us back to where we were? It is obvious who! So let us stifle them, snuff them out, kill them!

Terror was there at the smoking Bastille; it was there as drenched women drove the royal family from its resplendent seat in Versailles; it was there in street lynchings, in the hunt for bread, in severed heads suspended from Paris lamp posts, in the carnage at the Champs de Mars, the climactic 10 August onslaught on the Tuileries Palace, the September prison massacres that followed and the joyous promenading through the streets of Paris of the Princesse de Lamballe's filleted heart. And as Danton questioned himself on what part of the blame he carried, he could hardly miss the fact that the opening of the Revolutionary Tribunal had institutionalised the haphazard mix of political events, popular fury and revenge and given it a name.

Before working up the rapid rhythm that became its trademark, the Tribunal had made an almost lethargic start in mid-spring 1793. The first suspects it dealt with – individuals, couples, blueblood families – passed from the defendant's bench to the guillotine at the rate of a dozen or so persons a week, delivered to Fouquier, the chief prosecutor, from the prisons, by vigilante committees in the Paris sections and in some cases on the recommendation of the Convention and Danton's ruling committee. Now and then civil servants from the old order defeated the object of the Tribunal by getting themselves cleared, but that was before Fouquier truly mastered his art.

At first Danton was not averse to Fouquier as chief prosecutor. For one thing, he represented a small reverse for Robespierre, whose own candidate for the post, an expatriate Belgian from his close Jacobin circle, failed to win by a single vote. Once in office, however, Fouquier, who was nearing fifty, proved eminently acceptable to Robespierre, so that the only reason Danton had to favour him was that he appeared to be a distant cousin of Camille, who spoke up for him as a fellow Picard. The tall, angular chief prosecutor was a strange fellow. In court he looked like a vulture, with the black feather of office in his hat and black eyebrows so bushy that they almost knit with his thick black hair to conceal his forehead. He was a former police clerk who rose in revolutionary ranks through diligent work in the Paris Commune. At work in the Tribunal, his attention never slipped for a second. From his superior height he fixed defendants with a dark unwavering look until they lowered their eyes, at which point his accusing index finger rose to destroy them.

Exterminating 'enemies of the people' became Fouquier's whole life. At cruising speed six months into his mission he struck a rate topping fifty heads per week in Paris alone – royalty, blueblood soldiers, politicians, common folk who said the wrong thing before the wrong ears. He moved into sepulchral rooms at the Palais de Justice, where the Tribunal sat, leaving a wife and five children at home. The work consumed him. When not in court Fouquier was working up charges against suspects, tabulating denunciations from revolutionary committees and police informers in the Paris sections, writing orders to executioners for their next day's appointments and – each night without fail – taking the short carriage ride from the Palais de Justice to the Tuileries, to report on that day's tally to the Committee of Public Safety and hear its members' personal recommendations, for he developed the disconcerting habit of assuring the nine men each night that he would do exactly what they required of him. What patriot could blame the obsessive Fouquier if he stopped his carriage at a wine tavern on the way back from his late consultations at Danton's oval table? He invariably arrived alone at close to midnight, needing refreshment. Alas, the cheap tavern wine was bad for him, his bailiffs lamented, and as he returned for a final visit to the office he habitually made a scene, tearing folders, crushing boxes and dressing down underlings he insisted on keeping up until he went to bed.

It was hard to fault Fouquier in his professional endeavours, though. He was peculiarly fearsome – a zealous servant doing what was requested of him. He struck terror into the hearts of royalists who looked to civil war to overturn the republic. His performance followed Danton's original prescription to the impetuous letter.

Still, Danton applied the brakes to the Tribunal juggernaut when he saw it charging too far off course. He did not want it crushing loyal patriots who somehow found themselves in its path, whether his friends or his enemies. And what if he himself were the target! Among his most bitter Girondin critics were Breton representatives who even now talked of putting him before the Tribunal for supposed complicity with Dumouriez. So he contrived to pull his old antagonist Roland clear when petitioners from the Halles grain market burst into the Convention in early May calling for the Girondin leader to be delivered to Fouquier on some vague charge regarding past food distribution. On the other hand, this was no time to cross the sans-culottes. Danton was a master at appearing to speak on one side of an issue while in fact speaking on another. He never put the common people in the wrong. Ignore them and there was no prospect of prevailing either in the wars at home or against Europe's crowned heads. The great minds in the Riding School had to remember that. He kept drumming it into members: they must *be* the people, stay close to the people. They weren't fathers of the people; they were its children. A little excess on the people's part was only to be expected: 'When a people breaks the monarchy to create a republic it overshoots the goal by the very force of its momentum.'

Though he pulled Roland from Fouquier's clutches, and later spoke out against putting suspects on trial merely for uttering 'ill-digested phrases', he was in general very careful about blocking petitions from the Paris sections against supposed traitors. His position was: let the people's demands take their course. 'I know how this great drama will turn out. The people will stay free! I want the republic!'

At the head of the table in the green room, Danton was a hostage to contradiction. A conflict churned within him. He scorned government by fear, was repulsed by it, yet felt somehow compelled to roar it on.

# FIFTEEN

# *Exit Moderates*

It amazed Danton that the Girondin leadership – men (and, of course, a woman) of high ideas – could be so obtuse. There were not two but three wars he had to fight: after the monarchs of Europe and counter-revolution at home, he had a war on his hands against avowed republicans whose philosophy he fundamentally shared. He was with them on property, on education, on religion, on all manner of items that were going into the republic's slow-born constitution. How hard he had tried to bring them round. Perhaps Madame Roland, her husband and her adoring Buzot were beyond reach, but surely other leading Girondins could be made to see that their refusal to lock arms with fellow patriots in this perilous hour spelled doom for the new France they had created – and that their own doom would in all likelihood precede it.

Danton had done his damnedest to work for a truce. On the eve of his final trip to Belgium in early March 1793, heartbroken by Gabrielle's death not a month before, he and Camille had set up a secret meeting with the Girondins away from the angry ballyhoo of the Riding School. It took place a few miles outside the city walls at Sceaux, in a village house owned by Lucile's mother, Madame Duplessis. The Girondins who came were the movement's more approachable leaders, men whom Danton had dealt with, befriended even, before relations soured. Brissot and Vergniaud were there, and so was the courtly constitutionalist Condorcet, and Pétion, the Mayor of Paris. These were men of the progressive bourgeoisie with a dash of nobility in their ranks who did not necessarily share the Roland couple's snobbish abhorrence for Danton and the radical Jacobins. Still, the attempt at reconciliation failed. Danton was saddened: there was common ground, to be sure, but his adversaries refused to bury the hatchet with the Mountain, insisting that a truce would amount to giving immunity to the 'savages' who abetted the prison massacres, which they would not permit.

These Girondins were bitten after all by the Rolands' intractability.

They wanted power for themselves. Danton could not hide his frustration. To hell with them. They counted themselves reasonable men! Moderates! Their intolerance was criminal! And in a parting shot at Brissot, who had been particularly obstinate, he grasped his arm and said, 'You are wrong. You do not know how to forgive. You are pig-headed and you will die for it.' It was no threat, merely an awful premonition.

Danton's return to the head of the Revolution in the green room at the Tuileries was particularly hard to accept for the gentlemen Girondins who claimed paternity of the republic. It made their own abrupt exclusion from power all the more galling. Hostilities with Danton had reached a blazing climax at the Riding School just as the Revolutionary Tribunal got under way, for its creation fed feverish fantasies about who should be put before it.

A first candidate was the Duc d'Orléans, now Citizen Egalité, whom few cared to support these days, certainly not Danton, who had come to believe by now that the scourge of the Bourbons had in fact reverted to royal type and was secretly supporting the uprising in the west. Whatever his fault, the duke, in whose pleasure grounds the Revolution germinated, would be arrested on 5 April, after a snap vote by the Convention at Robespierre's behest, with Danton's full accord. The duke was a prize catch for Fouquier, though he was dispatched to prison in Marseilles out of the guillotine's immediate reach, this time at Danton's behest.

The Girondins had aimed for a still bigger catch for Fouquier. Having watched their war for universal liberty go disastrously wrong, they funnelled their bitter disappointment into an all-out assault on the largest of the Montagnards, Danton himself. His crime? High treason. Protecting the turncoat Dumouriez and refusing to arrest him while there was still time.

From the outset Roland and company were not on the firmest ground here. For one thing, in a moment of high drama at the end of March, Danton had been able to disclose to the Convention that Dumouriez had shown him a private letter he had received from Roland himself, a letter that concluded, 'You must join us in crushing this Paris party, and above all Danton.' Where, then, did the complicity lie?

Danton was beside himself with indignation. On 1 April he lowered his horns in fury, sarcasm and patriotic passion, and by the time his performance was over the Girondins were as good as finished as a revolutionary force. To make sure the performance had maximum effect, he had employed his favourite oratorical device – setting out his case in a preliminary session and whetting the public appetite for more by promising to get to the bottom of the matter in the following session, to establish where guilt truly lay.

A packed house was assured. Though it would still be a few days before Dumouriez joined the Austrian side, the public evidence that he intended to do so was already incontrovertible. At first, then, the high-treason motion appeared to place Danton on the defensive, for it was true that he had backed Dumouriez almost to the bitter end, which required an explanation. It was also true that long after Robespierre and Marat began clamouring for the soldier's head, Danton had continued to vaunt his military genius.

His defence was robust. Yes, he had admired Dumouriez's soldiering talents. He had lost faith in him, however, on his final hectic visit to Belgium, deciding it was time to arrest him and put him on trial; he had so informed the Riding School's defence committee on his return to Paris, and its records would confirm it. The general had become deranged, exposing himself as an outright enemy of the Convention and refusing to bow to 'an asylum of three hundred imbeciles led by four hundred brigands'. Why, then, had he not put Dumouriez under arrest when he was there on the spot as commissioner in Belgium? Well, that would have been difficult, Danton said, with a huge broken smile. He was no weakling himself, but there were physical considerations. It was not like arresting someone in the Faubourg Saint-Germain. This had been in a war zone and Dumouriez was surrounded by loyal officers protecting him. Besides, he would have had to pull the general off his horse to arrest him, for he was in the saddle day and night during that last visit, fighting one rearguard skirmish after another. 'Our duty was to combine prudence with republican firmness. If Dumouriez had been removed from the army in its presence, there would have been good reason to blame the army's disarray on the imprudence of your commissioners.'

No, he had not arrested Dumouriez, because to do so was impossible.

There were holes in the defence. The Girondins took his irony as a sign of embarrassment. They imagined they had him when the house voted to create a commission of inquiry into the general's defection. Danton's indignation was running so high, however, that he hardly bothered to tie up the loose ends. How dare the Girondins accuse him of treason! They were the traitors, and he would show the nation why. It was true that Dumouriez was gulled into treachery – but by them, not by him. They were the errant general's original allies. They were the most eager to court him; they monopolised his schedule when he was in Paris. And over their cosy suppers they ran down the Convention, they ran down the Jacobins and Cordeliers, they ran down Paris and they poisoned public opinion in the provinces against the capital. How different was this from betraying the Revolution? From encouraging the enemy in the civil war?

The closing stages of Danton's marathon riposte on 1 April produced the grandest, ugliest piece of theatre the Convention had yet witnessed.

The Girondin leaders left it to a tenacious lawyer, Marc-David Lasource, a deliberate speaker, to set out their side's treason case against him, and for good measure Lasource threw in the old accusation that never ceased to rile Danton – that he wanted to be king:

**Lasource**: Here is my argument. I say a plan was made to restore the throne, and Dumouriez was behind that plan. What was required to make it work? That Dumouriez be kept at the head of the army. Danton has been at the rostrum singing the praises of Dumouriez—

**Danton**: That is false! (*Shouts of 'false', 'lies' from the Mountain.*)

**Lasource**: I demand, then, in order to prove to the nation that we shall never capitulate before a tyrant, that each one of us here swear death to any man who would try to make himself king or dictator. (*Unanimous applause, members stand shouting 'Yes, yes!', placing hands oath-wise across their chests.*)

**Girondin voice**: Fabre, Danton's friend, has proposed a king—

**Danton**: This is vile rubbish! You have defended the king and now you cast your crimes upon us. (*Uproar, the president tries in vain to intervene.*)

**Lasource**: I demand that Danton be heard, and I assure you that I speak without passion.

**Danton**: (*Bounding to the rostrum, eyes turned to the left of the chamber.*) Citizens of the Mountain! You have been a better judge than I. For I have long thought that however impetuous my character I must temper the weapons nature has bestowed on me, that in the difficult circumstances in which my mission has placed me I should employ the moderation I presumed events called for. You have accused me of weakness and you are right. I admit it, before all France. For our task is to denounce those who through rashness or villainy always wanted the tyrant to escape the sword of justice. Well, here are those men! (*Swings to the right amid violent protests from that side.*) Yes, citizens, the same men who today assume the insolent role of accusers . . . Why do I abandon my course of silence and moderation? Because there is a limit to prudence, because when you are attacked by those who ought to applaud your circumspection, you have the right to attack in turn and to lose all patience—

**Girondin voice**: Don't talk so much. Answer!

**Danton**: I? Want a king? Only those stupid enough, craven enough to want to accommodate a king can be suspected of wanting to restore the throne . . . Only those who have clearly wanted to punish

Paris for its civil courage, to rouse the provinces against it— (*Huge commotion, members rise, pointing at the Girondins.*)

**Marat**: And their little suppers!

**Danton**: Only those who had secret suppers with Dumouriez when he was in Paris—

**Marat**: Lasource! Lasource was one of them. Aah! I shall denounce all the traitors.

**Danton**: Yes, they alone are accomplices in conspiracy. And it is me they accuse! Me! Well now! I say there can be no truce between the Mountain, between the patriots who wanted the death of the tyrant, and the cowards who have defamed us in all France in their effort to save him. We shall save the *patrie*!

**Girondin voice**: Cromwell!

**Danton**: What rascal calls me Cromwell? I cite you before the nation. (*Cries from the left for the culprit to be thrown into the Abbey prison.*) Yes, I demand that the foulmouth who has the gall to call me Cromwell be punished. To the Abbey with him! (*A hush as Danton strikes a calm pose, about to finish.*) I have taken my position in the citadel of reason. I shall come forth with the cannon of truth and pulverise the villains who accuse me.

The trumpet-blast finale brought Montagnards and citizens of the Marsh surging to his side; they embraced him, struggling mightily to lift his ox frame to their shoulders. Robespierre too would have joined the celebration in his manner, smiling a thin smile, extending an arm in tribute. Was he playing over to himself Danton's public admission that he, Robespierre, scourge of moderates, was the 'better judge' of things? The admission pleased him.

Thereafter the end of the Girondins came with cruel speed. They had succeeded in setting Paris against them and the people of Paris were unforgiving. The more spirited Danton grew in his praise of Paris, the deeper their jeopardy grew. For the sans-culottes, with their weight in the Paris sections, were working up that extra ounce of fury needed to get rid of them, by their own methods.

Madame Roland could turn up her beautiful nose at demagoguery and popularity-chasing, but Danton's belief in Paris was as heartfelt as it was practical. The tug of the Champagne country could not shake it. Indeed, the country roots were part of it, because it was his belief that what Paris had achieved through insurrection was good for every last province in France. Without the flood of volunteers from Paris there would have been no triumph at Valmy, no miraculous respite from foreign invasion. 'The republic has no worse enemies,' he declared with passion to the Riding School, 'than those who refuse to grasp that if Paris were to perish there would be no liberty in all the land. For there can be no liberty where there is no centre of enlightenment that draws on the lights of all our regions.' No, to hate Paris was to subvert the Revolution.

The Rolands and Brissotins raised a last hurrah in their battle with the Mountain; it was doomed to fail but it did not lack audacity. Already sinking, conspicuously excluded from Danton's new executive government, they went for the head of another idol of the street people – this time Marat, who had been branding *them* traitors ever since the king's execution. With assistance this time from the Marsh, where Marat was held in unanimous contempt, they managed to win a vote to send the voice of the *Ami du Peuple* before the Revolutionary Tribunal for acts of violence he had inspired and abetted. Danton had not remotely warmed towards Marat – to his mind he was still the malodorous homunculus who had spent too long in dank cellars – but he saw nothing to be gained from a Girondin resurrection at the expense of the scurrilous Montagnard. If they succeeded in eliminating Marat, they would surely come back for himself.

So it was that after Fouquier next came to the green room in the Tuileries for his nightly consultation, he went away knowing enough not to affect his standard dark stare when Marat entered the dock. Marat made the most of his acquittal on 24 April. He trotted in his soiled green frockcoat at the head of a triumphant sans-culotte procession from the Tribunal to the floor of the Riding School, where he bowed and clapped to the acclaim of the Mountain, still surrounded by pike-bearing insurgents from the street. The Girondins sat mortified. Since he had had a hand in the acquittal, Danton peppered his congratulations with sarcasm, hoping it would get the street people to leave: 'What a fine spectacle it is for all good Frenchmen to see the citizens of Paris demonstrating such high respect for the Convention that it becomes a public holiday when an accused deputy returns guiltless to its breast.'

This was making light of the episode, for Marat's acquittal was the trigger for an explosion of sans-culotte vengeance. Mad Tom Paine, who frequently sat with the Girondins and found himself branded a traitor too, saw it coming. He was already thinking of packing his revolutionary bags and returning not to Pitt's England, where he faced imprisonment for sedition, but to the United States. He wrote to Danton, 'I am exceedingly disturbed at the distractions, jealousies, discontent and unease that reign among us and which, if they continue, will bring ruin and disgrace on the republic . . . Such abominable internal aberrations discourage the progress of liberty all over the world.'

Danton could not have agreed more with his English ally of old. The incestuous political warring was indeed ruinous. Whose fault was it? Not his. He had implored the Girondins to compromise in order to protect the republic. Nonetheless, he remained a great admirer of the author of *The Age of Reason* and he weighed every word in Paine's letter. Perhaps because they came from an outsider, Paine's words stuck. Danton promised himself to shield the Englishman from personal danger if he could.

By chance, Madame Roland was among the first of the Mountain's adversaries to be eliminated from the Revolution. On the evening of 31 May, a rainy Friday, she was at home, alone, when Commune bailiffs came to the Rolands' latest apartment on the Rue de la Harpe, on the edge of the old Cordelier district. The couple had taken the apartment on the Left Bank merchant street after Roland grudgingly stepped down from Interior, obliging them to decamp from the ministerial suite in which her salon had acquired its full republican prestige. In the lesser glow of the Rue de la Harpe, the salon was taking a rest, awaiting better times.

Madame Roland was expecting the bailiffs' visit. They held a warrant for her husband, who had been tipped off that they were coming and had gone into hiding in a friend's cellar on the Paris outskirts. They left empty-handed on this first call, almost apologetic, as if relieved not to have had to arrest the ex-minister, their old employer. Later that night, though, they returned under the rain to arrest *her* – on suspicion of treason – and escorted her in a shabby police carriage to the nearby Abbey prison, which housed enemies of the Revolution.

There was nothing she could do to prevent it. The Paris sections had decided it. Legal recourse no longer existed. She was convinced she knew, though, who her captor was, pointing a slender finger at the 'coarse half-Hercules' she'd been fighting with for the past two years. 'I feel his hand tightening the irons that chain me, as I recognised his inspiration in Marat's first attacks against me,' she wrote as she collected her thoughts in prison. In her eyes, Danton was the cruel tyrant behind all her side's misfortunes. 'His intrigue keeps the people in ferment. His genius rules the committee they call Public Safety, in which all government power is concentrated. All order is gone and bloody men reign. Deceived by such a master, France is torn apart, exchanging one oppressor for another. That is Danton!'

This was unfair. Danton had no direct part in her arrest. But as ever in her strange dance with the Cordelier giant, Madame Roland exaggerated the turns. For all that divided them, they had this in common: they delivered opinions with purple abandon. What now put her and the entire

Girondin leadership behind bars, or on the run, was out of Danton's hands. The purge that eliminated them was organised and conducted by the sans-culottes of the Paris sections, backed by the cannon of a compliant National Guard. It would have been sheer revolutionary suicide for Danton, or for Robespierre, to stand in its way.

This was the tide in full flow. In mid-May the Convention had moved house from the Riding School to the old royal theatre at the Tuileries, re-constructed to improve conditions for deputies and the overflowing public gallery. On the day of Madame Roland's arrest the sans-culottes gave the new parliament a baptism of fire. Tocsins rang the alarm across the city that morning as street hordes bearing rifles and pikes besieged the building, demanding the heads of Girondins hostile to Paris and its Commune. Lacking a security force of a size or disposition to resist the siege, the Convention somehow managed to stave off an immediate sans-culotte putsch by sub-mitting to the insurgents' lesser demands, one of which was to annul a Girondin-led initiative to outlaw the *Père Duchesne* publisher, Jacques-René Hébert, newly elected to the post of deputy Paris prosecutor, Danton's old springboard, and since grown into twice the rabble-rouser for that.

Girondin deputies sat tight.

But two days later – on Sunday, 2 June – those who had not already made a run for it like Roland were swept away in a second, deadlier inva-sion of the Convention backed by scores of artillery pieces which the National Guard, under the command of Commune rowdies, rolled up to block the exits. This time the house surrendered, consenting by show of hands to the expulsion and arrest of twenty-nine Girondin members – the cream of the Revolution's original reform forces.

Danton watched, on his feet, following them out with a huge theatrical shrug as insurgent sans-culottes led them away. Brissot, Condorcet, Vergniaud, Pétion, Madame Roland's paramour, Buzot, the dogged Lasource . . . many of them were men he had admired and looked up to. He hated none of them and said so to an excited Camille, who was on his feet next to him, shouting something Danton was unable to catch. But best have them out of the way for a while – until the civil war was brought under control, until Lyons and the cities in revolt were pacified, until the republic had its new army in the field to defend itself – after which they could return and help determine the direction of it all. This was Danton at his most ambivalent: large heart and violent impulses in irresolvable conflict. He knew just what was going on; it was an immense jolt for the Revolution. He would have been remiss in his duties in the green room had he not kept himself informed of sans-culotte plans for the assault on parliament, or of the street people's will – which Robespierre and Marat manifestly shared

– to deliver the Girondin captives to the guillotine. The sans-culottes would not easily settle for less, yet Danton no doubt thought he could somehow resolve matters otherwise.

He was not for taking fellow patriots' heads. It was quite enough to neutralise the Girondins politically. He personally warned Tom Paine, for one, against attending the Convention session on 2 June, for he knew there was every chance that the Englishman's name would be added to the expulsion list if he were caught there. Seeing Paine approaching the entrance, Danton placed a broad forearm in his way and let him know with a growl that he risked his life to go in. He was glad to see the pop-eyed hero of the American Revolution make himself scarce. That Madame Roland had failed to do the same was not his fault; her crusty husband was quick enough to take the tip. She never listened.

All the same Danton gave his endorsement to the sans-culotte putsch, albeit after the fact. It was a spurious way to proceed, but action was the mother of all progress in his unencumbered political philosophy. As for Camille, he thought he could claim a direct part: though shaken by the strong-arm manner of the Girondins' fall, he wondered whether he was not personally responsible for the insurrection. In past weeks Camille had written a fast-selling pamphlet that nailed Brissot in particular for all the ills of the republic. 'My God, I have killed them!' he cried, pride mixed with regret, as insurgents wrestled Girondin leaders from the Convention benches. This is what he had been shouting at Danton's side. Danton's prescription for some form of banishment hardly registered with Camille, who was convinced they were bound for the scaffold.

But where would the crude dismemberment of the Revolution's liberal body lead? No one could tell for sure. While it certainly suited Danton to be rid of his antagonists for a while, it took some grand Dantonesque imagery to try making sense of it for a bewildered nation at large. 'We are surrounded by storms, the thunder groans,' he told the Convention some days after the street people's assault. 'Well then! It is from the thunder and lightning that an edifice will emerge to immortalise the French nation.'

The fratricidal manoeuvres to stifle conflict in Paris in fact succeeded only in worsening conflict across the land. The ouster of the Girondins further inflamed provincial hostility against Paris, where Montagnards now shared sovereignty with the Paris masses. Rather than containing civil war, such violently achieved unity in the capital let it loose. Anti-revolutionary forces in Brittany and Normandy formed a federation to join the Vendée crusade; regions further south in Catholic heartlands of the old kingdom rose against the republic's thinly spread troops; among rebellious cities, the biggest of them, Lyons, made itself the royalist capital. Moreover, the rebels now inherited some desperately committed leaders: a handful of expelled Girondin deputies – Brissot and Madame Roland's lover, Buzot, among them – escaped their captors while briefly left under house arrest before going to prison and, having fled the capital, took up arms against the Revolution in Normandy and in the south. Their new pursuit was a shred of satisfaction for the Montagnards, who could say they were right all along to regard them as traitors.

However awkward its outcome, Danton was relieved to have the second *coup d'état* of his revolutionary career behind him. Though he had not personally organised this one, as he had King Louis' overthrow, the long vendetta that the Roland and Brissot forces ran against him had taxed even his prodigious energies. The relief somehow affected his concentration at the Committee of Public Safety, where now and again he began skipping the decisive evening session that kept the ruling executive up into the small hours. He did not waver in his efforts to call every available citizen to arms – there were enough commissars in the field now to force up conscription rates in all but the regions lost to revolt – but there was a force pulling at him from another direction.

The pull came from the Cour du Commerce.

To be tied day and night to the Tuileries green room and the Convention rostrum was a trial for a man of outsize appetites. He caught only fleeting glimpses of Louise as she mothered his boys and those moments warmed him. This skinny girl was increasingly on his mind. He was thirty-three years old and he needed the closeness of a woman's body. The practical solutions he had turned to before Gabrielle – and in pliant Liège – no longer looked so open to him. To be sure, a thousand comely whores still walked the Palais Royal and half of them had a garret room or a closet nearby in which to work their arts, yet the perils facing the nation seemed to be playing on popular morals. The sans-culottes saw themselves as the true heroes of the Revolution and they made a republican virtue of their lowly existence; theirs was an underdog virtue that smiled on bloodlust but frowned on the Parisian lusting of old. At the Convention any number of petitioners from poor sections such as Saint-Antoine and Saint-Marcel were to be heard demanding strict regulation of republican society – fixed prices for food, fixed wages for labour, fixed profits for commerce.

Danton needed to be cagey to hold off these pressures, though hold them off he did, together with a campaign by poorer sections to place the ripe sisterhood of the Palais Royal in public homes equipped for the pleasures of sewing, flat-ironing and twice-daily reading of patriotic literature. It seemed no time, then, for the head of the Public Safety Committee, the people's champion, to seek satisfaction in the pleasure grounds thrown open to the public by the fallen Duc d'Orléans.

Danton took Louise for his wife on 12 June 1793. She was still only sixteen. It was four months since Gabrielle's death, not a fortnight since Danton's deliverance from the Girondins. News of the marriage caused a stir among patriots, for it seemed somehow expressive of his excesses: rutting bull and Paris sparrow – an intriguing union touched by the grotesque. In her prison cell Madame Roland, who, like everyone else, was apprised only of the civil act performed at City Hall, reared in derision. Where would the debauchery end! She refused to see the bourgeois solicitude in Danton's act.

The public stir would have been greater still had the full ceremonial circumstances of the marriage been divulged. Louise was more pious than Danton thought. Through her father, the navy official, she got the leading figure in the republic to agree to have a priest marry them – a 'proper' priest, one true to the old Roman Catholic Church, not the new kind betrothed to the Revolution. This was difficult for Danton; he should have refused. Religion was the anvil on which the civil war was being beaten out. Priests faithful to Rome were renegades, enemies of the new order – fodder for Fouquier when apprehended. But the beast was in love. His adolescent bride's demands showed that she was not afraid of him, which was good. And frankly this pious side charmed him; it was an extra endearment.

Still, the church ceremony had to go unseen. To avoid prying eyes, he insisted it be performed after dark. The priest the Gélys unearthed for the occasion, a former vicar from the home parish of Saint-Sulpice, was a survivor of the horrendous prison massacres the year before and had been in hiding ever since. He used an attic next to his old church to bless the couple according to the old Catholic rites. Danton's consent came with the proviso that no one but Louise's parents could attend; if even Camille were there, it was bound to reach Robespierre's ears.

While it was politic to keep the religious marriage secret, religion was of small consequence to him. He was a freethinker, a non-believer; he had taken his stand as a boy when talking his mother into removing him from that dreary seminary in Troyes. But it was a murderously divisive issue in the land. What havoc the *Ancien Régime* had bequeathed. There was no standing aside from this political battle. For the fanatical Hébert and hard-heads on the Mountain, it was not enough to have nationalised the Church, they were campaigning to abolish the Catholic faith altogether and shut down the churches: no matter how low the clergy were prepared to bow before the Revolution, they were finished. Robespierre, for his part, was reluctant to outlaw faith, since he had some odd notion of launching a new religion under a 'Supreme Being' untarnished by the *Ancien Régime* and was engaged in selling his new godhead to the Jacobins.

Danton took his customary practical line. He was damned if he would allow the Catholic religion or any other faith to hold a place in the republican constitution. Freedom of conscience began with the separation of Church and state, he was sure of it. This was a plank of the constitution which Convention specialists and his Committee of Public Safety aimed to wrap up before June was out, a timetable facilitated by the fall of the Girondins. The preamble Danton favoured – and which prevailed – made no mention of religion. It was obvious to him that Hébert's reverse bigotry was more likely to fuel civil war than halt it. At the same time, he instinctively shielded both God and Church against those who wanted to abolish them. He favoured continuing to pay priests who swore allegiance to the Revolution from state funds, on the common-sense grounds that if they were deprived of their means of subsistence they would be reduced either to dying of hunger or joining the Vendée rebels.

For a non-believer to explain these matters in heated debates at the Convention, where others howled for God's head, was not easy. Danton put himself in a Champagne peasant's shoes, waving a sprig of mockery. His view was that French traditions ran too deep to uproot in a trice. With or without revolution, most people's lives revolved around births, marriages and funerals. 'The people want a priest when they give up the ghost,' he had argued at the outset of the Convention, laying a hand across his barrel chest. 'Let them cling to their foolish dreams. It brings comfort and they need it in these hard times.' And at the same time he had allowed himself a poke at Robespierre: 'When morality officers have been around long enough to bring the light to our hovels, it might then be good to preach morals and philosophy to the people. But until then it is barbarous, a crime no less, to rob the people of men in whom they can still find some consolation.' The Revolution had not sought to destroy superstition so as to establish atheism in its place.

Meanwhile, it was wonderful to have a wife in his bed, however slight her proportions. To Camille and Fabre, who were no less intrigued by his marriage than the rest, he said with a pleasurable sigh: 'I can't live without women.' What he meant was that he could not live without a loving wife. He revelled in the new circumstances, now easing off on appearances at the Committee of Public Safety to spend days with Louise in the country – at Sèvres, where Gabrielle's parents, the Charpentiers, gave a warm welcome to their grandsons' adolescent stepmother at their forest villa, and at Choisy, a nearby village where Danton rented a house an hour removed from the violence and tensions of Paris. He settled 30,000 livres on his bride as a warrant of his husbandly intentions – her security in case the Revolution were to turn against him.

The bourgeois pleasures of marriage moved him to commission a fashionable artist, Louis-Léopold Boilly, to paint a portrait of his bride and she posed for him with girlish rectitude. Boilly specialised in portrayals of Parisian life. He painted Louise side-on but full-face, standing over Danton's elder son, Antoine, at a desk in a curtained corner of the Cour du Commerce home, turning the pages of a newspaper and teaching him to read, a violin at her side. Danton was happy with the artist's work: portrayed in her voluminous white skirt and bustle, long fair hair topped by coiled ribbons, his adolescent bride was a ripening beauty.

It perhaps failed to register with Danton that he was slowing down in his duties of state. Not neglecting them, but markedly easing off. Domestic pleasure was a powerful lure in these terrible times. Added to that, the weight of the people on his broad back was an exhausting burden that he could not throw off had he wished to.

But the summer of 1793 was a bad time to relax. A storm was brewing over his leadership. Word went round at the Jacobin club, from where Robespierre kept a jealous eye on his green-room activities, that Danton was losing his energy. Complaints grew that he never attended Jacobin club meetings these days to thrash out the arguments that shaped the affairs of state. Was he spurning his old colleagues? Indeed, Jacobins debated whether the whole of the Committee of Public Safety he headed had not gone to sleep. The renowned playwright Beaumarchais, who was playing a risky double-game of staying close both to Danton's ruling committee and to émigré forces, wrote to him at the end of June saying: 'I have scarcely seen you in several days at the committee, whereas in the past two months I saw not a single thing decided without you being consulted.' Perhaps the author of the popular comedies of intrigue *Barber of Seville* and *Marriage of Figaro* felt deprived of interesting material to report to the émigré camp. Marat, for his part, grabbed at the chance to avenge himself on his old Cordelier colleague for having publicly disowned him of late, renaming the Danton committee in the *Ami du Peuple* the 'Committee of Public Defeat'.

Danton allowed that he was 'whacked', that was all. He might have said overwhelmed.

The truth was that things were not going as well as his patriotic oratory led fellow radicals to hope in the two principal wars the republic faced. England under Pitt remained deaf to his soundings on negotiation, and as long as England was in the war, Austria and Prussia had little call to get out. That summer Germanic troops had broken back across the Rhine into

Alsace and into a wide strip of French Flanders in the north, while Spain was encroaching on the French Basque country and the English navy blocked the ports.

Danton's thoughts of regaining the upper hand through bargaining over the release of the Revolution's totemic hostage, Marie-Antoinette, came up against a granite wall of opposition from Montagnards and the poorer Paris sections. Accompanied by the trusty Lacroix, he nonetheless went to confer in secret with the fallen queen, still imprisoned in the Temple tower. They kept the conversation to themselves, never revealing a word. Danton wanted to save her if he could; she was desperate. What good would her execution do, except pander to a senseless lust for revenge? There was talk among Habsburg diplomats of arranging her escape with Danton's unspoken approval, so as to finesse popular resistance to her release, but this looked a hopelessly dangerous course. He could not outright defy the forces who supported him and get away with it. He was audacious, he championed audacity, but there were limits. Like the notion of arresting Dumouriez in his army's midst, to free the Austrian queen – however useful it might prove – was impossible.

In sum, Danton's leadership during this time produced little to cheer about. He had taken his seat in April, and July was now here. He would have been entitled to look on a brighter side. It seemed highly likely his total mobilisation measures would soon throw back foreign invaders. The republic would hurl half a million men at its aggressors, led by new dependable young generals. And the revolutionary armies would not overstretch themselves again by seeking to liberate foreign peoples. He had put the new principle to a chastened Convention, which accepted it: 'The French nation may never wage offensive war.' If the principle would not be honoured for long, it would at least outlast Danton.

But would total mobilisation resolve the civil war? The Convention had its doubts. For all his roaring rhetoric, hardcore Montagnards thought Danton soft on the rebels – a suspicion he appeared to encourage by talking of amnesty for ordinary folk led astray by villainous priests and nobles. The radicals wanted counter-revolutionary forces exterminated to a man. Montagnard doubts deepened when Danton's Cordelier protégé Westermann, promoted to army general after his fruitful behind-the-scenes dealings with the Duke of Brunswick a year before, went down to defeat at the head of a sizeable republican force in the Vendée in early July. Marat raged for Westermann to be sent to the guillotine, laying the blame on Danton for giving him so vital a command.

The rebels were in the ascendancy. Domestic contentment demanded a high price of the giant from Arcis and it was about to go higher.

# SIXTEEN

# The Rule of Terror

The fourth anniversary of the Revolution on 14 July 1793 was just days away, but France was in no mood to celebrate. Who would dance in the squares to celebrate a nation's fear? Who would sally forth to worship the murderous bloodletting among its citizens? It was an anniversary made to trouble the man at the head of the besieged republic.

Under the rules that created the Committee of Public Safety its membership was renewable by parliament each month. So far this had been a formality. But on 10 July a grim republican mood, made grimmer by the latest setbacks in the Vendée, upset the formalities. That day the Convention came to renew the 'Danton committee' for a fourth month. There was a warning of what was in store in an oblique no-confidence motion presented ahead of the vote by one of Robespierre's Jacobin lieutenants. Nonetheless, the result was a bolt from the blue: the nine members elected or re-elected included neither Danton nor any of his close allies who had dominated the committee thus far; only one of the new panel could he class a friend.

For once the Cordelier giant was speechless. He was relieved of power by fellow Montagnards who questioned the strength of his will to smite the forces of counter-revolution. It was the most abrupt and comprehensive of takeovers.

Control of the Committee of Public Safety went to Robespierre's pale young disciple Saint-Just and to Georges-Auguste Couthon, a half-paralysed arthritic who wheeled himself around after Robespierre at the Jacobins, and it was very soon extended to the Incorruptible himself, who overcame an initial reluctance to show his hand in the downing of Danton and joined the ruling body two weeks later, replacing a member compelled to resign.

Danton's rule in the green room at the Tuileries had lasted three months. This was longer than he had spent as justice minister at the head of the former cabinet of ministers, but he must have felt cheated, outmanoeuvred. The curtain had come down too soon. The republic to which he aimed to bring order and peace was still a violent madhouse. He restrained himself, with difficulty, from remonstrating with Montagnard colleagues for evicting him – indeed he declined to make a speech of any kind on his sudden exit – but he told the old Cordelier circle at the Procope that night, a spark of menace in his eye: 'I am not angry. I have no rancour, but I have a memory.'

Though his exclusion came as a shock, Danton must in fact have seen some challenge to his leadership coming. Only a month ago the Convention had stretched his green-room table to include three extra places, each of them filled by uncompromising Jacobins – Saint-Just already among them. These Robespierre supporters, seated temporarily to inject sterner purpose into proceedings, opposed any kind of negotiation with foreign powers that would not first recognise the sovereignty of the republic – a restriction tacitly absent from Danton's diplomacy. Then there was all that dark murmuring about his recent work-shyness, his neglect of the Jacobin club and his supposed leniency towards Vendée rebel foot soldiers 'led astray' by royalist masters.

But there was the difference. Behind his fierce, belligerent oratory, Danton was a peacemaker on both fronts – on the borders and in the provinces. To Robespierre and the Jacobin ideologues, on the other hand, clemency was an alien notion: there could be no compromise with either enemy. And perhaps what most worried the drudge from Arras was that he feared his time would never come if things quietened down on all sides.

Of course, things had not yet quietened down. Peace looked far off on either front, Danton had to acknowledge. But he had done the hard inspirational spadework: the total mobilisation that astonished William Pitt was under way, promising in weeks to come an overwhelming response to the threats facing the republic. No, these zealous mules were wrong for France. Their takeover was sabotage. Danton was never bitter, but he was inclined to agree with the assessment of his friend Garat, his successor at Justice: 'Robespierre came to government when there were no more great battles to fight, only scaffolds to erect.'

The 14 July anniversary produced a further shock. On the eve of that day of non-rejoicing Marat was murdered in his sit-up bathtub in the apartment he had lately rented close by the Cour du Commerce.

Danton shed no more tears than anyone at the Convention over the assassination, though the news alarmed the Paris sections and further whetted the sans-culotte appetite for revenge against internal enemies aiming to cast the people back into servitude. Still, even Fouquier had begun to roll his eyes at Marat's demands for traitors' heads, for the gnome threw out terrible numbers – first it was 600, then 10,000, then 40,000, then 270,000 heads he wanted – and he listed the street addresses of the more prominent of his prospective victims in the *Ami du Peuple* to promote rapid sans-culotte action.

The knife driven into Marat's scurvy chest by a distraught daughter of the Normandy gentry, Charlotte Corday, produced the beneficial effect for Danton of removing certain of the pressures that pushed him out of office. For Marat had lately been his most aggressive critic, mobilising the complaints against his leadership; the little man's intrinsic target for abuse was power, whoever held it, and his bloodthirsty energies were fed by flailing at it. But there were less welcome aspects to the assassination too. For one thing, the Corday girl ghosted into the capital from the Normandy city of Caen, where Buzot, Pétion and other Girondin fugitives were now busy fanning the flames of insurrection against Paris, so that her act seemed to symbolise the unfathomable determination of efforts to breach the Revolution. For another – and this struck Danton at once, as it struck all Paris – the elimination of Marat somehow refined the Revolution to a contest at the top between Robespierre and himself.

It was just the two of them now. The rivalry between them emerged in stark outline. Only the fanatical Hébert at the Commune, who swiftly appointed himself Marat's 'successor', was left to bedevil the outcome from the fringe. And between Danton and Robespierre it was evident at this moment who held the upper hand.

There was no use brooding over the green-room reverse. Danton made a point of not appearing to take offence. To do so would invite the old charges that personal power was all that mattered to him. Rather he conducted himself as Gulliver unbound, freed from the green-room chains.

It took some effort. His Jacobin critics were not altogether mistaken. They had spotted some change in him. There was a sense that a large part of his feeling derived from disillusion with the ritual violence which the Revolution was establishing as its standard – thanks in no small measure to his public incitements. Yes, by the sanguinary count of Jacobin terror-mongers, he probably *was* softening. The thought surely perplexed him. Nonetheless, he forced himself back into the melee, willed on by the Cordelier tribe. Right through the summer of 1793, while pursuing the honeymoon with Louise, he threw himself back into public oratory with what appeared to be his old vigour, holding fast to the people's cause.

At the Convention and the Jacobin club, where he repaired his attendance record, Danton concentrated his fire on two targets equally detested by sans-culottes: the rich and the hoarders. The rich were 'a sponge to squeeze'. Make them pay for the defence of the republic! Fine hoarders the value of the food they keep from the people and double it! Give them ten years in irons to rue their crime! Punish financiers who place their money abroad! With Danton's heavy palms pressing down on them, those who represented France's wealthy class – entrepreneurs, merchants, bankers and financial speculators, no longer the great aristocratic landowners and high clergy – were now subjected to levy after special tax levy to pay for the huge quantities of weapons, uniforms and supplies his *levée en masse* required.

This was populism of a high order. He clearly was not consulting with Fabre, who himself was under Jacobin scrutiny for happy-go-lucky involvement in dubious speculative ventures. But Danton did not condemn friends. He knew where he himself stood, and it was not with the rich. Indeed, he was apt to slip into humble exaggeration regarding his birthright and his oneness with the poor. Attacked at the Jacobin club over his softening attitude towards moderates, he roared: 'I was born a sans-culotte! A sans-culotte endowed by nature with the physical strength to safeguard my subsistence.'

Such signs that he was recapturing his old ebullience raised smiles and also raised him once more in his peers' esteem. His prowess as a performer very soon overcame the disgrace of his latest tumble.

How fickle the Revolution was. How quickly fortunes could change when the future was too hazardous to contemplate and men's frightened minds dwelt only on today. Thus it was that on 25 July, just a fortnight after his eviction from the green room, Danton was elected president of the Convention, a revolving post that allowed him to set the agenda for reform, if only through that sun-baked August to come. A certain equilibrium appeared to be restored in the rivalry with Robespierre. The Incorruptible was master of decisions taken in the stifling heat of the green room; Danton led parliament, which in principle retained oversight of Robespierre's actions. This was a chance for the orator to show that he was not all patriotic blow: he was aware that to stir French hearts and put the nation into uniform was not enough to create a republic in which free citizens led better lives.

Danton *did* contemplate the future: to lead better lives Frenchmen had to receive an education and the state must provide it. If education was to be fair, it must also be free. Danton's proposal that August for free education open to all entered French folklore as an abiding marker of the Revolution. Yes, it would be expensive, he told the Convention, left fist planted on hip, the right pumping to his best Ciceronian rhythm – expensive, but a thousand times worth it:

> When you sow in the vast field of the republic, you must not count the cost of the sowing. After bread, the people's first need is education . . . Let us advance therefore to public instruction. With education

in the home everything shrinks, with public education everything grows. I too am a father, and when I consider the public good I can say this with pride: my son belongs not to me, but to the republic! It is her job to inform him of his duties so that he serves her well.

*After bread, the people's first need is education* . . . It was not the first call for free public schooling to issue from the bourgeois combatants of 1789. But it was Danton's philharmonic way with words – straight, thunderous, rude, subtle, ironic, brimful of classical lore – that set it on its path.

The same skills allowed him to dissuade Montagnard fanatics from outlawing everyone of noble birth from the army or public service, whatever their leanings. He could skewer aristocrats with the best of them, but a blanket ban on blue blood struck him as an absurd waste. It was, though, an emotive issue that needed to be teased out if he was to make his point. Naturally the republic could not depend on nobles to safeguard its liberties, he allowed. 'But is there not one among them who should escape anathema? Is there no way to recover some zealous child of the *patrie* from their midst?' The argument led him on one of his spontaneous excursions to Ancient Rome: when a candidate for the post of Roman tribune came from a patrician family, Danton recounted, he was first obliged to have himself adopted by a plebeian, thus forfeiting the privileges of his high born caste and becoming one of the people for good. 'Might we not extend this example towards some who have every right to be counted among us?'

Though he was back on form, Danton's attitude towards power grew increasingly ambivalent after his eviction from the Committee of Public Safety. He both extolled power and rejected it, uncomfortably aware that any interest he displayed would be misinterpreted.

His foreshortened experience in the green room had not convinced him that a full solution to the problem of strong government was in place. The Committee of Public Safety was a de facto government with no established mandate to rule. Through the home-ground authority it gained from its secretiveness, it held sway in Paris to confront the bedlam in the capital. But to Danton it hardly seemed equipped to mobilise the energies of the French nation at large. Why not make it a bona fide government with full executive powers that the world could recognise? Why not make it a government equal in political weight to Pitt's across the Channel? No longer being part of the committee made it easier for Danton to propose the conversion to the Convention that August. It should halt any drift to federalism and division of the *patrie*, he argued. He proposed allotting the body generous commencement funds of 50 million livres to 'spend all in one day, if it sees fit', adding encouragingly: 'Immense prodigality in the cause of liberty is a paying investment.'

His proposal was not very carefully thought through, and it received a cool reception from a suspicious Robespierre and his green-room team, who had difficulty assessing Danton's motivations. 'It's a trap!' cried Saint-Just. The ruling committee's present nine members suspected the proposed funds were a poisoned gift which would be turned against them, were they ever to stand accused of misusing them. Barère, a founder member and still there, shouted that he would resign if Public Safety were burdened with such sums to dispense. They further suspected that Danton aimed to strengthen the ruling body to make it worth his while to force his way back on.

A return to the committee may indeed have been part of Danton's thinking; certainly his friend Lacroix, also a dispossessed member, was urging him to find a way back. However, the evident distrust his proposal encountered from the Robespierre camp drove him to tack on an oath of denial at the Jacobins. He assured the club: 'As one who has always been the target of slander, I declare that I shall never accept a role on this committee. I swear it by the liberty of the *patrie!*'

It was an impulsive vow straight out of the Danton oath chest which left him little room to change his mind. His bull pride bound him to it. It would be devilishly hard to maintain. The big test came in early September, as the house rocked with patriotic fervour following a series of Danton harangues on the war that had the Marsh eating out of his hand again. His physical presence, his great barrel chest, his gargoyle visage seemed to give his discourse extra welter, so that an excited deputy from the far south Pyrenean region, where bulls were appreciated, leaped to his feet amid the resounding applause and cried: 'Danton has the head of a revolutionary! He alone can execute his ideas! I demand that in spite of his wishes he be brought back to the Committee of Public Safety.'

The appeal caught on. On 6 September the house voted to reinstall Danton in the green room, creating an extra place for him.

Since he was liable to get a little drunk on applause, Danton acknowledged the vote with a victor's wave. The morning after left him clearer in the head, though undecided. By 9 September he was quite clear. He would not return, he announced to the house: 'I have made a vow and I stick to it. Not that I refuse to assist the committee in circumstances where I could be useful, but if I joined it you would have reason to argue, as some have, that Danton knows how to slip around a pledge.' For good measure, he noted with a broad grin that he hoped the Convention would not depart, in his case, from its excellent principle of never forcing a member to go against his wishes.

His friends, mystified, argued with him. By stepping aside from running the republic, they said, he was handing its destiny to Robespierre, probably for good. Indeed, Robespierre no doubt came into his reckoning, for the prospect of resettling into a committee now dominated by the Incorruptible and his disciples was less than appealing. Moreover, it surely occurred to him that he performed better in a great roiling public theatre where the people could hear him bellow for their liberties than in a room where discourse was locked within its stifling walls. When pressed in the Procope on his reasons for staying out, he took a light tone: 'Like Alcibiades, you sometimes have to know when to cut off the dog's tail.'

Flippancy was an instinctive recourse for Danton when unsure of his ground. It said a lot about him – and not only about his classical scholarship, for the Greek warrior-statesman to whom he referred was as prone to scandal as the Cordelier giant himself and capitalised on the celebrity: having bought himself a magnificent dog at a phenomenal price and paraded it before Athenians for their admiration, he cut off its tail when their attention began to wander to make them keep talking about it. It followed, then, that the coy offer to assist Robespierre's committee whenever his participation could be useful was a position Danton enlarged upon rather grandly in the days that followed. 'I wish to be a member of no committee, but I shall be a spur to all,' he promised. He was going to make sure that people kept talking about him.

He projected himself as the goad of the Revolution, the overseer of its progress. And he was not without credentials. In this early autumn of 1793 his reputation did seem to be riding high once more. His popularity with the masses was intact and there were even promising signs of a successful comeback by reinvigorated revolutionary armies against both Germanic forces encroaching on the borders and the Vendée rebels. Since August, the *levée en masse* obtained by his patriotic badgering had been geared to add 400,000 republican troops to the 300,000 first raised to stay the collapse that followed Dumouriez's defection.

'Let a rifle be the most sacred thing among us! Let every Frenchman rather lose his life than his rifle,' Danton roared to an applauding Convention. Members themselves seemed staggered by the scope of the mobilisation.

Still, the new role Danton envisaged for himself looked a lofty, nebulous mission for a man of action. In its imprecision there ran a certain resignation. His chances of prevailing were somehow receding and he surely sensed it. Perhaps, within himself, he preferred it that way. He was not made to direct the Terror from a closed room at the Tuileries, nor was he convinced that his presence there could stop it, or even slow it down. For all the high talk of being the spur of the Revolution, his Cordelier accomplices must have believed there was a deep malaise – the grain of a suicide wish – in Danton's refusal to rejoin the ruling committee and confront Robespierre when the golden opportunity called.

The upshot was brisk and inevitable. Whatever the puff surrounding it, Danton's demurral left Robespierre effectively in charge – and the only spur the Jacobin headman envisaged for the furtherance of the Revolution was more of the Terror.

Robespierre cut off the peace feelers that Danton had spread around Europe, terminating negotiations launched or sought with enemies who declined to recognise the sovereignty of the republic. Harmless Switzerland apart, the only state with which Robespierre's regime maintained diplomatic relations was another raw and unsettled republic, the United States of America.

The cause of Danton's malaise was not hard to find. The executions of the Girondins, those passionate souls who did more than most to launch the republic, were imminent. Leading army generals whose sin was to disappoint current hopes in the green room were hustled by Fouquier to the scaffold, among them the illustrious Adam-Philippe Custine, a noblemanturned-republican sentenced to death for retreating from positions won from the Prussians on the Rhine, and Jean-Nicolas Houchard, a man-mountain the size of Danton, who was first lionised for defeating an army led by England's Duke of York at Hondschoote in the Low Countries and just as quickly condemned for failing to pursue and destroy it. As for Marie-Antoinette, who was transferred in early August from the royal family's prison tower at the Temple, she now languished in the Conciergerie on the Île de la Cité, the departure point to the guillotine for enemies of the Revolution high and low.

Danton was privy to Fouquier's schedule for dispatching them all. There was nothing he could do for the queen save rue the lost chance to negotiate with the European powers. Nothing he could do for the Girondins save pointlessly ignite sans-culotte fury by speaking out for them in public. He was despairingly frank, in private, about his thoughts on the Girondins. 'Twenty times I offered them peace; they wouldn't have it,' he told Garat. 'They refused to believe me because they wanted to preserve the right to destroy me. It is they who forced us to resort to the sans-culottery that has devoured them; it will devour us all, devour itself.'

He felt helpless. 'I am sick of men,' he confided to Camille. For a prospective goad of the new order, it was an unpromising bill of health to give himself. His sickness surely welled from a sense that the vague, violent, furious hunger for liberty that dominated men's passions, not least his own, was somehow beyond definition and therefore unattainable, that there could never be the slightest agreement on how far the Revolution should go, how perfect its reach should be. Fall foul of the notion of the day and you lost your head. What *was* liberty? It featured high in the republican constitution that he had helped draw up, but giving it pride of place made it no more measurable. He himself, the instigator of the Revolutionary Tribunal, was an accomplice in its suppression.

Madame Roland's plight haunted him. He did not excuse her; with her admirers she had contrived to fracture the republic. That was *her* version of liberty. In her own manner she was as preposterously virtuous as Robespierre. Indeed, she had flagrantly courted the Jacobin grind with sloe-eyed persistence when she first opened her salon, presumably because she regarded him as easy prey for her exquisite browbeating. Even now, he heard, the lovely Madame Roland was poring over maps in her prison cell selecting likely regions to form the federation she favoured. She also fired off complaints to Convention members and journalists over her detention, though her pen-and-ink rancour had already brought her a cruel disappointment: having won her release in late June by decision of parliament's police committee, she was at once rearrested by order of the Commune on stepping out of the Abbey prison in the Saint-Germain district and shut away as a counter-revolutionary in grimmer confines.

Danton was aware, though, that her warders, once beholden to her husband at Interior, remained relatively lenient with her. They allowed her to receive visitors, whom she plied with notebooks filled with reminiscences and prison-cell thoughts on the course of the Revolution and the men in power. There was no respite for him in her hurried personal jottings. She dismantled him with the hellish fury of a mistress scorned: he was a brute, a terror-monger, a larcenist, a deceiver. With faintly more restraint, she wrote of him: 'In revolutionary movements the most active people are seldom the most pure. How many throw themselves forward simply to become something!'

Her extraordinary output included reckless love letters to the fugitive Buzot, who seemed to fill her thoughts as much as the waning prospect of her release. How was he? Did he think of her? Was his spirit as pure as the day he won her love? She prayed for his success in spreading the Normandy uprising. If Buzot ever received her letters, he was not able to reach her with replies, and when his Normandy venture faltered he moved to what he hoped was safer insurrectional territory in the Bordeaux vineyards. Madame Roland's heedlessness with her sentiments also served her cruelly, for the police intercepted her letters and signalled their content to Fouquier, who, with Robespierre's consent, hardened the loose existing charges against her to incitement to civil war and plotting against the republic, capital offences.

As autumn 1793 advanced and Robespierre knuckled down to accelerating the Terror, there occurred for the first time an unconscious fusion of Madame Roland's and Danton's sentiments. In what she called her last thoughts, she wrote: 'Now all is lost. Those now in power count the friends of humanity as conspirators . . . I know that their reign cannot long endure. Once they lose power such men almost always meet the punishment they deserve.' In his present mood Danton could hardly have expressed himself better. The high priestess of the Revolution and the beast from Arcis seemed joined in common disgust.

Abruptly, in mid-October, Danton signalled that he had had enough. It was more than he could stand to be present for the scheduled swathe of Girondin executions. His presence at the Convention with a gallery baying for blood would tell everyone that the wholesale slaughter of the Revolution's leading lights of moderation had his blessing. Founding the Revolutionary Tribunal put blood on his hands. He did not want more.

The fallback role he gave himself as goad to the Revolution, such as it was, had scarcely been put to the test when he packed Louise and his boys into the Champagne post-chaise on 13 October – the day before Marie-Antoinette was to pass before Fouquier at the Revolutionary Tribunal – and retired once more to Arcis, having first delivered an absence note to the Convention which read:

> I am stricken by a serious illness, according to professional advice, and in order to reduce the time of convalescence I need to leave to breathe my native air. I therefore ask the Convention to authorise my departure for Arcis-sur-Aube. Needless to say, I propose to return in all haste to my post as soon as my strength permits me to resume my work.

Technically, he was not a fugitive. On that dangerous score Robespierre had nothing on him. No doubt he was exhausted, but that would pass; he spent his first two days in Arcis in bed. The 'serious illness' was being sick of men.

Danton needed to be shot of the Revolution's fanatics in order to breathe, and once back among the fields and streams of Arcis, at the Danton family home, he was free of them. He refused to read the newspapers arriving with the daily mail coach; he refused to discuss the Terror and the civil war with friends of his mother and stepfather who called at the family home. He loved that home. He could relax there. The long stone building faced the Aube and had six bedrooms on two floors and a slate mansard roof; behind, it looked over the meadows he had purchased one by one since setting up his King's Council practice in Paris. It was the home of a man of property, *his* property, inhabited through the year by his mother and stepfather and the growing family of the eldest of his four sisters.

The season was turning colder but he went back to swimming in the swirling river below the grain mills, churning from bank to bank with his powerful stroke; physically, once the exhaustion had passed, he was in his prime. He was just about to turn thirty-four years old. He drove Louise and the boys around the little streets of Arcis in a one-horse trap the locals called a 'bumthumper' – a *tapecul* – and some mornings he set off early with peasant neighbours to hunt rabbit and wild boar, enjoying the chance to tread each new field and copse added to his adjacent acres over the past few years, and after the hunt he might knock at the Arcis notary's door to enquire about still another pocket of land that took his eye while out shooting.

And yet even as he breathed deep and free, the depression that brought Danton to Arcis refused to lift. Though he would not read the newspapers, he heard about events in the capital from callers: liberty was wallowing in blood. He heard how Marie-Antoinette went to the guillotine, with a certain Habsburg aplomb, straight from Fouquier's show trial. How two weeks later, on 31 October, the expelled Girondin deputies were executed to a man, all twenty-two of the liberal freethinkers who had failed to flee or go into hiding. This piece of news reached him as he worked in the courtyard in front of the house, repairing grass borders. A neighbour came by waving a newspaper.

'Good news!' the neighbour cried.

'What?' Danton said.

'Look. Read this! The Girondins have been condemned and executed.'

'Good news! You call that good news, my poor man!' Danton said with a sigh, tears welling in his eyes.

'Weren't they splitters? Dissenters?'

'Dissenters! Aren't we all dissenters?' Danton said. 'We all deserve to die as much as they do. One after the other, we shall all meet their end.'

He heard how the men in the green room sent tens of thousands of conscripts – the youth he had mobilised – to annihilate the population of dissident Lyons. He heard how the Duc d'Orléans went to the gallows just a week after the Girondins, his change of name to Philippe Egalité and his benevolent balcony appearances at the Palais Royal counting for nothing against suspicions that his sympathies sat on the wrong side in the civil war. And though he shared the suspicions against Orléans, Danton heard with a shudder how Madame Roland was executed two days after him, on 8 November, dispatched in a tumbrel to the guillotine on the Place de la Révolution with a trembling counterfeiter for company. How she had passed proud and beautiful before catcalling street crowds to her death, wearing a disdainful smile and crying out as her slim neck was pressed into the curve of the block: 'O Liberty, what crimes are committed in thy name!'

The execution of Madame Roland, expected though it was, staggered Danton. An illustrious procession of 'dissenters' and luckless army commanders followed her to the block in quick order, including Bailly, his old nemesis as Mayor of Paris from the days when he was a Cordelier roustabout. But the killing of the Roland woman moved him deepest. What sorcery she practised! What snobbery! But what persistence. What spirit. What thrusting ambition. What courage. What a woman. Madame Roland *was* the Revolution, its daring, seductive essence.

It would have been hard for Danton to take his thoughts off her death. Was it time to get back to Paris? Could he yet talk sense into the inhuman bunch at the helm of the Revolution?

He was surely still reflecting on these things several days later, while picnicking with Louise and some old Arcis friends in a copse near the house, when a horseman rode up between the poplars, dismounting in a hurry. It was a nephew of his on the Camut side, a serious boy who had settled in Paris and often called in at the Cour du Commerce. He was panting. 'Uncle, I have come from Paris. May I talk to you in private?'

'It's all right, these men are my friends,' Danton reassured him. 'What is it?'

'Your friends Citizen Fabre and Citizen Desmoulins ask you to return in all haste. Robespierre and his people are making a move against you.'

'What do they want? My head? They wouldn't dare!'

'Please, don't be so sure!' the youth said with urgent eyes. 'Come back, time is short.'

Still seated, Danton reared his bull head. 'Go and tell Robespierre I shall soon be there to crush him – him and his gang.'

Within two days he was back in Paris. He returned with Louise and the boys on 20 November to the stupendous stench and workshop roar of the capital, which penetrated the windows of their post-chaise before they were in sight of the walls. He had been absent for close to six weeks. It was a lifetime in the cut and thrust of revolution.

# SEVENTEEN

# *Fight to the Death*

If the long break in Arcis served Danton's health, it did not serve his political interest. This was the familiar outcome of retreats to the Champagne badlands. While the pull of the Arcis air was irresistible, he was surely aware by now of the trouble it was likely to blow his way in Paris.

His friends no less than his enemies had seen his 'serious illness' as a pretext for separating himself from events in the capital. He returned, therefore, to face wild rumours – which the Robespierre camp did nothing to discourage – that he had fled to Geneva or even joined the traitorous émigrés in London. How the Revolution worshipped rumour. Calumny – mocking, salacious, murderous – was first accomplice of the immense confusion that reigned. In describing it, the writer Beaumarchais perhaps had his old acquaintance Danton in mind: 'Calumny, sir? It leaps, spreads its wings, flutters, envelops, tears, pulls and becomes by Heaven's grace a general cry, a public crescendo, a universal chorus of hatred and condemnation. Who the devil could resist it?'

If Danton's reappearance went some way towards killing the rumours of his flight, the result of his absence was nonetheless as clear as day: Robespierre was indeed firmly enthroned at the Committee of Public Safety. Furthermore, the young Saint-Just had seized the opportunity, on the Incorruptible's behalf, to turn the committee into a fully fledged revolutionary government of the kind Danton had proposed in vain before his departure – with the difference that its powers were now little short of absolute and its re-election each month was no longer deemed necessary.

The Cordelier faithful had not been idle while he was away. Camille, Fabre and the journalist Fréron risked their heads by proposing an amnesty for 200,000 'suspects' who were held in prisons in the capital and across the country on the loose grounds of denunciation by fellow citizens or of hearsay reaching police ears. The amnesty campaign irked Robespierre, who was convinced that the Terror was a winning policy, especially since the situation on the frontiers and in the civil war showed further signs of rebounding in the republic's favour. He fended off the amnesty demands in the Convention with dark menace: 'Those who wish to free the guilty want counter-revolution.' Everyone knew the penalty for engaging in counter-revolution. Terrified deputies proceeded to block the Cordelier proposal as if it were their mass death warrant. And though Fabre, reverting from financial speculator to poet, temporarily improved his stock with the Robespierre regime by inventing an imaginative new calendar for the republic – the traditional Gregorian months giving way to months he named after the harvests, the hot times and the cold, the mists and rains – his splash of creativity, implemented during October, was of small assistance to the Cordelier clemency campaign.

Danton's talk of returning to crush Robespierre and his disciples sounded, then, like bluster. The Incorruptible was ensconced in power and meant to keep it: he stood by the Terror, revelled in it, twinning it with the moral virtue he aimed to impose on the Revolution. The civil war removed Robespierre's reluctance to shed blood, indeed made him insist on shedding all that was necessary to destroy the last vestiges of counter-revolution. The Terror over which Robespierre presided cleaved through the whole of society: in the twelve months that followed the spring of 1793, more than 2,300 people were guillotined in Paris alone, including – aside from suspect blue-bloods, politicians, defeated army officers and priests – nine soldiers who pricked their eyes with pins to avoid service, a youth who sawed down a 'tree of liberty', a widow convicted of hoping for the arrival of Austrian and Prussian armies, milliners and servants accused of writing bad things and a wine merchant convicted of selling bad wine. Robespierre's stated vision of good republican government was virtue and terror combined, for virtue had no power without terror and terror was disastrous without virtue. Though a strangely inhibited fellow, the Jacobin leader opened up on virtue. The soul of a republic was virtue: holy equality, love of the fatherland, high-minded devotion to the general interest above the private. The enemies of the republic were egoists, debauchers and ambitious, corrupt men.

For Danton this was utopian guff. Why, Robespierre envisioned laws to govern people's pleasures, to make honour the currency of the land in place of money. One night at the Jacobin club, Danton had collared Robespierre at the end of the session. 'What is your virtue?' he asked with a savage grin. 'There is no virtue firmer than what I show my wife in bed each night.' Robespierre had turned on his heel and walked away. For the Incorruptible there was room in France only for his brand of patriotism.

How easy it was, then, for Robespierre to situate Danton among enemies of the republic. Their rivalry was part classic power struggle – Robespierre regarded Danton as the only man capable of taking power from him – and part extreme difference of personality. Neither part augured well for a peaceable outcome.

With the Incorruptible seated so firmly on top of things, the Convention to which Danton returned from Arcis was a mangled shadow of its original self. Close to half of its 760 members were gone – guillotined, imprisoned, in hiding or dispatched as commissioners to the revolutionary armies to browbeat new generals into obeying triumph-or-perish standing orders. Nonetheless, Danton went straight before this rump parliament on 20 November – two days after his return from Arcis – to prove that he was back. There was nowhere else to go, and Robespierre's committee-cum-revolutionary government still in theory reported to it.

He was not without hope, moreover. There existed a silent majority in what remained of the house, he was sure, that repudiated the Terror and condoned it only out of fear. That day he stated frankly to the Convention the change of course he sought for the Revolution: 'I demand that we spare men's blood! Let the Convention be just to those who are not proven enemies of the people.' In this instance he was defending destitute priests who had lost their livelihood. There was no missing the broader reach of his appeal.

That same evening, at sundown, he walked home along the Seine in silence with Camille. It had been a clear blue November day and the setting sun shone bright red, casting its rippling hue over the river as they approached the Pont Neuf. There they met a juryman they knew from the Revolutionary Tribunal who was on his way home. The man stopped and – tired, not boastful – related that the court had sent fifteen people to the guillotine that day and was scheduled to dispatch twice that number tomorrow.

Danton turned his bull head. 'Look at the Seine!' he said, 'it's flowing blood.'

Camille nodded. The two friends stared at the waters, silent again.

At length Danton added, 'Too much blood has flowed. Come on, Camille, take up your pen! Write to demand clemency! I shall support you.' He raised his fist. 'You see my hand. You know how strong it is.'

Camille, never shying from a cause, got down that same night to preparing a successor to the famous *Révolutions de France et de Brabant* newspaper, which had made his reputation after the fall of the Bastille. Public speaking remained a trial for Camille with his semi-disciplined stammer – his adoring wife, Lucile, christened him 'Monsieur Hmm' – but his pen knew no hesitation. He owned the most eloquent style of all the Paris pamphleteers, passionate and ironic, aggressive and subtle. Not two weeks after Danton's return he was ready with a new newspaper, suggestively entitled the *Vieux*

*Cordelier*, the first issue of which appeared on 5 December. It sold out within an hour. Its mission was to halt the Terror.

Under Danton's phantom co-editorship, the *Vieux Cordelier* went about its task with a certain wariness, avoiding a head-on collision with Robespierre. The tactic was to set its sights first on Hébert, of the venomous *Père Duchesne*: as a Paris prosecutor and Commune headman, the eccentric Hébert surpassed the Incorruptible both in zeal for the Terror and in unabashed criticism of Danton, whom he daily lambasted for moderation. Besides, it was reasonable to suppose that Robespierre would be happy to see Hébert brought to his knees. With a lapsed nun for a wife, Hébert was the first trumpeter of atheism and rejected both the Catholic god and the Supreme Being, the new godhead whose worship Robespierre the prophet was presently imposing on republican France. Confusingly, the fanatical Hébert acknowledged but one idol: Reason.

So Camille, with Danton at his shoulder, wrote in respectful, even admiring, terms towards his old schoolmate Robespierre in that first issue of the *Vieux Cordelier*. When Robespierre asked to see the proofs prior to publication, Camille consented without a fuss. The damning rebuke it carried for Hébert's terror-mongering grew more pointed in the second issue, which Robespierre also insisted on scanning in advance. The Incorruptible rather approved of it, welcoming the campaign against Hébert.

It took a third issue before Robespierre, neglecting this time to ask for a preview of the proofs, came to suspect that Hébert might merely be a proxy target, for sharp irony over the current green room's 'purification' programme had cut into Camille's prose. And in the fourth issue – published on what was previously Christmas Day, now another grey day during Nivôse, Fabre's month of snows – the co-editors of the *Vieux Cordelier* could no longer hold back. With the rhythm of a Danton speech, Camille's editorial purred, then roared:

O my dear Robespierre, my old college friend, you whose eloquent speeches posterity will read and reread, remember the lessons of history and philosophy: that love is stronger, more enduring than fear . . . Why would clemency be a crime in our republic? Open the prisons to the two hundred thousand citizens you call suspects, for in the Declaration of Rights there is no house of suspicion. You wish to exterminate all your enemies by the guillotine! Was there ever any greater folly? For do you send a single soul to the scaffold without making ten new enemies for yourself among their families and friends? Do you believe they are dangerous, these women, these old men, these morons, these self-servers, these foot-draggers of the Revolution you are locking up?

No, the strong and the brave among them have emigrated. The rest do not merit your anger. Let us create a Committee of Public Clemency and, believe me, liberty will be strengthened and Europe will be vanquished.

Robespierre had not pre-examined this issue either. It caused pandemonium at the Jacobin club, where Robespierre's supporters demanded that the editors of the *Vieux Cordelier*, whose sales were bounding ahead, be put on trial.

The uproar put Robespierre on the spot, for Camille at once let it be known that the Jacobin headman had been reading the proofs. After some hesitation, Robespierre told members that instead of a trial it was best to burn the offensive issue, since Camille, he allowed, had otherwise served the Revolution well. Camille was not assuaged. 'To burn is not to answer,' he cried during an ugly session at the club, holding his ground. Camille's retort cut the Incorruptible short, for it reiterated Rousseau's famous jab at the *Ancien Régime* officials who burned his bold novel *Émile*. For a while the matter went unresolved; Camille prepared his next issue.

Judging by his hesitations over the *Vieux Cordelier*, Robespierre indeed appeared more interested that winter in eliminating Hébert than in crushing Danton and his Cordelier friends. For his part, Danton, despite his malaise, still thought he was stronger than Robespierre, stronger in every sense. He stood well over a head above Robespierre; in his antagonist's flaccid eyes, he had read puniness from the day they first met. The feeling of superiority never left Danton. He was a man; the other, something less than a man. Whatever political heights the chaste inquisitor from Arras scaled, he remained in Danton's eyes the pasty-faced 'eunuch' he had taken him for from the start.

In the New Year of 1794 the rivalry had the deceptive air of a fencing match with blunted foils. Danton, had he realised it, was on the back foot. The certainty of his superiority planted him there. For Robespierre seemed able to do as he liked. Deliberately confusing all things foreign with danger and sabotage, the suspicious Jacobin leader had marked the old Yuletide by having the Convention expel its foreign members, of which there were two – Mad Tom Paine, who had dallied too long over leaving Paris, and a rich, eccentric German, Jean-Baptiste Clootz, who had rebaptised himself 'Anacharsis' for revolutionary purposes. Paine and Anacharsis were locked up in prison for their efforts to build the republic. If Robespierre's lusts were few, he did lust for power and this gave him an advantage: he had a clear objective. And Danton? Though he was a creature of outsize appetites, hunger for personal power was not the first of them. The repeated getaways to Arcis proved it. Would a man in love with power have disappeared on a love-struck honeymoon when all was to play for?

The rules of the fencing match did not prevent Danton from roaring. Supporting the *Vieux Cordelier*, he warmed the winter benches of the rump Convention with insistent calls for a turn to clemency. France no longer needed to terrorise her citizens to defeat her enemies! He told deputies: 'If it is the pike that vanquishes, it is the compass of reason and the genius of humanity that raises and consolidates the edifice of society.' No, Danton had not metamorphosed from bull to lamb. But like the opening issues of the *Vieux Cordelier*, he preferred to make Robespierre an indirect target.

His demands for clemency were most often the prelude to a frontal attack on Hébert and his Commune terror-mongers. Danton grew exasperated by the circus-tent antics to which Hébert resorted in his attempts to abolish religion: each day recently the Paris prosecutor produced a gaggle of supposed priests who tore off their churchly robes on the floor of the Convention, or sent deputations from city wards to parade before deputies bearing saintly relics from desecrated parish churches. The Cordelier giant exploded:

We are here to serve the people. I demand an end to these anti-religion masquerades in the well of the Convention. Let those individuals who want to place church spoils at the altar of the *patrie* stop making a trophy game of it. Our task here is not to receive endless deputations all mouthing the same thing. There is an end to everything, even to self-satisfaction. I demand that we close the door on it now.

*An end to everything!* He surely meant the Terror too.

For his part, Robespierre feigned support for Danton in public as Montagnard hardheads assailed his push for clemency as the work of a traitor. The Incorruptible's support was delivered poison-tipped at the Jacobin club, where these days his word went unchallenged. He well knew what they said of Danton. Danton had emigrated! Danton faked his illness! He plotted with Pitt, with Austria, with Prussia, to destroy the Revolution! He was the king of conspirators! In a word, he asked to be executed! But was all this not a smear against a man of courage, a patriot? 'I may be wrong about Danton,' Robespierre said, 'but, as a family man, he deserves nothing but praise. In the political arena, we have had differences that have made me look at him closely, sometimes in anger, but if he hasn't always shared my opinion, must I conclude that he has betrayed the *patrie*? No, I say that he has always served it with zeal!'

Robespierre was adept at damning with praise. His tribute to Danton the family man stirred dissent among Jacobins; they muttered about the impropriety of taking a girl-child in marriage. But while the tone of Robespierre support was not calculated to lift Danton to the skies, the conclusion sounded sincere. To the capital's intrigued gaze, the fight to the death – for that is what it was – between the Revolution's Goliath and its chaste moralist remained cagey in the extreme. They appeared to be circling each other, each reluctant to go for the kill.

Their wary game did bring a kill, however, and it was a momentous one. On the night of 13 March Hébert was arrested, with a score of his Commune henchmen. The arrest order came from the Committee of Public Safety.

The republic looked on stunned as the publicist it knew as Père Duchesne and his tribe of *enragés*, sentinels of the Terror, filed in short order before Fouquier's court on their way to the guillotine, paying with their heads for a vain attempt to drum up yet another sans-culotte insurrection – this time aimed at overthrowing the revolutionary government. Hébert had rated Robespierre's green room far too slow in disposing of traitors in the ever larger numbers he desired. His execution was Robespierre's response to the dawdling charge.

Danton refrained from proposing clemency for Hébert. There were limits. The Hébert crowd had been screaming for his own head, depicting him as an outright accomplice of Dumouriez, and their hatred had grown as the *Vieux Cordelier* set about ending the Terror they worshipped. There could be no end to the reign of fear, Danton recognised, as long as the foul-mouthed Père Duchesne was there to promote it.

All the same, Danton's public reaction to his death was careful. The sans-culottes had been too confused – perhaps too exhausted – to respond to the Hébert faction's call to rise against their green-room masters. But who could tell how they would respond to the master rabble-rouser's execution? Danton made it his task to head off mass violence. Without gilding Hébert's reputation, he depicted his fate as part of the mystique of popular revolt. Speaking straight to the sans-culottes from the Convention rostrum, he urged:

> Frenchmen! Do not take fright at the effervescence of this first age of liberty. It is like a strong new wine that ferments until purged of all its froth . . . I foresee that enviable time when all masks shall fall away, when there remain only those men worthy of the values that reign in our republic. But this moment we live through is necessary for the destruction of those who have merely aped patriotism and borrowed its clothes. At last we shall distinguish false revolutionaries from the true!

The house grasped Danton's objective. His unrehearsed peroration that March day on the nature of popular revolt went down so well with the Convention that the parliament voted to have it printed and dispatched around the country for the people's edification, a rare honour for a speech from the rostrum. In the president's chair was a white-haired Montagnard, Philippe-Jacques Rühl, a normally calm Alsatian who also sat on Robespierre's ruling committee. In tribute to the orator, he invited him to take his chair, which Danton graciously declined. To loud applause, they clasped each other in an emotional embrace at the foot of the Mountain.

It turned out to be Danton's last speech to the Convention.

Robespierre had already identified a lot more froth to be purged. In the New Year of 1794, as the fencing with Danton continued, he had recalled his handsome young disciple Saint-Just to Paris from an important political mission in the east. The Jacobin headman had a strategy for the bigger kill and was counting on Saint-Just to implement it.

Danton perhaps missed the significance of the recall of the young man at first. Saint-Just returned to Paris at the age of just twenty-six with his reputation as a stern disciplinarian enhanced, having stopped a revolutionary-army haemorrhage on the Rhine by sending irresolute officers and local republican administrators to the gallows. At the time, Danton was busy rescaling his abandoned political heights after the latest retreat to Arcis. But the purpose of Saint-Just's presence soon grew ominously clear to him. One after the other, his close accomplices, the Cordelier pioneers, began stumbling and falling around him, and throwing out his barrel chest to protect them no longer seemed to work.

Robespierre's strategy was this: still too wary to strike at Danton's head, he and Saint-Just would hack at the base of the people's idol, calculating that if they chopped with precision the giant pillar would topple of itself.

A first swing caught a plain-speaking Convention ally of Danton, a provincial lawyer named Pierre Philippeaux. Though not a member of the Cordelier inner circle, Philippeaux had worked closely with Danton when he was master of the green room, which got him named commissioner to the Vendée. His task there was to lift the republic's fortunes in the civil war. Philippeaux grew disgusted by what he saw. He sharply criticised the incompetence and thievery of the newly promoted sans-culotte officers who held command, and ultimately penned a report laying blame for the continuing civil-war fiasco in large part on tactics pursued by Danton's successors at Public Safety.

The report stung Robespierre, the more so because of the author's links with Danton, and at the Jacobin club the troublesome commissioner had come under ferocious attack even before Saint-Just's return. The charges flew. Philippeaux was a Vendée sympathiser. Philippeaux supported counter-revolution. Philippeaux was a traitor.

Over Christmas Danton hastened to the club to defend his colleague, though his opening sounded unusually limp: it was up to the Vendée commissioner to prove the accusations in his report, Danton allowed, or lose his head. But much more to the point, Danton continued, warming up, the whole ugly dispute over Philippeaux was a disservice to the republic. 'Why! When the Romans argued publicly over the affairs of state and over the conduct of individuals, they dropped their quarrels as soon as the enemy was at the gates of Rome. Then they vied with each other in courage and heart alone to repel the enemy hordes. Now the enemy is at *our* gates and we tear ourselves apart. Do all our arguments kill a single Prussian?'

The Danton-at-the-Forum act never failed to impress, though this time it only half succeeded. His intervention temporarily saved Philippeaux from arrest, imprisonment and worse, but not from expulsion from the Jacobin midst. His ally was in disgrace with the masters of the Terror. The disgrace could not but damage Danton too.

Philippeaux's plight prompted Danton to try to have things out in private with Robespierre. It was time to put the welfare of the republic before the hatred that welled at its summit. The two of them seldom conversed, though had they reached out they could practically have joined hands from where they sat on the Mountain. When they did briefly exchange words, Danton found it hard to resist mocking his rival's obsession with virtue, for he was always hearing of how Robespierre groused in private about his deficient morals.

But there were graver issues to consider, and in January several concerned fellow Jacobins, wishing to act as peacemakers, got them together over dinner a mile or so outside Paris in the hamlet of Charenton, where the gentle Marne flowed into the Seine, there to escape mischievous eyes. The guests made strange table partners: one picked, the other ate with relish; one seemed fearful, his hands trembling, the other jovial, a little overdoing his natural bonhomie. The signals were unpromising. Still, the atmosphere remained polite enough, until Danton spoke his thoughts on the Terror.

'It is absolutely right to suppress royalists,' he said, spreading his large palms, 'but let us not confuse the innocent with the guilty!'

Robespierre's pallid face tightened. 'What makes you think we have killed a single innocent?'

Danton was aghast. 'Did you hear that?' he said, turning to their umpire hosts. 'Not one innocent soul has perished!' Exasperated, he got up to leave, but turned back to deliver a warning to Robespierre, who was scratching busy notes on a piece of paper, head down. Danton persisted: 'If we cannot get together to slow this down it will end up killing us both.'

The meeting ended there. Afterwards Danton talked it over with Camille, once so friendly with the Incorruptible. Camille had always been convinced that love of the republic would unite them. So why had the meeting achieved nothing? Camille contended that Robespierre was envious of Danton, and frightened.

Danton nodded. He had never admired Robespierre, now he was saddened by him. The man who had taken charge of France wanted a Revolution without moral blemish. He wanted what was humanly impossible. And he was ready to kill for it, a thousand, ten thousand times over, until everything conformed to his censorious view of liberty. He sought the salvation of the French people through his own freakish ideals. The fool! It was France the nation, France the land, that needed saving, not the French people's soul.

Danton had never aspired to save the people. Never imagined cleansing the nation's soul. His revolutionary aims, if indeed he could define them, stretched to giving the people a better life, free of the yokes he had helped them throw off.

The first of the Danton inner circle to fall was Fabre. The poet-rebel was among the closest and the worst of Danton's accomplices. If a man was judged by the company he kept, Danton always rather risked being pulled down by Fabre, who was forever in debt. Fabre had been at his side from the first wild days with the Cordeliers: during the clashes with La Fayette, the toppling of the monarchy, at the summit of government, warding off Brunswick and the Prussians, on the benches of the Convention. Fabre had genuine revolutionary passions, but they were bedevilled by a passion for lucre, which he had lately pursued via speculation in public funds and dalliances in a series of commercial enterprises – army boot supplies among them – that in his political position he would have done better to shun. Robespierre was known to despise Fabre: if he thought Danton immoral, he thought Fabre utterly corrupt. Moreover, Fabre intensely irritated the Jacobin chief by posing at the club with a lorgnette, turning it ostentatiously this way and that, as though he were treating the critical debates as a piece of boulevard theatre.

It was financial scandal that now caught up with the creator of the new republican calendar. His name became implicated in shady activities surrounding the collapse of a prominent trading company, the East India Company, whose share values yo-yoed alarmingly as its day of reckoning neared in the New Year of 1794, producing large profits for financiers and Convention deputies involved in manipulating the price. The East India Company, once the flagship of France's international trading prowess, had a business pedigree reaching back to the reign of the Sun King, Louis XIV, and now here it lay dead, a fat goose throttled and plucked by financial grafters with the Revolution in full flow. The manner of its collapse confirmed the sans-culotte masses in their grudge against speculators, whom they hated as much as they did hoarders.

Public resentment over the East India Company scandal grew when police discovered that in proceedings for the closure of the company a document was falsified at the last minute to switch control of the liquidation from the Convention to the company itself, promising a further take for insiders. The police report hinted that Fabre may have been the tamperer. Robespierre and Saint-Just jumped on the disclosure, which Fabre denied. No matter. The East India Company fraud, in Robespierre's view, was a counter-revolutionary act that damaged the republic's economy to the benefit of William Pitt and the English paymasters who financed Europe's war against the Revolution. Indeed, Robespierre's accusations against Fabre became so pointed at the Jacobin club that an aroused member cried, 'To the guillotine with him!' Fabre paled, dropping his lorgnette. Soon other voices joined the terrible shout.

Fabre was arrested on 13 January by order of the green room, with the Convention appending its accord. Again, Danton tried to prevent it. He was horrified by the prospect of his companion-in-arms, however remiss, being carted off and guillotined without being able to put up a defence. While accepting that a fraud had occurred, he went before the Convention to demand that Fabre and fellow deputies accused with him be given the chance to defend themselves before their peers at the rostrum. The right of self-defence was a precious liberty that each and every member of the house had fought for. He urged: 'Let them be judged before all the people, so the people can know those who still merit its trust.' Furthermore, he said, the Committee of Public Safety and its police offshoot, the Committee of General Security, should carry out a proper inquiry into the scandal to untangle all its financial threads and determine where they led.

The Convention would not have it. For once he was shouted down. A Robespierre supporter yelled: 'You're Fabre's dupe, Danton! You have sat beside him. He has cheated the best patriots!' Fabre was taken to the Luxembourg prison that same day. The idol's base was cracking.

The next friend to go was Danton's one remaining link with the green room, Marie-Jean Hérault de Séchelles, a former *Ancien Régime* magistrate of noble blood who had turned to revolution and worked with Danton on producing the new republic's constitution. Hérault was a disarming fellow, learned and clever but happy-go-lucky. He had served as Convention commissioner on the Rhine to pursue Danton's peace-seeking diplomacy, an occupation that came to Robespierre's disapproving ears through Saint-Just, who replaced him there. Now Robespierre summoned Hérault to resign from Public Safety for having made contact with foreign agents. Hérault informed Danton that he was 'on the razor's edge', then consented to resign. Robespierre called his departure an expulsion and placed him under close police surveillance.

The president of the Committee of General Security, Marc Vadier, a greybeard terror-monger privy to Robespierre's plan to cut away Danton's support, revelled in the Cordelier giant's discomfort. 'Now we'll gut this big stuffed turbot!' This choice taunt found its way into the Paris news-sheets, which enraged Danton. He felt doubly aggrieved: not only were these fanatics deaf to his calls for moderation, they dared belittle him and crow about it in public. To Vadier's outburst he reacted in kind, swearing to his diminishing Procope circle: 'Tell that swine that the day I need to fear for my life I shall be worse than a cannibal with him – I'll eat his brains and shit in his skull!' His friends had to calm him down, walking him twice up and down the Cour du Commerce before letting him go home to Louise.

And then it was Camille's turn.

The blow Camille received was worse than arrest: his writing hand was severed, his bold pen crushed at the nib. He had managed to get a fifth issue of the *Vieux Cordelier* off the presses, but when he presented his manu-script of a sixth in late January, his printer refused to take it. No printer in Paris dared publish it. Robespierre had overcome his hesitation in dealing with the insolent newspaper. He attacked Camille before the Jacobin club as a spoilt child misled by bad company. He cut Camille off, disowned their past. In February, when a motion was put to expel the spirited journalist from the Jacobin midst, Robespierre dismantled in a curt phrase their long friendship – their years as schoolmates, his part as best man at Camille's wedding, as a godfather to his son – observing frigidly: 'Whether you throw Desmoulins out or keep him, what should I care? He is just an individual.'

After the jolt of Hébert's execution, Danton was able to measure how completely Robespierre had outmanoeuvred him. Perhaps he was right to proclaim Père Duchesne's fall as a chance at last to separate false revolu-tionaries from the true. All the same he had never felt more isolated.

The spring of 1794 was the loveliest in years, warmer and sunnier than any springtide since the birth of the Revolution. In Paris the chestnuts gave leaf in March, city squares blossomed and the fields beyond the walls were a rich fresh green. The Seine flowed high and clean under the bridges of the capital and the barques and coloured barges bumped the stone arches as they chased each other through. Even the great municipal stench held back, reluctant to spoil the show. The almanacs had it that Mother Nature was consoling the world for the terrible deeds of society.

In Danton the sap was slow to rise. Was the people's idol broken? Those who remained free to support him feared it was so.

Yet if the plight of Fabre, Camille and the rest was a heavy blow to his prestige, he found his personal standing at the Convention almost miraculously intact. The deputies were a frightened pack, but his belief that a majority among them repudiated the Terror in their hearts seemed strengthened by the applause he heard each time he spoke for clemency. He warned them: 'You need to be very sure of your facts to bring counter-revolutionary accusations against ardent friends of liberty, or to treat mistakes they make with greater gravity than you would treat your own.' He had gone further, demanding a clean-out of the police authority, Vadier's Committee of General Security, and the removal of 'false patriots in red caps' – a disdainful challenge to Robespierre's green room.

Danton tried hard not to let the hunting-down of his friends by the 'red caps' affect his public discourse. The practical affairs of state powered his lungs, as did brave new plans for spreading human liberty: he pushed through bonuses for peasant farmers who increased their livestock production to feed the republic, and he took the lead in securing the abolition of slavery in France's colonies in the new world. The ardour of his anti-slavery speech, which he pitched against William Pitt and England's enduring domestic quarrels over abolition, electrified the house. He boomed:

> Representatives of the French people, until now we have selfishly decreed liberty for ourselves alone. Today we proclaim it to the universe, for the glory of future generations. We proclaim universal liberty!

And a month later, when finally he was locked in that embrace with the president of the Convention following his discourse on Hébert's execution and the mystique of revolt, there was surely not a witness in the public gallery who imagined it could be the giant orator's last performance at the rostrum.

Only the mutilated Cordelier tribe thought they knew what silenced Danton. He had come off the wave he had been riding for four years, of his own volition. The ride no longer thrilled, it drowned a man's soul. Universal liberty was a wondrous goal. His fellow deputies were right to applaud. But it was a chimera.

The sickness was back with him. Danton had felt he was getting over it, but the fear that infected the capital brought it back, and the glorious spring somehow made it worse. Speeches were his stock in trade – he seemed unable to make a dull one – but while his recent stirring orations hid his gloom they could not shake it off. For he was also a penitent. How could he forget the harm he had inflicted on men and women who shared his goals – on the nation itself – by his creation of the Revolutionary Tribunal and the despotic committee rule that accompanied it? And what surely sickened him further was that his efforts to repair the harm were baulked by survivors' fears for their own lives.

For himself, Danton was not afraid of Robespierre's hold on power. When the butcher-statesman Legendre, now thoroughly reconciled, and Fréron, the Cordelier pamphleteer, warned him that the Incorruptible was conspiring to kill him, having axed his support, he refused to believe it, or pretended not to. 'If I thought the idea even crossed his mind, I'd eat his entrails,' he barked. This was his ruffian pose; it usually signalled that he was not minded to act half as rough as his words promised. He seemed convinced, as ever, that Robespierre would not dare touch him: he was too large a figure for that.

Fréron was worried for him. Why did he not pre-empt his adversary? Why not strike first?

Danton heaved his bull shoulders. 'And spill more blood!' he said. 'There's enough as it is. I have spilled my share when I thought it was useful.' And when Legendre too pressed him, he added wearily, 'Better to be guillotined than to guillotine.'

A further private meeting with Robespierre was arranged on 22 March at the home of Edmé Courtois, a fellow Montagnard perturbed by the fatal course the two rivals looked to be set upon. Danton managed to act his cordial, frank self. He arrived accompanied by Camille, who, though chastened, remained free to move about, and two or three other supporters. Danton did most of the talking, addressing Robespierre by the familiar '*tu*' commonly used in these republican times, but which his pent-up rival nonetheless seemed uneasy with, for he reverted to the discarded '*vous*'. They came quickly to the point:

Danton: Since we are in the presence of patriots who are veterans of the Revolution, like ourselves, I think I may say what I want. Believe me, Robespierre, I know why you are against me. I have never complained about the absurd charges made against me, regarding my missions in Belgium or the fortune I'm supposed to have acquired, because I have never bothered with personal things and because everyone knows that not only have I not increased my fortune, which is very modest, but I have sacrificed part of what I had before the Revolution.

Robespierre: So you say.

Danton: I don't doubt that you love your country and serve it in good faith. But I have often been pained at how willing you have been to take the gossip of imbeciles and the mischievous insinuations of a few intriguers as proof of crime.

Robespierre: (*Making notes on a piece of paper.*) Ah.

Danton: Come on now, Robespierre, halt this intrigue! Join the patriots. Let us march together in good faith. Let us tread the same line. Punish the guilty, yes! Punish the leaders! But pardon the mistaken. Then you'll see, our republic will triumph and win respect abroad, and soon it will win the love of those at home who fight us.

Robespierre: So by your principles, by your morality, there would no more guilty to punish!

Danton: That would upset you? To have no more guilty to punish?

Despite the sharp irony in their tussle, their seconds believed they were close to reconciliation, for they embraced at the close. The optimism was inspired mainly by Danton's creature instincts. Visibly moved, he grasped his slight adversary in an emotional bear hug. It looked amicable enough, but those who looked closer saw that Robespierre remained as cold as a slab of marble.

# EIGHTEEN

# The Cornered Bull

The Revolution appeared in its confusion to accelerate things, cramming a year into a week, a week into an hour. And in that caressing spring of 1794, the speed picked up still further. To Danton it became a blur.

On the night of 30 March, as the last meeting with Robespierre turned fresh and not altogether bleak in his mind, he sat at home on the Cour du Commerce in consultation with Camille and Lacroix, half-listening to Louise playing with the boys before bedtime in the next room, when a messenger came. The nervous caller delivered an urgent warning: the Committee of Public Safety had signed a decree for Danton's arrest; he was to go before Fouquier's tribunal forthwith.

The messenger was sent by Rühl, the courtly Alsatian who had embraced him at the rostrum days before. A Public Safety committee member as well as rotating Convention president, the Alsatian was sworn to secrecy, like the rest of Robespierre's green room, on that evening's arrest decision, but felt compelled to alert Danton all the same. In view of the source, Danton had no doubt that it was true. Camille's and Lacroix's names were also on the arrest list. Indeed, the whole of the old Cordelier tribe was bound for the guillotine unless he could slow time down.

It was clear that Robespierre's part in that last meeting had been a murderous sham: the Jacobin headman had indeed been engaged with Saint-Just in arranging Danton's death before he went to Charenton. Those notes Robespierre took! The Incorruptible's pockets bulged with them. They filled the drawers in his cramped lodgings at the carpenter Duplay's home, ready for presentation in chronological bunches to Saint-Just, his master inquisitor, who would draw up the case for the extermination of the last man to obstruct his rule of virtue.

The charge sheet Saint-Just had put before the green room earlier that day was a compendium of all the adverse rumours, gossip and allegations that Robespierre had collected concerning Danton's engagement in the

Revolution. The list went back to his first harangues in the pleasure grounds of the Palais Royal. Robespierre's jottings contained conclusions he had drawn largely from listening to what people said, such as the charge that Mirabeau had 'bought' Danton, which he noted thus: 'Friends of Mirabeau boasted loudly of having shut Danton's mouth: as long as Mirabeau lived, Danton stayed quiet.'

Tactfully omitted from the Saint-Just presentation was Robespierre's declared belief in Danton's outstanding patriotic zeal, voiced to the Jacobins only three months earlier; deleted the 'undying love' Robespierre had pledged to Danton on the death of Gabrielle. In his indictment Saint-Just added little, in fact, to the Jacobin headman's bundles of damnation, which he presented with a quiet, searing conviction that his extreme youth rendered the more terrible to committee men's ears: Danton was an enemy of the Revolution and must die for it.

Even so, the arrest decree for the Danton circle was not unanimous. Two committee men, including old Rühl, braved their fears of retaliation and refused to sign. They held public office to feed the deprived citizenry, the hold-outs argued, not to kill patriots. The rest signed, the boldness of their pen strokes betraying the depth of their purpose. Saint-Just, the cripple Couthon and Vadier, co-opted from the police committee to 'gut the turbot', wrote their names with a firm hand. The shyest hand of all, appearing in small, thin script in a bottom corner of the arrest document, was that of Robespierre, as if his fear of Danton would never leave him.

The decree signed and the committee men sworn to secrecy, all that remained was for Saint-Just to run it past the Convention on the morrow. However, the signatories were unnerved by what they had done. As a precaution, they pre-empted Convention debate, ordering the arrests made that same night for fear of giving their main target time to stir up the Paris street crowds.

Even with the advance warning Danton had little time to react. Two hours perhaps, three at most. Ever since Hébert's execution, his Cordelier friends had been telling him it would be his turn next. Between them Robespierre and Saint-Just controlled all the levers of state; it was time to leave the country. The thought of flight repelled him. It was unthinkable that he, Danton, would run away, fleeing like the émigrés whose treachery he thundered against. No, they could threaten him all they liked. When it came to it, they would never dare touch him! Such was his conviction on the night of 30 March, as Camille and Lacroix, perplexed, returned to the prospect of making an escape. Danton dismissed it with a proud heave of his chest: 'You can't take the *patrie* with you on the soles of your shoes.'

As startled as he was, sick of men as he felt, Danton told his companions they need not fear. Was his head not still on his bull shoulders? Why would they want to kill him? What good would it do? What purpose would it serve? No, they would defend themselves before the people and show who truly carried the Revolution in their hearts. Though Louise, weeping, implored him to go into hiding, and Lucile, who arrived from upstairs, was also in tears tugging at Camille to get away to her mother's house in the country, Danton strode around the living room repeating, 'They wouldn't dare!'

The headmen of the Cordelier tribe determined to take their chance before the people.

An hour or so after midnight a company of gendarmes came to arrest all three of them, escorting them on foot through dark and empty streets to the prison fashioned out of the old Luxembourg Palace close by. The gendarmes already had Philippeaux and the soldier Westermann in manacles and the five of them walked under escort together. Danton went quietly, wearing his favourite red frockcoat, which he thought fitting for the occasion; he was in full charge of his volcanic temper, having sought to comfort Louise with a promise to return home very soon.

As news of the arrests, released by one of Danton's jabbering kitchen maids, spread through the streets of Paris that morning, deputies hastened to the Convention to seek confirmation. Legendre, as stupefied as anyone, was first to the rostrum. The butcher was unsure of his facts. 'Citizens, four members of this house were arrested overnight,' he affirmed in his rough sans-culotte tones. 'I know Danton is one of them. I don't know the names of the others. What do names matter if they are guilty? But I stand here, citizens, to ask you to bring the arrested members before the bar of the house, where you can hear them, where you will then charge them or free them.' The stocky Legendre owned that he was uneducated and relied on his native wit to get by, so he was not equipped to put up an eloquent defence. But he was sure of one thing: 'Citizens, I declare that I believe Danton is as pure as I am! And I don't think any of you can accuse me of an act that has wronged the Revolution.'

Legendre seemed fearless. He said he believed that the government committees were acting out of personal spite and hatred for men who had done the republic proud. Why, it was Danton's energy, he declared, that stirred the nation to overthrow the monarchy in August 1792; it was Danton's vigour that mobilised the entire people, his forcefulness that sentenced to death able-bodied Frenchmen who refused to defend France against her foreign foes. 'The enemy was at the gates of Paris. Then came Danton, and his actions saved the *patrie*!'

The Convention, aroused by the butcher's plea, was moving towards a vote on his motion to hear Danton and his arrested friends when Robespierre, alerted to what was happening, hurried white of face into the chamber and went straight to the rostrum. At the sight of the Incorruptible, a shiver seemed to run across the suddenly silenced benches. In his sharp, dry voice, he demanded to know why the Convention would even consider taking it upon itself to judge Danton and his fellow deputies. Had it not very recently rejected a request from Danton himself to hear Fabre, also a deputy? It was an outrage against liberty to favour one citizen over another. If the house took the place of the Revolutionary Tribunal as Danton's judge, it would simply revive the rule of privilege. 'No! We want no more privilege,' Robespierre cried, his thin voice rising. 'No! We want no more idols! This day we shall see if the Convention knows how to smash a supposed idol long gone to rot, or if the falling idol crushes the Convention and the French people with it.' The small, slight figure fixed the massive butcher with a stare, adding with menace: 'He who trembles is guilty.'

The Jacobin headman's new-order logic was greeted in continued petrified silence. Even the Mountain remained hushed. No one dared step up to contest it. A deflated Legendre all at once felt acutely vulnerable. Alas, Robespierre misunderstood him, he said, returning gingerly to the rostrum. Naturally he, Legendre, was not privy to the evidence that the Committee of Public Safety possessed. 'Anyway, I don't mean to defend any particular person here,' he said, his humiliation complete as the house voted by show of hands to reject his initiative to free Danton.

Now it was Saint-Just's turn to address the hushed chamber. With strangely measured violence, barely changing his tone throughout, Robespierre's inquisitor spent an hour and a half presenting his labyrinthine indictment, twisting this way and that through diverse conspiracy theories and every insinuation ever thrown at Danton but coming back to a half dozen central charges: Danton was the enemy of liberty from the start – 'the tiger stalking liberty for his prey' – who conspired with Mirabeau, the Duc d'Orléans and Dumouriez to maintain the throne in whatever form appeared possible; Danton plotted in secret with foreign enemies, through agents and negotiators, to undo the Revolution; Danton sought with his Cordelier friends, once excluded from the Committee of Public Safety, to overthrow it and sabotage the revolutionary government; Danton abandoned the people's cause by retreating to Arcis whenever crisis struck; Danton enriched his friends when justice minister and head of government; and most criminal of all, Danton did his utmost, like Brissot and the Girondins, to impose a policy of moderation and clemency to destroy the republic and wreck its liberties.

If deputies found it hard to believe their ears as Saint-Just droned on, they did not show it.

Though it was hard to recognise the Danton they knew in the indictment, they chose to suspend their incredulity and hold mute, or indeed applaud Saint-Just. Hardly a gasp of dissent greeted the youthful inquisitor when he depicted Danton's drive for total mobilisation – the *levée en masse* that was turning the tide in the war against Europe – as a treacherous scheme to send all patriots and sans-culottes to the frontiers so as to leave an unprotected Paris open to a royalist takeover. The one familiar accusation the inquisitor refrained from throwing at Danton was that of lawless extravagance with state monies, perhaps because it was the allegation favoured by the Rolands and by the Girondin leaders whom he and Robespierre had exterminated.

Had Danton the barrister been present he might have marvelled, roared with laughter even, at Saint-Just's reliance on moral conviction to make his case, for not a shred of material evidence was produced on any count. The youth incriminated the Cordelier giant's entire public life without a fact in support: all was suspicion, conjecture, innuendo and insinuation reduced at the close to a broad two-line decree to deliver the Cordelier leaders to the Revolutionary Tribunal: 'They have participated in a conspiracy to maintain the monarchy and to destroy national representation and republican government.'

The Convention approved the decree, again by a show of hands. Robespierre, having so often heard it applauding Danton to the rafters, appeared surprised by the house's submissiveness. Returning to his lodgings on the Rue Saint-Honoré, he sniffed to his landlord, 'I must say, Danton has spineless friends.'


If there was ever a propitious time for Robespierre to rid himself and his moral crusade of Danton it was now.

That the Revolution had no more battles to fight, only scaffolds to raise, seemed close enough to the truth. By that spring of 1794 the revolutionary forces were holding the armies of the European monarchies on every front, even driving them out; at the same time, they were at last suppressing the popular revolts at home to end the civil war. Superior troop numbers driven into the field by Danton's lungs, coupled with the scythe of the Terror, were paying off for the new republic.

For William Pitt and the England with which Danton had sought to negotiate the year before, it was a calamitous time. Pitt's cold shoulder to Danton's unconventional diplomatic advances betrayed a blindness, for all the English leader chose to see across the Channel was a republic imploding from the impossible pressures of national bankruptcy and the abominable scare of the guillotine, which he wagered would kill the French people's spirit. Things had been going wrong for England at the head of the grand European coalition since the end of the previous year. It was during Christmas 1793, that the English fleet and a sizable Anglo-Spanish occupation force were unfestively driven out of Toulon, despite the allegiance of the city fathers. And it was at Toulon that a republican gunnery captain named Napoleon Bonaparte, barely into his twenties, first tasted victory. Alas for Pitt's future career, Bonaparte left the field with an ugly gash in the leg from an English bayonet that nourished a lifelong animosity towards the old foe.

Pitt's main problem in confronting the Revolution was that the French forces, led by generals who knew they were bound for the guillotine if they failed to win, were now at least twice as numerous as the combined 300,000-strong force that the coalition allies could agree to muster. There were embarrassing debacles too, besides Toulon. An English force that landed on France's Channel coast in January to link up with anti-revolutionary columns led by fugitive Girondins – Madame Roland's lover, Buzot, among them – failed to make contact and eventually sailed back home, sealing the rebels' fate in Brittany and Normandy. Furthermore, the chief allies Pitt was financing, Austria and Prussia, increasingly had their eyes elsewhere – this time as rivals dividing up Poland between themselves and Russia. The allied effort to undo the Revolution was in danger of falling apart. London clubs and coffee houses buzzed with rumours that hostilities had reached a point where the invasion boot was on the other foot: it was not England that was about to invade France, it was sans-culotte hordes with pikes and cannon that were about to burst upon the shores of England. In response to such feverish rumours, Pitt was obliged through the spring to hasten measures for home defence, including the deployment of gunboats and floating batteries along the Kent and Sussex coasts.

Pitt's problems were Robespierre's gains. Still, gaining the upper hand on the home front was greater satisfaction than foiling England for Robespierre, who never looked far beyond stamping out traitors at home. His gaze remained fixed there as republican troops now tightened a merciless vice on the Vendée and on the breakaway cities of the republic in the west and the south. From the very beginning of 1794 the peasant army of the Vendée was defeated and then obliterated by superior republican forces in a series of battles in the Loire marshlands; the Vendée cause had been lost after the rebels tried to move north of the great river that mothered their insurrection in the vain hope of joining up with an English fleet at Granville, on the Cotentin Peninsula, a departure point for the Channel Islands.

Robespierre's green room declined to leave the republic's civil-war victory at that, as Danton wanted. During the spring of 1794 the Committee of Public Safety unleashed the Terror on the entire Vendée region, ordering the indiscriminate destruction of the land and its population. Large republican forces sent to the region under sans-culotte generals split into a dozen marching columns – 'Columns of Hell' – with orders to kill every man, woman and child in their path, to burn every dwelling, every farm, every village, every crop. And that is what they did. If obliterating the Vendée region cost 100,000 lives, the Terror's toll was high too in bringing royalist-leaning Lyons to its republican senses. After revolutionary troops retook France's second city in the closing weeks of 1793 – renaming it 'Ville Affranchie' (Freetown), as instructed by Paris committee men – the real punishment began. Right up to the time of Danton's arrest, the green room's two commissioners in Lyons – the Shakespeare adapter Collot d'Herbois and a priestly ex-teacher named Joseph Fouché, who was launching a sinister career as France's most efficient policeman – set about sacking the southern capital. Over a period of two months Collot and Fouché demolished the houses of the rich, the Lyons silkmen's great riverbank mansions, and sent 3,000 citizens to the guillotine or, when the swish of the blade seemed too slow, disposed of them in mass groups before firing squads.

Things were tilting back in favour of the revolutionary regime in Paris, so long accustomed to adverse happenings.

In the minds of Robespierre and Saint-Just there existed a pervading conspiracy against the Revolution – spread through Paris, the provinces, among all foreigners – that had to be endlessly crushed to make way for the perfect society. Danton was at the head of that notional conspiracy.

A soft dawn broke on 31 March as Danton entered the gates of the Luxembourg prison. The rooms and cells of the former palace were crammed with inmates of all kinds, though it was supposedly reserved for prisoners with a Revolutionary record to their name – Convention deputies who fell foul of the green room, government officials, defeated generals, nobles and foreigners. Fabre and Hérault de Séchelles had already been shut up there for some weeks now.

Despite the hour, prisoners crowded the cobbled forecourt as warders ushered in the Atlas of the Revolution and his Cordelier friends. Amid the hollering that greeted their arrival, Danton heard a cry in English and turned on his heel. It was Mad Tom Paine, the thorn in Pitt's flesh, incarcerated since Christmas at Robespierre's bidding. The Englishman had been detained there in black fear for three months, his sleep shattered by the shrieks and sobs of fellow prisoners being taken away in the darkness to the guillotine, certain that his turn must come next. Danton reached out to clasp Mad Tom's hand, greeting him with the shout: 'What you have done for the liberty and happiness of your country, I have tried to do for mine.'

While some of the prisoners kept their distance, others mobbed Danton now, clutching at his red frockcoat. Still addressing Paine, he added, 'I have been less fortunate in my endeavours, but no less innocent. They send me to the scaffold. Very well, my friend, I shall go in good spirit.' Then to the prisoners in general he bellowed, raising an arm above his massive head: 'I was hoping to get you all out of this soon, but here I am myself. Who knows when it will all end!'

This was a bluffing Danton making out that he somehow had matters in hand. Perhaps he believed it. His conviction that the puny Robespierre would not dare exterminate someone of his size, his record, his popularity with the people, sustained his spirits despite his patently perilous situation. If he had to die, though, he would die as the people would expect him to – loud, full-voiced, scornful of his executioners. And what could he expect of the people, *his* people? Would they surge to his side? Would they rise with him against Robespierre's law?

Two days passed in a flash in the Luxembourg cellars. Fabre, reunited with his tribe, was sardonic, trying to make light of things: they could kill him, he said, but not his theatrical works. Camille wrote tender, painful letters to Lucile, who went to Robespierre's lodgings, tugging Louise Danton with her, hoping to weaken the Incorruptible's resolve by reminding him of his part at their wedding. His landlord, Duplay, answered the women's knock and, after establishing who they were and returning inside to consult with his tenant, sent them away: Robespierre did not wish to see them.

Danton's mood took him up and down – now buoyant, now ribald, now rueful, now bluff. 'I'm leaving everything in a horrible mess,' he shrugged. Occasionally he took an ironic lunge at the 'half-men' in the green room who aimed to kill him: 'If I left my balls to Robespierre and my legs to Couthon, that committee might go on working for a while.' It was a year almost to the day since Danton took the initiative in creating the Revolutionary Tribunal and he remarked on the anniversary to his jailers, adding under his breath, no doubt in earnest if rather out of character, 'I ask the pardon of God and of humanity.'

At dawn on 2 April, the third day of confinement, the Cordelier prisoners were transferred together to the Conciergerie fastness on the Île de la Cité, where the guillotine tumbrels were lined up. From there it was a step across a gaunt courtyard to the Palais de Justice, where in another world, as a barrister's clerk, Danton had done the rounds of the law courts for Maître Vinot, and where Fouquier in his black-feathered hat now sat to open his trial.

# NINETEEN

## Trial and Execution

The trial of Danton was bound to be a spectacle. The giant jousting with death. An enthralled public crammed Fouquier's vaulted courtroom in the Palais de Justice, filled the streets outside and spilled in their thousands on to the cobbled quays of the Seine to witness what promised to be one of the greatest shows of the Revolution.

In those blue early days of April 1794 the windows of the tribunal were thrown open, so that Danton's famous roar carried at times across the river to the Cordelier constituency on the Left Bank. Those who heard, or thought they heard, spread their version of what he said to the surrounding crowd, transforming what occurred inside the court into a rushing, babbling swell of conjecture outside.

The first thing they heard was Danton's booming response to his judges' request to identify himself: 'I am Georges-Jacques Danton, thirty-four years old, born in Arcis-sur-Aube, barrister, Convention deputy.' With proud disdain, he added his address: 'Soon to be the Void, and my name will dwell in the pantheon of history.' Camille responded in similar vein: 'I am Camille Desmoulins, I am thirty-three years old, the age of the sans-culotte Jesus Christ when he died.'

It was hard not to treat the trial with scorn. Prosecutor Fouquier swore in just seven jurors, for the most part tradesmen he believed he could depend on, instead of the statutory twelve. Danton and the Cordelier brethren were among sixteen prisoners in the dock, half of whom, including two Austrians, a Spaniard and a Dane, were businessmen and speculators of one kind or another who faced fraud charges stemming from the East India Company fiasco, with no link – except through Fabre's presence – to the separate political conspiracy charges brought against Danton.

But why not compromise Danton by roping him in with the fellowship of financial fraudsters whom the sans-culottes so detested? That seemed the purpose of the presiding judge, Armand Herman, Robespierre's straight-backed personal appointee, and of Fouquier, both of whom received an implicit prior warning from the green room that they would be removed and arrested if they showed signs of weakening towards the Cordeliers or failed to obtain a guilty verdict. At any rate, judge and prosecutor ignored indignant protests from Camille. 'Let us be sacrificed alone!' he cried. 'What do we have to do with these rogues?' In the audience sat four committee men, including Vadier, to ensure that judge and prosecutor met their obligations.

The trial went on for four days, rather longer than intended in view of the court's predispositions. At the opening on 2 April a junior judge laboriously read out Saint-Just's long charge sheet, as well as charges against the financial defendants – a disappointment to the vast crowd outside, which expected permanent fireworks from the start. The litany of accusation had its effect, though. It had the crowd murmuring and somehow tilted the public mood against Danton.

General Westermann, brought to the tribunal after the others and uncited in the group indictment, protested that he had neither been notified of charges against him nor been asked to identify himself. Herman shrugged, calling his request a pointless matter of form. Danton surged to his feet with a roar: 'Form! We're all of us here only for form!' The tribunal erupted in laughter as Herman called on the defendants to obey their duty to respect the court, at which Danton rose again, shouting: 'And I, Your Honour, I remind you of yours. We have the right to speak here!' He was acting as his own defence counsel, having refused a court-appointed advocate. Turning to the jury, he added with a monstrous scowl, 'I'm the one who created this tribunal, so I know something about it.'

Herman rang his bell for order but the hubbub continued. 'Don't you hear the bell?' he asked, glaring around the court. Still on his feet, Danton countered: 'A man defending his life does not care about a damn bell. No, he keeps shouting! If we are allowed to speak, and freely, I am sure to beat my accusers – and if the French people are what they ought to be, I shall be asking for clemency for those who accuse me.'

Was he hinting at how he hoped the great crowd surrounding the Palais de Justice would react to this programme to kill him? He had seen popular insurrections. Why not one on his behalf? But this was perhaps a fleeting thought. Danton was prepared for the worst. Still, Westermann too showed that he had it in him to fire public sympathy. Having at length been taken away to an ante-room to have his alleged crimes read to him – that he, like Danton, had plotted with Dumouriez to restore the monarchy – the soldier returned angrier than before. He said: 'I have received seven wounds fighting for the republic, all of them from the front. I have received only one from behind – this accusation!' Roars of support from the public benches were soon echoing through the streets outside.

Fouquier, unhappy with the way things were going, opted to address the financial scandal first, where he felt on reasonably strong ground, since it was not part of the indictment against the vehement Danton. The prosecuter called in a notable witness for the prosecution, Joseph Cambon, the Convention's finance brain. Cambon was a Montagnard who backed the Terror but was not enamoured of Robespierre and had been as loath as Danton to see the Girondins sent to the guillotine. As Cambon approached his seat, Danton called out: 'Ah, Cambon, it's you. Do you believe we are conspirators?'

Cambon could not hide a smile.

Danton erupted: 'Look! He laughs! He laughs! He doesn't believe it! Let it be recorded that he laughs.'

The hilarity was not to last. Cambon's expert testimony helped Fouquier construct a passable case against those involved in the East India Company manipulations. This took up most of the second day of the trial, during which Danton hardly had a chance to present his defence, and although he was in no way incriminated in the financial misdoings, he sat frustrated at the lost opportunity to keep the momentum on his side. He and Camille were chafing to call witnesses in their defence; they had a score of them lined up. Furthermore, they wanted to force Robespierre and Saint-Just into the witness box, aiming to expose the futility of their actions. Where was their murderous virtue taking France? What destination did they seek? Danton doubted there was one.

Only in the third day's session did a wary Herman direct the tribunal to address the case against the Cordelier giant. His crisp summation of the charges brought further uproar:

**Herman**: Danton, the Convention accuses you of supporting Dumouriez, of failing to inform it of his intentions and of participating in his plans to destroy liberty, to wit, marching his army on Paris in order to overthrow the government and restore monarchy.
**Danton**: My voice has too often spoken out in defence of the people's cause to have to hear this slander. I reject it! Do the cowards who vilify me dare attack me face to face? Let them show themselves! I shall cover them in their own shame and ignominy. I have said so and I repeat it: my domicile is the Void. My head is there, which answers everything! Life weighs heavy, I look forward to leaving

it!

**Herman:** Danton, your audacity is the mark of crime. The mark of innocence is moderation . . . I invite you to justify yourself as to the charges made against you. I invite you to be precise, and above all to address the facts.

Danton saw red. This robed puppet was maligning his nature, criminalising his audacity in restoring backbone to a quaking Revolution: *Be bold! Bolder still! Ever bolder! And France is saved.* Here was this slave of Robespierre talking of facts and courtroom propriety! It was a fact that Robespierre called in the seven jurymen to brief them each evening at the end of the session, and that Fouquier repaired to the jury room each time he left his desk.

Still, Danton composed himself:

**Danton:** Personal audacity is no doubt reprehensible, and I have never been accused of it. But audacity for the nation, the audacity for which I have so often tried to set an example, the audacity that has served the republic, yes, that is permissible. Indeed, it is necessary in revolution, and that audacity I own to with honour. (*Throwing out his hands, and raising his stentorian voice.*) When I see myself so grossly, so grievously accused, how do you expect me to control my indignation? You expect a cool response from a revolutionary like me! Men of my stripe cannot be bought, the seal of liberty is printed in indelible letters on their brow!

**Herman:** The duty of a defendant, his personal interest, is to explain in a clear and precise manner . . .

But now the courtroom was in tumult once more. Herman halted proceedings to call for order. He scribbled a note to Fouquier, saying that he intended to suspend the defence. Meanwhile, Danton, on his feet, demanded that Robespierre and Saint-Just show 'proof, half-proof, a clue even' that he had sold out to Mirabeau and the royalist side. 'Bring them on! Come, vile imposters! I shall tear off the masks that hide you from public condemnation.'

Herman was sounding his bell again. When a relative quiet returned, Fouquier joined the magistrate in reiterating the rumours about Danton's supposed dealings with Mirabeau. Danton had already been through this in a rambling explanation of his conduct at the time of the violent overthrow of the monarchy, as head of the revolutionary government, as commissioner in Belgium, in his relations with Dumouriez, his friendship with Fabre ('I still believe Fabre is a good citizen') and his frequent retreats to Arcis, and now, a little fatigued, he turned to heavy irony:

I do in fact recall bringing about the restoration of royalty. Indeed, I do remember reviving the power of the throne – when I opposed with all my might the tyrant's flight to Saint-Cloud, when I had his path blocked with pikes and bayonets, when I seized the reins of his spirited horses to stop him. If that is being a friend to royalty, if those are the acts of a man who supports tyranny, then in that case I confess I am guilty!'

The confession brought raucous applause. Herman was alarmed. While warning Danton against his 'indecent outbursts', he proposed that since the Cordelier chief's voice was turning hoarse it was time for a rest, so he would suspend the session. Danton did not object to a break, he told Herman, as long as he and his co-defendants could call their own witnesses at the resumption.

Herman stared at him. His evident reluctance brought Danton back to his feet. 'You refuse me witnesses! All right, I shall no longer defend myself! A thousand pardons, I must add, if I have been overheated. It's my character! The people will tear my enemies to shreds before three months are out.'

During the suspension, Fouquier penned a hurried message to the Committee of Public Safety, describing how the trial had run into a 'terrible storm'. Maddened defendants insisted on calling witnesses, he reported, and were appealing to the people to support their demand. What should he do? His note ended: 'We invite you to lay down how we should respond to their claim, since judicial procedure provides no means to motivate a refusal.'

The prosecution seemed overwhelmed. The public was worked up. Acquittal stared the green room in the face.

Robespierre and the committee men were looking for a quick solution even before receiving Fouquier's appeal. The Incorruptible made himself scarce during the trial; apart from one appearance at the Convention, he was not seen outside his committee chambers, and he spent the rest of the time alone in his lodgings. It was safer there. Saint-Just, though, was a venomous whirlwind. It was he who believed he had hit upon the required solution. Whether genuine or fabricated – perhaps simply dictated by Saint-Just – a report came through from an inmate at the Luxembourg prison, named as a foreign service functionary, that an uprising was imminent at the jail: the objective was to deliver a popular assault on the Revolutionary Tribunal to liberate Danton. According to the prisoner's report, Lucile Desmoulins, desperate to free her husband, had come to the gates of the jail with a large sum of money to reward a detained army general, the head of the planned uprising.

As Fouquier's pleading letter landed, Saint-Just secured green-room agreement to go straight before the Convention to divulge his prison-uprising tale. In a grim voice he announced the uncovering of a plot to assassinate patriots and crush the Tribunal, and with it moved for a decree devised to close the Danton trial there and then. His motion, approved by the Convention, empowered the Tribunal to remove from the courtroom any defendant who resisted or insulted the bench. The effect of this gag order, which left Herman and Fouquier to interpret at will what constituted resistance or an insult, was to cut off all further debate on charges against the Cordeliers.

A committee man with a place reserved beside Vadier in the trial audience hastened from the Convention floor to plant the order in Fouquier's hand. 'My God, citizen, we needed it,' said the prosecutor. At that same moment Lucile, publicly incriminated by Saint-Just, was herself arrested and locked up in the Sainte-Pélagie jail, where Madame Roland had spent her last days. Saint-Just trusted that Lucile's arrest would help validate the prison revolt story.

The final session of the trial on 5 April, was a curt affair, though no less turbulent for that. As Saint-Just intended, the rumour of the jailbreak conspiracy left the sans-culottes perplexed as it spread around Paris. They regarded the Luxembourg prisoners as a gang of blueblood traitors and their perplexity at the supposed plot again tilted the popular mood against Danton. In the courtroom, Herman, shielded by Saint-Just's decree, ruled that there would be a fair exchange concerning witnesses: the prosecution would surrender its right to introduce them, in return for which Danton and company would forfeit the right to call theirs. The Cordeliers were enraged by the ruling. Camille, beside himself with grief and anxiety over Lucile's arrest, had composed a memoir rebutting Saint-Just's accusations; he tore the paper up and screwed it into a ball which he tossed at the bench. Herman reminded the defendants of the insult decree, then bid the jury to retire to determine whether they had heard enough and were ready to reach a verdict. A few minutes later the seven jurymen returned, saying they were ready, upon which Herman declared: 'The jury being satisfied, the pro-ceedings are closed.'

Danton sprang to his feet one last time. 'Closed! How closed? They haven't even begun. No proof! No witnesses!'

Camille, Lacroix, Hérault, Philippeaux and Westermann were also on their feet, shouting: 'We're being judged without being heard!' Fouquier intervened to demand that in view of the prisoners' unbecoming behav-iour they should be removed from court before the jury pronounced its verdict, to which Herman consented. A platoon of bailiffs bundled them back to the Conciergerie.

Danton's reaction to his removal was raucous even by his standards. He took it as an assault on his manhood. The whole trial, he felt, was an assault on his manhood. On Danton the human being. He was no saint, but he was a man. 'Me, a conspirator? I bed my wife every day!' he yelled in the departure hall, the urge to distinguish himself from Robespierre welling into incongruous frenzy. 'My name is engraved on every institution of the Revolution – the revolutionary army, the *levée*, the committees, the Revolutionary Tribunal. I have killed myself!'

Still, it took the jury longer than expected to deliver the verdict it had pronounced itself ready to reach. While jurymen wanted to do right by Robespierre's committee, two or three of them found it hard to accept that Danton was guilty. At length Vadier and his committee men broke into the deliberations. What? Not guilty? they cajoled. Had public opinion not already judged Danton? What were they waiting for? Only traitors would acquit him!

The open threat did it. The jury returned, its headman drawing a flat hand across his throat on entering the box. Then the verdict. A conspiracy existed to corrupt and defraud the nation; how did the jury find? Guilty. A conspiracy existed to restore the monarchy; how did it find? Guilty. Herman pronounced the death sentence on the absent defendants, to be carried out forthwith. Only one of the sixteen – an obscure lawyer placed late in the dock with Westermann – received an acquittal.

At four o'clock that same afternoon the condemned Cordeliers and financiers began the tumbrel ride through the streets of Paris from the courtyard of the Conciergerie to the Place de la Révolution, where the guillotine awaited them. Crowds lining the route were strangely subdued, neither shouting support nor sneering and catcalling, the ritual street response to carts seen bumping towards the guillotine. Danton rode in the last of three red-painted tumbrels, each drawn by a pair of horses at walking pace and carrying five condemned men. Several dozen gendarmes accompanied the convoy on foot.

By now the Cordelier giant had regained his composure: he stood with his broad thighs against the backboard, his enormous head fixing the crowd with a proud stare. Now and then he threw an arm around Camille, who was flinging himself about the cart, sobbing over Lucile. Across the bridge from the Conciergerie the convoy rolled past the Parnasse café, where he had wooed Gabrielle at Madame Charpentier's till. Poor Gabrielle. Was it his leap on to the tide of Revolution that killed her? And poor Louise, left with his boys. Still only at walking pace, they came on to the Rue Saint-Honoré, passing the gates of the Palais Royal, where he had learned his revolutionary arts. The Duc d'Orléans' pleasure grounds looked unswept and miserable now. Further along the Rue Saint-Honoré they passed the carpenter Duplay's house, where Robespierre lodged, its shutters closed. Danton couldn't resist a bellow; the crowd would expect it of him. 'You're next!' he roared, pointing a finger. 'You will follow me!' Then the carts turned left onto the Rue Royale, down to the great square on the river beside the gardens of the Tuileries, where the guillotine rose in silhouette against the deepening blue of the late-afternoon sky. Close by, at the heart of the Place de la Révolution, as high as the scaffold, rose a white plaster Statue of Liberty that feted the end of monarchy. Perhaps Danton's thoughts turned for a moment, and not unsweetly, to Madame Roland – that pretentious goddess of revolt who refused to look past his hideous face and his outsize appetites to take a measure of his worth. Who could forget her last words at that same scaffold? *O Liberty, what crimes are committed in thy name!* She might have said the same of patriotism.

One after the other, condemned Cordelier heads began thudding into the bucket at the foot of the guillotine. Danton was listed by Fouquier as the last of the fifteen to go. Blood slewed across the platform where the next man up awaited his turn. The executioner was in a hurry now; he had to finish his task before nightfall and the sky in the west was reddening fast. Hérault, when his turn came, went to embrace Danton but the executioner pulled him away. 'Fool!' Danton growled to the spattered functionary. 'You won't keep our heads apart in the bucket.'

The huge crowd that had surged into the square from the tumbrel route, now stretching down to the bank of the Seine, still struck him as eerily quiet. Was it for these gapers – the people – that he had jumped on to the tide? Or because of his impetuous nature? And were they now with him? Or were they against him? It was hard to tell, for they seemed paralysed by the Terror.

He felt the guillotine crew pulling at him, baring the nape of his bull neck. As his Gorgon head touched the block, he reared round to squint up at the exhausted executioner, telling him: 'Make sure you show it to the people. It is worth a look.'

# EPILOGUE

Four months pass before Danton's death writes humanity into the rulebook of the Revolution as sister to liberty. The immediate aftermath of his execution, however, is a bloodbath of still greater proportions, baptised the Great Terror by those who live through it. During these four months Robespierre's rule of virtue turns into the rule of fear absolute.

The Incorruptible and his green-room disciples stand unchallenged. They simplify the statutes of Fouquier's court by removing all vestiges of judicial process. The Revolutionary Tribunal acquires a blunt catch-all purpose: to punish the 'enemies of the people'. With defence rights abolished, it becomes a political court charged in effect with political extermination. Thus will Robespierre's theories serve the public interest. There are plenty of candidates for extermination, since the number of counter-revolutionary 'suspects' languishing in dungeons across the land has risen to half a million. Ultimately, the majority of them will manage to hang on and survive. Still, during the four months of the Great Terror, starting with Danton's execution, the bulk of the 2,300 citizens guillotined in Paris alone are rushed past Fouquier without a hearing. The Revolution has run amok, disposing not only of the *Ancien Régime* but of its own liberal origins. Across France 16,600 people are dispatched by drumhead revolutionary justice, not counting the massive death toll run up by the 'Columns of Hell' in the Vendée and ruthless commissioners in Lyons.

It cannot last.

The Revolution has brought about stupendous change but the population no longer knows what purpose it serves, except vengeance and repression. The counter-urge for moderation and clemency that Danton endeavoured to instil in the Convention finally boils over in late July. Convention members, each of them feeling perilously close to the guillotine, turn on Robespierre to a man and vote to arrest him, together with Saint-Just and the cripple Couthon. Robespierre's voice cracks when he takes the rostrum attempting to defend himself. Someone shouts: 'It is the blood of Danton that chokes you!' The Incorruptible croaks back: 'Danton! Is it Danton you regret? Cowards! Then why didn't you defend him?'

The arrest of Robespierre is hideously bungled and half his jaw is shot away before he goes to the guillotine, heavily bandaged, the following morning, 28 July 1794 – 10 Thermidor by Fabre's evocative calendar. A trial is deemed unnecessary. Saint-Just, Couthon and a score of committee men are guillotined with him. Robespierre's fall is a *coup d'état* that heralds serener times. Among the first actions taken by the Terror's survivors is abolition of the Revolutionary Tribunal.

Many, indeed most, of those deeply involved with Danton in making the Revolution have died. Here is what befalls those whose fate is left hanging:

**Lucile Desmoulins** – Saint-Just allows little time for doubts to grow over his story of Lucile's efforts to promote a prison uprising to free Camille and Danton; she goes to the guillotine, aged twenty-four, a week after Camille's execution, accompanied, in a fiendish piece of green-room stage management, by the widow of Jacques-René Hébert, the butt of Camille's *Vieux Cordelier*.

**Louise Danton** – A widow at sixteen, Louise is allowed to leave in peace for Arcis after Danton's execution. At eighteen she marries a young provincial administrator who is promoted to prefect under Napoleon and ennobled as a baron of the empire. On his death in 1828, the baroness settles in Niort, near the Atlantic coast. She dies in 1856, aged seventy-eight, seldom having spoken of her first husband – except to the second, who forbade her to mention the name 'Danton' in public.

**Buzot** – After fleeing to Normandy, where his efforts to rouse the province against Paris are blocked, Madame Roland's lover escapes to Bordeaux, but is forced to go into hiding in the Saint-Emilion vineyards as the city submits to the Revolution. Cornered by Robespierre's republican trackers in June 1794, he commits suicide, aged thirty-four, having learned of the execution two months before of his mistress's nemesis and remarked on it thus: 'I am surprised to find that I regret Danton's death. What a crowd the people of Paris are! How shallow. How capricious.' Of Saint-Just's charge sheet he adds: 'With such a report and such a tribunal you can have half of France killed whenever you want.'

**Roland** – 'Old Roland', having eventually made good his escape to Rouen, commits suicide, aged fifty-nine, in a cellar hideout in the Normandy city the day he learns that his wife has gone to the guillotine.

**Condorcet** – The liberal philosopher, mainstay of the early Revolution and the Convention, manages to go into hiding in Paris when his fellow Girondins are arrested and later executed. So high is his reputation that the Convention makes no serious effort to find him and he has time to write a long essay, *Esquisse d'un Tableau de Progrès Humain*, in which he establishes three proper aims for the Revolution: reason, tolerance and humanity – a list close to Danton's latterday hopes. Though he disguises himself in workman's clothes, he is eventually recognised on the street and arrested a few days before Danton's execution; he poisons himself to thwart the guillotine. Only after Robespierre's death does Condorcet's wife discover that he too is dead, aged fifty – and not, as she thought, a refugee in Switzerland.

**Dumouriez** – Having fled to the Austrian side, the first soldier of the republic fails to see eye to eye with the Austrians on how to restore a monarchy in France and moves from country to country before settling in England in 1804, where Pitt grants him a pension in return for his professional advice on prosecuting the war against Napoleon. He dies at Henley-on-Thames in 1823, aged eighty-four.

**La Fayette** – Switching to the enemy proves small relief for Danton's long-standing adversary, since the wary Austrians hold him in castle dungeons for the next five years, releasing him only after Napoleon, fresh from a first military triumph over Austrian arms, takes power in France. Napoleon doesn't take to him, however, and only after the emperor's fall does the hero of the American Revolution resume a now modest political career as assembly deputy, nonetheless recapturing some of his old prestige on reappointment as Commander of the National Guard in 1830, at the age of seventy-three. He dies four years later.

**Fouquier** – The personification of the Terror – a man of no party – is in difficulties when Robespierre's execution puts an end to his Revolutionary Tribunal. Put on trial for his own life by the Convention, he throws all blame its way: 'I have been the hatchet of the Convention. Can you punish a hatchet?' The house, relieved of its fears, nonetheless sends him to the guillotine. He dies aged forty-nine.

**Vadier** – Though he turns against Robespierre in the end, Danton's persecutor with the fishwife mouth is tried as a leader of the Terror by the Convention and sentenced to deportation to Guyana, the Caribbean jungle-colony stockade which few survive. He escapes before departure, however, and hides until an amnesty frees convicted Terrorists in 1795.

He dies in exile in Belgium aged ninety-two – the record age reached by a Terrorist.

**Legendre** – Having recovered some of his courage after letting down Danton at the last, the butcher restores his influence in the Convention as it summons the will to dispose of Robespierre. He leads troops a year later in putting down a revolt against parliament, then takes a seat in Napoleon's obsequious chamber, the Council of Five Hundred, bequeathing his body to medicine at his death in 1797, aged forty-five.

**Paré** – Danton's old schoolfriend, while maintaining their close personal ties, pulls away from the Cordelier clan to take up public-service duties. During Robespierre's green-room dictatorship, he holds the post of interior minister, by then purely administrative. During Napoleon's reign he becomes director of military hospitals, a demanding post under the warrior emperor.

**Tom Paine** – On meeting and bidding farewell to Danton in the Luxembourg prison, the pioneer of revolution is certain he will die. The Englishman's name comes up for execution on 25 July 1794, as the Great Terror rages. By chance, the door to his cell is open when warders come by to chalk a guillotine number on it; thus they chalk it on the inside of the door. When the executioners come by later to escort him to the scaffold, the door is closed and they pass his cell by. Two days later Robespierre's arrest and rapid execution make Mad Tom's miraculous reprieve permanent. He resumes his seat in the Convention, leaving France when Napoleon takes power. He dies back in America, his first adopted homeland, in 1809, aged seventy-two.

**William Pitt** – Despite the incredible disarray in Paris, England's fortunes in her war on the Revolution seldom pick up after the total mobilisation inspired by Danton, and things do not improve when Napoleon brings his military genius to bear on the conflict. On hearing of Napoleon's crushing victory at the Battle of Austerlitz in December 1805 – a victory that sends asunder the Continental coalition Pitt has laboured long and hard to maintain against France – the prime minister falls mortally ill, at the age of forty-five. He dies months later, his friends concur, of a broken heart, though his doctors add to the diagnosis a chronic excess of port wine.

# NOTES

In place of a formal bibliography I have endeavoured to cite in the notes that follow each of the works I have read or referred to in writing this life of Danton. Those not mentioned in the notes are listed at the end. I have quoted from very many of Danton's speeches, invariably giving sources for those delivered at critical moments in the Revolution – most of them addressed to the national parliament or the Jacobin club. Where such quotations are not separately sourced, it will be clear from the text that they come from lesser speeches before the same houses.

Translation from the French is mine throughout. With Danton, this is a humbling task.

## Prologue: Paris: 15 July 1789 (pages 1–8 )

**Page 3** *Jules Michelet, a great romancer . . .* : Michelet's stupendous *Histoire de la Révolution Française* (first published 1847, reprinted many times over, among them Laffont, Paris, 1979 – a two-volume edition which I have used) is a mainstay work on the Revolution, subjectively capturing all its colour, tension, action, violence and players large and small.

**Page 3** *a phenomenon as awesome and irresistible . . .* : Eric Hobsbawm, *The Age of Revolution 1789–1848* (Weidenfeld and Nicolson, London, 1962), p. 94.

**Page 4** *'the greatest master of revolutionary tactics . . .'*: Hobsbawm, *Echoes of the Marseillaise* (Rutgers UP, 1990), p. 80. The tribute is found in Lenin's collected papers.

**Page 5** *'Nothing better explains provincial life . . .'*: Balzac, *Le Député d'Arcis* (de Potter, Paris, 1853).

**Page 7** *Alphonse Aulard (1849–1928) and Albert Mathiez (1874–1932) . . .* : Aulard's Danton opus includes *Études et Leçons sur la Révolution Française* (9 vols., 1893–1924), *Histoire Politique de la Révolution Française* (1901), *Danton* (1908) and *Les Grands Orateurs de la Révolution* (1914).

Mathiez's assaults on Danton include his major work, *La Révolution Française* (3 vols., 1922–7), as well as *Le Club des Cordeliers* (1910), *Annales Révolutionnaires* (1919) and *Autour de Danton* (1926).

An earlier nineteenth-century Danton specialist, Jean Robinet, is so admiring of Danton as to make his views a little embarrassing to read at times. That aside, his comprehensively researched works contain rich archive material. In particular, his *Danton: Homme d'État* (Charavay, Paris, 1889) reproduces invaluable chronological transcripts of Danton speeches – major and minor – to the Convention and the Paris political clubs.

Alfred Bougeart, a Belgian historian and contemporary of Robinet, is also an exhaustive compiler of Danton speeches, verbal sallies and documents relating to him; his *Danton* (Lacroix and Van Meenen, Brussels, 1861) has been of great help to me.

**Page 8** *a youthful Hilaire Belloc produced* . . . : Belloc's engaging work is entitled *Danton: A Study* (Duckworth, London, 1899).

**Page 8** *Danton is a figure made for the theatre* . . . : on the cinema screen the best-known offering is *Danton* (1982) by Polish director Andrzej Wajda, starring the French actor Gérard Depardieu: between them, in my view, they rather misconstrue Danton.

## Chapter 1: Bullfights (pages 9–17)

**Page 10** *He carried the vivid scar* . . . : Alexandre Rousselin de Saint-Albin, *Fragments Historiques* (Dentu, Paris, 1873), p. 168. Rousselin, a revolutionary civil servant, is a contemporary of Danton from the same Champagne region, albeit his junior by several years. His record of Danton's childhood and school years on which this chapter is based derives from unpublished notes kept by Louis Béon, an Arcis classmate of Danton and otherwise the sole direct source for his early years.

**Page 12** *At ten, he caught a chest infection* . . . : Alphonse Aulard, *L'Enfance et la Jeunesse de Danton; Études et Leçons sur la Révolution Française* (4th series, Paris, 1904), p. 73. Aulard notes that the smallpox leaves Danton 'severely pockmarked' – the lot of several other leading figures in the Revolution, notably Mirabeau, also to a lesser degree Robespierre.

**Page 13** *His recitations* . . . *had his classmates clapping* . . . : Rousselin, p. 170.

**Page 13** *recent discoveries of extraordinary ruins at Pompeii* . . . : some French historians hold that the discoveries (starting in 1748) contributed greatly to the intellectual climate that brings the Revolution. It is true that revolutionary speechmaking and news-sheets will hum with Roman references. Children are christened Scaevola, Gracchus and so on.

**Page 14** *'I want to see how a king is made'*: Rousselin, p. 170.

Page 15 *He was excited by the monarchy* . . . : Rousselin, p. 170. Rousselin's source, Béon, attests to Oratorian distaste for *lettres de cachet*.

Page 15 *'May God cure thee, the King doth touch'* (Que Dieu te guérisse, le Roi te touche): Aulard, *L'Enfance et la Jeunesse*, p. 76.

Page 15 *Danton won the essay prize* . . . : Aulard, p. 78.

Page 16 *In years to come Danton kept Shakespeare* . . .' Robinet, *Danton: Homme d'Etat*, p. 29.

## Chapter 2: Doing the Palais (pages 18–23)

Page 18 *The long day's ride was free* . . . : Louis Madelin, *Danton* (Hachette, Paris, 1914), p. 9.

Page 18 *Danton was astonished at the noise and bustle* . . . : Louis Mercier, *Tableau de Paris à la Révolution* (Michand, Paris, 1884), p. 18.

Page 19 *'Good God, man. What an atrocious fist!* . . . *Hah, I like a little cheek'*: Rousselin, p. 172.

Page 21 *Clearly she was not put off by his looks* . . . : Robert Christophe, *Danton* (Perrin, Paris, 1964), p. 82. Mademoiselle Duhauttoir's main business in Paris is by all accounts to seek a wealthy husband.

Page 21 *'I hate that bloody place* . . .': Rousselin, p. 173.

Page 22 *he came in full curiosity to Montesquieu, Voltaire* . . . : Aulard, *L'Enfance et la Jeunesse*, p. 80.

Page 22 *law degrees from Reims were up for sale* . . . : Madelin, p. 11. Some of the principal figures of the Revolution take their law degrees at Reims, among them the Girondin leader Jacques-Pierre Brissot, who disarmingly owns to 'purchasing' his, and the Girondin minister Jean-Marie Roland, who says he completed his in five days.

Page 23 *debtors became Danton's standby clients*: Christophe, p. 31. During Danton's political career his enemies pour scorn on this early defence of debtors.

## Chapter 3: Questions for a Bourgeois Gentleman (pages 24–36)

Page 26 *a regular seat at the Théâtre Français* . . . : the theatre is the home of the Comédie Française until the state troupe moves across the Seine after the Revolution to its present location at the Palais Royal, after which the Left Bank playhouse – still a foremost Paris landmark – takes its current name of the Odéon.

Page 27 *'We were raised in the schools of Rome* . . .': Jules Clarétie, *Étude sur les Dantonistes* (Plon, Paris, 1875), p. 42. Clarétie is an excellent source on the Desmoulins couple – Camille and his future wife, Lucile Duplessis – and their intimate ties to Robespierre that turn sour.

**Page 28** *If people whispered . . . how hideous he was . . .* : Rousselin, p. 177.

**Page 29** *The council was limited to seventy-three members . . .* : Christophe, p. 40.

**Page 29** *a standard decree declaring the monarchy's 'full and entire trust . . .'* : Madelin, p. 14.

**Page 30** *'It had me walking on razors'*: Rousselin, p. 178.

**Page 30** *'Woe to those who provoke revolution . . .'*: Rousselin, p. 179.

**Page 32** *Desmoulins, so eager to release . . .* : Clarétie, p. 84.

**Page 33** *ninety-one separate lodges . . .* : Robinet, p. 38.

**Page 34** *'The people will never be happy . . .'*: Robinet, p. 39.

**Page 34** *'A time will come when our outraged offspring . . .'*: abbé Sieyès, *Essai sur les Privilèges* (Bibliothèque Nationale de France [BNF], 1788). This is a short pamphlet which made a large impact among bourgeois intellectuals.

**Page 35** *the price of a regular loaf rose . . .* : Georges Rudé, *The French Revolution* (Weidenfeld and Nicolson, New York, 1988), p. 29. Rudé cites the price of a 4lb loaf.

**Page 35** *In Paris alone, 80,000 were out of work*: Rudé, p. 30.

## Chapter 4: Jumping upon a Tide (pages 37–52)

**Page 38** *Rights of the people . . . Power of the people . . .* : see Robinet, Cordelier assembly records, pp. 247–60. Here Danton's speeches to the Cordeliers show him defending *le peuple* at every turn; there is no record of the random speeches delivered at the Palais Royal, but it is logical to suppose he will have used the same technique in addressing crowds there.

**Page 39** *Barentin . . . invited him on the strength of it to consider joining his ministry . . .* : Rousselin, p. 180.

**Page 39** *'What! Can't you see the avalanche coming?'*: Rousselin, p. 181.

**Page 43** *'. . . we can only be removed by the power of his bayonets.'*: François Furet, *The French Revolution* (English translation: Blackwell, Oxford, 1992), p. 64.

**Page 44** *'What is the Third Estate? Everything . . .'*: Sieyès first sets the tone for revolution with his *Essai sur les Privilèges*; his clinching *Qu'est-ce que le Tiers État?* is published in January 1789.

**Page 44** *a giant fellow with a frenetic voice . . .* : Madelin, p. 19. The astonished barrister acquaintance is Christophe Lavaux, whose account may be politically biased: a staunch royalist, Lavaux later asks to defend Louis XVI when he comes to trial.

**Page 45** *'I saw an irresistible tide sweep by . . .'*: Jacques Roujon, *Ce Bon M. Danton* (Plon, Paris, 1929), p. 31.

**Page 45** *much gold changed hands . . .* : Adolphe Thiers, *Histoire de la Révolution Française* (Furne, Paris, 1846), vol. 1, p. 67. Thiers, journalist and politician, is a fair-minded student of the Revolution later to become prime minister, then president, of France. As a record of the Revolution seen from close quarters, his history rivals Michelet's more famous work.

**Page 46** . . . *a feline aspect, with joyless eyes*: Michelet, vol. 1, p. 382.

**Page 47** *It publicly 'sentenced' King Louis* . . . : Robinet, pp. 45–8. Robinet unearths this 'judgement' from contemporary documents published by a Palais Royal printing shop.

**Page 48** *'Citizens, I have just come from Versailles* . . .': Clarétie, p. 53.

**Page 48** *'I was choking with a host of ideas I had to get out* . . .': Clarétie, p. 55.

**Page 48** *now its inmates were mainly* . . . *men of letters*: Michelet, vol. 1, p. 88.

**Page 51** *Danton scowled. 'Whose orders?* . . .': Madelin, p. 20.

## Chapter 5: The Cordelier Republic (pages 53–68)

**Page 54** *'To release revolution* . . .': Madelin, p. 21.

**Page 56** *'Please send me shirts* . . .': Clarétie, p. 106.

**Page 56** *'This year the harvest is good* . . .': Christophe, p. 97.

**Page 61** *The march on Versailles* . . . : Robinet, pp. 52–3. The events that bring King Louis and Marie-Antoinette back to Paris and the mothballed Tuileries Palace are also nicely recorded in *Fatal Purity* by Ruth Scurr (Chatto & Windus, London, 2006) pp. 93–5.

**Page 61** *'Monsieur Marat is a bolt of lightning* . . .': Desmoulins, *Révolutions de France et Brabant, no. 47.*

**Page 62** *the capital* . . . *was the most splendid and most filthy of cities* . . . : Mercier, p. 12. Soon after King Louis' return to the Tuileries he is so disgusted by the fumes that he establishes a row of public latrines – never sufficient – along the outside walls. The Duc d'Orléans has installed public latrines at the Palais Royal from its opening as public pleasure grounds.

**Page 63** *He wore his ceremonial best* . . . : Christophe, p. 94.

**Page 63** *'Sire, Your Majesty's capital greets you* . . .': Madelin, p. 22.

**Page 63** *'two English individuals named Dantonne and Parr* . . .': Georges Lefebvre, *Sur Danton* chapter: *'Études sur la Révolution Française'* (Paris, 1932), p. 85.

**Page 64** *'His unanimous election in vote after vote* . . .': Bougeart, p. 30, citing Cordelier district assembly record for 11 January.

**Page 64** *Supposing he* had *accepted funds* . . . : there is no proof that Danton receives funds from the Orléans purse. Studies by hostile historians (e.g. Mathiez, *Autour de Danton, Annales de Danton*, etc.) and by some less biased ones (Lefebvre, *Sur Danton*) conclude that circumstantial evidence points to Danton receiving Orléans money to finance the Cordeliers.

This may be so, yet Danton's later relations with Orléans indicate that he in no way feels beholden to the duke.

**Page 66** *The decree savaged the Commune hierarchy* . . . : Bougeart, p. 30, citing Cordelier assembly record for 12 January.

**Page 66** *'What are all these troops for?* . . .': Bougeart, p. 31.

**Page 68** *The Great Inquiry* . . . : Madelin, p. 41.

## Chapter 6: Travails of a People's Champion (pages 69–84)

**Page 69** *'That fellow will go far* . . .': Michelet, vol. 1, p. 386.

**Page 70** *'We must regard as a vile traitor* . . .' : Bougeart, p. 35, citing a Cordelier district decree signed by Danton.

**Page 70** *'O my dearest Cordeliers* . . .': Robinet, p. 70, quoting article from Camille's *Révolutions de France et de Brabant*.

**Page 71** *The humiliation did not end there* . . . : Christophe, p. 120.

**Page 71** *only 14,000 Parislans* . . . *had the vote* . . . : Robinet, p. 70.

**Page 72** *'Tremble, you tyrants* . . .': Madelin, p. 46.

**Page 74** *Of necessity the meeting was secret* . . . : numerous references and allusions to the secret Mirabeau–Danton encounter appear in the contemporary press, taking one or the other participant's side. See Henri Avenel, *Histoire de la Presse Française* (Flammarion, Paris, 1900).

**Page 75** *'I do believe that his over-elegant, overloaded table* . . .': Clarétie, p. 109.

**Page 77** *The massive Cordelier had chosen his attire* . . . : Roujon, p. 83.

**Page 79** *'The man's a eunuch'*: Michelet, vol. 1, p. 720.

**Page 80** *a 'pack of donkeys'*: Madelin, p. 61. The members of the Paris department assembly who select Danton are for the most part moderates whose overt royalist inclinations he finds outdated and out of place.

**Page 80** *'Whatever the ebb and flow of opinion* . . .': Bougeart, p. 44, extract from speech published in the newspaper *Orateur du Peuple*, no. 45.

**Page 81** *'O Mirabeau! Patriot, people's tribune* . . .': Clarétie, p. 109, citing *Révolutions de France et de Brabant*, no. 72.

**Page 81** *'The royal family is lost* . . .': Christophe, p. 138. Mirabeau's warning is relayed to King Louis by a courtier who handles financial transactions with the dying orator.

**Page 82** *harried by crowds to 'swear or swing'*: Furet, p. 90. Only seven of France's legion of bishops took the revolutionary oath. Parish priests were more flexible, given that state 'salaries' they received were often higher than their lowly Church incomes of old.

**Page 83** *'Only a coward deserts his post* . . .': *Révolutions de France et de Brabant*, no. 74.

Page 83 *'Keep away from the enemies...'*: *Révolutions de France et de Brabant*, also no. 74.

## Chapter 7: A Wilful Woman in the Way (pages 85–100)

Page 85 *Paine had in fact first come to France...*: John Keane, *Tom Paine* (Bloomsbury, London, 1996), p. 283.

Page 86 *The conflict came to a head...*: House of Commons record for 6 May 1791. Burke has laid the ground for his Commons rant with his essay *Reflections on the Revolution in France* published six months earlier, an uncannily precise preview, as it turns out, of the eventual terror and bloodshed to befall France.

Two separate books in English that examine cross-Channel confrontation at this time – by William Morris Laprade and by Stephen Prickett – bear the same title: *England and the French Revolution*.

Page 88 *... 'as a people becomes truly great...'*: Robinet, p. 279, extract from Jacobin club record for 20 June 1791.

Page 88 *they heard muffled activity...*: Desmoulins, *Révolutions de France et de Brabant*, no. 82.

Page 89 *Danton was woken by Fabre...*: Christophe, p. 144.

Page 90 *'You're right. You're right. Your leaders have betrayed you!'*: Madelin, p. 66.

Page 91 *You have sworn that the king would not leave*: Robinet, p. 286, citing account in *Révolutions de France et de Brabant* of Jacobin club session on 21 June 1791.

Page 91 *He regarded Danton as an anarchist...*: La Fayette, *Mémoires, Correspondence et Manuscrits* (Paris, 1837), vol. 3, p. 83. In his memoirs La Fayette self-importantly refers to himself throughout in the third person.

Page 91 *... the head of the 'beast king'*: Christophe, p. 151.

Page 91 *'... declare France a republic without further ado ...'*: Madelin, p. 69, citing Cordelier manifesto addressed to parliament on 22 June 1791.

Page 92 *'What is a republic?'*: Madelin, p. 69.

Page 94 *the couple had separate beds...*: Michelet, vol. 1, p. 523. The romantic historian is a specialist on Madame Roland's private life.

Page 95 *'However much I told myself...'*: Madame Roland, *Mémoires* (Mercure de France, Paris, reprinted 1986), p. 74.

Page 95 *My mouth is a bit large...*: Madame Roland, p. 43.

Page 96 *'If we have energy, let us show it ...'*: Madelin, p. 73.

Page 97 *to head off any attempt by City Hall to arrest them...*: Desmoulins, *Révolutions de France et de Brabant*, no. 86.

**Page 99** *Gabrielle sobbed when she glimpsed the pistol* . . . : Christophe, p. 174.

**Page 99** *On arriving in London* . . . : Robinet, p. 93. Robinet enlarges on Danton's stay in London, which lasts six weeks or so, in a separate booklet entitled *Danton Émigré* (Soudier, Paris, 1887). Some of this is pure conjecture as to whom he meets and what he does there, though it is certain that he stays at the liberal activist home of Dr Thomas Christie.

**Page 99** *Mad Tom was the most controversial figure* . . . : Keane, pp. 287–357. For Pitt's quickening hostility to both the Revolution and Paine see also: William Hague, *William Pitt the Younger* (Harper Collins, London, 2004), pp. 329–47.

## Chapter 8: The Revolution at War (pages 101–115)

**Page 102** *'Dictatorship! What a present* . . . *'*: Roujon, p. 89.

**Page 104** *pictured him as Hercules* . . . : article in the newspaper *Orateur du Peuple* (BNF), no. 9, vol. 9. The *Orateur*'s editor, Stanislas Fréron, is at this time a Cordelier regular.

**Page 105** *his share was calculated at 69,031 livres* . . . : Lefebvre, p. 72.

**Page 106** *'Danton will save France* . . . *'*: Bougeart, p. 80.

**Page 107** *'. . . immense estates paid for by God knows what* . . . *'*: Camille publishes this speech in full in *Révolutions de France et de Brabant*, no. 128, cited by Bougeart, pp. 81–4.

**Page 107** *Nature has given me the frame of an athlete* . . . : ibid.

**Page 109** *brigands terrorised the villages* . . . : Furet, p. 69.

**Page 109** *the price of sugar tripled* . . . : Rudé, p. 89.

**Page 109** *They had settled on a uniform* . . . : Albert Soboul, *Les Sans-Culottes* (Seuil, Paris, 1968), pp. 214–21.

**Page 111** *'you can pay Danton 80,000 livres* . . . *'*: Lefebvre, p. 72, citing Lord Henry Holland, *Foreign Reminiscences*, a souvenir published in London in 1851.

**Page 111** *towering new machine they called the guillotine* . . . : the apparatus is named after Joseph-Ignace Guillotiu, a Parisian physician-politician who sells the revolutionary parliament on the supposedly merciful invention before it is tested: 'With my machine I shall knock heads off in the blink of an eye, and they'll never feel it.' The guillotine is first used in public on 25 April 1792 to execute a condemned murderer on the Place de la Grève, in front of the Paris City Hall; a little later it is moved for big-name executions to the Place de la Révolution, the future Place de la Concorde.

**Page 112** *'We must have war* . . . *'*: Bougeart, p. 87, citing Jacobin club record.

**Page 113** '*Monsieur Robespierre has never imposed . . .*': Jacobin club record for 10 May 1792.

**Page 115** *At the very sight of weathered Austrian and Prussian professionals . . .*: *Dictionnaire Critique de la Révolution* (Flammarion; Paris, 1988), under heading '*Guerre Révolutionnaire*'.

### Chapter 9: The End of a Thousand-Year Throne (pages 116–129)

**Page 116** '*Listen to us. You are here to listen . . .*': Pierre-Louis Roederer, *Mémoires sur la Révolution* (Plon, Paris, reprinted 1942), p. 141. Roederer, a lawyer and an administrator of the Paris department (a rank Danton has also held), is close to the court and serves as a reliable eyewitness to events. He is the source for the account of the Tuileries invasion.

**Page 117** *. . . a promise to 'bring terror' . . .*': Madelin, p. 93, citing Jacobin club record for 13 June 1792.

**Page 118** *M. Danton spoke concerning a law . . .*: Robinet, p. 302, citing Jacobin club session of 14 June 1792. Danton's intervention on a Roman citizen's right to kill is recorded only in indirect speech.

**Page 119** '*Let the reign of the clubs . . . yield to the reign of the law*': Monitor record, 20 June session of parliament (Bougeart, p. 98).

**Page 120** '*Either way, all his plots are aborted . . .*': Bougeart, p. 98, quoting Jacobin assembly record, no. 217.

**Page 121** *Robespierre . . . dandled the baby on his thin knee . . .*: Clarétie, p. 169.

**Page 121** '*Their Majesties will hold personally responsible, on pain of death . . .*': Brunswick's 1000-word text can be seen in French on the Internet, under the heading *Manifeste de Brunswick*.

**Page 122** *Robespierre hesitated over how to counter . . .*: Scurr, p. 194.

**Page 122** '*This bugger couldn't cook an egg*': Michelet, vol. 1, p. 742.

**Page 123** *Paris sans-culottes . . . called it the Marseillaise . . .*: France's future national anthem is the work of Claude-Joseph Rouget de Lisle, an army engineer garrisoned in Strasbourg in the spring of 1792 to guard against possible attack. Asked to compose a war song in a hurry, he wrote the words and strummed the tune out on his violin overnight; troops from the south based on the Rhine took it home with them.

**Page 125** *Lucile giggled . . .*: the story of Danton's movements on 10 August and the previous night is sourced on personal notes left by Lucile Desmoulins, published in full in Bougeart, pp. 101–3, and on the recollections of Roederer (pp. 29–50), who is once more an observant eyewitness at the Tuileries that day.

**Page 126** *. . . her ministers were offering them 20,000 livres . . .*: Roederer, p. 33.

**Page 126** '*Danton will save us*': Lefebvre, p. 81. Madame Elisabeth's pathetic remark is sometimes cited to support rumours that Danton is in the king's pay. Its origin, though, is La Fayette, who misses no opportunity to defame Danton and is, besides, absent from Paris at the time he recalls Elisabeth saying it.

**Page 127** '*Traitor! You will learn to obey . . .*': Madelin, p. 106.

**Page 127** '*Sirs, I have come here to avoid a great crime*': Roederer, p. 49.

**Page 128** '*You're a minister*': Madelin, p. 108.

**Page 129** '*We need a man who has the confidence . . .*': Madelin, p. 108, citing Monitor record.

## Chapter 10: Courage, Patriots! (pages 130–144)

**Page 130** '*In all times, and especially at present . . .*': Monitor record, 13 August 1792 session of parliament (Bougeart, p. 112).

**Page 131** *La Fayette . . . galloped to the Austrian camp . . .* : the Austrians, suspicious, imprison La Fayette in a castle dungeon.

**Page 131** '*It is a national convulsion . . .*': Monitor record, 28 August session of parliament (Robinet, p. 305).

**Page 132** '*He smites with his trident . . .*': Dominique Garat, *Mémoires sur la Révolution* (Poulot-Malassis, Paris, 1862), p. 21. Garat, who succeeds Danton as Justice Minister, is a perceptive eyewitness to Danton's time in power; he sympathises with the moderates who take the name Girondists (soon Girondins), though does not join their party.

**Page 133** '*we must be bold! Bolder still!*': Monitor record, 2 September session. It is hard to render in English the full, eloquent force of the French: '*Il nous faut de l'audace! Encore de l'audace! Toujours de l'audace! Et la France est sauvée.*'

**Page 133** *She had a premonition . . .* : Roujon, p. 164.

**Page 134** '*Because he scares the hell out of me . . .*': Madame Roland, p. 74. The intimidated minister she quotes is Gaspard Monge, who will later join Napoleon Bonaparte as head of his ambitious scientific research projects.

**Page 134** '*We shall not retreat . . .*': Thiers, vol. 2, p. 260.

**Page 135** '*We must strike fear . . .*': Thiers, vol. 2, p. 261.

**Page 135** '*I come to ask for supper*': Madame Roland, p. 208.

**Page 136** '*We're trash. We come from the gutter*': Christophe, p. 238.

**Page 136** *Important correspondence from provincial administrators . . .* : Madelin, p. 152.

**Page 137** '*Swear you love liberty!*': Thiers, vol. 2, p. 283.

**Page 138** *A dark blanket fell . . .* : Garat, p. 21.

Page 138 '*You know my passion for the Revolution* . . .': Madame Roland, p. 310.

Page 139 '*To hell with the prisoners* . . .': Madelin, p. 167. As told, scarcely reliably, to Madame Roland by a fellow Girondist. The French is: '*Je me fous bien des prisonniers: qu'ils deviennent ce qu'ils pourront.*'

Page 139 '*No power on earth could have stopped* . . .': Robinet, p. 338. This explanation encapsulates Danton's views on the prison massacre and is offered a little later to the Convention (see session of 21 January 1793).

Page 139 '*Those men are guilty enough*': Madelin, p. 170.

## Chapter 11: Long Live the Republic (pages 145–159)

Page 145 *voting rights were finally extended* . . . : *Dictionnaire Critique de la Révolution*, p. 618.

Page 146 *Robespierre, remaining bitter, put it around* . . . : Madelin, p. 182.

Page 147 '*I now stand before you* . . .': Monitor, Convention record for 21 September 1792 (Robinet, p. 307).

Page 148 '*Let the law be terrible* . . .': Convention record for 22 September 1792 (Robinet p. 308).

Page 149 '*I need your head!*': Madelin, p. 183.

Page 150 '*A word of advice before you go* . . .': Mathiez, *Autour de Danton* (Payot, Paris, 1926), p. 146. The altercation with the young Duc de Chartres sounds authentic, though it is recorded by him from memory many years later, prior to his enthronement as the liberal monarch Louis-Philippe in 1830. Mathiez cites the exchange as damning for Danton.

Page 151 *In souvenirs she would write* . . . : Madame Roland, p. 207.

Page 152 '*I believe the caves* . . .': Bougeart, p. 150, extract from Convention record for 26 September 1992.

Page 153 '*As for myself I do not belong to Paris* . . .': Bougeart, pp. 150–1.

Page 153 *A nervous figure entered* . . .: Alexandre de Lameth, *Mémoires* (Paris, 1913), pp. 239–44. Lameth (1760–1829), who recounts the conversation with Danton in full from memory, is, like his older brother Charles, among prominent early Jacobin club members who break away to form the Feuillants. After his quest for a constitutional monarchy fails, he flees to the Austrian side, like La Fayette, and is received no better: the Austrians hold him in prison for three years.

Page 155 *The braver you were with this fearful man* . . . : Lameth, p. 200.

Page 156 '*Who did you think I should use? Young ladies?*': Madelin, p. 159.

Page 157 *As the stuff of scandal* . . . : full list as handed to the Convention (Robinet, p. 314).

Page 158 '*Remember! The* patrie *was in danger* . . .': Robinet, p. 316.

Page 158 *Only later, when on the defensive* . . . : François Topino-Lebrun,

*Notes sur le Procès de Danton* (BNF, undated, probably first printed 1795), p. 20.

**Page 159** '*No one gives Roland his due more than I . . .*': Bougeart, p. 152.

## Chapter 12: The Execution of a King (pages 160–173)

**Page 161** *Paine . . . campaigned for a show trial . . .*: Keane, pp. 357–60.

**Page 161** *A letter . . . was delivered by messenger . . .*: Lefebvre, p. 71.

**Page 162** *The letter was certainly founded on trickery . . .*: Bougeart, p. 178. Molleville of course never presents to the Convention the letter he sends to Danton. The letter is contained in Molleville's souvenirs, alluringly entitled *Mémoires Sécrètes pour Server à l'Histoire de la Dernière Année du Regne de Louis XVI*, published from exile in London, where he flees after the king's trial and wherein he confesses that he has tried to fool Danton into thinking he has the 'incriminating' documents to hand.

**Page 162** *In mid-November, a safemaker . . .*: see Michelet, vol. 2, p. 200, for a lively account of the discovery of the king's *armoire de fer*.

**Page 164** *declining to sit with 'women of low appearance . . .*': Michelet, vol. 2, p. 68.

**Page 164** '*that vile eunuch of the Revolution . . .*': Jacobin club record for 14 October 1792 (Robinet, p. 325).

**Page 165** *a republic was somehow against human nature . . .*: Charles-François Dumouriez, *Mémoires* (Librairie Historique, Paris, 1821), p. 20.

**Page 166** *an 'oaf endowed with great energy . . .*': Dumouriez, p. 81.

**Page 167** *He wined them at his well-laden table . . .*: Christophe, p. 306, quoting reports home from a visiting pair of French Convention deputies.

**Page 167** *Their accounts reached the ears of Madame Roland . . .*: Madame Roland, p. 218.

**Page 167** '*Don't forget to look after my trees . . .*': Madelin, p. 208. This and his follow-up note are among the very few private letters Danton is known to have written.

**Page 169** '*I am not one of that throng . . .*': Convention record of 16 January 1793 (Robinet, p. 337).

**Page 169** '*You're not yet king, Danton!*': Monitor record of 17 January 1793 Convention session (Bougeart, p. 176).

**Page 172** *Danton had 'hypnotised 600,000 imbeciles' . . .*: François Buzot, *Mémoires* (Librairie Privat, Toulouse, 1908), p. 19. Buzot pens his memoirs while on the run from the guillotine between June 1793 and early summer 1794.

**Page 173** '*My sole aim was to preserve . . .*': Madame Roland, p. 342. Here the memoirs also announce her love for Buzot and her admission to her aggrieved husband.

Page **173** *he the abominable 'genius'*...: Madame Roland, p. 213.

Page **173** *He was Tiberius*...: Buzot, p. 49.

## Chapter 13: Flames in Flanders (pages 174–187)

Page **174** *'When I die*...': Joseph Granata, *Danton* (Imprimerie Pellet, Arcis, 1990), p. 50. Granata establishes a genealogy of Danton family descendants, their roots moving from France to Chile. His direct line ends with the death of his two childless sons by Gabrielle, who after Danton's execution eventually return to live quiet lives in business in the Champagne country.

Page **175** *'The boundaries of France*...': Convention record for 31 January 1793 (Robinet, p. 340).

Page **176** *'An insurrection! Where is it?'*: House of Commons record, security debate, December 1792.

Page **176** *'the foulest and most atrocious deed*...': Hague, p. 329. This and following Pitt quotes are from the House of Commons record for 1 February 1793.

Page **177** *Dumouriez saw large*...: Dumouriez, p. 42.

Page **177** *'Today's Paris is the most wretched*...': Dumouriez, p. 81.

Page **180** *Among the letters*...*was one from Robespierre*: Madelin, p. 217.

Page **180** *'You could tear the flesh off Robespierre*...': Clarétie, p. 171.

Page **181** *Lacroix*...*informed Danton in a note urging him*...: Madelin, p. 218.

Page **183** *The thrust of Dumouriez's missive*...: Jean-Pierre Bois, *Dumouriez: Héro et Proscrit* (Perrin, Paris, 2005), p. 305.

Page **183** *By three in the morning*...: Monitor, reporting an intervention by Lacroix at the Convention (Bougeart, p. 196).

Page **184** *'Paris is engulfed by tyranny*...': Bois, p. 323.

## Chapter 14: In the Green Room (pages 188–201)

Page **188** *'I summon all good citizens*...': Monitor record of Convention late-night session, 10 March 1793 (Robinet, p. 346).

Page **190** *the tribunal was to take the heads of sixty*...: Bois, p. 323.

Page **191** *'He acted barbaric*...': Garat, *Mémoires*, p. 315.

Page **191** *the theatre and the arts were lonely survivors*...: Thiers, vol. 3, p. 29.

Page **191** *Louise was a competent girl, slim*...: see portrait of Louise Gély with Danton's son Antoine by the fashionable contemporary artist Louis-Léopold Boilly' (Musée Carnavalet, Paris).

Page **191** *she seemed a little afraid of him*...: Madelin, p. 242.

**Page 193** '*A nation in revolt is like boiling bronze* . . .': Robinet, p. 350, with Monitor record of Convention session for 27 March 1793.

**Page 193** *Robespierre . . . obsessed with fears that he would be assassinated* . . . : Scurr, p. 237.

**Page 194** '*Vanquish our enemies* . . .': Monitor record of Convention session for 10 April 1793.

**Page 195** *On average the committee issued thirty decrees* . . . : Lefebvre, p. 76.

**Page 195** '*Each one of our soldiers believes* . . .': Monitor record of Convention session for 21 January 1793.

**Page 197** '*It is time, citizens* . . .': Monitor record of Convention session for 13 April 1793.

**Page 197** *Fox . . . sent Danton a letter* . . . : Madelin, p. 239.

**Page 198** *the iron merchant who 'acted high and mighty* . . .': Soboul, p. 141.

**Page 200** *From his superior height he fixed defendants* . . . : Gérard Walter, *Actes du Tribunal Révolutionnaire* (Mercure de France, Paris, 1986), p. 11.

**Page 201** '*When a people breaks the monarchy* . . .': Monitor record of Convention session for 10 April 1793.

**Page 201** '*I know how this great drama will turn out*': Monitor record of Convention session for 10 April 1792 (Robinet, p. 365).

## Chapter 15: Exit Moderates (pages 202–215)

**Page 203** '*You are wrong. You do not know how to forgive* . . .': Michelet, vol. 2, p. 126.

**Page 203** '*You must join us in crushing* . . .': Monitor record of Convention session for 27 March 1793. Danton offers no corroboration of his disclosure and the record gives no indication that anyone requests it, which suggests that Roland is disinclined to dispute it.

**Page 204** *His defence was robust* . . .: Monitor record of Convention session for 1 April 1793.

**Page 205** *Lasource: Here is my argument* . . . : Robinet, pp. 151–63, from an exhaustive separate report of 1 April 1793 Convention debate produced by *logotachigraphe*, a new transcription method.

**Page 207** '. . . *if Paris were to perish there would be no liberty* . . .': Monitor record of Convention session for 28 May 1793.

**Page 207** *Paine . . . wrote to Danton* . . .: Keane, p. 377.

**Page 208** '*I feel his hand tightening the irons* . . .': Madame Roland, p. 213.

**Page 209** *He hated none of them* . . . : Madelin, p. 234.

**Page 210** *Seeing Paine approaching...*: Keane p. 380.

**Page 210** *We are surrounded by storms...*: Monitor record of Convention session for 14 June 1793 (Robinet, p. 390).

**Page 211** *A campaign...to place the ripe sisterhood...in public homes...*: Soboul, p. 231. This particular sans-culotte petition comes to nothing.

**Page 213** *'The people want a priest...'*: Convention session of 30 November 1792 (Robinet, p. 335).

**Page 213** *'I can't live without women'*: Madelin, p. 242.

**Page 214** *'I have scarcely seen you in several days...'*: Madelin, p. 245. Soon after this, Beaumarchais goes into exile in Hamburg, where he becomes destitute, returning to Paris in 1796 to die three years later.

**Page 215** *'The French nation may never wage...'*: Monitor record of Convention session for 15 June 1793.

## Chapter 16: The Rule of Terror (pages 216–227)

**Page 217** *'I am not angry...'*: Madelin, p. 247.

**Page 217** *'Robespierre came to government'...*: Garat, p. 315.

**Page 218** *The rich were a 'sponge to squeeze'*: Robinet, p. 377.

**Page 219** *'I was born a sans-culotte...'*: Jacobin club record for 26 August 1793.

**Page 219** *'When you sow...'*: Monitor record of Convention session for 13 August 1793. The declaration 'After bread, the people's first need is education' (a slogan to be seen pinned up in today's French schoolrooms) is inscribed on the pedestal of Danton's statue at the modern-day Odéon crossroads on the Boulevard Saint-Germain; the statue marks the site of his Cour du Commerce home, which will be demolished under Baron Haussmann's vast reconstruction programme for the capital in the second half of the nineteenth century.

**Page 221** *'It's a trap!'*: Madelin, p. 247.

**Page 221** *'...I shall never accept a role...'*: Jacobin club record for 1 August 1793.

**Page 221** *'Danton has the head of a revolutionary!'*: Madelin, p. 249. The deputy who moves the motion – M. Gaston, from the Ariège department in the far south – hails from a bourgeois royalist family and has an émigré brother, a combination that perhaps induces him to display a maximum of Montagnard fervour to conceal his roots.

**Page 221** *'I have made a vow and I stick to it...'*: Frédéric Bluche, *Danton* (Perrin, Paris, 1984), p. 378.

**Page 222** *'Like Alcibiades...'*: Robinet, p. 194. The Alcibiades reference appears to be fashionable in educated revolutionary circles; another who alludes to it is Talleyrand (currently in exile in the United States).

**Page 222** *'Let a rifle be the most sacred thing...'*: Monitor record of Convention session for 4 September 1793.

**Page 223** *'Twenty times I offered them peace...'*: Garat, p. 317.

**Page 223** *'I am sick of men'*: Madelin, p. 251.

**Page 224** *'In revolutionary movements the most active people...'*: Madame Roland, p. 352.

**Page 225** *In what she called her last thoughts...'*: Madame Roland, p. 34.

**Page 226** *'Good news!' the neighbour cried...*: Madelin, p. 255.

**Page 227** *'O Liberty, what crimes are committed...'*: Madame Roland, p. 5.

**Page 227** *'Uncle, I have come from Paris...'*: Christophe, p. 370.

## Chapter 17: Fight to the Death (pages 228–242)

**Page 228** *'Calumny sir? It leaps...'*: Frédéric Grendel, *Beaumarchais ou la Calomnie* (Paris, 1973), p. 14.

**Page 229** *an imaginative new calendar...*: Fabre's names for the twelve months come into official use on 24 October 1793. Starting in the autumn (22 September), they are: Vendémiaire, Brumaire, Frimaire, Nivôse, Pluviôse, Ventôse, Germinal, Floréal, Prairial, Messidor, Thermidor, Fructidor. The republican calendar endures for fourteen years before Napoleon drops it at the height of his power, finding it inconvenient for commerce and too redolent of revolution.

**Page 229** *nine soldiers who pricked their eyes...*: Scurr, p. 2.

**Page 229** *Robespierre's...*: *vision of good republican government was virtue and terror...*: Scurr, p. 275, citing Robespierre's address to Convention on 5 February 1794.

**Page 229** *Robespierre envisioned laws to govern people's pleasures...*: Scurr, p. 275.

**Page 229** *'There is no virtue firmer...'*: Madelin, p. 282. The taunt so shocks Robespierre that he notes it down, including it in the prosecution dossier later used to send Danton to the guillotine.

**Page 230** *'I demand that we spare men's blood!...'*: Monitor record of Convention session for 22 November 1793.

**Page 230** *'Look at the Seine!'*: Clarétie, p. 252.

**Page 232** *'To burn is not to answer'*: Albert Soboul, *Portraits de Révolutionnaires* (Seuil, Paris, 1968), p. 73.

**Page 233** *'If it is the pike that vanquishes...'*: Monitor record of Convention session for 1 December 1793.

**Page 233** *'I demand an end...'*: Monitor record of Convention session for 20 November 1793.

**Page 233** '*I may be wrong about Danton . . .*': Jacobin club record for 3 December 1793.

**Page 234** '*Frenchmen! Do not take fright . . .*': Monitor record of Convention session for 19 March 1794 (Robinet, pp. 445–7).

**Page 235** *a white-haired Montagnard, Philippe-Jacques Rühl . . .* : Rühl blows hot and cold over Robespierre's actions, at length committing suicide with a dagger when Robespierre is executed.

**Page 236** '*Do all our arguments kill a single Prussian?*': Jacobin club record for 23 December 1793.

**Page 236** *one picked, the other ate with relish . . .* : Madelin, p. 277.

**Page 238** '*Let them be judged . . .*': Monitor record of Convention session for 13 January 1794.

**Page 238** '*You're Fabre's dupe, Danton!*': ibid.

**Page 239** '*Now we'll gut this big stuffed turbot!*' (Alors on videra ce gros turbot farci!): Madelin, p. 266. Vadier's colourful threat appears in every account pertaining to Danton's life published since the early nineteenth century. It probably originates from contemporary news-sheet reports. With his own 'Be Bold! Bolder still! Ever bolder!' it is a line that clings to the Danton legend – as does his retort below to Vadier, a favourite with contemporary memoirists: 'I'll eat his brains and shit in his skull.'

**Page 239** '*Whether you throw Desmoulins out . . .*': Christophe, p. 386.

**Page 240** *The ardour of his anti-slavery speech . . .* : Monitor record of Convention session for 6 February 1794. The republic's abolition of slavery is annulled a decade later by Napoleon, who decides that, like the use of the Revolutionary calendar, it puts France at a commercial disadvantage.

**Page 241** *he was also a penitent . . .* : Garat, p. 320.

**Page 241** '. . . *I'd eat his entrails . . .*': Madelin, p. 284.

**Page 241** '*Better to be guillotined than to guillotine*': Madelin, p. 284.

**Page 241** *A further private meeting . . . was arranged . . .* : Aulard, *Danton* (Paris, 1908), pp. 63–6. The conversation quoted by Aulard is recorded in souvenirs by the host, Courtois, coincidentally a native of Arcis and the official who will take charge of Robespierre's private papers after his death.

### Chapter 18: The Cornered Bull (pages 243–251)

**Page 244** '*Friends of Mirabeau boasted loudly . . .*': Bougeart, p. 343, citing Robespierre's surviving notes published in 1841.

**Page 244** '*You can't take the* patrie *with you . . .*': Madelin, p. 285. The Courtois notes are the origin of this enduring Danton remark on fleeing one's country, which in French runs: '*On n'emporte pas la patrie à la semelle de ses souliers.*'

**Page 245** *Legendre . . . was first to the rostrum*: Monitor record of Convention session for 31 March 1794, containing Legendre's defence and Robespierre's stark rebuttal.

**Page 246** *Now it was Saint-Just's turn . . .* : Décembre-Alonnier, *Dictionnaire de la Révolution Française* (BNF), pp. 549–54. This subjective dictionary runs Saint-Just's indictment verbatim.

**Page 247** '*I must say, Danton has spineless friends*': Christophe, p. 400. This from Robespierre to his landlord M. Duplay.

**Page 247** *For William Pitt . . . it was a calamitous time . . .* : Hague, pp. 347–9.

**Page 249** *If obliterating the Vendée region cost 100,000 lives . . .* : Furet, p. 140.

**Page 249** *Danton heard a cry in English . . .* : Keane, p. 408.

**Page 250** '*If I left my balls to Robespierre . . .*': Christophe, p. 402 (French: '*Si je laissais mes couilles à Robespierre, mes jambes à Couthon . . .*').

**Page 250** '*I ask the pardon of God and of humanity*': Madelin, p. 292. The supplication appears in contemporary accounts as hearsay, probably based on reports by Danton's jailers – or on the invention of well-meaning supporters.

## Chapter 19: Trial and Execution (pages 252–259)

**Page 252** *Danton's famous roar . . . carried at times across the river*: Décembre-Alonnier, p. 544. Reports that Danton's voice carries across the Seine to the Cordelier district are certainly exaggerated, though his highest bellows may have been audible.

**Page 252** '*I am Georges-Jacques Danton . . .*': No reliable account of the trial exists. Two sources are available.

Certainly the more authentic, though alas disjointed and fragmentary, is the account of the aforementioned Topino-Lebrun, a Paris artist and relatively impartial juryman who takes his own secret notes of the exchanges, published after the Revolution in a thirty-page booklet entitled *Notes sur le Procès de Danton*.

The second, more expansive source is the official bulletin of the Revolutionary Tribunal, whose scribes – beholden to Fouquier and Herman – are flagrantly partial and whose record is reproduced extensively by Bougeart, pp. 352–67. The account of the trial in this chapter is a sifting from the two, made in all awareness of the deficiencies of the official bulletin, and supported by reminiscences of the trial published later by contemporary memoirists.

**Page 252** '*. . . Camille Desmoulins, I am thirty-three years old . . .*': Camille has in fact just turned thirty-four, but one year less affords him a memorable martyr's line.

**Page 253** *both of whom received an implicit prior warning . . .* : Madelin, p. 294, citing a Public Safety committee paper.

**Page 253** *'Let us be sacrificed alone!'*: Bougeart, p. 365.

**Page 255** *Robespierre called in the seven jurymen . . .* : Madelin, p. 295. Here the source is testimony given in the trial later that year of Fouquier himself.

**Page 256** *. . . a report came through from an inmate . . .* : the warning is contained in a letter to the Convention from the Paris Commune police, published by Bougeart, p. 361.

**Page 258** *'I bed my wife every day!'*: Topino-Lebrun, p. 26. In French, the juryman conveys Danton's outcry thus: *'Je baise ma femme tous le jours.'*

**Page 258** *What? Not guilty?*: Madelin, p. 310.

**Page 258** *Crowds lining the route were . . . subdued*: Bougeart, p. 366.

**Page 259** *'You will follow me!'*: Michelet, vol. 2, p. 754.

**Page 259** *'It is worth a look'*: Danton's last words are part of revolutionary legend, quoted by every memoirist and historian who has written on him (cf. Michelet, vol. 2, p. 754).

## Epilogue (pages 261–264)

**Page 261** *'It is the blood of Danton that chokes you!'*: Bougeart, p. 387.

Works consulted but not cited in the preceding notes include, in alphabetical order:

Olivier Bernier, *Lafayette*, Dutton, New York, 1983

Jacques-Pierre Brissot, *Mémoires*, Ladvocat, Paris, 1832

Edmund Burke, *Reflections on the Revolution in France*, British Library, London

Pierre Caron, *Paris pendant la Terreur*, Paris, 1948

Norman Hampson, *Danton*, Duckworth, London, 1978

Jacques Hérissay, *Cet Excellent Monsieur Danton*, Paris, 1960

Stanley Loomis, *Paris in the Terror*, Lippincott, Philadelphia and New York, 1964

Edmund Morgan, *Benjamin Franklin*, Yale University Press, New Haven, 2002

Jérôme Pétion, *Recit du 10 Août*, Plon, Paris, 1866

Nicolas Restif, *Les Nuits de Paris*, first published 1786, BNF

Jean-Jacques Rousseau, *Du Contrat Social*, Flammarion, Paris, reprinted 2001

Michel Vovelle, *La Mentalité Révolutionnaire*, Eds. Sociales, Paris, 1985

Hermann Wendel, *Danton* (French translation from German), Payot, Paris, 1932

# INDEX

INDEX

14–15; taxation, 24; and social unrest, 26, 38, 47; enrols Danton as Council member, 29; authoritarianism and powers, 32–3; and trade treaty with England, 35; and Third Estate's National Assembly, 42–3; on state of nation, 43; condemned by Palais Royal committee, 47; troops desert service, 47; foreign mercenary troops, 49; and storming of Bastille, 49; Danton considers position of, 53, 59, 62–3; remains at Versailles, 58, 60; encourages counter-revolutionary sentiments among officers, 60; taken from Versailles to Paris, 62–3, 65; Danton meets in Tuileries, 63; as potential constitutional monarch, 65, 74–6, 81, 88; and Commune's arrest warrant against Danton, 68; power of veto over parliament, 75; ministers dismissed, 77–8; Danton pledges loyalty to, 80; apprehension at Mirabeau's death, 81; frustrated attempt at sortie from Tuileries, 81–3; religious devotion, 81–2; flight and recapture, 89–90, 92–3; Danton attacks, 92–3; popular hostility to, 92; Jacobin petition against, 96–7; appoints ministers, 106; contributes to Nancy troops relief fund, 111; and war with Austria and Prussia, 112–14, 116; and mob attack on Tuileries, 116–17, 120; Duke of Brunswick protects, 121; and Danton's planned attack on Tuileries, 126; leaves Tuileries for Riding School, 127; imprisoned in Temple, 129; and Brunswick's negotiations for settlement, 143; fate discussed, 150–1, 155, 160; Alexandre de Lameth pleads for, 155; trial, 160–3, 166, 168; private papers discovered, 162–3; Dumouriez supports, 165–6; condemned to death, 169; executed, 170, 174, 176
Lyons, 113, 226, 249

Mandat, Marquis Jean-Antoine de, 126–7
Marat, Jean-Paul: in Cordeliers, 40–1, 55; qualities and activities, 41–2; journalism, 42, 54–5, 59, 199; encourages riotous behaviour, 59; on rumours of Louis XVI's plans to flee, 60; accompanies women's march on Versailles, 61; La Fayette and Commune seek arrest of, 65–7; demands La Fayette's head, 76; Madame Roland dislikes, 95; absolved by Constituent Assembly for attempted flight, 96; Danton mistrusts, 98; advocates Danton for dictator, 101–2; conspires against Danton, 101;

persecutions and demands for death penalty, 115, 133, 153, 217–18; uncertainties, 117; provokes September massacres, 136–40; and Danton's protection of royalist suspects in provinces, 140; elected to Convention, 145, 152; power, 147; Danton breaks with, 152; demands death of Louis XVI, 160, 163; Buzot's antipathy to, 172; attacks Dumouriez, 176, 182, 204; and sans-culottes support, 199; acquitted by Revolutionary Tribunal, 207; supports purge of Girondins, 209; satirises Committee of Public Safety, 214; attacks Westermann for Vendée defeat, 215; murdered, 217–18
Marie-Antoinette, Queen of Louis XVI: loathes Duc d'Orléans, 32; remains at Versailles, 58; and women's march on Versailles, 61; attempted sortie from Tuileries, 81; flight and recapture, 89; Danton demands return to Austria, 118; Duke of Brunswick protects, 121; and Danton's planned attack on Tuileries, 126; imprisoned in Temple, 129, 137, 196; and death of Princesse de Lamballe, 137–8; Austrian interest in liberation of, 196–7; Danton seeks release, 214–15; transferred to Conciergerie, 223; tried before Fouquier, 225; executed, 226
'Marseillaise' (song), 123
'Marsh' see 'Plain'
Marx, Karl, 3
Mathiez, Albert, 7–8
Michelet, Jules, 3
Mirabeau, Honoré Gabriel Riqueti, Comte de: appearance and voice, 7; defies Louis XVI at Versailles, 43, 50–1, 57; and National Assembly, 43–4, 57, 59, 69; oratory, 43, 63; principles and policies, 43, 59, 65, 74, 145; Danton admires and supports, 44, 77, 81; warns Louis XVI, 47; admiration for Danton, 64–5; disapproves of Louis XVI's detention in Tuileries, 65; weakening health, 65; on Robespierre, 69; postpones Paris election, 70; and revision of suffrage, 71; Danton meets, 74–5; favours constitutional monarchy, 74–6, 81; death, 80–1; on Paris council, 80; incriminated by king's private papers, 162; reinterred in unknown site, 163; Danton's supposed conspiracy with, 244, 255; in Robespierre's notes, 244
Molleville, Bertrand de, 161–2, 168
monarchy: justice mocked, 46–7; Danton's view of, 55, 59, 64, 91, 109–10; future

291